THE CONTESTED PAST:
Reading Canada's History.

This collection of selected excerpts focuses on the *Canadian Historical Review*'s contribution to the study of Canadian history from the journal's founding in 1920 to the present. Using the *CHR*'s own interconnected objectives as a benchmark – the promotion of high standards of historical research and writing in Canada, and the fostering of the study of Canadian history – Marlene Shore analyses the varying degrees of success the journal had in meeting those goals. Her introductory essay explains how the *CHR* was shaped not only by its own editorial policies, but by international currents affecting the discipline of history and its practitioners.

Shore chose the excerpts as representative of the major trends, crucial studies, and heated controversies in Canadian historical writing and arranged them chronologically and thematically into four sections: Nation and Diversity, 1920–1939; War, Centralization, and Reaction, 1940–1965; The Renewal of Diversity, 1966 to the Present; and Reflections. Integrating discussions of key themes such as Native–European contact, society and war, the nature of Canadian and Quebec nationalism, class-consciousness, and gender politics, *The Contested Past* offers an excellent introduction to Canadian history and historiography.

MARLENE SHORE is an associate professor of history and chair of the Department of History at York University. Her first book discussed the origins of social research in Canada; she has also published in numerous Canadian and international scholarly journals. Her area of specialty is modern cultural history.

The Contested Past: Reading Canada's History

Selections from the *Canadian Historical Review*

Edited by Marlene Shore

UNIVERSITY OF TORONTO PRESS
Toronto Buffalo London

© University of Toronto Press Incorporated 2002
Toronto Buffalo London
Printed in Canada

ISBN 0-8020-4305-4 (cloth)
0-8020-8133-9 (paper)

Printed on acid-free paper

National Library of Canada Cataloguing in Publication Data

Main entry under title:

The contested past : reading Canada's history : selections from
the Canadian historical review

Includes bibliographical references and index.
Includes some text in French.

ISBN 0-8020-4305-4 (bound)   ISBN 0-8020-8133-9 (pbk.)

1. Canada – History.   I. Shore, Marlene, 1953–   II. Canadian
historical review.

FC176.C66 2002   971   C2001-900976-3
F1026.6.C66 2002

University of Toronto Press acknowledges the financial assistance
to its publishing program of the Canada Council for the Arts and
the Ontario Arts Council.

University of Toronto Press acknowledges the financial support for its
publishing activities of the Government of Canada through the Book Publishing
Industry Development Program (BPIDP).

Contents

PREFACE xiii
ACKNOWLEDGMENTS xv

Introduction 3

PART ONE: NATION AND DIVERSITY, 1920–1939

Commentary 65

The Purpose of the Past

Some Vices of Clio (1926) 71
W.S. Wallace

The Beginnings of Historical Criticism in Canada:
A Retrospect, 1896–1936 (1936) 73
George Wrong

Past Historians and Present History in Canada (1941) 77
Gustave Lanctôt

Dollard des Ormeaux and the Fight at the Long Sault:
A Reinterpretation of Dollard's Exploit (1932) 80
E.R. Adair

Was Dollard the Saviour of New France? (1932) 82
Gustave Lanctôt

Women of New France (Three Rivers: 1651–63)
(1940) 84
Isabel Foulché-Delbosc

The Historian and Society (1933) 87
Charles Beard

The Historian and Society (1933) 90
George M. Wrong

Defining the Canadian Nation

Canada and the Imperial War Cabinet (1920) 93
George M. Wrong

The Growth of Canadian National Feeling (1920) 99
W.S. Wallace

Canada as a Vassal State (1920) 101
Archibald MacMechan

Nationalism and Self-Determination (1921) 104
W.P.M. Kennedy

Canada's Relations with the Empire as Seen by the
Toronto *Globe*, 1857–1867 (1929) 107
F.H. Underhill

Some American Influences upon the Canadian Federation
Movement (1924) 110
R.G. Trotter

The Struggle for Financial Control in Lower Canada,
1818–1831 (1931) 112
D.G. Creighton

Canadian Migration in the Forties (1928) 115
Frances Morehouse

The Beginnings of Nova Scotian Politics, 1758–1766 (1935) 115
W.S. MacNutt

The Environment and Natural Resources

The Assault on the Laurentian Barrier, 1850–1870 (1929)   118
A.R.M. Lower

Economic Factors in Canadian History (1923)   120
W.A. Mackintosh

The Extermination of the Buffalo in Western Canada (1934)   124
Frank G. Roe

Native–European Contact

Review of Harold A. Innis, *The Fur Trade in Canada* (1931)   127
W.A. Mackintosh

Social Revolution in Early Eastern Canada (1938)   129
Alfred Goldsworthy Bailey

PART TWO: WAR, CENTRALIZATION, AND REACTION, 1940–1965

Commentary   135

Society and War

The Social Sciences in the Post-War World (1941)   140
A.R.M. Lower

Response to Lower, 'The Social Sciences …' (1941)   145
H.A. Innis

The Need for a Wider Study of Military History (1944)   147
A.E. Prince

In Defence of Political History (1950)   149
G.P. de T. Glazebrook

Redefining the Nation

Sir John Macdonald and Canadian Historians (1948)   152
D.G. Creighton

Toronto vs Montreal: The Struggle for Financial Hegemony,
1860–1875 (1941)   156
D.C. Masters

Agriculture in the Red River Colony (1949)   159
W.L. Morton

The Origins of Public Broadcasting in Canada (1965)   162
Margaret Prang

Nationalism Challenged

Chapleau and the Conservative Party in Quebec (1956)   168
H. Blair Neatby and John T. Saywell

Review of Guy Frégault, *La Guerre de la Conquête* (1958)   170
G.F.G. Stanley

The British Conquest: Canadian Social Scientists and the
Fate of the *Canadiens* (1959)   171
Michel Brunet

Le Nationalisme canadien-français: De ses origines à
l'insurrection de 1837 (1964)   176
Fernand Ouellet

The Concept of Social Class and the Interpretation of
Canadian History (1965)   183
S.R. Mealing

The Lachine Strike of 1843 (1948)   186
H.C. Pentland

The National Policy, the Workingman, and Proletarian Ideas
in Victorian Canada (1959)   189
F.W. Watt

PART THREE: THE RENEWAL OF DIVERSITY, 1966 TO THE PRESENT

Commentary   195

Contents

Limited Identities

The People of a Canadian City: 1851–2 (1972) 202
Michael Katz

Halifax Merchants and the Pursuit of Development, 1783–1850 (1978) 206
David Sutherland

Never the Twain Did Meet: Prairie–Maritime Relations, 1910–27 (1978) 208
Ernest R. Forbes

Industry and the Good Life around Idaho Peak (1985) 212
Cole Harris

Of Inequality and Interdependence in the Nova Scotian Countryside, 1850–70 (1993) 217
Rusty Bitterman, Robert A. MacKinnon, and Graeme Wynn

Quebec and Nationalism

The Defeat of George-Etienne Cartier in Montreal-East in 1872 (1970) 224
Brian J. Young

Religion and French-Canadian Mores in the Early Nineteenth Century (1971) 227
Jean-Pierre Wallot

The Agricultural Crisis in Lower Canada, 1802–12: A Review of a Controversy (1974) 232
T J A LeGoff

Revisionism and the Search for a Normal Society: A Critique of Recent Quebec Historical Writing (1992) 235
Ronald Rudin

Class Consciousness

Aid to the Civil Power: The Canadian Militia in Support of Social Order, 1867–1914 (1970) 242
Desmond Morton

The Shiners' War: Social Violence in the Ottawa Valley in the 1830s (1973) 247
Michael S. Cross

Through the Prism of the Strike: Industrial Conflict in Southern Ontario, 1901–14 (1977) 253
Craig Heron and Bryan D. Palmer

E.P. Thompson vs Harold Logan: Writing about Labour and the Left in the 1970s (1981) 259
Kenneth McNaught

Paternalism and Politics: Sir Francis Bond Head, the Orange Order, and the Election of 1836 (1991) 262
Sean T. Cadigan

The Return of Native History

The French Presence in Huronia: The Structure of Franco–Huron Relations in the First Half of the Seventeenth Century (1968) 267
Bruce G. Trigger

Amerindian Views of French Culture in the Seventeenth Century (1974) 269
Cornelius Jaenen

The Historians' Indian: Native Americans in Canadian Historical Writing from Charlevoix to the Present (1986) 273
Bruce G. Trigger

Gender Politics

Writing Canadian Women's History, 1970–82: An Historiographical Analysis (1982) 278
Eliane Leslau Silverman

The Skilled Emigrant and Her Kin: Gender, Culture, and Labour Recruitment (1987) 282
Joy Parr

Gender History and Historical Practice (1995) 285
Joy Parr

Cultural History

The Methodist Church and World War I (1968)   289
J.M. Bliss

The Social Gospel in Canada, 1890–1928 (1968)   292
Richard Allen

French Canada and the Prairie Frontier, 1870–1890 (1969)   295
A.I. Silver

Some Quebec Attitudes in an Age of Imperialism and Ideological Conflict (1976)   298
A.I. Silver

Speaking Modern: Language, Culture, and Hegemony in Grocery Window Displays, 1887–1920 (1989)   302
Keith Walden

PART FOUR: REFLECTIONS

Commentary   309

On Canadian History

Canadian History in Retrospect and Prospect: An Article to Mark the Completion of the First Twenty-Five Years of the *Canadian Historical Review*, 1920–1944 (1944)   312
George Brown and D.G. Creighton

Canadian History in the 1970s (1977)   315
H.J. Hanham

A Belated Review of Harold Adams Innis, *The Fur Trade in Canada* (1979)   318
W.J. Eccles

One Step Forward, Two Steps Back: Innis, Eccles, and the Canadian Fur Trade (1981)   322
Hugh M. Grant

The Second Time Around: Political Scientists Writing
History (1986)   326
John English

Where to Begin and How: Narrative Openings
in Donald Creighton's Historiography (1991)   328
Kenneth C. Dewar

1837–38: Rebellion Reconsidered (1995)   332
Allan Greer

INDEX   337

Preface

This volume of selected readings from the *Canadian Historical Review* (*CHR*) reveals the array of approaches to history featured in the journal since its inception in 1920. Short excerpts from numerous articles, from letters to the editors, and from Notes and Comments highlight the two principal objectives that the *CHR* has pursued throughout its history: to promote high standards of historical research and writing in Canada that were in step with approaches and methodological developments elsewhere and to foster the study of Canadian history. The readings selected for this volume appear in chronological and thematic categories, reflecting major trends in Canadian historical writing, pathbreaking studies, and controversies. The volume demonstrates that the *CHR*, the flagship journal of the Canadian historical profession, has presented a picture of the Canadian past that is anything but monolithic. Divergent views about the writing of Canadian history have engaged the *CHR* and its editors and contributors ever since its founding.

This collection can serve as a point of entry to Canadian history and historiography for Canadian and international audiences alike. Newcomers will find a tour through the trends and debates that have shaped Canadian history, while specialists will be prompted to revisit and reconsider some long-held assumptions about Canadian historical writing.

The volume opens with an introductory essay by the editor, which presents the history of the *CHR* in the context of broader efforts to professionalize the discipline of history and the issues that have shaped historical practice. The rest of the volume is divided into four parts. In addition to three parts that accord with the major themes highlighted in the introductory essay – Nation and Diversity, 1920–1939; War, Centralization, and Reaction, 1940–1965; and The Renewal of Diversity, 1966 to the Present – there is a concluding section entitled 'Reflections.' The first three parts are divided into subsections containing representative works on topics such as, the purpose of the past, environmental history, Native–European contact, Canadian and Quebec nationalism, regional history, class consciousness, gender politics, cultural history, and debates over the status of political history. All four parts begin with a commentary written by the editor, summarizing the excerpts and relating them to the themes raised in the volume introductory essay. For reasons of space, I was compelled to omit numerous significant *CHR* contributions, but I mention some particularly notable ones in the introduction and the commentaries, in the hope that readers will consult them, along with the articles excerpted here, in back issues of the journal.

Acknowledgments

This volume would not have been possible without the assistance of numerous people. For prompting me to pursue the project, I thank Mitchell Shannon; for supporting it through various stages of production at University of Toronto Press, I am grateful to Gerry Hallowell, Emily Andrew, Wally Brooker, Siobhan McMenemy, Frances Mundy, and John Parry. I am fortunate to be a member of the Department of History at York University, among whose ranks are many former editors of the *Canadian Historical Review*. Along with colleagues in an array of fields, they have created a lively departmental atmosphere conducive to thinking about the discipline and practice of history. For their engagement with this project in different ways, I particularly thank Christopher Armstrong, Bettina Bradbury, Stephen Brooke, Kathryn McPherson, H.V. Nelles, Nicholas Rogers, John T. Saywell, and Adrian Shubert. Craig Brown, at the University of Toronto, and Ian McKay, at Queen's University, also provided invaluable help, as did Janet Miron, my research assistant. In the final analysis, everything in this volume is owed to decades of contributions made to Canadian historiography by those whose work has appeared in the *Canadian Historical Review*.

THE CONTESTED PAST:
Reading Canada's History

Introduction

At the beginning of the twenty-first century, despite pronouncements of its death, history is still alive and at the centre of popular and academic interest – and contention.¹ The past couple of decades have witnessed history's ever-growing presence in international developments and its marketability in popular culture.² Obsession with the past is apparent throughout the Western world: from family genealogies and antique industries and roadshows, through history theme parks, museums, and monumental art, to retrofashion, television, and movies. The Canadian Broadcasting Corporation's sixteen-episode *Canada: A People's History* is a local contribution to this phenomenon. Meanwhile, works of historical fiction by front-ranking Canadian novelists – Margaret Atwood, Wayne Johnston, Anne Michaels, and Michael Ondaatje – have reached the top of international bestsellers lists, capturing accolades and prestigious awards. Media creations of neo-traditions, such as anniversaries marking the Kennedy assassination, the Gulf War, and so on, abound.³

A memory boom also pervades the academy, centred on the production of texts about memory and commemoration and individual and collective representations of the past. Even the recent lying-in-state and funeral of Pierre Elliott Trudeau evoked the aura of a commemorative event in its manipulation of cultural symbols and in the reflections that poured forth about the kind of nation that the former prime minister had tried to shape and define.

Ironically, this phenomenon coexists alongside expressions of concern among professional historians about a seemingly shrinking audience for their scholarship. Across North America and much of the

Western world, the trend towards globalization and economic integration has prompted governments to embrace market-driven forces and to emphasize science, technology, and practical education in secondary and higher education. As these developments operate to marginalize such disciplines as history, privately funded historical institutes, backed by substantial donations from entrepreneurs and business elites, attempt in a number of countries to promote the revival of a so-called national history and to educate the public about civics and citizenship. Has this situation emerged because the demands of academic specialization have rendered the work of many professional historians intellectually inaccessible, as many critics have argued? Or is it attributable to the professional historians' abdication of their role as spokespersons for the nation and to their retreat from political and national history, as these same critics have also charged?

In the last decades of the twentieth century, debates on these issues intensified and became more heated. During the 1980s and early 1990s, it was not unusual in Canada to hear the comment that the field of Canadian history, fragmented by specialization, no longer spoke to the concerns of the country as a whole. And from that, the inevitable parallel was drawn – as Canadian history went, so went the nation.[4] In 1998, the furore grew louder when J.L. Granatstein, in his polemical book, *Who Killed Canadian History?*, assailed social, working-class, and gender historians for destroying Canadian history.[5] In response, the *CHR* presented readers with two thoughtful and provocative interpretations of this viewpoint. A.B. McKillop explained how the new historical approaches had not only enriched ideas about what constituted politics but, following trends in international scholarship, had destroyed the possibility that a single narrative voice could tell the story of Canada's past.[6] Bryan D. Palmer, while acknowledging McKillop's sometimes-fine denunciation of Granatstein's book, cautioned historians not to celebrate their fracturing of the Canadian story. For one thing, he argued, this had merely reversed the fabric of consensus historiography; for another, it failed to confront the fact that women, workers, immigrants, and transgressors perhaps did not revel in their peripheralization but rather wanted into the story or, at least, to rewrite it. Most significantly, abhorring the depoliticization of historical practice, Palmer called on historians to turn their attentions once again to the state and to issues of political power and authority. Ideas of nationhood, he explained, may be discussed not only as a form of universalizing pride but as an example of class tragedy.[7]

Such contentiousness about the state of Canadian historical writing is nothing new, however much observers point to the last three decades as the era when it all supposedly fell apart. Similar arguments appeared through most of the twentieth century. In fact, there never was a golden age when all historians of Canada were devoted to constructing a national chronicle, nor was there agreement on the fundamentals of that narrative. At the height of nationalist consciousness in English Canada – Expo 67 – and the celebration of the hundredth anniversary of Confederation, some Candian historians pondered over the limitations of nationalist approaches. Only three years later, on the occasion of the fiftieth anniversary of the *Canadian Historical Review*, it was apparent that the traditional mission for historians of new nations such as Canada – to chronicle a national history – had come to an end.[8] Even the *CHR*, long regarded as 'the' national historical journal, was promoting 'limited identities.' Within a decade it was publishing numerous articles in social and working-class history. Some issues were so specialized that the journal's editors were concerned that not only general audiences, but even some historians, were losing interest in the field and, hence, in the *CHR*.

During the 1970s and early 1980s, the *CHR* endured a troubled period as it tried to confront and adjust to the demographic and intellectual changes in the profession; Canadian historical scholarship has indeed changed over the past quarter-century. Although the *CHR* initially did not seem hospitable to these developments, eventually it incorporated the new fields of specialization without abandoning its efforts to be a general, national journal. Close scrutiny of editorial policy, articles, book reviews, and correspondence in the journal since 1920 reveals that there have been certain continuities in the *CHR* over its history. Its contents have reflected the tendency of Canadian historians to write about the past with an eye to the present and the future. To that degree, the traditional mission of Canadian historians to be custodians of the past and moral leaders of society has persisted: where once they wrote out of concern for the nation, they were now interested in a multiplicity of futures – that of regions, communities, classes, and genders. A similar kind of diversity, which included attention to the work of scholars in other disciplines, had characterized the *CHR* in the 1920s and 1930s, before events surrounding the Second World War and subsequent developments narrowed it. What currently looks like fragmentation may turn out to be rather a renewed diversity of approaches.

Diversity in the Early Decades

Divergent views about the writing of history have engaged the *CHR* since its inception. The *CHR* has always been more than a journal of Canadian history; it has sought to convey by example and instruction the proper methods and forms of historical scholarship. This goal was reflected in its founding objectives – to raise the standard of historical scholarship in Canada and to promote Canadian history – and in the manner in which those two functions were consistently interconnected.

In the period between 1920 and the late 1930s, when the *CHR* was establishing itself as the national historical journal, its two objectives were closely entwined. The *CHR* was a continuation of the annual *Review of Historical Publications Relating to Canada*, founded in 1896 by George Wrong. As professor of history at the University of Toronto, and an active participant in the American Historical Association (AHA), Wrong had been influenced by the inauguration of the *American Historical Review* (*AHR*) in 1895 and of the *English Historical Review* (*EHR*) a decade earlier.[9] This founding of journals was one facet of the professionalization of history that occurred at the turn of the century, aiming to foster the profession's skills, raise its status, ensure its autonomy, and, above all, establish its objectivity. The notion that objectivity conveyed authority and gave history the credibility of science led many historians to accept objectivity as the hallmark of the professional craft. An assumption that scientific method entailed factual and empirical investigation that shunned hypotheses contributed to the belief that systematic investigation of historical documents would result in a definitive history. Leopold von Ranke's dictum to describe history '*wie es eigentlich gewesen*' (as it essentially was) was the rallying call, but many English-speaking historians misunderstood the vestiges of German idealism in Ranke's thought: he believed that historians, through a process of romantic or mystical insight, would see within the documents a progressive course of development.[10]

Wrong's annual review began the process of professionalization through critical reviews of publications, but after the First World War it could no longer accommodate the proliferation of books dealing with Canada. The efflorescence of writing on Canadian history and culture stimulated by Canadian participation in the war necessitated expansion to a quarterly that could also carry original articles. The absence of outlets for the publication of articles in Canadian history, apart from the French-Canadian *Bulletin des recherches historiques*, *Canada français*, and *Revue canadienne*, influenced the decision to concentrate on Canadian history and related subjects. The postwar spirit of English-Canadian nationalism also played a part in that policy.[11] Although the University of Toronto Press owned the *CHR*, a board of editors who lived in

Toronto (among them, George Wrong) controlled it: the board met frequently with the journal's first managing editor, W.S. Wallace, who was a member of the University of Toronto's history department and university librarian. When George Brown took over as managing editor in 1930, the board of editors was broadened to include members from other provinces and disciplines. The board met to discuss general policy at the annual meetings of the Canadian Historical Association (CHA), although the *CHR* was never officially linked to the CHA, which was founded in 1923. Finally, in the spirit of *bonne entente* – the effort to heal the rift caused by the conscription crisis of 1917 – the *CHR* began to work on bridging the divide between French and English Canadians.[12]

During the interwar years, the *CHR*'s contributions covered a broad range of topics and reflected a variety of beliefs about the purpose and methods of history. This eclecticism stemmed from the lack of agreement among Canadian historians about certain aspects of professionalization. By the 1920s, supporters of scientific methods in history existed alongside those who were sceptical about the absolute veracity of its findings and those who had never abandoned the idea that history belonged to the realm of literature. There was widespread agreement about the need to correct distorted views of the Canadian past through documentary research, as manifested in demands for the preservation of records of all kinds and greater access to archives.[13] William Wood best expressed this pursuit of 'truth' about the past through investigation of original archival material in his three-stage description of historical study: 'The first is of little archives and much prejudice. The second is that of more archives; but not enough to lighten truth and blacken prejudice. The third is that in which the original evidence of the archives is strong enough to convince all but those who shut their eyes.'[14]

During the interwar period, historical relativism and the development of pragmatism in the social sciences challenged such certainties regarding truth by emphasizing the social nature of knowledge. Contributors to the *CHR* saw other kinds of limitations in historical findings based solely on documents. One reviewer thought it regrettable that historians were shying away from studying tradition, embedded in things such as folklore, at a time when such sources were being used by ethnologists and psychologists.[15] George Brown warned that documents could never reveal a complete picture. Regarding the events that preceded the outbreak of the First World War, he cited Lord Morley, 'The truth can *never* be known. It will never overtake the legend ... Far more depended on the negotiations of half an hour ... than ever appeared in letters and dispatches.'[16]

The most strongly expressed concern about scientific history came from historians who thought it important to appeal to a wide audience. They believed that historians, as custodians of the past, were natural leaders of society, whose duty it was to create stories that would stimulate Canadians' interest in the past while imparting moral lessons. For that reason, Stewart Wallace (September 1926) was disturbed that trends in academic history were resulting in dissertations that had all the required components in the form of copious citations and phalanxes of facts, but nothing that made them great books. To his mind, they belonged to what British essayist Thomas De Quincey had called 'the literature of knowledge,' as opposed to 'the literature of power': the former was information, science, the kind of knowledge that could be easily apprehended and constantly revised; the latter was eternal, expressing a deep sympathy with truth.[17] Even Dominion Archivist Gustave Lanctôt (September 1941), who believed that the hallmark of 'real history' was a 'judicious use of documents,' urged Canadian historians to infuse their studies with 'a spirit and colour befitting the great achievements narrated and the greater future looming ahead.'[18]

Contributors to the *CHR* were well aware of the public's taste for certain kinds of history and biography throughout the English-speaking world. Particularly in Britain, the war had stimulated an interest in readable historical explanations that was filled by such writers as H.G. Wells and Lytton Strachey because the scientific approach had made professional history unappealing. The *CHR* nevertheless warned of the consequences of heeding popular trends. On the sixtieth anniversary of Confederation, the journal noted clamours in the schools for patriotic literature and cautioned that patriotism buttressed by distortions of fact would create an atmosphere that bred 'bitter iconoclasts.' In the United States during the 1920s, various groups demanded that textbooks be purged of the influence of scholars who disputed long-accepted legends. Any belief that Canada would not experience this situation was premature, the *CHR* noted: the country was entering a period of constitutional development when the pressure to write history to suit the demands of various groups and doctrines was likely.[19]

During the 1920s, many American historians and popular writers engaged in debunking heroes, traditions, and myths. The iconoclasm of this decade was a reaction against the distortions of history perpetrated by George Creel's wartime propaganda. (Creel, a Denver progressive journalist, directed the U.S. government's Committee on Public Information, which set professors from leading universities to writing propaganda to mobilize public opinion in favour of the war.) Nevertheless, many traditionalists regarded myths and heroes as integral to the nation's heritage and condemned attempts at revision.[20] A smaller-scale version of this conflict played out in the *CHR*. In its first year, the journal observed that while many of the accepted beliefs about Canadian history required revision, this was bound to be unpopular with the public: 'Few people like to be told that Wolfe did not recite the lines from Gray's *Elegy* as he floated down the Foulon on the night before the battle of the Plains of Abraham, or that Brock did not say, as he fell at Queenston Heights, "Push on, brave York Volunteers."'[21] Articles in the debunking style inevitably met with objections. Lawrence J. Burpee took issue with A.S. Morton's depiction of La Vérendrye as a soldier of fortune, and no mere fur-trader, declaring that Morton had joined 'the ranks of the iconoclasts.'[22] And there was an even stronger reaction to E.R. Adair's (June 1932) demonstration that Dollard des Ormeaux's title as saviour of New France had to be 'relegated to the museum of historical myths' – Dollard, he said, not understanding Indian warfare, incurred unneccessary losses in the battle with the Iroquois at the Long Sault in 1660, which encouraged the Iroquois in their attempts to destroy the St Lawrence settlements the next year. Appealing to postwar sensibilities, Gustave Lanctôt (June 1932) pointed out that to refuse Dollard the title of saviour of New France meant that 'we cannot say that the first Canadian division saved the allies at Ypres, for more Canadians than ever were killed the next year.'[23]

The issue of debunking and demythologizing was prominent in discussions at the annual meeting of the AHA in Toronto in December 1932.[24] Addresses by AHA vice-president Charles Beard (March 1933) and by George Wrong (March 1933) appeared together in the *CHR* under the title 'The Historian and Society.' From different perspectives, both argued that history served a higher morality that often involved challenging prevailing beliefs. Beard pointed to the role that historians had played in reconciling the North and South by seeing the Civil War not as an issue of right versus wrong but as an antagonism of cultures. Wrong spoke of the historian's role as storyteller, providing the traditions by which people governed their lives. This meant that historians had a duty not to falsify or distort the record, but to do more than provide facts. Influenced by Lord Acton, Wrong believed that history had to help develop social conscience, which required the historian to make moral judgments and, if necessary, to attack the reputation of popular heroes and to wound national pride.[25]

To some degree, the *CHR* had been born out of national pride, but in the task of fostering Canadian history during the 1920s and 1930s, it achieved a breadth not evident in subsequent decades. There were criticisms about the journal's narrow, national scope – criticisms that Canadian history was an insignificant subject and that Canadians needed a journal that informed them about other countries. To this, the editors responded that they saw no point in duplicating the *AHR* and *EHR*, which covered the whole range of ancient and modern history. They likened the *CHR* to the *Mississippi Valley Historical Review*, which began publication in 1914 as the periodical of the Mississippi Valley Historical Association, organized in 1907 to serve the interests of professional historians of mid-America.[26] The *CHR* met the same kind of need, its editors insisted, making a distinctive contribution to a local field while demonstrating its wider significance. Editors George Brown and Donald Creighton (December 1944) also had a liberal view of what fell within the journal's publishing range and invited contributions from geography, economics, archaeology, ethnology, law, education, imperial relations, aspects of British and American domestic history, pre-revolutionary France and its colonies, and international relations as they impinged on Canada.[27] Even so, by another measure of breadth, the *CHR* mirrored the Anglo-Canadian university establishment at that time: female contributors and articles dealing with the history of women were few.

In support of their argument that there were truly significant aspects of Canada's past that demanded notice, the editors pointed to the country's distinctive constitutional development. Canada had a unique form of federalism; it was in Canada that responsible government was first worked out in the colonial sphere; and Canada had played a leading part in the evolution of the British Commonwealth.[28] An article in the first issue, George Wrong's 'Canada and the Imperial War Cabinet' (March 1920), signalled the importance of the approach, and numerous articles in constitutional history followed.[29] In the second issue, Stewart Wallace (June 1920) stressed the growth of national feeling as the 'central fact' of Canadian history. Contributions reflected the range of ideas about Canadian nationalism being expressed in English-Canadian intellectual circles during the interwar years: in numerous ways, concern with Canada's colonial mentality, the negative influence of American popular culture, and Canada's position as a North American nation influenced interpretations of episodes in Canadian history.[30]

Other voices in the *CHR* cautioned against excessive nationalism. Constitutional historian W.P.M. Kennedy (March 1921) warned that the doctrine of national self-determination threatened 'a higher human solidarity.' He explained that in North America, the lack of a common history to provide a foundation for nationalism promoted a search for other unifying bonds, such as language and religion. The effect was to exclude groups of people when it was preferable to have more than one type of national feeling in a state: what was needed was a supranationalism that would lead to internationalism.[31] The argument – significant in discussions of Woodrow Wilson's doctrine of self-determination, with which Kennedy disagreed – also had ramifications for Canadian politics.[32] The *CHR* noted that the Great War had heightened debates between nationalists and internationalists about the nation-state and about whether nationalism was the highest good or a crime against civilization. If the arguments of the extreme nationalists were admitted, then French Canada should be allowed to withdraw from Confederation and become a separate and independent state, if it so desired. But if Lord Acton and his intellectual heirs were correct in seeing a multinational state as a better protection of individual liberty, there was room for more than one kind of national feeling in Canada, and emphasis should be placed not on nationalism but on toleration.[33]

The *CHR*'s tolerance of French Canada was accompanied by its distaste for extreme expressions of French-Canadian nationalism. Because the dominant interpretation in French-Canadian historical writing was Roman Catholic and *nationaliste*,[34] few articles by French-Canadian historians appeared in the journal during this period; those that dealt with French Canada accorded with the dominant trends in English-Canadian historiography. Lanctôt argued that the elective council of Quebec of 1657, which regulated and administered trade and financial policy for the colony, was in an embryonic way the first Canadian parliament; Hilda Neatby contended that events in Lower Canada since 1763 had to be seen in the context of the triangular connection of Canada with Britain and the United States. Donald Creighton sounded another note in 'The Struggle for Financial Control in Lower Canada, 1818-1831' (June 1931), arguing that French Canadians impeded efforts at economic development because they did not share the values of the English industrial revolution; their entire outlook was shaped by the France that the French Revolution had destroyed.[35]

Interpretations of Canadian history that had less divisive implications for relations between French and English Canadians were those, like the Laurentian thesis, that saw geography as central to the nation's development and identity. 'History is emphatically not "past politics"; it is the life of yesterday in the present,' W.A. Mackintosh asserted in his pathbreaking article (March 1923), which put forward the staples theory. He urged Canadian historians to study economic and geographical factors in Canadian history, demonstrating how North American geographical features had shaped economic, social, and political development in Canada, including constitutional crises.[36] The relationship between geographical conditions and settlement patterns concerned many scholars during the 1920s; A.R.M. Lower's *CHR* article, 'The Assault on the Laurentian Barrier' (December 1929), was the first example of a Canadian historian's interest in the subject. Lower thought it was necessary to understand the contact of the first settlers with the Canadian Shield, because the Shield was the most important factor in the country's past and future growth.[37] Indeed, the role of geography in Canadian history did not escape the attention of the journal's editors during the 1920s: 'In the beginning was geography,' Stewart Wallace had proclaimed in 'The Growth of National Feeling'; (June 1920); he stressed the profound influence of geography on Canadian history, especially in stimulating the growth of Canadian national consciousness. George Wrong suggested that the new scientific way of studying human society was to link history and geography: history was the study of a completed past that could not be altered, and geography was the study of 'the forces of nature which will mould the yet unformed future.'[38]

In a period when boundaries between disciplines were not rigid, the *CHR* recognized the value of other social sciences and benefited from connections with their practitioners. Before 1950, when Canada had few formally trained geographers, historians (along with economists and sociologists) made significant contributions to geographical literature on the Canadian past. They were acutely aware of such factors as distance and climatic conditions in their studies of historical events, as shown by *CHR* articles that dealt with environmental history or were influenced by interpretations of American history that accorded a central role to the environment in shaping human society.[39]

During the 1920s and 1930s, historians of Canada were also attuned to the work of political scientists, with whom they shared a common interest in constitutional history. This was facilitated by close relationships – personal and disciplinary – between history and political economy at such institutions as McGill University and the University of Toronto. Historians also saw work in anthropology and ethnology valuable to the study of the Canadian past. Until the mid-1950s, the *CHR* featured an annual list of publications in Canadian archaeology, anthropology, and ethnology, which from 1925 onward was prepared by T.F. McIlwraith. The relationship with anthropology was a legacy of Daniel Wilson, who before the days of George Wrong, taught history and ethnology at the University of Toronto; while striving to establish history's autonomy, Wrong also continued to lecture in ethnology.[40] *CHR* readers kept up to date with developments in anthropology through book reviews by leading American figures in the field – Franz Boas, Robert Redfield, and Robert Lowie – along with significant contributions by Canadian scholars, such as McIlwraith, Marius Barbeau, and Alfred G. Bailey.

The recognition accorded to Native history in the *CHR* during the interwar years stemmed from links with anthropology. 'The beginnings of Canadian history must be sought in the customs and practices of the Canadian aborigines,' an item in Notes and Comments announced in 1929.[41] Although most of the items dealing with Native history were written by anthropologists and ethnologists,[42] book reviews mentioned a few significant exceptions. In *The Fur Trade in Canada* (1930), Harold Innis demonstrated how fur, as a commodity, dominated and shaped the life of Canada. But, as W.A. Mackintosh's review noted (March 1931), Innis also saw the fur trade as the nexus between the mature mercantile and industrial culture of Europe and the primitive culture of the North American Indians and emphasized the role of the Indians therein. Innis, in turn, praised J.B. Brebner for the attention that he accorded to Indians as middlemen in North American exploration.[43]

The *CHR* also published some pathbreaking articles by historians who offered new interpretations of Native populations in Canada. In 'The Half-Breed "Rising" of 1875' and his book *The Birth of Western Canada* (1936), G.F.G. Stanley argued that the troubles in the North-West were not primarily racial or religious, but a clash between a primitive and a civilized people that was characteristic of frontiers. More than an extension of the frontier theory, Stanley's argument reflected theories that had been developing in anthropology and sociology through the 1920s and 1930s and that stressed the primacy of culture over biological traits.⁴⁴ In 'Social Revolution in Early Eastern Canada' (September 1938), A.G. Bailey employed those theories to explain the fusion of cultural traits that resulted from contact. Robert Redfield in the *CHR* hailed his masterly *Conflict of European and Eastern Algonkian Cultures, 1504–1700* (1937) as a 'historian's contribution to an ultimate comparative study of culture contacts.'⁴⁵

These approaches broadened the horizons of Canadian history, but by the time of the *CHR*'s twenty-fifth anniversary, editors Brown and Creighton (December 1944) commented that the journal's interest lay with 'the centre rather than the periphery.' This was evident, even during the 1920s and 1930s, in the small number of articles dealing with regions outside central Canada. Already in 1926, the journal was being criticized for its inattention to western history and for its domination – even in the book-review section – by the 'the Wise Men of the East.'⁴⁶ Several articles on British Columbia appealed to the taste for epic: F.W. Howay and Walter Sage dealt with the fur trade on the coast, Spanish exploration, and the search for gold; and the colony's entrance into Confederation could not go unnoticed.⁴⁷ In his article on the beginnings of Nova Scotia politics, W.S. MacNutt (March 1935) alluded to the scant attention that Canadian historians paid to the Atlantic provinces. Nova Scotia had been neglected, he commented, because the colony had not been part of the main line of Canadian or European economic development, had nothing in common with Quebec, and, compared with the more opulent and advanced United States, was the 'Cinderella' of the imperial family.⁴⁸

Economic and social history fared better, with numerous articles demonstrating the limitations of political history for explaining the Canadian past. In dealing with Canadian migration in the 1840s, for instance, Frances Morehouse (December 1928) pointed out that migrants could not afford political preferences; they wanted land and lived wherever they could find work. She confessed to finding something 'grimly humorous in the contrast between the conscious nationalism of the migrations planned by government officials and philanthropists and the movements which actually took place.'⁴⁹ Isabel Foulché-Delbosc (June 1940) observed that the emphasis historians had placed on documents relating to political rather than simple household affairs explained why colonial domestic life was rarely studied. By using notarial and law-court records, and records of dispute, she was able to present a history of the women of New France, rather than just the customary heroines.⁵⁰

The *CHR* conceded that local history held some importance, but local historians had a secondary role, as providers of 'facts' for 'the grand scheme of history,' to be written by general historians with broad vision.[51] By the late 1930s it was becoming clear just who those visionaries were. On the publication of *The Commercial Empire of the St Lawrence, 1760–1850* (1937), Arthur Lower praised Donald Creighton for producing a book with popular appeal, thereby rescuing Canadian history from its status as 'the Cinderella of studies, confined to the safe scullery of the academic world, unknown to, and unsought by the average intelligent citizen.' Lower found Creighton's occasional use of melodrama and 'purple patches' excusable.[52]

By that time, signs of the *CHR*'s direction over the next decade were also becoming evident. Not only did the onset of the Second World War strengthen the determination of many English-Canadian historians to craft a past to guide Canada's future, but it also prompted a re-examination of the methods and purpose of historical scholarship. An item in Notes and Comments in 1938 observed that once-accepted canons such as objectivity were being thrown away in the face of utilitarian demands and repeated crises: perhaps historical writing had never been as objective as its nineteenth-century practitioners had hoped, but at least historians had agreed to use evidence honestly, even if they could not rid themselves of all preconceptions. Now, in many places, the sole concern of scholarship was to bolster some theory or dogma.[53]

The Centralizing Tendencies of the Middle Decades

During the war years, numerous contributions to the *CHR* spelled out the duty of Canadian historians on the home front. Associate editor G.P. de T. Glazebrook called for them to contribute to the literature on international relations, as befitted the country's separate declaration of war.[54] While the *CHR* noted the impediments to research during the war years, there were suggestions that historians write about the war itself and not leave the task to moralists or philosophers.[55] Reginald Trotter argued that social scientists should explain what was at stake in the conflict and shape public opinion for post-war reconstruction.[56] Arthur Lower (March 1941) thought that social scientists should be formative agents in a new order, preserving freedom and the values of Western civilization in a world in which society's needs would take precedence over individual rights.

Lower believed that it would fall to a small group of historians to create a Canadian version of Western civilization. Because Canada was a practical country, cut adrift from its British moorings, he thought that this national history had to be built on a liberal education, but not treat grand and universal themes. It should be 'a kind of ready-made history, awaiting the arrival of a people to purchase it,' he suggested. He seemed to imply that all previous treatments were lacking and that Canada – a society in the making – needed a new history. Indeed, Lower commented, Canadian historians stood at the beginning of an evolution, rather than at some distance along its course. In writing the history of Canada, they faced the conundrum of just what it was that constituted Canada: he warned that the necessity of treating the British in the Maritime provinces, the French on the St Lawrence, and the Loyalists in Upper Canada could result in 'several histories running alongside each other rather than one integrated story.'[57]

Lower's view did not pass without criticism. Percy Corbett noted that Lower had long been 'a patriot in search of a *patria*' and that he sought it in Canada, where he and his kind could play a role in its creation. Harold Innis (June 1941) thought the best means of ensuring the survival of Western civilization was through individual scholarship: the social scientist should adhere to the traditions of his subject and mind his own business.[58]

The results of a survey conducted by the bilingual journal *Culture*, and sent to all history departments in Canadian universities in 1941, indicated that many historians agreed that Canada needed a history that would give roots to its population and foster unity.[59] Similar sentiments emerged in the *CHR*'s survey in 1944, which solicited comments from 150 men and women in Canada, the United Kingdom, and the United States about the state of Canadian historical studies and the journal itself. Respondents demanded more attention to new interpretations and philosophical issues: one commented that the *CHR*'s lack of attention to the history of ideas reflected a general Canadian attitude. Some urged more studies in local and social history, while others warned against overemphasizing modern trends. In that regard, it was suggested biography would be a useful corrective to the mechanistic approaches of economics, sociology, and psychology and their tendency 'to weigh, measure, and classify human activities in the mass.'[60]

More than just the rising prestige of the social sciences prompted the criticism of such 'mechanistic' approaches. Contributions to the *CHR* demonstrated that attitudes fostered by the war and, later, the Cold War were also influential in turning historians away from some interwar interpretations, particularly economic and social history. A.E. Prince (March 1941) condemned the rejection of military history as part of the

'Great-Man nonsense.' The dismissal of the study of war, he charged, had led the 'aggressive imperial nations' to conclude that liberal democracies would not fight. He also outlined the ways in which the wars of the twentieth century had undermined the discipline, exposing the limitations of scientific history through the inability of historians to explain them and shattering the faith in human progress that had underlain historical interpretations by demonstrating that 'history is quite as much cataclysmic as evolutionary.' (It was Arnold Toynbee's ability to evoke these kinds of widely shared anti-rationalist, anti-scientific, and anti-democratic sentiments that Frank Underhill thought explained Toynbee's popular appeal in this period.)[61]

In this atmosphere, the significance of the Harvard Committee's *General Education in a Free Society* (1946), popularly known as 'The Harvard Report,' was not lost. Its recommendation for compulsory courses in 'Western Thought and Institutions,' to instill a central core of common convictions, reinforced many Canadian historians' view of history as the guardian of tradition.[62] The dominance of the state in the twentieth century, and its role in promoting militant ideologies, prompted George Glazebrook's plea for renewed attention to political history. In a letter to the *CHR*'s editors (December 1951), Glazebrook lamented its overshadowing by social and economic approaches. He castigated social historians for unfairly linking political history to the mid-nineteenth-century form that concentrated on government. Modern political history, he argued, dealt with the state and therefore involved analyses of private citizens as well as holders of public office and of both groups' thoughts, problems, and activities.[63] During the 1940s, the *CHR* reflected the shift in Canadian historical writing produced by such concerns. Donald Creighton, associate editor from 1939 to 1945 and thereafter a member of the editorial committee, and George Brown, in a key editorial role, were well placed to shape this development. Brown believed that Canada could not be seen in isolation and that its external relations, particularly with the United States, always had to be considered. The conviction that Canada's North American heritage was of prime importance in understanding its past, shared by many Canadian historians during the interwar years, grew stronger in the 1940s and 1950s with the rapid increase in U.S. power, as the *CHR*'s publication of numerous articles on Canadian-American relations makes clear.[64] Creighton, however, could not countenance this approach, as his article 'Sir John Macdonald and Canadian Historians' (March 1948) demonstrated. He believed that a Liberal nationalist interpretation had distorted Canada's past: the allegiance of Canadian historians to the Liberal Party had led to the dismissal of Sir

John A. Macdonald as a subject worth treating; a continentalist outlook contributed to the discrediting of Canada's British past and efforts 'to rehabilitate it as a decent American community.' The result was the use of American terminology and concepts in Canadian history, environmental determinism, and a failure to pay attention to cultural baggage, ideas, and people. Political biography, which placed the individual at the centre of events and as the focus of interpretation, was the solution to these failings.[65]

Creighton sought to bolster British traditions in a country where they were still strong but lacked their former force. Writing biography also helped to differentiate history from the social sciences and ensured its autonomy.[66] But the rhetoric surrounding his elevation of biography evoked the Cold War, particularly in its portrayal of individuals as much more than the product of economic and social forces. Moreover, Creighton wanted politically suitable subjects for biographical treatment. He was irate about the money spent on the series on the Social Credit Movement in Alberta because it focused on the likes of Henry Wise Wood and William Aberhart. He even noted that, in comparison, the memorials to the 'trivial radicals and sectional leaders of the East' resembled 'tombstones in a pauper's cemetery.'[67]

Creighton was not alone in reasserting the place of the individual in history. Vernon Fowke thought that the violent reaction against the 'great man theory of history' had 'left students of North American agrarianism with too little awareness of the personal element in agrarian leadership.'[68] W.L. Morton in turn criticized Fowke's *National Policy and the Wheat Economy* for using an Innisian interpretation (to Morton, a form of non-liberal economics), which ignored character.[69]

The approaches to Canadian history suggested by Creighton appeared in the *CHR* immediately. In one of the most important, J.M.S. Careless refuted the centrality of frontier influences in mid-nineteenth-century Upper Canada. His examination of agrarian radicalism in the Toronto *Globe*, which demonstrated the strength of urban influences, laid the foundation for his ideas about the influence of the metropolis over the hinterland (or frontier) that he first presented in the *CHR* in 1954.[70] These studies served to dismantle the environmental and Turnerian frontier interpretations that Creighton thought had warped the view of the Canadian past. Another departure was W.L. Morton's challenge to interpretations that attributed the troubles in the Red River Valley in 1869-70 to the forward movement of the frontier, which supposedly thrust Canadian political and religious issues onto a primitive and isolated society. Morton showed the Red River settlement instead as a civilized society disintegrating from within as the old order could no longer be sustained by the buffalo hunt and subsistence agriculture.[71]

New syntheses of Canadian history began appearing in the late 1940s: Lower's *Colony to Nation* (1946) and Edgar McInnis's *Canada: A Political and Social History* (1947). These works and the press's attention to them signalled to *CHR* reviewers that Canadian history had finally advanced beyond primary research to interpretation. C.P. Stacey saw Canadian historians as poised to make significant contributions to Canadian culture, even influencing thought on national problems.[72] Creighton's *Sir John A. Macdonald: The Young Politician* (1952) was the crowning achievement. Stacey praised it lavishly, not only for its extensive archival research but because it was a model biography.[73]

These accomplishments put some English-Canadian historians in a celebratory mood. For that reason, Lower was disappointed by Hilda Neatby's treatment of Canadian historical writing in the 1951 report of the Royal Commission on National Development in the Arts, Letters and Sciences (Massey Commission). He thought that Neatby consistently wrote off 'her fellow-craftsmen,' making false distinctions between specialists ('experts') and generalists ('popular writers'). The mere fact that Canadians wanted to read about themselves gave their historians a right to be conceited, Lower argued. 'What class of person has done more for Canadian culture in the last thirty years,' he asked, 'than the Canadian historian?'[74]

While English-Canadian historians were congratulating themselves for their contribution to Canada's national culture, French-Canadian historians were organizing for similarly nationalistic purposes. The *CHR*'s efforts to bridge the gap between French- and English-Canadian historical scholarship had not amounted to much by the 1940s, and the war deepened divisions. Although the CHA had anglophone and francophone members, English Canadians played a larger role; in the Royal Society of Canada, historians were divided into two separate sections; and few historians contributed to both the *CHR* and the *Bulletin des recherches historiques*.[75]

In 1946 the Institut d'histoire de l'Amérique française was created to foster the study of the French presence throughout North America. Its founding and that of its journal, the *Revue d'histoire de l'Amérique française* (*RHAF*), could not pass without notice in the *CHR*. The *nationaliste* historian Lionel Groulx had been instrumental in creating both enterprises, and his Université de Montréal disciples Guy Frégault and

Maurice Séguin also played prominent roles. Groulx's involvement led Richard Saunders, a member of the *CHR*'s editorial committee, to express the hope that the *RHAF* would be able to rise above Groulx's nationalism. In fact, the *RHAF* was concerned with improving historical scholarship, and it gave more prominence than the *CHR* to articles on methodology. The importance attached to theory would differentiate French-Canadian from English-Canadian historical scholarship even more sharply in the future.[76]

As much as the *CHR* in the late 1940s and the 1950s brought forward new work, it also narrowed its focus. The elevation of biography and the assault on Innisian interpretations further weakened Canadian economic history. The abandonment of economic and geographic conceptualizations made consideration of the natural environment unimportant to the work of most English-Canadian historians. The rejection of social science theories boded ill for rapprochement with political science, and the schism deepened with that discipline's turn to studies of political behaviour. In 1955 the *CHR* dropped its anthropology section, explaining that the development of 'strictly historical work' had put demands on space, but the effect was to reinforce a view that Native history was not a fitting subject for Canadian historians.[77]

By the Second World War, Canadian historians had all but lost interest in Native history. Bruce Trigger later explained (September 1986) that the 'invisibility' of Natives in the Canadian mainstream had facilitated the rejection of Native history by professional historians by the early twentieth century. Natives' increasing isolation on reserves, the rise of notions of the biological superiority of Europeans, and a historiography that celebrated Europeans' achievements all marginalized Indians, who became the concern primarily of anthropologists.[78] It is clear, however, that Canadian historians' growing emphasis on political and biographical history, as well as their push for disciplinary autonomy, also contributed to the dismissal of Native history.

There was little innovation in the *CHR* of the 1950s. Most contributions came from an older generation dealing with familiar topics. An advisory board had replaced the board of editors but seemingly had no function. The journal did not reflect new developments, particularly research in twentieth-century political history as the relevant government documents opened in the archives. If the *CHR* was arid, it mirrored the times. When Kenneth McNaught's biography of J.S. Woodsworth was published in 1959, Underhill wondered how contemporary Canadians – 'prosperous, complacent, conformist, conservative' – could appreciate the radical unrest of the 1920s and 1930s, and a man who was always challenging society's ideals.'[79]

The University of Toronto Press invited John Saywell to become editor in 1958 in order to enliven the journal. Saywell immediately sought out younger scholars working on modern Canadian history. By 1959 an array of new names and approaches was appearing. Frank Watt's 'The National Policy, the Workingman, and Proletarian Ideas in Canada' (March 1959) and Bernard Ostry's 'Conservatives, Liberals and Labour in the 1870s,' which appeared in June 1960, were only two of the numerous contributions that Saywell solicited. He initiated other changes as well. While still publishing only Canadian articles, he widened the fields covered in the book review section, bringing in new reviewers and ending the dominance that the University of Toronto history department had exercised over that aspect of the journal. No new appointments were made to the advisory board, which expired when the last of the three-year appointments ended.[80]

Contributions to the *CHR* in the early 1960s initiated changes in Canadian historical writing that became more pronounced in the 1970s. There was increased attention to provincial history and a more complex view of nationalism. Saywell's stress on provincial history was evident in the article he wrote with Blair Neatby, 'Chapleau and the Conservative Party in Quebec' (March 1956). It argued that one of the most significant developments in Canadian political history – Quebec's switch in federal allegiance from the Conservatives to the Liberals in the late nineteenth century – lacked adequate explanation because Canadian historians had focused on national parties and leaders: in so doing, they oversimplified provincial politics in Quebec, where the origins of the shift really lay. Saywell was elated by W.L. Morton's *Manitoba: A History* (1957): to him, it demonstrated that the most marked contribution to Canadian history would come from studies of the provinces.[81]

The new, pluralistic view of Canadian society held by this generation of historians blended with provincial history to produce a more nuanced treatment of nationalism. The recoil from excessive nationalism after the Second World War also added a critical edge to those interpretations. These influences were particularly manifested in examinations of the impact of the First World War on Canadian society and politics. In 'Clerics, Politicians, and the Bilingual Schools Issue in Ontario, 1910–1917,' Margaret Prang showed how Unionist candidates exploited the issue of French-Canadian participation in the war to win the election of 1917, aided in Ontario by the provincial parties' virtually identical policy on the bilingual problem that bolstered Ontarians' desire to make the French Canadians 'do their duty.'[82] Ramsay Cook insisted that the understanding of conscription, union government, and the racial rupture of 1917 required closer examination of Manitoba and Ontario politics. He demonstrated through his examination of J.W. Dafoe's attitudes towards these events, however, that Canadian nationalism had greater subtleties than historians had recognized. Dafoe's belief that Canada's national status implied international interests and responsibilities was more realistic than Laurier's, which saw Canada isolated from the world, concentrating on solving its own difficult problems.[83]

Debates regarding the nature of French-Canadian nationalism held prominence in this period of the *CHR*'s history because of the work of the historians at the Université de Montréal. Since the mid-1940s, Maurice Séguin, Guy Frégault, and Michel Brunet had been revising the image of New France as a clerically dominated society; the publication of Frégault's *La Guerre de la Conquête* in 1955 marked the end of the dominant Catholic nationalist interpretation of French Canada's past.[84] Reviewing Frégault's book for the *CHR* (March 1958), G.F.G. Stanley took issue with the main hypothesis; he could not understand how the surrender in 1763 could be viewed as the death blow to French Canada as a living society when its roots in the North American continent were so deep that it had developed its own sense of national consciousness.[85]

Even if English-Canadian historians did not agree with the Montreal school, the *CHR* acknowledged its importance by naming Frégault, in 1953, and Michel Brunet, in 1958, to the advisory board. The relevance of their work to modern Quebec was clear to Saywell, who, as organizer of the Toronto history department's Gray Lecture series, invited Brunet as speaker in 1958 and published the address in the *CHR* (June 1959). Brunet explained that French Canada was doomed to anaemic survival after the Conquest: its economic leaders migrated to France, and the rest submitted to the British crown; it was deprived of links to its own metropolis; and responsible government was granted only after the French Canadians constituted but a minority. Condemning English-Canadian interpretations of French Canada for their Victorian idealism, Brunet urged historians to become social scientists and to study the past in ways that provided solutions for the problems of urban, industrial life.[86]

As Brunet's address hinted, the Montreal historians had retained Groulx's nationalism while accepting the reality of urbanization and industrialization. Their work was geared to explaining Quebec's alleged economic inferiority and, by implication, offered solutions, which required state intervention. Frank Underhill detected anti-clericalism and yearnings for state socialism in Brunet's *La présence anglaise et les Canadiens* (1958), particularly in Brunet's suggestion that the post-conquest elevation of 'l'agriculturalisme, l'anti-étatism et le messianisme' had inhibited state action. In view of that, Underhill wondered why Brunet and his colleagues had adopted an isolationist stance and dismissed the efforts of English-Canadian intellectuals to build a bicultural Canada.[87]

The work of the Montreal school also generated conflict among historians of Quebec, which was linked to political debates over the province's future. Those who supported liberal or social democratic principles found their intellectual milieu in *Cité libre* circles, where they took issue with the Montreal school's interpretations and implicit nationalist solutions. Part of this conflict revolved around interpretations of New France's economic development and turned into arguments about the origins of French-Canadian nationalism. W.J. Eccles, whose *Frontenac: The Courtier Governor* (1959) also challenged dominant interpretations of New France, outlined the two sides of the debate to *CHR* readers in his review of Jean Hamelin's *Economie et société en Nouvelle-France* (1960). While the Montreal school contended that New France had a large Canadian commercial class that was destroyed by the Conquest, Hamelin, using the research methods of the Ecole pratique des Hautes Etudes at the Université de Paris, disputed the existence of a Canadian bourgeoisie: his evidence indicated that the sizeable group of wealthy men in the colony did not act like good bourgeois because they spent their profits, instead of using them to expand their commercial and industrial enterprises.[88]

As these interpretations turned into debates about the origins of nationalism, the separatist cause intensified in Quebec. Signalling where its sympathies lay, the *CHR* reprinted, as its first item in French, an article by Ouellet that had appeared in *Liberté* in March 1962 – 'Les Fondements historiques de l'option séparatiste dans le Québec,' which highlighted the connection between historical interpretations and the political situation in Quebec. Ouellet noted that French-Canadian nationalism characteristically displayed separatist tendencies in periods of economic difficulty. After explaining the dominance of nationalism as an ideology in Quebec – in the Montreal school and in the movement for reform after the death of Maurice Duplessis – he postulated other ways of dealing with the imperatives of the modern world.[89] His interpretation of the origins of French-Canadian nationalism appeared in the *CHR* two years later. Ouellet argued (December 1964) that nationalist historians tended to find the beginnings of nationalism back in New France because they believed that nationalism was indispensable to all collective existence. His research found its emergence in the period between 1802 and 1837, first within the liberal professions, and then, in the 1830s, when the first bishop of Montreal, Mgr Lartigue, separated it from its liberal attachments to make it accord with a theocratic vision of society.[90]

When Ouellet's *Histoire économique et sociale du Québec, 1760–1850* (1966) appeared, Jacques Monet's *CHR* review hailed it as one of the era's most important scholarly works on nineteenth-century Quebec. It not only shattered the Conquest hypothesis, but its argumentation and its use of the quantitative methods of the Annales school – facts, charts, and price indices – represented a turn from the '*terribles simplificateurs*' towards scholars who 'understand the past as a complex story in which the truth is seldom simple and the choices always difficult.'[91] Monet's own *CHR* article, in September 1966, on the annexation crisis of 1848–50 attempted to demonstrate another dimension of that complexity in its suggestion that the British constitution had always served as the best protection for French Canadians and their nationality.[92]

As the nationalist interpretations of Quebec history proliferated, the *CHR*'s ability to attract articles from francophone historians worsened. When Ramsay Cook spoke about the journal at an AHA meeting in Toronto in 1967, he described this as one of the *CHR*'s greatest failings. As editor from 1963 to 1968, he also worried about the lack of outside stimulus on Canadian history.[93] Out of that concern, and pressure from subscribers, he continued to invite ranking historians in other fields to review books.[94]

Specialization and the Renewal of Diversity in Recent Decades

The pressure on the *CHR* to reconsider its Canadian-only policy on articles stemmed from the university expansion of the mid-1960s, which saw the hiring of numerous scholars outside Canadian history. One result was the appearance in March 1966 of a journal devoted to fields of history other than Canadian – the *Canadian Journal of History/Annales canadiennes d'histoire*, published at the University of Saskatchewan.[95] Growth of the profession and changes in the discipline also brought forward scholars posing questions not normally pursued in Canadian history. This was reflected in a number of contributions to the *CHR* in the mid-1960s, which suggested the need for discussions of class and social structure. Outlining how the dominant concerns of Canadian historiography had inhibited such analyses, S.R. Mealing (September 1965) demanded more attention to cultural change, intellectual history, social structure, and ordinary people.[96] A Soviet critique of the *CHR* attributed its neglect of theoretical issues, class struggle, mass movements, and their economic underpinnings to the journal's idealistic adherence to objectivity and its political and biographical focus.[97] With its treatment of class and social structure, John Porter's *The Vertical Mosaic* (1965) did not escape the *CHR*'s notice. While Arthur Lower attacked its turgid prose, Margaret Prang argued that it demonstrated the need for work on social structure, ethnic pluralism, working-class and trade union history, the social consequences of migration, and religious history. She declared that it was time for Canadian historians to abandon national history, and instead give priority to regional and local themes.[98]

By the time of the nation's centennial celebrations in 1967, it was already clear that Canadian history was moving away from national history. Under Saywell's editorship in the late 1950s, awareness of the necessity of studying provincial and regional history had been established in the *CHR*. In a review article written for the *International Journal* during the centennial year, Ramsay Cook provided the metaphor that symbolized the trend. Tired of books that deplored Canada's lack of national identity and unity, he suggested that efforts should be made to understand regional, ethnic, and class identities: it was in those more limited identities, he commented, that 'Canadianism' might be found. In 1969, J.M.S. Careless's 'Limited Identities in Canada' promoted that approach in the *CHR*. It also noted that in dealing too wishfully with nationalism, Canadian historiography had 'produced expectations and discouragements out of keeping with realities.'[99]

The enormous impact that Louis Hartz had on North American history in the mid to late 1960s was apparent in Careless's suggestion that Canadian historians turn to Hartz's work on culture fragments as a way to understand Canadian regions and their social and political cultures. Not surprisingly, an article by Hartz immediately appeared in the *CHR*, but it dealt with violence in the supposedly consensual North American polity. It argued that the fragment culture, in containing only one aspect of the European social universe, heightened consensus but also produced new sources of violence lacking in Europe. His article was followed by Robin Winks's discussion of the segregation of Blacks in Ontario and Nova Scotia schools.[100]

As such articles showed, the political and intellectual tumult of the late 1960s was shaking Canadian history. If it was ending consensus history in the United States, it was shattering the minimal consensus in the Canadian field. Many young Canadian historians and graduate students were attuned to the worldwide shift away from political history to economic and social approaches that emphasized class and social structure. This was particularly pronounced in Quebec, where the influence of Annales school helped turn historians to the everyday life of communities. These intellectual currents disturbed many Canadian historians. In his presidential address to the CHA in 1967, Richard Saunders noted that the promise of scientific history had not succeeded: mountains of research and specialization had brought not truth but 'a steadily intensifying centrifugal tendency' that caused tension among historians, students, and staff alike. 'Where, they ask, is the common bond that holds us all together?' He reminded his audience that historians had once had an important role in imparting to succeeding generations what it meant to live in a nation.[101]

The *CHR* celebrated its fiftieth anniversary in 1970 with its editors aware of what these tensions meant for the 'national' historical journal. Craig Brown and Michael Cross invited contributions in social, religious, educational, legal, medical, and cultural history; they urged those working in local history not to assume that, because the *CHR* had always 'exulted in the title of "national" journal of Canadian history,' it published only political and national history.[102] The same year saw political turbulence and violence in Quebec that culminated in the invocation of the War Measures Act; this only served to underline the *CHR*'s concern about the implications of neo-nationalist scholarship. In the March 1970 issue, a commissioned article by eminent French historian Robert Mandrou evaluated French-Canadian historical writing since 1945. An advocate of the social scientific approach, Mandrou praised Marcel Trudel, Jean Hamelin, Fernand Ouellet, W.E. Eccles, and Cole Harris, for their extensive and meticulous research and criticized the Université de Montréal historians for their apocalyptic visions of the Canadian future.[103] Similar criticisms were directed against the Montreal school on the eve of the October crisis, in the book-review section of the September 1970 issue. Yves Zoltvany called on Frégault's followers to substantiate his provocative hypothesis before it became 'a platitudinous cliché.'[104]

Articles in Quebec history in the *CHR* during the next year displayed growing diversity in the field and a less monolithic view of Quebec society. They demonstrated that, by the nineteenth century, the supposed foundations of French-Canadian life – the church, the seigneuries, the clerical and political élite – were weak. The *habitants* were not exceptionally religious or virtuous (Wallot, March 1971); Louis-Joseph Papineau's *seigneurie* had experienced extreme poverty and numerous other institutional weaknesses; Montreal had been alive with industrial, religious, and nationalist tendencies, with shifting political alliances (Young, December 1970).[105] The picture of New France was still changing: W.J. Eccles argued that military interests ran the fur trade a close second as the mainstay of the colony and shaped its ethos and social structure. And L.R. MacDonald, making explicit reference to the work of a Soviet historian and to Marxist theory, concluded that mercantilism and French policy towards New France had inhibited the development of the necessary pre-conditions for the emergence of capitalism.[106]

The highly politicized arguments about Quebec's economic development and the origins of nationalism did not disappear; indeed, they became more complex as historians fought over economic and quantitative approaches – as in the controversy over the state of Lower Canadian agriculture at the turn of the nineteenth century; see T.J.A. LeGoff in the *CHR* (March 1974). Gilles Pacquet and Jean-Pierre Wallot dismissed Ouellet's thesis that an agricultural crisis produced the discontent that fostered nationalism and the rebellions of 1837–8. They charged that Ouellet did not understand Lower Canada's multifaceted economy and attributed too much importance to agriculture. Their work saw the Lower-Canadian economy as a vulnerable part of a larger transatlantic economic system: agricultural difficulties intensified social discontent and formalized political tensions, but they did not produce nationalism; it already existed.[107]

A few years after the launch of the journal *Histoire sociale / Social History*, *CHR* editors made efforts to include articles in quantitative history. Through 1972 and 1973, Michael Katz, David Gagan, and others offered insight on the history of ordinary people and instruction on how to approach it. Influenced by U.S. scholarship on urbanization and industrialization and their effects on equality and social mobility, Katz presented material from the Social History Project on Hamilton. David Gagan's Peel County project focused on the family as the fundamental unit of social, economic, and cultural organization, following lines of inquiry established by such historians as Lawrence Stone. Both articles explained how the data for such investigations, obtained from censuses, parish records, assessment rolls, city directories, and land registry records, were assembled and manipulated through use of computers.[108]

The *CHR*'s application for Canada Council funding in 1971 may have influenced the decision to include these kinds of articles. Although the assessments were favourable and the funds were granted, the preponderance of political history in the journal was noted, as was its inattention to newer social science methodologies, historical sociology, and philosophy. These were seen as faults of the Canadian field more generally, which the *CHR* was well placed to correct.[109] The *CHR*'s application for Canada Council funds in 1975–6 produced positive comments – the *CHR* was the bell-wether for Canadian scholarly journals – but it was criticized as being dominated by the University of Toronto's history department. In response, the University of Toronto Press (UTP) established an advisory board, with five members representing the regions of Canada, to be appointed by UTP on the advice of the *CHR*'s editors.[110] The *CHR* would continue to maintain an office in Toronto, with at least one editor who resided in the area. In 1979, however, because of the continued perception that the *CHR* was a Toronto product, the board decided that the journal should have two co-editors, one of whom was from Quebec, the east, or the west. After 1976, because of the enormous backlog of accepted material, it once again confined book reviews to the Canadian field.[111]

The *CHR*'s status as a general journal in a time of increasing specialization helped generate criticism. The *AHR* experienced difficulties throughout the early 1970s for the same reason. A committee's review of that journal in 1975 found the criticisms symptomatic of profound changes in the historical profession, among them the influence of the social sciences. The committee received one letter that made the telling point: 'the *AHR* has always presupposed the existence of a universe of discourse' among historians. The committee accordingly urged the *AHR* to explain various areas of specialization as a way of dealing with the fragmentation of the discipline.[112]

With similar intentions, *CHR* editors supplemented specialized pieces with articles of general interest and frequently reminded readers and contributors that they were seeking a middle ground. In 1977, editors David Bercuson and Robert Bothwell emphasized the *CHR*'s status as a national journal, reflecting Canada's best historical writing: political history would continue to find a home in the *CHR* but would 'share the limelight with newer approaches.'[113] In an effort to broaden and improve the journal, they established an annual prize for the best article and commissioned historiographical pieces on labour and the left, women and the family, and disciplines related to history. After a readers' survey in 1978, they redoubled their efforts to use a broader range of appraisers and reviewers and to publish articles in social history and on eastern and western Canada.[114]

Even these changes did not guarantee all-inclusiveness. Editors often observe that a journal is only as good as its submissions. The *CHR* received few articles in some fields and often rejected pieces in others. One underrepresented area was the history of ideas: Canada had only a few specialists, and many English-Canadian historians had never accepted it as a valid approach. As trends shifted from political to social history, the position of intellectual history deteriorated. Social historians objected that it dealt with élites, focused on nationalist themes, and was not grounded in material reality. Although the September 1950 issue of the *CHR* had been devoted to aspects of nineteenth-century central Canadian cultural and intellectual developments,[115] studies on cultural institutions such as public broadcasting, the press, and magazines started appearing only in 1965.[116] Religious history fared better, particularly those topics that dealt with the social reform tradition.[117]

The history of ideas had deeper roots in French-Canadian historiography, and the *CHR*'s items in the field were among its most intellectually wide-ranging. A.I. Silver's treatment (March 1969) of French-Canadian attitudes towards western expansion was set in the context of a wider discussion of the mentality of colonization. Later, Silver (December 1976) showed how late-nineteenth-century cultural conflict was fuelled by conflicting ideologies of imperialism and mission and thereby challenged the accepted notion of Quebec as an insular society.[118]

The *CHR* presented few articles in working-class history in the 1970s despite the field's rapid growth. Its practitioners' ideological position seemed to cause resistance. The approach that began in western Europe, Britain, and the United States in the 1960s dealt with the totality of working-class life. It saw the industrial revolution's disciplining of the workforce as a cultural rather than as simply an economic process and the evolution of class consciousness as a cultural expression of resistance to industrial capitalism. This approach required international context – an understanding of class as a culture with its own dynamics, as well as attention to local texture, which in Canada accorded well with the shift to 'limited identities.' Many young Canadian historians were attracted to working-class history at a time when the New Left, the war in Vietnam, trends in social history, and Marxist critiques of capitalism and imperialism raised new questions about the Canadian past. Their studies were influenced by the work of Antonio Gramsci, who stressed the cultural underpinnings of capitalism; by E.P. Thompson, E.J. Hobsbawm, Raymond Williams, and Gareth Stedman Jones, who endeavoured to rediscover British working-class life; and by Melvin Dubofsky's and Herbert Gutman's work on American working-class culture. They also had Canadian forebears in H.C. Pentland and Frank Watt.[119]

Articles by Pentland and Watt were among the very rare treatments of class found in the *CHR* before the 1960s. Pentland, a labour economist and historian, demonstrated that an oppositional working class, shaped by industrial development, existed in Canada. His article (September 1948) on the Lachine Strike of 1843 saw the 1840s as the transitional decade in the emergence of large-scale wage labour, which would forge itself into a self-conscious, independent force. Watt (March 1959) treated the cultural expression of radicalism, challenging assumptions that class-conscious social ideals were imported to Canada from the Russian Revolution or were attributable to the Depression. He identified a tradition of radicalism in the Canadian labour press that borrowed from American and English radical thought; he showed that it ran counter to the nation-building aspirations of the mainstream political parties and foreshadowed the radicalism that developed in the twentieth century after Macdonald's National Policy did its work.[120]

The conviction that radicalism was alien to Canada may well have hindered the development of class analysis in Canadian history, particularly during the Cold War. An approach closer to mainstream historiography found greater acceptance: it treated labour as part of political–economic development and focused on industrial relations, the growth of trade unions, social democratic leadership, the evolution of collective bargaining, and parliamentary reforms. Within this tradition, Martin Robin's 1966 *CHR* article corrected the assumption that organized labour's resistance to mobilization efforts during the First World War was a sectional rather than a class phenomenon – with Quebec nationalism posing the only obstacle. He showed that opposition was widespread, culminating in organized labour's stand against conscription and the entry of the Trades and Labour Congress into independent politics.[121] Nevertheless, the trade union approach, exemplified by H.A. Logan, was subject to criticism from all sides. In a *CHR* book review in 1969, Walter Young complained that Canadian labour history, in its concern with numerous trade union organizations (referred to by acronyms) was dull, convoluted, and 'pock-marked with initials.'[122] Michael Bliss praised Martin Robin's *Radical Politics and Canadian Labour*

1880–1930 (1968) for its 'lack of ideological overlay' but criticized it for its insignificance. In Bliss's view, more could be learned about Canadian society in the late nineteenth and early twentieth-century through a study of the temperance movement. He suggested that Canadian historians turn to the work of E.P. Thompson and Herbert Gutman for methodological approaches that would reveal more about the lives of working-class people.[123]

This endeavour was well under way in the early 1970s, despite scant evidence in the *CHR*. Articles by Michael Cross (March 1973), which dealt with the Shiners' War in the Ottawa Valley, and Desmond Morton (December 1970), on the Canadian militia, illustrated the dimensions of class conflict and violence in nineteenth- and early-twentieth-century Canada.[124] In a 1975 issue of the *CHR*, however, Morton suggested that the emotional demand for Canadian labour and working-class history was not being met in the production of manuscripts.[125] The Canadian Committee on Labour History formed in the early 1970s to foster work in the area, and by 1976 there was enough material to support the creation of *Labour / Le Travailleur* (later renamed *Le Travail*), a journal dedicated to the interdisciplinary study of Canadian labour history.[126] Shortly thereafter, products of the new approach began to appear in the *CHR*: Peter N. Moogk examined craftsmen's associations in early French Canada; and Craig Heron and Bryan Palmer dealt with industrial conflict in southern Ontario between 1910 and 1914, demonstrating the existence of class consciousness in the centre of maturing industrial capitalism.[127]

As social and working-class history made its way into the *CHR*, hostility and contentiousness became palpable. Some historians were disturbed by the Marxist overtones in treatments of class and class conflict. As John Cairns observed in a more general way in his review of Geoffrey Barraclough's *Main Trends in History* (1979), what came to be referred to as the 'New History' – 'global, quantitative, scientific (social), and collaborative' – was attempting to finish what Marxism began: 'What Marxism began in a sectarian way has now developed and broadened into powerful rivers of social, psychological, and mathematical inquiry, at once complementary and fragmenting, overturning conventional structures, discovering new courses.'[128] When H.C. Pentland reviewed *Essays in Canadian Working Class History* (1976), he referred to the animosity that Canadian working-class historians had produced with their 'revolutionary aspirations.' He thought the reaction misplaced, since the collection's essays were mostly straightforward studies in labour history.

Reviews of other working class histories made the same observation.[129] For example, in a historiographical article on labour and the left that received a *CHR* prize, Kenneth McNaught (June 1981) commented that, despite their neo-Marxism, these historians' most significant work hardly drew on Marxist theory at all, or even on the methodology of the new social history: it looked at local communities using a narrative approach.[130]

The new political economy, centred in the University of Toronto's Department of Political Economy, was the target of similar rebukes. A revival of economic history that began in the 1960s, this approach combined Innisian interpretations with Marxist theory to study Canadian economic dependency. Whereas Innis focused on the staple, the new political economy attempted to understand the transition from commercialism to capitalism by examining the way in which capital was accumulated; where Innis saw the staple as the tie that bound the periphery to the centre, capital served that function in the new political economy.[131] Innis's continuing influence concerned W.J. Eccles, who called for a reassessment of *The Fur Trade*. In a prize-winning article for the *CHR* (December 1979), Eccles charged that Innis, with his economic determinism and *a priori* assumptions, had promulgated incorrect views of the fur trade: he had overrated the role of the fur trade in New France, failing to recognize other crucial factors, including France's interest in the fur trade as a way to facilitate military alliances with the Indians. Eccles also thought that Innis was responsible for fostering the myth that the fur trade's incompatibility with agriculture, industry, and other forms of external trade had hampered New France's economic development.[132]

Eccles's article met with immediate criticism from the new political economists. A doctoral candidate in the field, Hugh Grant (September 1991), criticized his misunderstanding of Innis's intentions. Innis had articulated a framework in which historical problems were to be perceived, Grant explained: he saw the fur trade as 'a product of the spatial extension of European empires in their search for staple products'; his interest was to emphasize 'the discrepancy between the centre and the margin of western civilization which was the result.' This was not economic determinism but an attempt 'to define the limits which material conditions imposed upon the range of human activity.'[133]

By the late 1970s anthropologists and historical geographers were finding this approach useful for their studies, as Cole Harris's prize-winning *CHR* article (September 1985) on Idaho Peak in the BC interior made clear. Harris thought Innis's analytical framework invaluable and criticized its dismissal by a generation of Canadian scholars. Modern British Columbia was a product of the same pattern that had shaped Canadian society since the early sixteenth century – the entrance of capital and labour into 'the recesses of Canadian space.' In a process that Innis had identified, first the fur trade and then gold rushes, fishing, logging, and hardrock mining attracted capital and labour close to resources but far from markets. The result was creation of settlements of migratory workers from different ethnic backgrounds, where the 'technic of labour' overrode culture.[134]

Since the 1970s, the work of historical geographers Cole Harris, John Warkentin, and Graeme Wynn has reviewed important recognition from the Canadian historical profession. Harris and Warkentin's *Canada before Confederation: A Study in Historical Geography* (1974), Wynn's *Timber Colony: A Historical Geography of Early Nineteenth-Century New Brunswick* (1981), and the *Historical Atlas of Canada, I: Canada before 1800* (1987), edited by Cole Harris, all received high praise for their illuminating treatment of early Canadian history. Canadian historical geography has been concerned with the modification of environments and with the ways in which people have made sense of their settings and conducted themselves within them; the development of community, region, and nation has also been of central concern.[135] *CHR* articles in the field have examined subjects that professional historians have failed to treat. Most recently, Graeme Wynn (March 1993), drawing on the work of Rusty Bitterman and Robert MacKinnon, presented a microanalysis of the Nova Scotian countryside in the mid-nineteenth-century, which refutes the notion of a pre-Confederation 'Golden Age' for the Maritimes. The image, spawned during the 1920s in a period of economic and social disruption, had served emotional needs by holding out the promise of a better future, but it belied the social and political instability of life experienced by the rural majority.[136]

Other forgotten and neglected aspects of the Canadian past re-emerged in the 1980s and 1990s, stimulated by developments outside Canadian history. A second edition of Bailey's *Conflict of European and Eastern Algonkian Cultures* came out in 1969, followed by several other studies chronicling Native history. This renewed interest came on the heels of a U.S. revival that started in the 1950s, when social scientists working on theories of personality development and acculturation began to look at

Native groups. In the 1960s the increasing visibility of Native groups in American society – the result of a growing population and heightened activism – attracted historians and anthropologists interested in class, gender, and racial and ethnic groups to Native history. As Native peoples became more prominent in Canadian political and economic affairs – especially in court cases dealing with treaties and land claims – anthropologists and ethnohistorians took an interest in their history; later, historians worked to integrate these findings into the framework of Canadian history.[137]

One of the roles of ethnohistory, according to anthropologist Bruce Trigger (September 1986), was 'to free mainstream North American history from its legacy as a colonial ideology.' It accomplished this by developing outside the mainstream of the historical discipline and by bringing the history of the Natives back from the peripheries where it had been relegated. It sought to understand Native culture from within rather than through the views of Europeans and, by using the methods and material of history and other disciplines, to understand the nature and causes of change in a culture, as defined by ethnological concepts and categories.[138]

Trigger brought Native history back to the *CHR* in the late 1960s. In 'The French Presence in Huronia: The Structure of Franco–Huron Relations in the First Half of the Seventeenth Century' (September 1968), he emphasized the centrality of Native peoples to the history of Canada. Since European colonizers, traders, and missionaries knew that their success depended on an ability to understand and accommodate themselves to Native customs and networks of political and economic relationships, modern historians must study the Indians' customs, behaviour, and values.[139] In that context, he reminded *CHR* readers of a tradition of Canadian scholarship that had been ignored for decades: in 1931, T.F. McIlwraith had argued in the *CHR* that 'an accurate interpretation of the first two hundred years of Canadian history must take cognizance of the Indian point of view as well as that of the white man.'[140]

Trigger thought that Canadian historians had neglected Native history because of their Eurocentric concerns but also because of their reluctance to learn the requisite skills from anthropology and ethnology. Cornelius Jaenen noted the same faults. In 'Amerindian Views of French Culture in the Seventeenth Century' (September 1974), he assailed Canadian historians' one-sided view of Native–European contact: failure to examine both parties defied 'the most elementary canons of historical interpretation.'[141] He also drew historians' attention to the cross-cultural and interdisciplinary interpretations of ethnohistorians. He argued that Trigger's *The Children of Aataentsic* (2 vols., 1976) would dictate much of future scholarship on the subject and praised James Axtell's *The Invasion Within: The Contest of Cultures in Colonial North America* (1985) for transforming colonial history.[142]

These social and ethnohistory approaches combined to produce interpretations of the fur trade as a social system that was mutually beneficial for Europeans and Natives. Sylvia Van Kirk's *'Many Tender Ties'* (1980), which treated the role of women in the economy and society of the western fur trade, brought that interpretation to prominence.[143] In turn, an appreciation that the fur trade had produced a unique, racially mixed society contributed to the growth of Métis history. The *CHR* acknowledged these fields by devoting a special issue to Louis Riel and Métis history in March 1988 and to Native and fur trade history in June 1992. The hundreth anniversary of Riel's hanging and the publication of his collected writings contributed to the reassessment of Riel, but the new lines of interpretation in Métis history borrowed from working-class and women's history. As advisory board member Jim Miller, a scholar in the field, explained, this approach forsook climactic events and political organization to deal with everyday experience.[144]

As with a few other fields, women's history, already rare in the *CHR*, disappeared from the journal in the late 1940s and the 1950s. This was a reflection of its absence from Canadian history more generally, although Frank Underhill's review of Catherine Cleverdon's *The Woman Suffrage Movement in Canada* (1950) applauded it for rescuing Canadian history from dullness.[145] Through the 1970s, as women's history grew in Britain and the United States, reviews of the major studies appeared in the *CHR*. In 1976, *Women at Work* was noted as 'a long overdue and exciting historical anthology of the involvement of women in the development of Canada.'[146]

It was only in the 1980s, however, that the growth of Canadian women's history became evident in the *CHR* in the form of articles. Lack of submissions may explain the earlier absence of women's history in the journal, and the existence of *Atlantis*, *Labour* and *Social History* may have drawn away contributions. A likely obstacle was the reformist and revolutionary objective of women's history. Susan Mann (Trofimenkoff) made these clear to *CHR* readers in her review of *L'Histoire des femmes au Québec depuis quatre siècles* (1982): 'From the beginning, back in the late 1960s, women's history has harboured the premise that oppression or at least inferior status is the common lot of the female half of humanity. Once documented, that oppression would become an intellectual and political weapon, first to change the past and then to change the future.'[147]

In her historiographical article on women's history, Eliane Leslau Silverman (December 1982) expressed hope that the field would not be feared but integrated into the mainstream of Canadian history. She explained that women's history ran a separate but parallel line with general Canadian history: it was the story of the female majority living in tension with the institutions that contained them in subsidiary and auxiliary positions, but it was also the history of their own culture.[148] Over the next decade, women's history and the concerns of female historians in Canada's institutions of higher learning attained prominence in the *CHR*. The CHA's 1989 survey on the status of women historians, reported by Linda Kealey, revealed that women had been appointed at lower ranks and were promoted more slowly than their male colleagues and that the place of women's history in the curriculum had to be considered.[149]

The diversity of Canadian women's history was evident in the *CHR*'s issue of December 1991, which was devoted to the field. In her treatment of the literature since the 1980s, Gail Cuthbert Brandt noted that the simplicity of earlier studies was gone and that the later ones resembled a patchwork quilt – of the crazy-quilt variety. She attributed this to the influence of postmodernism, which many feminist historians found attractive in its emphasis on difference, its recognition of the way in which social and cultural factors created historical 'fact,' its rejection of linear, all-encompassing interpretations, and its use of deconstruction.[150]

There is little doubt that the editorial and advisory board structure implemented in the late 1970s contributed to the increasing diversity of the *CHR*'s articles in the 1980s and 1990s. Many issues reflected the interests of editors and advisory board members. In 1983, when the *CHR* was under the editorship of J.L. Granatstein and Douglas McCalla, there were numerous articles in political, diplomatic, and military history. When H.V. Nelles was involved, first as an advisory board member and then as an editor, economic history made a stronger appearance in a dialogue on Ontario's industrial revolution and in articles dealing with economic inequality and the distribution of wealth. During Colin Howell's tenure as a co-editor, the Atlantic provinces' role in Confederation was discussed.

The inclusion of an array of fields did not mean that the *CHR* had abandoned its mission to be a general and national journal or that political history was absent. At the start of the *CHR*'s seventh decade, editors Robert Bothwell and David Bercuson declared that they would not allow the journal to become 'the prisoner of one position.' They expressed concern that 'sectarian interests' had diminished awareness of the variety and scope of Canadian history and led to an 'erosion of knowledge in its broadest sense,' and the editors committed the *CHR* to a broad understanding of Canada's past.[151]

Some readers equated that 'broad understanding' with national, political history, as indicated by a CHA session in 1984 entitled, 'What's Wrong with the *CHR*?' In response, editor Douglas McCalla presented a statistical profile to demonstrate that the geographical and subject spread of *CHR* contributions had never been more diverse. The journal had touched on most fields of history and was balanced between political and economic or social items; half the articles were not classifiable in regional terms – understandable, McCalla thought, for a national journal. The institutional affiliations of contributors indicated a preponderance from Ontario, but McCalla noted that the province probably had the largest number of historians. It was the near absence of francophone writing and the small number of French-language books reviewed that concerned the editors and the advisory board.[152] Nevertheless, the readers' survey that same year revealed subscribers' displeasure. Some wanted greater effort to include new subjects and methodologies, while others complained about too much social history. McCalla and co-editor Robin Fisher, however, worried: 'The effort to please everyone may well result in satisfying no one.'[153]

It is clear that through the 1980s and the early 1990s, the *CHR* tried, with varying degrees of success, to deal with diversification in the field of Canadian history. It was presenting divergent views of the past from historians concerned with different subjects and issues. But what had happened to its status as a national journal and to historians' (and thus the *CHR*'s) concomitant role in leading the Canadian public? The widely expressed concern about the profession's diminishing public stature suggested a desire that historians engage a wider public.

John English (March 1986) regarded the dismissal of political history since the late 1960s as symptom and contributing factor in the profession's apparent decline. This dismissal went hand in hand with the end of the nationalist mission, precipitated by change in the university – where historians and future prime ministers once shared the same classrooms and the same vision of Canada, which they worked together to support, politics had lost its charm. The student protest movement and the hiring of American faculty members, who brought their own distrust of politics and opposition to the war in Vietnam, contributed to its rejection, while attacks all across Canada against Ottawa and centralization reinforced the shift to 'limited identities.' In English's view, this specialization had not made history more attractive for undergraduates, the reading public, or other disciplines.[154]

The actions of university and government institutions added to fears of the profession's weakening. Throughout the 1980s, the *CHR* documented retrenchment in the universities – few tenure-track appointments, promotions, or transfers – in its 'Historians in Canada' surveys. Many historians saw the efforts of the Social Sciences and Humanities Research Council of Canada to push research in certain directions through its strategic grants program, and to favour group projects, as government interference. Reduction in service at the Public Archives of Canada, restricted access to government documents, and Freedom of Information legislation (with sections aimed at the protection of privacy) posed additional impediments to research, and editors David Bercuson and J.L. Granatstein called on the CHA to lobby in Ottawa on behalf of professional historians.[155]

Other evidence of history's declining status was the absence of historians from important legal and political decision-making bodies. Advisory board members Gregory Kealey and Rosemary Ommer noted that historians were rarely appointed to royal commissions any longer. For this, historians were partly to blame, they argued, because of their failure to demonstrate that interpretation and analysis were central to the discipline and their ambivalence about history's value for dealing with the present and the future.[156] Similarly, Canadian historians were urged to serve as expert witnesses in litigation. By participating in cases arising out of the Charter of Rights and Freedoms, they would have an opportunity to 'educate the litigants and the courts on important matters to Canadian society.' The example of the U.S. case *Equal Employment Opportunity Commission v. Sears, Roebuck*, however, in which two specialists in women's history, Rosalind Rosenberg and Alice Kessler-Harris, offered conflicting interpretations of working women's occupational mobility gave pause. Participating in an alien intellectual environment, with different rules of evidence, could weaken historians' effectiveness in their own forum.[157]

Canadian historians were also concerned about the ground they were losing to popularizers. Although they were reluctant to write contemporary history, they complained about its superficial treatment in the hands of journalists and autobiographers. With the publication of Peter C. Newman's widely selling book on the fur trade, *Company of Adventurers* (1985), Jennifer Brown observed a gulf – 'two solitudes'– between the book's journalistic reviewers and promoters, who praised it lavishly, and specialist-historians, who criticized its approach. Newman dismissed these criticisms as the 'standard academic attack on popular historians' and declared: 'Canadian history belongs to all of us.' Brown agreed but argued that this implied 'a sacred trust to treat it fairly.' For Newman, the controversy indicated that academic and popular history would never coexist: professional historians, wedded to the concept of objectivity, did not infuse their tales with the bounce and bravado characteristic of popular history. He regretted that the Canadian historical community had so few successors to Donald Creighton, W.L. and A.S. Morton, Chester Martin, and Arthur Lower, 'writers who combined academic integrity with an ability to write evocative prose.'[158]

In its effort to be a national journal, the *CHR* continued through the 1980s and 1990s to attempt to bridge English- and French-Canadian historical scholarship. Having English-Canadian historians review books on Quebec and francophones deal with English-Canadian publications, however, seemed only to accentuate differences and exacerbate tensions. Quebec historical writing in the 1980s was characterized by economic and social analyses of the post-Confederation period, which focused on class conflict, the status of women, and the role of the state, as reflected in Paul-André Linteau, Jean-Claude Robert, and René Durocher's *Histoire du Québec contemporain*.[159] In his review of Robert Bothwell, John English, and Ian Drummond's *Canada since 1945*, Robert criticized its centralist approach; he thought that it displayed ignorance of Quebec and other regions of the country; and he could not understand how the only significant socio-cultural cleavage that it treated – in a country with classes and persistent inequality – was the anglophone–francophone divide. The authors replied that Robert was confusing objectivity with his own subjective view of events.[160]

In a review of *Le Québec depuis 1930* (1986), John Thompson explained why these different views of modern Canada existed alongside each other. In the tradition of the Annales school, Robert and his colleagues looked at the *longue durée*: they were interested in the modification of a traditional society; they saw this not as an abrupt transition dating from the Second World War or the Quiet Revolution but as a gradual one, with roots in the past. In contrast with the authors of *Canada since 1945*, they did not write a narrative of events; they emphasized structures more than conjunctures; their principal characters were not people but fundamental processes: industrial capitalism, urbanization, technological change, demographic fluctuations, and class formation.[161]

The pluralistic view of twentieth-century Quebec emerging from the work of Quebec historians did not necessarily mean that support for the nationalist cause had disappeared. Ronald Rudin explained in the *CHR* (March 1992) that the efforts of Quebec politicians to promote Quebec as a 'distinct' society and those of revisionist historians (among them, Allan Greer, Jean-Claude Robert, Normand Séguin, and Brian Young) to show that it was 'normal' were not contradictory but dedicated to the same ends. The effort of revisionists to prove that the myths about Quebec's distinctive past were false and that Quebec experienced the same processes of industrialization and urbanization as the rest of the Western world had to be read correctly. Although the analyses were not directly linked to political issues, Rudin noted, the emphasis on Quebec's normality was intended to demonstrate that it had the preconditions to achieve the status of all 'normal' societies – statehood.[162] The close relationship between politics and interpretations of history was nowhere more evident than in the aftermath of the provincial election victory of the Parti Québécois in September 1994, when Jacques Parizeau suggested that Quebeckers would become 'a normal people' when they regained their confidence in the future. He reiterated the argument in subsequent discussions of plans for the Quebec sovereignty referendum.[163]

If some divides were intractable, there were signs in the *CHR* during the late 1980s and 1990s that fragmentation in the discipline was lessening. Joy Parr (December 1987) introduced *CHR* readers to a sophisticated form of social history that incorporated working-class, economic, and women's history to examine how gender, as a social – not a biological – construct, affected lives, work, and social relationships. The article demonstrated that gender was confounded by time, class, and place.[164] Working-class historians' increasing attention of late to the state defies criticism that their field neglects politics. British sociologists Philip Corrigan and Derek Sayer suggested important new lines of inquiry in *The Great Arch: English State Formation as Cultural Revolution* (1985), but, as Sean T. Cadigan's *CHR* article (September 1991) on Sir Francis Bond Head and the Upper Canadian general election of 1836 made clear, an interest in the state was always implicit in the field's Marxist approach. Cadigan saw events surrounding the election as part of an ongoing conflict between Tories and Reformers – a facet of a paternal order in the throes of dissolution.¹⁶⁵ Such treatment views politics not as a distinct activity but as part of a larger totality, in which politics may represent the exercise of power in any sphere. A concern with cultural hegemony similarly informs the new approach to cultural history, which combines social and intellectual history to look at the language of texts, written and unwritten: one of its concerns is to illuminate what language and texts reveal about class mediation. Keith Walden (September 1989) explained how grocery-store window displays in the late nineteenth and early twentieth centuries defined for a generation of Canadians what it meant to be 'modern': the image was promoted for different reasons by merchandise producers, trade journalists, and some grocers to condition an acceptance of industrial society and to bolster their authority within that system.¹⁶⁶

An interest in texts has also focused attention on narratives and thus on the dominant style of English-Canadian historical writing. In the 1930s, J.B. Brebner explained that in writing a narrative, the historian had to maintain interest, provide convincing explanations for the exploits described, relate them to each other, and enable them to be followed by map. This was a difficult process, he suggested, akin to describing 'the vagaries of ants attracted by sugar irregularly distributed on an inverted saucer, with a lump of sugar at the top centre.'¹⁶⁷ More recently, Hayden White demonstrated that the form of historical writing conveys as much meaning and explanation as the content. Within this context, Kenneth C. Dewar (September 1991) analysed Donald Creighton's narrative style and showed that the popular idea of narrative as story telling was incorrect. Using narrative form required the historian to make choices, informed by ideological predisposition, about how to arrange conditions, circumstances, setting, character, human actions, intentions, and experiences in a multiplicity of relationships. He or she then had to set these complex relationships in discursive form.¹⁶⁸ Careful examination of the form of historical writing, then, exposed its underlying ideological intentions and demonstrated the weakness of claims to objectivity.

The revival of interest in narrative style and the integration of what were once separate fields of specialization do not necessarily point to the production of a new synthesis of Canada's history. Particularly in their interest in expressions of cultural hegemony, many recent contributions to the *CHR* display a concern with themes and issues that transcend national boundaries. Canada is no longer a new nation, and many of its historians no longer see themselves as its chroniclers. But the *CHR* is not alone among national historical journals in having to contend with the consequences of a decline in the national tradition in historical writing and with the effects of specialization. In Australia, New Zealand, and the United States, the historical profession is experiencing the same kinds of strains and tensions; a review of their national historical journals shows that they too worry about the consequences of specialization, the declining public role of historians, and their disengagement from the public arena.

In Australia, where the number of professional historians has tripled since 1960, senior historians have spoken about 'intellectual ennui,' loss of a sense of purpose, and a changed social role. Whereas a generation ago those who studied Australian or New Zealand history were concerned with the problem of national identity, the connection between national purpose and historical inquiry has almost dissolved. Australian historians have become critics of society, one observer has commented; social history has become their orthodoxy, and if they champion a cause, 'it is more likely to be that of a class, a party, an ethnic or racial, group, a locality or a gender than that of a nation as a whole.' Social and political divisions within Australia created by the war in Vietnam and the constitutional crisis of 1975 diverted historians from their national purpose, as have changes in the discipline and international trends, including widening research interests of Australian scholars and the hiring of faculty members from outside the country.[169]

Contributions to the Australian and New Zealand historical journals reflect these changing trends. Born in the late 1930s, *Historical Studies: Australia and New Zealand* was designed to raise the standards of professional history. While its first editors wanted to cultivate higher standards of research, they did not see history as merely a body of technical knowledge nor historians as abandoning their humanist concern with moral purpose. Accordingly, the journal was meant to serve both the specialist and the general reader of history. The founders were also wary of narrow local specialization and wanted Australian historians to keep in touch with their intellectual heritage. In addition to topics in the two countries' history, the journal has always contained articles on English and Renaissance history; and in the last thirty years the number of articles outside the domestic fields has grown. As the historical profession in Australia expanded in the 1950s, *Historical Studies* helped liberate Australian history from its imperial context. In the 1960s new journals emerged in Pacific and New Zealand history and in specialist branches.[170] *Historical Studies* began paying less attention to the Pacific region and changed character. In 1972 it abandoned its policy of ensuring a regional and topical range of articles and began to welcome material in any field of history written in any part of the world. Now, wrestling with specialization, its editors also express the desire to maintain 'a universe of discourse.' General national historical journals, they state, 'ignore new work at their peril' – a lesson that they learned from the example of the 'ossified' *English Historical Review*.[171]

In recent years, the *Journal of American History* (*JAH*) has made perhaps the most concerted efforts to come to grips with specialization. Its pages are a window on the astounding diversification of American historical inquiry over the past quarter-century. A national ideology of exceptionalism had once promoted a forward-looking view of the past, encouraging American historians to neglect diversity on the assumption that it would dissolve as a singular national ideal developed. Republican institutions, a continent of virgin land, and capitalist development had set American history on a millennial course. But as this idea declined, the historic diversity of American life emerged from the shadows.[172]

Surveys of *JAH* readers in the past two decades reveal that American historians generally welcome this development. They regard their field's attempts to understand more diverse people from the past through a wide range of sources, methods, and ideologies as its greatest strength. But they also see diversification as 'a double-edged sword,' which has eroded valued traditions of historical practice, harbouring such weaknesses as overspecialization, politicization, and fragmentation. Overspecialization in particular had broken American history into so many small pieces that it had become impossible to master anything but one area of specialization.[173]

In interpreting these comments, former *JAH* editor David Thelen observed that developments in American history had to be understood in a broader context – historians' institutional structures and professional milieu. History, like other disciplines in the social sciences and humanities, has come to value the erudite, the unfamiliar, the 'original,' and the exploration of new methods. These are now more highly prized than telling a good story or 'distilling wisdom.' The once-important challenge of revealing the past in original ways to non-specialists, Thelen argued, 'has flattened into the task of writing things whose originality is defined and appreciated by a handful of specialists in a subdiscipline.' But this trend has echoes in the wider public and political sphere as well: the tendency for historians to communicate in small, self-enclosed arenas parallels the isolation of professionals in many aspects of American life. Underlying all of this, Thelen believed, has been the erosion of popular political participation and a narrowed political debate. In response, the *JAH* encouraged historians to broaden their perspectives and sought to internationalize itself, drawing foreign scholars into book reviews and publishing articles in comparative history. The hope was that American history would benefit from the approaches that foreign scholars had developed in their efforts to introduce texts and events from one culture to audiences of another.[174]

The circumstances that prompted these readjustments have some relevance for the *CHR*, especially since the *CHR* once so closely identified with the *JAH*'s predecessor, the *Mississippi Valley Historical Review*. Moreover, the same kinds of institutional and professional developments have affected Canadian historians. If isolation and insularity have become problems in the Canadian historical discipline, internationalization may be useful for the *CHR*. The *CHR* attempted to use the book-review section for such purposes but abandoned this policy when the literature of Canadian history proliferated. Nevertheless, as a few recent excellent articles in the *CHR* demonstrate, some of the new scholarship in Canadian history is attuned to a wide array of cultural and literary theory outside the field. While some might regard the accompanying decline of the national tradition as a loss, it is a sign of the maturity of the Canadian field that many of its historians are attuned to such trends. To the extent that the journal reflects this kind of inquiry, it signifies a return to its interwar breadth.

If Gail Cuthbert Brandt was correct about postmodernism's attractiveness to feminist historians because of its emphasis on difference and multiple perspectives, the trend towards diversity will continue. Postmodernism has only recently captured the attention of some Canadian historians, but its wide acceptance in other areas of cultural study warrants attention. Encompassing myriad theories and views, postmodernism is an indictment of modernism, which it views as positivistic, technocentric, rationalistic, and characterized by notions of linear progress and absolute truth. Postmodernism celebrates heterogeneity and difference, as well as the relativism and fragmentation that were actually part of modernism, but rather than attempting to understand modern society or to transcend it, postmodernism insists on facing up to the fact of relativism in human knowledge. Its hallmark is a distrust of all 'totalizing' interpretations – large-scale 'stories' about the development of progress or humanity, bearing such labels as 'the Enlightenment' or 'capitalism' – which it calls 'master' narratives or metanarratives.[175]

Postmodernism arose as a number of intellectual developments in the second half of the twentieth century challenged the assumptions underlying many disciplines. These included the re-emergence of pragmatism in philosophy, the shift of ideas in the philosophy of science put forward by Thomas Kuhn, Michel Foucault's rejection of simple and even complex causality in history in favour of multitudinous correlations and the recognition of discontinuity, and new developments in mathematics and science that emphasized indeterminacy. These ideas, along with the concern in ethics, politics, and anthropology for the dignity of 'the other,' dovetailed with international political developments – the end of colonialism, the expression of strong sentiments of nationalism, ethnicity, and race – to cause many social scientists to doubt their ability to interpret and to establish facts, theories, and conclusions.[176] But postmodernism is also a misunderstanding of modernism, which was never as 'totalizing' as the postmodernist critique implies. More than just an artistic movement, modernism was the product of the rapid industrialization of the second half of the nineteenth century, which disrupted traditional time–space perceptions in science, art, literature, and philosophy. As a result, intellectuals in many fields questioned the notion of fixed and universal truths and linear and chronological explanations, and they adopted more relativistic interpretations, which considered how social, economic, political, and religious factors shaped 'facts,' ideas, and cultures.[177] One could argue that the willingness of many interwar *CHR* contributors to understand Canada's past from a number of different perspectives accorded with the main trends of modernist culture. Into the 1940s, there were statements in the journal about indefinitude and flux in history. Not even the voluminous literature dealing with the American Revolution had clothed that era 'in the garments of finality,' Winfred Trexler Root observed. 'Change is one of the rights of men,' she added, 'and the law of impermanence applies equally well to a knowledge of the past as to pulsing life itself.'[178]

Whether or not historians accept postmodernism, its understanding and treatment of history require members of the discipline to confront it. In positing a breakdown of temporal order, it challenges all sense of historical continuity. In seeing history as disconnected episodes, it gives postmodernists licence to plunder history for examples to use in any aspect of their work while insisting that historians should do no more than dig up the remnants of the past, withholding all critical and aesthetic judgment.[179] Postmodernism also makes sweeping and incorrect generalizations about historical practice. The degree to which historians ever resorted to metanarratives is debatable: studies of 'progress' and 'capitalism' have been moderated by attention to cultural, regional, and local differences; the meaning of concepts and words has also been interpreted within smaller contexts. However, postmodernism demands consideration of things that many historians have always heeded – the nature of interpretive assumptions, the strategies used in constructing texts, the pervasiveness and expression of authority and power in all aspects of society.[180]

Without necessarily accepting postmodernism's radical relativism, Canadian historians could reflect on the issues and problems that it raises and demonstrate that some of them have always concerned the historical discipline. They might also cease downplaying intellectual and cultural history, which explores the foundations of knowledge in history, philosophy, and other realms of culture.

Given the constantly shifting trends that affect historical inquiry, it is not surprising that journals such as the *CHR* have sometimes found it difficult to define what it means to be 'general' or 'national.' As against the view that the decline in the national tradition has caused the *CHR* to lose its moorings, this essay and the volume of selected readings from the journal that follow attempt to demonstrate that the current diversity is not entirely a radical departure. But in addition to being a national journal, the *CHR* was committed from the start to raising the standard of Canadian historical scholarship.

To be a discipline's leading journal is a major responsibility, not without inherent problems, which have been the source of past – and probably future – conflicts. Raising the standards of a discipline requires the promotion of excellence. This might mean presenting articles that are models of certain approaches. But it also necessitates the publication of material whose content, or method, or approach is unfamiliar or represents a departure from, or a challenge to, the mainstream. Over the course of its history, the *CHR* has published a few pathbreaking articles – perhaps the most notable was Mackintosh's (March 1923), which introduced the staples approach. Many other innovations in the field first appeared in other journals; many more were published as monographs and so received attention in the *CHR*'s book-review section, which was meant to play a crucial role. It offers a window on the state of Canadian historical scholarship, in terms of both the books treated and the assessements of reviewers – the discipline's practitioners.

If the *CHR* has failed at times to be a leader in Canadian historical scholarship, this is owing to a number of obstacles.[181] Perhaps some editors or appraisers failed or were unable to recognize the significance of material submitted for consideration. Other obstacles lie in the perception of the journal held by members of the Canadian historical profession. Where once the journal was condemned for publishing only political history, it more recently has been criticized for publishing only social history. Neither view is entirely correct, but their articulation points to how important it is for editors and advisory board members to be more active in encouraging the submission of the best work that is being done in Canadian history.

One more responsibility lies with all historians of Canada – to make a greater effort to explain and to demonstrate the significance of our work in a larger context. This does not necessarily imply a return to national history, but it does ask practitioners to remember the diversity of our audiences – differences in culture, language, region, class – and to speak beyond our respective subdisciplines, including to those outside Canadian history. And in the midst of current government agendas to marginalize the liberal arts, we must investigate and explain the workings of power – whether we label it politics, authority, or the state – in all realms of the historical past.

Notes

I would like to thank Ken Dewar, Arthur Silver, Veronica Strong-Boag, Graeme Wynn, and two anonymous *CHR* appraisers for their helpful comments on an earlier version of this essay.

The *CHR* editors and the University of Toronto Press granted me access to the Press's restricted archival records dealing with the *CHR*, which I was permitted to use subject to restrictions of confidentiality.

1 An earlier version of this essay appeared as '"Remember the Future": The *Canadian Historical Review* and the Discipline of History,' *Canadian Historical Review* (*CHR*) 76 (Sept. 1995): 410–63; translated into Spanish as '"Recuerdo el futuro": La escritura de la historia canadiense desde 1920,' *Historia y grafia* 11 (1998): 89–112, and 12 (1999): 179–218.
2 This was the subject of a conference held at York University, Toronto, 13–15

April 2000, organized by Nicholas Rogers and Marlene Shore: 'Historians and Their Audiences: Mobilizing History for the Millennium.'
3 Pamela Ballinger, 'The Culture of Survivors: Post-Traumatic Stress Disorder and Traumatic Memory,' *History and Memory* Vol. 10 no. 1 (1998): 99
4 See, for example, Michael Bliss, 'Privatizing the Mind: The Sundering of Canadian History, the Sundering of Canada,' *Journal of Canadian Studies* 26 (winter 1991–2): 5–17.
5 J.L. Granatstein, *Who Killed Canadian History?* Toronto: HarperCollins, 1998
6 A.B. McKillop, 'Who Killed Canadian History? A View from the Trenches,' *CHR* 80 (March 1999): 269–99
7 Bryan D. Palmer, 'Of Silences and Trenches: A Dissident's View of Granatstein's Meaning,' *CHR* (Dec. 1999): 677–8; 680–5
8 H.J. Hanham, 'Canadian History in the 1970s,' *CHR* 58 (March 1977): 2–6, 9, 17–18
9 George Wrong, 'The Beginnings of Historical Criticism in Canada: A Retrospect, 1986–1936,' *CHR* 17 (March 1936): 4–7; William Bennett Munro, review of R. Flenley, ed., *Essays in Canadian History: Presented to George Mackinnon Wrong for His Eightieth Birthday* (Toronto: Macmillan, 1939), in *CHR* 21 (March 1940): 68; W.S. Wallace, 'The Life and Work of George M. Wrong,' *CHR* 29 (Sept. 1948): 234–5
10 Peter Novick, *That Noble Dream: The 'Objectivity Question' and the American Historical Profession* (Cambridge: Cambridge University Press, 1988), 28–9, 37, 48, 525; Dorothy Ross, *The Origins of American Social Science* (Cambridge: Cambridge University Press, 1991), 19–20
11 Notes and Comments, *CHR* 8 (Dec. 1927): 281
12 Ibid.; Notes and Comments, *CHR* 10 (Dec. 1929): 289–90; G. de T. Glazebrook, 'George Williams Brown,' in Notes and Comments, *CHR* 45 (1964): 88–90; 'Notes and Comments' *CHR* 1 (March 1920): 1–2; Notes and Comments, *CHR* 7 (Sept. 1926): 195; Notes and Comments, *CHR* 10 (Dec. 1929): 289–90; University of Toronto Archives (UTA), University of Toronto Press (UTP) Papers: CHR Papers, Acc. A79-0004, box 2, file: Correspondence 1972, Robert Craig Brown to John Banks, executive secretary SSRC, 6 Dec. 1972
13 Lawrence J. Burpee, 'A Plea for a Canadian National Library,' *CHR* 1 (June 1920): 191–4; Notes and Comments, *CHR* 10 (Sept. 1929): 194–5
14 William Wood, 'The New Provincial Archives of Quebec,' *CHR* 2 (June 1921): 126, 136–7
15 J.D. Robins, review of *Ballads and Sea Songs of Newfoundland* (Cambridge, Mass.: Harvard University Press, 1933), in *CHR* 14 (Dec. 1933): 440

16 Cited in George Brown, 'The St Lawrence in the Boundary Settlement of 1783,' *CHR* 9 (Sept. 1928): 237
17 W.S. Wallace, 'Some Vices of Clio,' *CHR* 7 (Sept. 1926): 199–202; W.S. Wallace, review of *Three Centuries of Canadian Story: From John Cabot to John Franklin* (Toronto: Musson, 1928), in *CHR* 10 (June 1929): 171; Sigmund K. Proctor, *Thomas De Quincey's Theory of Literature*, reprint ed. (New York: Octagon Books, 1966), 3–5, 16, 112, 117
18 Gustave Lanctôt, 'Past Historians and Present History in Canada,' *CHR* 22 (Sept. 1941): 241–9, 251–3; Gustave Lanctôt, review of Alfred Leroy Burt, *The Old Province of Quebec* (Minneapolis: University of Minnesota Press, 1933), in *CHR* 15 (June 1934): 196
19 Notes and Comments, *CHR* 8 (Dec. 1927): 282–3
20 Michael Kammen, *Mystic Chords of Memory: The Transformation of Tradition in American Culture* (New York: Vintage, Random 1993), 299, 497–501; Charles F. Mullett, 'Tory Imperialism on the Eve of the Declaration of Independence,' *CHR* 12 (Sept. 1931): 262
21 Notes and Comments, *CHR* 1 (June 1920): 134–5
22 A.S. Morton, 'La Vérendrye: Commandant, Fur-Trader, and Explorer,' *CHR* 9 (Dec. 1928): 282–4, 297; 'Correspondence: Professor Morton and La Vérendrye': Lawrence J. Burpee to the editor, 15 Jan. 1929, in *CHR* 10 (March 1929): 53–5
23 W.J. Eccles, 'Edward Robert Adair,' *CHR* 46 (Sept. 1965): 296–7; E.R. Adair, 'Dollard des Ormeaux and the Fight at the Long Sault: A Reinterpretation of Dollard's Exploit,' *CHR* 13 (June 1932): 135–8; Gustave Lanctôt, 'Was Dollard the Saviour of New France?' *CHR* 13 (June 1932): 138–43
24 See 'Program of the Forty-Seventh Annual Meeting of the Association Held in Toronto, Canada, December 27–29, 1932,' *Annual Report of the American Historical Association for the Year 1932* (Washington, DC, 1934), 33–40, 88–93.
25 'The American Historical Association,' *CHR* 13 (Dec. 1932): 363; Charles Beard, 'The Historian and Society,' *CHR* 14 (March 1933): 1–2; George Wrong, 'The Historian and Society,' *CHR* 14 (March 1933): 4, 8; Carl Berger, *The Writing of Canadian History: Aspects of English-Canadian Historical Writing since 1900*, 2nd ed. (Toronto: University of Toronto Press, 1986), 15
26 Notes and Comments, *CHR* 1 (Dec. 1920): 343; Notes and Comments, *CHR* 6 (March 1925): 1–2
27 Notes and Comments, *CHR* 1 (March 1920): 2; Notes and Comments, *CHR* 11 (March 1930): 3; George W. Brown and D.G. Creighton, 'Canadian History in Retrospect and Prospect: An Article to Mark the Completion of the First Twenty-Five Years of the *Canadian Historical Review*, 1920–1944,' *CHR* 25 (Dec. 1944): 359

28 Notes and Comments, *CHR* (Dec. 1920): 343; Notes and Comments, *CHR* (March 1930): 3
29 George Wrong, 'Canada and the Imperial War Cabinet,' *CHR* 1 (March 1920): 20; Arthur Berriedale Keith, 'Recent Changes in Canada's Constitutional Status,' *CHR* 9 (June 1928): 102–16; John S. Ewart, 'Canada's Political Status,' *CHR* 9 (Sept. 1928): 194–205; W.M. Whitelaw, review of Arthur G. Doughty and Norah Story, eds., *Documents Relating to the Constitutional History of Canada, 1819–1828* (Ottawa: King's Printer, 1935), in *CHR* 17 (March 1936): 76
30 W.S. Wallace, 'The Growth of National Feeling,' *CHR* 1 (June 1920): 136; F.H. Underhill, 'Canada's Relations with the Empire as Seen by the Toronto Globe, 1857–67,' *CHR* 10 (June 1929): 106–7; Archibald MacMechan, 'Canada as a Vassal State,' *CHR* 1 (Dec. 1920): 351, 353; R.G. Trotter, 'Some American Influences upon the Canadian Federation Movement,' *CHR* 5 (Sept. 1924): 213–14; Chester Martin, 'British Policy in Confederation,' *CHR* 13 (March 1932): 14–15, 18; Chester Martin, 'The United States and Canadian Nationality,' *CHR* 18 (March 1937): 10; Chester Martin, 'By-Products from British and American Books on the Eighteenth Century,' *CHR* 15 (March 1934): 62
31 W.P.M. Kennedy, 'Nationalism and Self-Determination,' *CHR* 2 (March 1921): 6–10
32 Berger, *Writing of Canadian History*, 40–1
33 Notes and Comments, *CHR* 1 (June 1920): 132–3
34 Dale Miquelon, review of Mason Wade, *Francis Parkman: Heroic Historian*, reprint ed. (1972), in *CHR* 65 (March 1974): 86
35 Gustave Lanctôt, 'The Elective Council of Quebec of 1857,' *CHR* 15 (June 1934): 123, 132; Hilda Neatby, 'The Political Career of Adam Mabane,' *CHR* 16 (June 1935): 137, 150; D.G. Creighton, 'The Struggle for Financial Control in Lower Canada, 1818–1831,' *CHR* 12 (June 1931): 120–1, 143–4
36 W.A. Mackintosh, 'Economic Factors in Canadian History,' *CHR* 4 (March 1923): 12–14, 25
37 Notes and Comments, *CHR* 10 (Dec. 1929): 292; A.R.M. Lower, 'The Assault on the Laurentian Barrier,' *CHR* 10 (Dec. 1929): 294
38 Wallace, 'The Growth of National Feeling,' 138–40; George M. Wrong, 'The Teaching of the History and Geography of the British Empire,' *CHR* 4 (Dec. 1924): 297–8, 301, 311
39 Graeme Wynn, 'Geographical Writing on the Canadian Past,' in Michael P. Conzen, Thomas A. Rumney, and Graeme Wynn, eds., *A Scholar's Guide to Geographical Writing on the American and Canadian Past* (Chicago and London: University of Chicago Press, 1993), 96–7, 99. See R.M. Saunders, 'The First

Introduction of European Plants and Animals into Canada,' *CHR* 16 (Dec. 1935): 388; Frank G. Roe, 'The Extermination of the Buffalo in Western Canada,' *CHR* 15 (March 1934): 1, 10; 'Correspondence: The Extermination of the Buffalo in Western Canada,' *CHR* 15 (June 1934): 213–18; F.G. Roe, 'Buffalo and Snow,' *CHR* 17 (June 1936): 125, 139, 146.

40 Berger, *Writing of Canadian History*, 8–9
41 Notes and Comments, *CHR* 10 (Dec. 1929): 290–1; see also S.B. Watson, 'A Layman's View on the Teaching of History,' *CHR* 15 (June 1934): 155–70.
42 See, for example, Marius Barbeau, 'Asiatic Migrations into America,' *CHR* 13 (Dec. 1932): 403, 417; T.F. McIlwraith, reviews of Edward Moffat Weyer, Jr, *The Eskimos: Their Environment and Folkways* (New Haven, Conn.: Yale University Press, 1932), in *CHR* 15 (June 1934): 211, and of Frank G. Speck, *Naskapi: The Savage Hunters of Labrador Peninsula* (Norman: University of Oklahoma Press, 1935), in *CHR* 19 (March 1938): 85.
43 W.A. Mackintosh, review of Harold A. Innis, *The Fur Trade in Canada: An Introduction to Canadian Economic History* (New Haven, Conn.: Yale University Press, 1930), in *CHR* 12 (March 1931): 65–7; H.A. Innis, review of John Bartlet Brebner, *The Explorers of North America, 1492–1806* (London: A. & C. Black, 1933), in *CHR* 15 (March 1934): 71
44 G.F.G. Stanley, 'The Half-Breed "Rising" of 1875,' *CHR* 17 (Dec. 1936): 399–400; R.O. MacFarlane, review of George F. Stanley, *The Birth of Western Canada: A History of the Riel Rebellions* (Toronto: Longmans, Green, 1936), in *CHR* 17 (Dec. 1936): 454. The influence of sociology and anthropology is also evident in Stanley's review article, 'The Metis and the Conflict of Cultures in Western Canada,' *CHR* 28 (Dec. 1947): 428–33.
45 Alfred Goldsworthy Bailey, 'Social Revolution in Early Eastern Canada,' *CHR* 19 (Sept. 1938): 264; Robert Redfield, review of A.G. Bailey, *Conflict of European and Eastern Algonkian Cultures, 1504–1700: A Study in Canadian Civilization* (New Brunswick: Museum, 1937), in *CHR* 19 (March 1938): 83
46 J.N. Wallace to Editor, in *CHR* 7 (25 Sept. 1926): 321–4; Notes and Comments, *CHR* 8 (Dec. 1926): 273–5
47 F.W. Howay, 'Early Days of the Maritime Fur Trade,' *CHR* 4 (March 1923): 26–44; articles by Walter N. Sage included: 'The Gold Colony of British Columbia,' *CHR* 2 (Dec. 1921): 340–59; 'The Early Days of Representative Government in British Columbia,' *CHR* 3 (June 1922): 143–80; 'Spanish Explorers of the British Columbia Coast,' *CHR* 12 (Dec. 1931): 390–46. See also J.A. Maxwell, 'Lord Dufferin and the Difficulties with British Columbia, 1874–7,' *CHR* 12 (Dec. 1931): 364–89; Margaret Ormsby's 'Prime Minister Mackenzie, the Liberal Party, and the Bargain with British Columbia,' *CHR* 26 (June 1945): 148–73.

48 W.S. MacNutt, 'The Beginnings of Nova Scotian Politics, 1758–1766,' *CHR* 16 (March 1935): 41, 53
49 Frances Morehouse, 'Canadian Migration in the Forties,' *CHR* 9 (Dec. 1928): 309–29. On migration history in this period, see also A.R.M. Lower, 'Canada and the Problems of the World's Population and Migration Movements,' *CHR* 12 (March 1931): 55–9; Paul W. Gates, 'Official Encouragement to Immigration by the Province of Canada,' *CHR* 15 (March 1934): 24–38.
50 Isabel Foulché-Delbosc, 'Women of New France (Three Rivers: 1651–1663),' *CHR* 21 (June 1940): 132–49
51 D.C. Harvey, 'Local History Societies: The Importance of Local History in the Writing of General History,' *CHR* 13 (Sept. 1932): 244–6. On the need for local history, see also G.P. de T. Glazebrook, review of Ontario Historical Society, *Papers and Records*, vol. 25 (Toronto, 1929), in *CHR* 10 (Sept. 1929): 273–4.
52 A.R.M. Lower, review of D.G. Creighton, *The Commercial Empire of the St Lawrence, 1760–1850* (Toronto: Ryerson, 1937), in *CHR* 19 (June 1938): 207–8
53 'History in a World of Crisis,' *CHR* 19 (Dec. 1938): 454; 'The International Congress of Historical Sciences,' *CHR* (Dec. 1938): 392
54 G.P. de T. Glazebrook, 'Canada and Foreign Affairs,' *CHR* 21 (June 1940): 180
55 Eric Harrison, 'The Anatomy of War,' *CHR* 24 (March 1943): 48
56 Reginald Trotter, 'Canada and Commonwealth Affairs,' *CHR* 22 (Sept. 1941): 302
57 A.R.M. Lower, 'The Social Scientists in the Postwar World,' *CHR* 22 (March 1941): 1–13; A.R.M. Lower, 'The Social Sciences in Canada,' *Culture* 3 (1942): 433–8; A.R.M. Lower, review of Alfred Leroy Burt, *A Short History of Canada for Americans* (Minneapolis: University of Minnesota Press, 1942), in *CHR* 23 (Sept. 1942): 327
58 P.E. Corbett, H.A. Innis, and F.H. Soward, 'The Social Sciences in the Post-War World,' *CHR* 22 (June 1941): 117–24
59 Archange Godbout, 'L'histoire dans nos universités,' *Culture* 2 (1941): 41–50
60 UTA, UTP Papers, CHR Papers, Acc. 73–023, box 4, file: CHR 1970, copy of Brown and Creighton, 'Canadian History in Retrospect and Prospect,' 362–4
61 A.E. Prince, 'The Need for a Wider Study of Military History,' *CHR* 25 (March 1944): 20–2; Frank H. Underhill, 'Arnold Toynbee, Metahistorian,' *CHR* 32 (Sept. 1951): 201–2, 213
62 George W. Simpson, review of *General Education in a Free Society: Report of the Harvard Committee* (Cambridge, Mass.: Harvard University Press, 1945), in *CHR* 27 (Dec. 1946): 446; see also W.L. Morton, 'Canada and Foreign

Affairs,' *CHR* 28 (June 1947): 183; B.S. Kierstead, 'Canada and Foreign Affairs: The Cold War,' *CHR* 30 (June 1949): 144–6.
63 G.P. de T. Glazebrook, 'In Defence of Political History,' *CHR* 31 (Dec. 1950): 443–5
64 'Relations of Canada and the United States': J. Bartlet Brebner, 'I: Persistent Problems,' and R.G. Trotter, 'II: Reciprocity of Attitudes,' *CHR* 24 (June 1943): 117–25; Richard Van Alstyne, 'New Viewpoints in the Relations of Canada and the United States,' *CHR* 25 (June 1944): 109–30; James T. Shotwell, 'A Personal Note on the Theme of Canadian-American Relations,' *CHR* 28 (March 1947): 31–43
65 D.G. Creighton, 'Sir John Macdonald and Canadian Historians,' *CHR* 29 (March 1948): 1–12
66 See also D.G. Creighton, Presidential Address, Canadian Historical Association *Annual Report* (1957): 3.
67 D.G. Creighton, review of W.L. Morton, *The Progressive Party in Canada* (Toronto: University of Toronto Press and Saunders, 1950), in *CHR* 32 (March 1951): 70–2
68 Vernon Fowke, review of S.W. Yates, *The Saskatchewan Wheat Pool: Its Origin, Organization and Progress, 1924–1935* (Saskatoon: United Farmers of Canada, 1947), in *CHR* 28 (Dec. 1947): 446
69 W.L. Morton, review of [Vernon Fowke], *The National Policy and the Wheat Economy* (Toronto: University of Toronto Press, 1957), in *CHR* 39 (Dec. 1958): 342–3
70 J.M.S. Careless, 'The Toronto *Globe* and Agrarian Radicalism,' *CHR* 29 (March 1948): 15–16, 39; J.M.S. Careless, 'Frontierism, Metropolitanism, and Canadian History,' *CHR* 35 (March 1954): 1–21. The foundation of this approach, taken from N.S.B. Gras and the Chicago school of sociologists, was evident in D.C. Masters, 'Toronto vs. Montreal: The Struggle for Financial Hegemony, 1860–1875,' *CHR* 22 (June 1941): 133–46.
71 W.L. Morton, 'Agriculture in the Red River Colony,' *CHR* 30 (Dec. 1949): 305, 321
72 C.P. Stacey, review of *Colony to Nation: A History of Canada* (Toronto: Longmans, Green, 1946), in *CHR* 28 (June 1947): 194; John Irwin Cooper, review of Edgar McInnis, *Canada: A Political and Social History* (Toronto: Clarke Irwin, 1947), in *CHR* 28 (Dec. 1947): 434
73 C.P. Stacey, review of Donald Creighton, *John A. Macdonald: The Young Politician* (Toronto: Macmillan, 1952), in *CHR* 34 (March 1953): 55
74 A.R.M. Lower, review of *Royal Commission Studies: A Selection of Essays Prepared for the Royal Commission on National Development in the Arts, Letters and Sciences* (Ottawa: King's Printer, 1951), in *CHR* 32 (Dec. 1951): 381–3

75 E.R. Adair, 'The Canadian Contribution to Historical Science,' *Culture*, 67–9, 74–5, 78, 82–3
76 Richard M. Saunders, review of *Revue d'histoire de l'Amérique française* (June 1947), in *CHR* 29 (March 1948): 78–9
77 Notes and Comments, *CHR* 36 (March 1955): 91
78 Bruce Trigger, 'The Historians' Indian: Native Americans in Canadian Historical Writing from Charlevoix to the Present,' *CHR* 67 (Sept. 1986): 317–24
79 Frank Underhill, 'Canadian Political Protest,' in *CHR* 41 (March 1960): 48–9, 53
80 Interview with John Saywell, 20 July 1994
81 H. Blair Neatby and John T. Saywell, 'Chapleau and the Conservative Party in Quebec,' *CHR* 37 (March 1956): 1–22; John T. Saywell, review of W.L. Morton, *Manitoba: A History* (Toronto: University of Toronto Press, 1957), in *CHR* 38 (Dec. 1957): 326–7; see also Ramsay Cook, review of Margaret A. Ormsby, *British Columbia: A History* (Toronto: MacMillan, 1958), in *CHR* 42 (March 1961): 53–4.
82 Margaret Prang, 'Clerics, Politicians, and the Bilingual Schools Issue in Ontario, 1910–1917,' *CHR* 41 (Dec. 1960): 307
83 Ramsay Cook, 'Dafoe, Laurier and the Formation of Union Government,' *CHR* 42 (Sept. 1961): 185–6, 208
84 Dale Miquelon, review of Mason Wade, *Francis Parkman: Heroic Historian*, reprint ed. (1972), in *CHR* 65 (March 1974): 84
85 G.F.G. Stanley, review of Guy Frégault, *La Guerre de la Conquête* (Montreal: Fides, 1955), in *CHR* 39 (March 1958): 67–9
86 Michel Brunet, 'The British Conquest: Canadian Social Scientists and the Fate of the *Canadiens*,' *CHR* 40 (June 1959): 93–107
87 F.H. Underhill, review of Michel Brunet, *La présence anglaise et les Canadiens: études sur l'histoire et la pensée des deux Canadas* (Montreal: Beauchemin, 1958), in *CHR* 40 (June 1959): 160–2
88 W.J. Eccles, review of Jean Hamelin, *Economie et société en Nouvelle-France* (Quebec: Les presses de l'Université Laval, 1960), in *CHR* 42 (Dec. 1961): 335–6. The position argued by Hamelin had already been suggested by Fernand Ouellet in *Bulletin des recherches historiques* in 1956.
89 Fernand Ouellet, 'Les fondements historiques de l'option séparatiste dans le Québec,' *CHR* 43 (Sept. 1962): 185, 203
90 Fernand Ouellet, 'Le nationalisme canadien-français: de ses origines à l'insurrection de 1837,' *CHR* 45 (Dec. 1964): 277–92
91 Jacques Monet, review of Fernand Ouellet, *Histoire économique et sociale du Québec, 1760–1850: structures et conjonctures* (Montreal: Fides 1966), in *CHR* 49 (June 1968): 176–8

Introduction 55

92 Jacques Monet, 'French Canada and the Annexation Crisis, 1848–1850,' *CHR* 47 (Sept. 1966): 264
93 Ramsay Cook, 'Good-Bye to All That,' *CHR* 49 (Sept. 1968): 275. The article originated as remarks to a session, 'Historians and Editors: The Changing Functions of Historical Journals,' AHA Meeting, Toronto, Dec. 1967.
94 Notes and Comments, *CHR* 46 (March 1965): 98
95 UTA, UTP Papers, CHR Papers, Acc. A-73-023, box 1, file: Correspondence, 1964–5, Ivo Lambi, Peter Bietenholtz, and Peter Marsh to T.A. Sandquist, n.d.; Historians in Canada, *CHR* 46 (Sept. 1965): 298–9; Notes and Comments, *CHR* 48 (Sept. 1967): 306
96 S.R. Mealing, 'The Concept of Social Class and the Intepretation of Canadian History,' *CHR* 46 (Sept. 1965): 201–7, 214–18
97 O.S. Soroko, 'A Soviet Critique of the Canadian Historical Review,' trans. R.H. McNeal, *CHR* 47 (March 1966): 50–2, 58
98 Margaret Prang and Arthur Lower, 'Sociology and History,' *CHR* 47 (June 1966): 156–61
99 Ramsay Cook, 'Canadian Centennial Cerebrations,' *International Journal* 22 (autumn 1967): 659–63; J.M.S. Careless, '"Limited Identities" in Canada,' *CHR* 50 (March 1969): 1–5, 8
100 Louis Hartz, 'Violence and Legality in the Fragment Cultures,' *CHR* 50 (June 1969): 123; Robin W. Winks, 'Negro School Segregation in Ontario and Nova Scotia,' *CHR* 50 (June 1969): 164–91
101 Richard M. Saunders, 'Presidential Address: The Historian and the Nation,' Canadian Historical Association *Historical Papers/Communications historiques* (1967): 1, 6
102 UTA, UTP Papers, CHR Papers, Acc. A73–023, box 4, file: CHR 1970, Draft for 1970 anniversary retrospective: 'Watch That First Step – It's Fifty Years Long'
103 Robert Mandrou, 'L'historiographie canadienne française: bilan et perspectives,' *CHR* 51 (March 1970): 5–18
104 Fernand Ouellet, review of *Les Canadiens après la Conquête (1759–1775): de la Révolution canadienne à la Révolution américaine* (Montreal: Fides, 1969), in *CHR* 51 (Sept. 1970): 312–16; Yves Zoltvany, review of Guy Frégault, *Canada: The War of the Conquest* (Toronto: Oxford, 1969), in *CHR* 51 (Sept. 1970): 319–20
105 Jean-Pierre Wallot, 'Religion and French-Canadian Mores in the Early Nineteenth Century,' *CHR* 52 (March 1971): 51–2, 77–90; Cole Harris, 'Of Poverty and Helplessness in Petite-Nation,' *CHR* 52 (March 1971), 24–50; Brian J. Young, 'The Defeat of George–Etienne Cartier in Montreal-East in 1872,' *CHR* 51 (Dec. 1970): 386, 406

106 W.J. Eccles, 'The Social, Economic, and Political Significance of the Military Establishment in New France,' *CHR* 52 (March 1971): 3–22; L.R. MacDonald, 'France and New France: The Internal Contradictions,' *CHR* 52 (June 1971): 121–43
107 Gilles Paquet and Jean-Pierre Wallot, 'The Agricultural Crisis in Lower Canada, 1802–1812: *mise au point.* A Response to T.J.A. LeGoff,' *CHR* 56 (June 1975): 133–61; see T.J.A. LeGoff, 'The Agricultural Crisis in Lower Canada, 1802–1812: A Review of a Controversy,' *CHR* 55 (March 1974): 1–31.
108 Michael Katz, 'The People of a Canadian City,' *CHR* 53 (Dec. 1972): 402–3, 426n37; Jacques Légaré, Yolande Lavoie, and Hubert Charbonneau, 'The Early Canadian Population: Problems in Automatic Record Linkage,' *CHR* 53 (Dec. 1972): 427–42; David Gagan and Herbert Mays, 'Historical Demography and Canadian Social History: Families and Land in Peel County, Ontario,' *CHR* 54 (March 1973): 27–8
109 UTA, UTP Papers, CHR Papers, Acc. A79-0004, box 1, file: Canada Council 1971, Assessments, n.a.
110 Ibid, file: Correspondence – Jan.–June 1976, report of Assessor A, n.d., n.a.; Report of Assessor B, n.d., n.a.; Summary of Comments of Jury for Learned Journals, 30–31 Oct. 1975; Robert Bothwell, Michael Cross, and Paul Rutherford to H. Bohne, associate director, University of Toronto Press, 3 Feb. 1976; M. Jean Houston, executive editor, University of Toronto Press, to Michael Cross, Robert Bothwell, and Paul Rutherford, 29 June 1976; Michael S. Cross and Robert Bothwell, 'An Editorial,' *CHR* 58 (March 1977): 1
111 J.L. Granatstein, 'The CHR, the University of Toronto Press, and the Profession,' *CHR* 65 (Dec. 1984): 546–9
112 UTA, UTP Papers, CHR Papers, Acc. A79-0004, box 1, file: Correspondence Jan.–June 1976, xerox copy of 'The Research Committee's review of the American Historical Review,' 5 Jan. 1975
113 Robert Bothwell and David Bercuson, 'Some Frank Words about the *Canadian Historical Review*,' *CHR* 58 (March 1977): 1–2
114 See, for example, David Sutherland, 'Halifax Merchants and the Pursuit of Development,' *CHR* 59 (March 1978): 1–17; Ernest R. Forbes, 'Never the Twain Did Meet: Prairie–Maritime Relations, 1910–27,' *CHR* 59 (March 1978): 18–37.
115 See *CHR* 31 (Sept. 1950): 221–87; John Irving, 'The Development of Philosophy in Central Canada'; J.M.S. Careless, 'Mid-Victorian Liberalism in Central Canadian Newspapers, 1850–1867'; and Claude Bissell, 'Literary Taste in Central Canada.'

116 Margaret Prang, 'The Origins of Public Broadcasting in Canada,' *CHR* 46 (March 1965): 1; P.F.W. Rutherford, 'The Western Press and Regionalism,' *CHR* 52 (Sept. 1971): 286–305; Mary Vipond, 'Canadian Nationalism and the Plight of Canadian Magazines in the 1920s,' *CHR* 58 (March 1977): 43–63

117 See *CHR* 49, no. 3 (Sept. 1968): Judith Fingard, 'Charles Inglis and His "Primitive Bishoprick" in Nova Scotia' 247–66, and J.M. Bliss, 'The Methodist Church and World War I,' 213–33; Richard Allen, 'The Social Gospel and the Reform Tradition in Canada, 1890–1948,' *CHR* 49, (Dec. 1968); 381–99.

118 A.I. Silver, 'French Canada and the Prairie Frontier, 1870–1890,' *CHR* 50 (March 1969): 11–36; A.I. Silver, 'Some Quebec Attitudes in an Age of Imperialism and Ideological Conflict,' *CHR* 57 (Dec. 1976): 458–60

119 Alan F.J. Artibise, review of Bryan Palmer, *A Culture in Conflict: Skilled Workers and Industrial Capitalism in Hamilton, Ontario, 1860–1914* (Montreal: McGill-Queen's University Press, 1979): 88–90; Kenneth McNaught, 'E.P. Thompson vs Harold Logan: Writing about Labour and the Left in the 1970s,' *CHR* 62 (June 1981): 142–3; Bryan D. Palmer, review of H. Clare Pentland, *Labour and Capital in Canada* (Toronto: Lorimer, 1981), in *CHR* 64 (June 1982): 227

120 H.C. Pentland, 'The Lachine Strike of 1843,' *CHR* 29 (Sept. 1948): 255, 277; F.W. Watt, 'The National Policy, the Workingman, and Proletarian Ideas in Canada,' *CHR* 40 (March 1959): 1–2

121 Martin Robin, 'Registration, Conscription, and Independent Labour Politics,' *CHR* 47 (June 1966): 101, 118

122 Walter Young, review of Gad Horowitz, *Canadian Labour in Politics* (Toronto: University of Toronto Press, 1968), in *CHR* 50 (March 1969): 86

123 Michael Bliss, review of Martin Robin, *Radical Politics and Canadian Labour 1880–1930* (Industrial Relations Centre, Queen's University, 1968), in *CHR* 51 (June 1970): 195–6

124 Desmond Morton, 'Aid to the Civil Power: The Canadian Militia in Support of Social Order, 1867–1914,' *CHR* 51 (Dec. 1970): 407–8, 424; Michael S. Cross, 'The Shiner's War: Social Violence in the Ottawa Valley,' *CHR* 54 (March 1973): 4, 25–6

125 Desmond Morton, review of Richard Desrosiers and Denis Héroux, *Le travailleur québecois et le syndicalisme* (Montreal: Les Presses de l'Université du Québec, 1973), in *CHR* 56 (March 1975): 71

126 Notes and Comments, *CHR* 57 (March 1976): 111

127 Peter N. Moogk, 'In the Darkness of a Basement: Craftsmen's Associations

in Early French Canada,' *CHR* 57 (Dec. 1976): 399–439; Craig Heron and Bryan D. Palmer, 'Through the Prism of the Strike: Industrial Conflict in Southern Ontario, 1910–1914,' *CHR* 58 (Dec. 1977): 423

128 John C. Cairns, review of Geoffrey Barraclough, *Main Trends in History* (New York: Holmes & Meier, 1979), and Emmanuel Le Roy Ladurie, *The Territory of the Historian* (Chicago: University of Chicago Press, 1979), in *CHR* 61 (Sept. 1980): 361

129 H.C. Pentland, review of Gregory S. Kealey and Peter Warrian, eds., *Essays in Canadian Working Class History* (Toronto: McClelland & Stewart, 1976), in *CHR* 59 (March 1978): 95; Michael Piva, review of Gregory S. Kealey, *Toronto Workers Respond to Industrial Capitalism, 1867–1892* (Toronto: University of Toronto Press, 1980), in *CHR* 62 (June 1981): 209–11

130 McNaught, 'Thompson vs Logan,' 147, 167–8

131 Daniel Drache, review of R.T. Naylor, *History of Canadian Business, 1867–1914, I: The Banks and Finance Capital, II: Industrial Development* (Toronto: James Lorimer, 1975), in *CHR* 59 (March 1978): 83

132 W.J. Eccles, 'A Belated Review of Harold Adams Innis, *The Fur Trade in Canada*,' *CHR* 60 (Dec. 1979): 420–3, 436–7, 441

133 Hugh M. Grant, 'One Step Forward, Two Steps Back: Innis, Eccles, and the Canadian Fur Trade,' *CHR* 62 (Sept. 1981): 306, 319–22

134 Cole Harris, 'Industry and the Good Life around Idaho Peak,' *CHR* 66 (Sept. 1985): 316, 343

135 Wynn, 'Geographical Writing on the Canadian Past,' 116

136 Rusty Bitterman, Robert A. MacKinnon, and Graeme Wynn, 'Of Inequality and Interdependence in the Nova Scotian Countryside,' *CHR* 74 (March 1993): 1–5, 39–41

137 G.F.G. Stanley, review of George E. Simpson and J. Milton Yinger, eds., *American Indians and American Life* (Philadelphia: *Annals of the American Academy of Political and Social Science* 311, May 1957), in *CHR* 39 (June 1958): 163; Trigger, 'The Historians' Indian,' 315–18, 320–4

138 Trigger, 'The Historians' Indian,' 336–8; Cornelius Jaenen, review of Bruce Trigger, *The Children of Aatensic: A History of the Huron People to 1660*, 2 vols. (Montreal: McGill-Queen's University Press, 1976), in CHR 59 (March 1978): 220–1

139 Bruce G. Trigger, 'The French Presence in Huronia: The Structure of Franco–Huron Relations in the First Half of the Seventeenth Century,' *CHR* 49 (June 1968): 107–8; Trigger pursued this theme further in his *Natives and Newcomers: Canada's 'Heroic Age' Reconsidered* (Kingston: McGill-Queen's University Press, 1985).

Introduction

140 Bruce G. Trigger, review of Alfred Goldsworthy Bailey, *The Conflict of European and Eastern Algonkian Cultures, 1504–1700: A Study in Canadian Civilization*, 2nd ed. (Toronto: University of Toronto Press, 1969), and Anthony F.C. Wallace, *The Death and Rebirth of the Seneca* (New York: Alfred A. Knopf, 1970), in *CHR* 53 (June 1971): 183–4

141 Cornelius J. Jaenen, 'Amerindian Views of French Culture in the Seventeenth Century,' *CHR* 55 (Sept. 1974): 262, 293

142 Jaenen, review of *Children of Aataentsic*, 220–1; Cornelius Jaenen, review of James Axtell, *The Invasion Within: The Contest of Cultures in Colonial North America* (New York: Oxford University Press, 1985), in *CHR* 68 (March 1987): 120

143 Robin Fisher, review of Sylvia Van Kirk, *'Many Tender Ties': Women in Fur-Trade Society in Western Canada, 1670–1870* (Winnipeg: Watson & Dwyer, 1980), in *CHR* 64 (June 1983): 237

144 Gerald Friesen, review of George F. Stanley, general editor, *The Collected Writings of Louis Riel / Les écrits de Louis Riel*, vols. 1–5 (Edmonton: University of Alberta Press, 1986), in *CHR* 69 (March 1988): 88; J.R. Miller, 'From Riel to the Metis,' *CHR* 69 (March 1988): 1–13

145 Frank H. Underhill, review of Catherine Lyle Cleverdon, *The Woman Suffrage Movement in Canada* (Toronto: University of Toronto Press–Saunders 1950), in *CHR* 31 (Dec. 1950): 422

146 Kathryn Peterson, review of *Women at Work: Ontario 1850–1930* (Toronto: Women's Press, 1974), in *CHR* 57 (June 1976): 206

147 Susan Mann Trofimenkoff, review of Micheline Dumont, Michele Jean, Marie Lavigne, and Jennifer Stoddart (Le Collectif Clio), *L'histoire des femmes au Québec depuis quatre siècles* (Montreal: Les Quinze 1982), in *CHR* 64 (Dec. 1983): 562–3

148 Eliane Leslau Silverman, 'Writing Canadian Women's History, 1970–82: An Historiographical Analysis,' *CHR* 63 (Dec. 1982): 514–33

149 Linda Kealey, 'The Status of Women in the Historical Profession in Canada, 1989 Survey,' *CHR* 72 (Sept. 1991): 370–88

150 Linda Kealey, 'Special Issue on Women's History,' *CHR* 72 (Dec. 1991): 437–40; Gail Cuthbert Brandt, 'Postmodern Patchwork: Some Recent Trends in the Writing of Women's History in Canada,' *CHR* 72 (Dec. 1991): 440, 445, 467

151 Robert Bothwell and David J. Bercuson, '*The Canadian Historical Review* and the State of the Profession: A View on Our Sixtieth Birthday,' *CHR* 61 (March 1980): 1–2

152 Douglas McCalla, 'The *CHR* since 1978: A Statistical Overview,' *CHR* 65

(Dec. 1984): 549–56; John English, 'The Second Time Around: Political Scientists Writing History,' *CHR* 67 (March 1986): 2–4

153 Robin Fisher and Douglas McCalla, 'A Journal for All Seasons?' *CHR* 66 (Dec. 1985): 441–2

154 English, 'The Second Time Around,' 1, 16

155 David J. Bercuson and J.L. Granatstein, 'The Public Archives of Canada and the Historical Profession,' *CHR* 62 (March 1981): 1–2; David Bercuson and J.L. Granatstein, 'A CHA for the 80s,' *CHR* 64 (March 1983): 1–2

156 Gregory Kealey and Rosemary Ommer, 'The Practical Historian,' *CHR* 68 (Sept. 1987): 430–4

157 Donald Bourgeois, 'The Role of the Historian in the Litigation Process,' *CHR* 67 (June 1986): 195–205; G.M. Dickinson and R.D. Gidney, 'History and Advocacy: Some Reflections on the Historian's Role in Litigation,' *CHR* 68 (Dec. 1987): 578, 584–5

158 W.J. Eccles, review of Peter C. Newman, *Company of Adventurers* (Markham, Ont.: Viking, 1985), in *CHR* 67 (Sept. 1986): 399–400; Jennifer Brown, 'Newman's *Company of Adventurers* in Two Solitudes: A Look at Reviews and Responses,' *CHR* 67 (Dec. 1986): 562–78

159 Ronald Rudin, 'History from Quebec, 1981,' *CHR* 63 (March 1982): 34–44

160 Jean-Claude Robert, 'Quelques reflexions sur l'historiographie canadienne récente,' *CHR* 63 (March 1982): 47–56; letter of Robert Bothwell, Ian Drummond, and John English to CHR Editors, *CHR* 63 (Sept. 1982): 409

161 John Herd Thompson, review of Paul-André Linteau et al., *Le Québec depuis 1930* (Montreal: Les éditions du Boréal express, 1986), in *CHR* 60 (Sept. 1988): 432–4

162 Michael D. Behiels, 'Recent Contributions to the History of Twentieth-Century Quebec,' *CHR* 68 (Sept. 1987): 393–4; Ronald Rudin, 'Revisionism and the Search for a Normal Society: A Critique of Recent Quebec Historical Writing,' *CHR* 73 (March 1992): 30–4; Ronald Rudin, review of Paul-André Linteau et al, *Quebec since 1930* (Toronto: Lorimer, 1991), in *CHR* 74 (March 1993): 105

163 See, for example, 'Parizeau Exhorts Quebeckers to Regain Their Confidence,' *Globe and Mail*, 13 Sept. 1994, p. A7.

164 Joy Parr, 'The Skilled Emigrant and Her Kin: Gender, Culture, and Labour Recruitment,' *CHR* 68 (Dec. 1987): 530–1

165 Sean T. Cadigan, 'Paternalism and Politics: Sir Francis Bond Head, the Orange Order, and the Election of 1836,' *CHR* 72 (Sept. 1991): 320–2

166 Keith Walden, 'Speaking Modern: Language, Culture, and Hegemony in Grocery Window Displays, 1887–1920,' *CHR* 70 (Sept. 1989): 285–7; on cul-

tural hegemony, see also Tina Loo, 'Dan Cranmer's Potlatch: Law as Coercion, Symbol and Rhetoric in British Columbia,' *CHR* 73 (June 1992): 129–65.
167 J.B. Brebner, review of Jeannette Mirsky, *To the North! The Story of Arctic Exploration from Earliest Times to the Present* (New York: Viking Press, 1934), in *CHR* 16 (June 1935): 195
168 Hayden White, *The Content of the Form: Narrative Discourse and Historical Representation* (Baltimore: Johns Hopkins University Press, 1987); Kenneth C. Dewar, 'Where to Begin and How: Narrative Openings in Donald Creighton's Historiography,' *CHR* 72 (Sept. 1991): 348–51, 368
169 Graeme Davison, 'Slicing Australian History,' *New Zealand Journal of History* 16 (April 1982): 3–5
170 *Historical Studies: Australia and New Zealand* 1 (April 1940–Oct. 1941): 1; Stuart Macintyre, '*Historical Studies*: A Retrospective,' *Historical Studies* 21 (April 1984): 1, 3, 6–7. The journal was renamed, simply, *Historical Studies* when the *New Zealand Journal of History (NZJH)* was founded in 1967.
171 John Rickard, 'Introduction,' to John Rickard and Peter Spearritt, eds., *Packaging the Past: Public Histories* (Australian Historical Studies, Melbourne University Press, 1991), 9–10; see also Keith Sinclair, 'Editorial: The First Twenty Years,' *NZJH* 20 (Nov. 1986): 107–8.
172 Joyce Appleby, 'Rediscovering America's Historic Diversity: Beyond Exceptionalism,' *JAH* 79 (Sept. 1992): 419–20, 424–6, 430; Ross, *Origins of American Social Science*, xiv–xv
173 David Thelen, 'The Practice of American History,' *JAH* 81 (Dec. 1994): 933, 935–7
174 Ibid., 956, 959; David Thelen, 'Of Audiences, Borderlands, and Comparisons: Toward the Internationalization of American History,' *JAH* 79 (Sept. 1992): 432–5, 439, 451
175 David Harvey, *The Condition of Postmodernity: An Enquiry into the Origins of Cultural Change* (Cambridge: Blackwell, 1989), 9; Michael R. Curry, 'Postmodernism, Language, and the Strains of Modernism,' *Annals of the Association of American Geographers* 81 no. 2 (June 1991): 213–14, 224
176 See Marlene Shore, review of William R. Everdell, *The First Moderns: Profiles of the Origins of Twentieth-Century Thought* (Chicago: University of Chicago Press, 1997), and Elazar Barkan and Ronald Bush, eds., *Prehistories of the Future: The Primitivist Project and the Culture of Modernism* (Stanford, Calif.: Stanford University Press, 1995), in *Journal of the History of the Behavioral Sciences* (summer 1998); Harvey, *Condition of Postmodernity*, 9; Wynn, 'Geographical Writing on the Canadian Past,' 122–3.

177 There is an enormous body of literature on the subject: Stephen Kern, *The Culture of Time and Space, 1880–1918* (Cambridge, Mass.: Harvard University Press, 1983) is particularly insightful.
178 Winfred Trexler Root, 'The American Revolution in New Books and Light,' *CHR* 23 (Sept. 1942): 308
179 Harvey, *Condition of Postmodernity*, 54–56, 61
180 Curry, 'Postmodernism,' 211, 221
181 An anonymous *CHR* appraiser urged me to consider this issue.

PART ONE

NATION AND DIVERSITY, 1920–1939

COMMENTARY

The Purpose of the Past

The *Canadian Historical Review (CHR)* was born in a period of national consciousness within English and French Canada. Throughout the Western world, remembrance also occupied popular and academic attention. The aftermath of the Great War had stimulated the desire to commemorate, but preoccupation with history and memory stretched back to the late nineteenth century, when the experience of rapid industrial and technological change, along with political upheaval, fostered concern about the erasure of the past.[1] By the 1920s, history was competing with other social and behavioural sciences to explain the impact of the past, and of memory, on individuals as well as on entire societies.

The excerpts in this part show that the *CHR*'s objectives – to stimulate an interest in Canadian history and to promote high standards of historical research – were embedded in this culture of remembering. It underlay the concern expressed by some *CHR* contributors that even though professional historians were producing narratives of the nation's past, they should avoid propagating myths and untruths. These considerations – reflected below in W.S. Wallace's 'Some Vices of Clio' (September 1926), George Wrong's 'The Beginnings of Historical Criticism in Canada' (March 1936), and Gustave Lanctôt's 'Past Historians and Present History in Canada' (September 1941) – also help explain professional historians' emphasis on archival research and careful use of documents.

In a 1947 *CHR* article, James T. Shotwell, a Canadian-born historian who was appointed full professor at New York's Columbia University in 1908, reminisced about his undergraduate studies at the University of Toronto in the 1890s. A course in elementary psychology with James Gibson Hume led him to question the veracity of certain kinds of texts. He was shocked at Hume's maxim 'that memory and imagination were psychologically akin, the only difference being that memory held imagination down to scenes and happenings which one could identify with one's own experience.' Admitting a lack of familiarity with the ways in which contemporary psychologists dealt with that theory decades later, Shotwell concluded that Hume's maxim 'at least provides a useful criterion for historians and a warning not to take too literally memories that are not controlled by documentary evidence.'[2]

In addition to vying with other academic disciplines as arbiters of memory, professional historians had to contend with the popularity of biographers, novelists, and amateur historians. R.O. Flenley, an Englishman who taught historiography at the University of Toronto, explained that modern historians faced a tension between demanding exactitude and impartiality and appealing to the popular: as they became more scientific, they ceased being interesting, and others – such as H.G. Wells – stepped into the breach, supplying the public demand for readable history and for historical explanations of the world around them.[3] Radio programs and motion pictures were also invading the historian's terrain, as frequent *CHR* contributor and artist C.W. Jefferys noted. Adding that movies were often 'travesties of facts and history,' he singled out for criticism a few that had Canada as their subject: *Hudson's Bay, Northwest Passage, North West Mounted Police,* and *Prime Minister.*[4] Jefferys was nevertheless a staunch advocate for the visual representation of history, believing that visual reconstructions of the past could assist the popular imagination.[5] Some *CHR* contributors rejected the idea of appealing to popular audiences altogether, abhorring the themes of 'sex and sanitation'[6] found in much realism; others worried that writing biographies for popular consumption could foster blind patriotism.

Many historians chose to focus on conspicuous personalities, A.S. Morton once explained in the *CHR*, because it was an easy way to write history. Indeed, he suggested, it had enabled French-Canadian historians to celebrate the struggle of their 'race' to master the continent. They were fortunate to have access to colourful archival documents that recorded those achievements. (Morton used this example to plead with the Hudson's Bay Company in London to open its private archives, to reveal the English side of the struggle for the fur trade.[7]) All these issues helped to frame the controversy over whether or not Dollard des Ormeaux was the saviour of New France – a debate played out in the *CHR* in articles by E.R. Adair (June 1932) and Gustave Lanctôt (June 1932). In one of the more innovative studies to appear in the journal, however, 'Women of New France,' Isabel Foulché-Delbosc (June 1940) chose *not* to celebrate the few familiar heroines of the colony in favour of examining colonial domestic life.

French-Canadian historians rarely appeared in the CHR during this period, even though then English-Canadian counterparts recognized that their predecessors had been Canada's earliest historians – the first to realize a consciousness of corporate identity. (During this period, awareness of collective identity was regarded as a necessary precursor for writing history.) And, as *CHR* contributor D. McArthur noted in 1927, it was English-Canadian intolerance that helped this consciousness develop. It took the rapid settlement of the prairies, beginning in the late nineteenth century, and the ordeal of the First World War to produce the counterpart in English Canada.[8]

The annual meeting of the American Historical Association (AHA) in Toronto in 1932 provided a unique setting for more general reflections on the purpose of history. The convention banquet in the Great Hall of Hart House at the University of Toronto was especially interesting to Americans, one observer commented, because they were 'strangers from a country whose traditions and customs have suffered a losing fight. The roast, the pudding, and the great ram's head snuff box were brought in to the sound of the pipes and drum.' Toasts to the King, to the AHA's president, and to Clio, the muse of history, were followed by an address by AHA Vice-President Charles A. Beard, who remarked that historians 'often had the task of courageously recording truths unpalatable to the interests of the hour.'[9]

In papers presented to the AHA, both Beard (March 1933) and George Wrong (March 1933) argued that history dealt with 'universals,' although each saw these differently. Wrong regarded the historian as an interpreter-guardian of the past, a moral guide for the present and future; yet he held that historians should write in an attractive style, free of excessive footnotes. The public, he said, wanted a finished product, 'not an exposition of the methods of the workshop ... The cook ... peels the potatoes but he does not do it on the dining room table.'[10] Beard argued that history was never about the particular, even when it dealt with specific localities, but transcended time and space, serving the highest morality when it was immoral and challenged presuppositions.

Defining the Canadian Nation

In the first two decades of the *CHR*'s existence, numerous contributors grappled with ideas to shape and define the Canadian nation politically and culturally. Excerpts from articles by George Wrong, 'Canada and the Imperial War Cabinet' (March 1920), and by 'W.S. Wallace, 'The Growth of National Feeling' (June 1920), reflect these trends. English-

Canadian historians differed strongly, however, regarding the nature of nationalism. Some, such as Archibald MacMechan (December 1920), sounded the alarm over American popular culture. MacMechan feared that U.S. influences were swamping indigenous Canadian traditions in sports, clothing, and holiday celebrations: he decried the borrowing of American Thanksgiving Day, which he called 'a heathen festival of autumn,' Labour Day, and Mother's Day. From a wholly different perspective, W.P.M. Kennedy (March 1921) warned that nationalism was too frequently used and manipulated by political quacks as a modern cure. Nationality, he commented, could easily become pharisaical and block the path of social solidarity, while self-determination conceivably covered everything 'from a child sulking in a nursery' to calling into being 'the hell of civil war.'

By the late 1920s, other forms of more critically edged nationalism appeared in the *CHR*. Frank Underhill's 'Canada's Relations with the British Empire as seen by the Toronto *Globe*, 1857–1867' (June 1929) reflected broader efforts within Canadian artistic and literary circles (in the work of the Group of Seven, or the McGill poets, for example) to break the hold of the colonial mentality on Canadian national consciousness.[11] Historians such as Reginald Trotter (September 1924) and C.P. Stacey recognized that much Canadian history, including Confederation, could be read only with an eye on the United States.

At the same time, the journal reverberated with concerns about tensions between English and French Canadians. While the journal officially tried to foster *bonne entente*, such articles as Donald Creighton's 'The Struggle for Financial Control in Lower Canada, 1818–1831,' (June 1931) must have added fuel to the strained relationship. Vaguely reminiscent of Lord Durham and his report, Creighton argued that the struggle represented 'a difference of social heritage as fundamental as the differences of race, language, creed.' This collision of heritages, he continued, had given 'the petty racial conflict' more constitutional importance than it deserved. Frances Morehouse's article (December 1928) on Canadian migration in the 1840s, however, provided a unique example of social–economic history that eschewed nationalist considerations, by implicitly suggesting that nationalism was unimportant to ordinary people. In 'The Beginnings of Nova Scotian Politics,' W.S. MacNutt (March 1935) demonstrated that excessive attention to political developments in central Canada ignored the history of the so-called peripheries.

The Environment and Natural Resources

By stressing land, place, and geography in Canada's past, some contributors to the CHR circumvented these vexed issues. A.R.M. Lower (December 1929) described how geography had determined the nature of Canadian settlement while, in 'Economic Factors in Canadian History,' W.A. Mackintosh (March 1923) argued that even constitutional crises were products of economic conditions related to natural resources. In three *CHR* contributions, one excerpted here, Frank G. Roe (December 1935) offered interpretations for the destruction of the buffalo in the U.S. northwest and western Canada – a subject of great interest at the time to western Canadian historians.

Native–European Contact

In this period, and especially in the 1930s, cultural anthropology held a prime place in the *CHR*. This was part of the legacy established by Daniel Wilson, who had taught history and ethnography at the University of Toronto. As interwar pieces by W.A. Mackintosh (March 1931) and A.G. Bailey (September 1938) indicate, contributions acknowledged the role that Natives had played in the early Canadian economy as middlemen and interpreters and thus in the development of its natural resources.

Notes

1 Marlene Shore, 'Memory in the Midst of Change: The Social Concerns of Late 19th-Century North American Psychology,' in Christopher Green, Marlene Shore, and Thomas Teo, eds., *The Transformation of Psychology: Influences of 19th-Century Natural Science, Technology, and Philosophy* (Washington, DC: American Psychological Association [APA] Books, 2001).
2 James T. Shotwell, 'A Personal Note on the Theme of Canadian-American Relations,' *CHR* 28 (March 1947): 31–43
3 R.O. Flenley, review of C.H. Williams, *The Modern Historian* (London: Thomas Nelson & Sons, 1938), in *CHR* 20 (March 1929): 77–8
4 Charles W. Jefferys, 'History in Motion Pictures,' *CHR* 22 (Dec. 1941): 361
5 Charles W. Jefferys, 'The Visual Reconstruction of History,' *CHR* 17 (Sept. 1936): 264
6 C.H. Snider, review of Archibald MacMechan, *There Go the Ships* (Toronto: McClelland and Stewart, 1928), in *CHR* 10 (Sept. 1929): 268–9

7 Review article, A.S. Morton, 'The Early History of the Hudson Bay,' *CHR* 12 (Dec. 1931): 412, 414, 427–8
8 D. McArthur, 'Some Problems of Canadian Historical Scholarship,' *CHR* 8 (March 1927): 3–4
9 Information on the meeting appears in 'Toronto Meeting: American Historical Association,' *American Historical Review* 38 (April 1933): 431–2; *Annual Report of the American Historical Association for the Year 1932* (Washington, DC: United States Government Printing Office, 1934), 'Program of the Forty-Seventh Annual Meeting of the Association Held in Toronto, Canada, December 27–29, 1932,' 33–40, 88–93; 'The American Historical Association,' *CHR* 13 (Dec. 1932): 363
10 George Wrong, 'The Historian and Society,' *CHR* 14 (March 1933): 4, 7–8
11 See Marlene Shore, '"Overtures of an Era Being Born." F.R. Scott: Cultural Nationalism and Social Criticism, 1925–1939,' *Journal of Canadian Studies* 15 (winter 1980–1): 31–42.

THE PURPOSE OF THE PAST

Some Vices of Clio

W.S. WALLACE

(September 1926)
CHR 7, no. 3: 197–203. Excerpt: 197–8, 201.

There have recently come from the press two books which will provide much matter for thought among those who are interested in present-day tendencies in historical study, especially in Canada and the United States. The first of these is *The Art of History* (London, 1926), by Professor J.B. Black, formerly of the department of history in Queen's University, Kingston, Canada, and now professor of modern history in the University of Sheffield; and the second is *The Art of Thought* (London, 1926), by that dean of English political thinkers, Professor Graham Wallas, of London University.

Professor Black's book is a study of the work of four eighteenth-century historians – Voltaire, Hume, Robertson, and Gibbon. But it is more than this. It is an attempt to bring the historians of to-day back to the ideals which actuated the historians of the Age of Enlightenment. 'The motive lying behind the entire essay,' confesses the author, 'is that the intimate union of literature, philosophy, and history, so amply demonstrated in the writings of Voltaire and his "school," is not merely an ideal of the eighteenth century, but one which bears validity for all time. Or, more explicitly, history devoid of philosophic and literary interest, which concerns itself only with the establishment of the fact, however scientifically handled, has always seemed to the writer to be blind of an eye and lame of gait: a study, in short, of contracting horizons and diminishing cultural value' (p. vii). And he expresses the hope that 'when the humanist has come into his own once more, we shall see the subject, freed from excessive subserviency to "science," rise again to the commanding position it held in the days of Voltaire and Gibbon – the indispensable passport of every educated person, and a social force of the first magnitude' (p. vii).

In developing this thesis, Professor Black deals the so-called 'scientific' school of historians some shrewd blows. 'The facts of history,' he reminds us, 'are infinite; and if, as a French historian assures us, they are "everything", the labour of collecting and interpreting them becomes infinite also. In fact, there is presented to us the impressive spectacle of whole armies of collaborators grappling with the great historical synthesis of the future, and the individual sinking into comparative insignificance. And a question naturally suggests itself. Assuming that the final synthesis will be achieved – at present it is a matter of faith – may we presume that it will be, not only comprehensive, but readable and compassable as well? If so, who will read, comprehend, and compass it? In the eighteenth century, the study of history was well within the scope of every educated person; to-day it is written by specialists primarily for specialists' (p. 5).

...

Some Vices of Clio

It is worth while inquiring why this is so. One is loath to be dogmatic; but one ventures to raise the question whether, on the whole, the historians of to-day have not lost the art of telling a story. Herodotus, the father of history, was a story-teller; and every great historian since his time has been a story-teller, in greater or less degree. The story may be simple or involved; but it is none the less a story, and in it the facts fall into their proper place and perspective. The Anglo-Saxon chronicler was not a story-teller; he merely gave the story-teller the facts from which he might draw. Perhaps the modern doctor of philosophy is also not a story-teller, but is content to provide the facts of which the story-teller may make use. If so, his ambition is less than it ought to be. Story-telling is a branch of literature; and the historian who abdicates the function of story-teller, places himself outside the pale of literature.

The average Ph.D. thesis, moreover, has, as the French say, the defects of its qualities. It is well to add something to the sum of human knowledge; but this does not mean that one should drag from oblivion solid phalanxes of meaningless and unimportant facts. It is well to cite authorities; but this does not mean that one should annotate every statement, or give the source of every chance quotation. Indeed, nothing damns a book so quickly as excessive and indiscriminate annotation and citation of authorities: one might as well bring the kitchen utensils into the dining-room. Lastly, it is well to be thorough and exhaustive; but this does not mean that one should narrow the field in which one is working until it becomes insignificant. The graduate schools of history are not perhaps so guilty in this respect as some other graduate schools one might mention ...

The Beginnings of Historical Criticism in Canada: A Retrospect, 1896–1936

GEORGE WRONG

(March 1936)
CHR 17, no. 1: 1–8. Excerpt: 1–2, 4–7.

The first volume of the annual *Review of Historical Publications Relating to Canada*, the parent of the *Canadian Historical Review*, appeared in 1897. It reviewed the books which were published in 1896, and the present year may therefore be taken as the fortieth anniversary of the founding of a journal of historical criticism in Canada. Historical journals are now legion but in 1896 they were few in number and of comparatively recent growth. There were, however, in the 1890s many evidences of a new activity in the field of history in Canada as well as in other countries. The *Bulletin des recherches historiques*, which has for over forty years performed a most valuable service in publishing the results of research in the history of French Canada, was begun in 1895 by M. Pierre-Georges Roy who is still its editor. The influence of the rapidly growing collections in the Public Archives at Ottawa was beginning to make itself strongly felt.[1] Important works touching Canadian history and using materials recently made accessible were appearing not only in Canada, but elsewhere and especially in the United States. Writers whose names were to be prominent in the dominion's historical literature during the next generation were beginning their effective work.

It is beyond our scope to attempt to analyse fully the reasons for this new growth. It was part of a wider movement observable in many countries and drawing its inspiration from a variety of sources – not least from the example provided by research in natural science. The development in Canada doubtless owed something also to the growing spirit of national consciousness which was a characteristic of the time. Probably, too, it owed something to the new imperialism. The diamond jubilee [of Queen Victoria] and the imperial conference in 1897 were among the many signs indicating that the dominions were about to play a part more distinctive and on a larger stage than in the past. Whatever may be the explanation of the new development, there can be no question as to the importance of the 1890s in the growth of Canadian historical scholarship.

Professor George M. Wrong, who was head of the department of history in the University of Toronto from 1894 to 1927, founded the *Review of Historical Publications* and edited the first volume himself. It is not surprising that he should have felt that there was need for such a publication but, everything considered, the venture was an ambitious one, and in undertaking it Mr. Wrong displayed no little initiative and courage. The annual series which he thus began contained reviews only,[2] but the policy of the present historical quarterly is, in many respects, an elaboration of the policy which Mr. Wrong laid down at the beginning: there was included, for example, not only Canadian history in the strict sense of the term but public affairs, imperial relations, economics, and other subjects closely related to history. Over a period of forty years the reviews and bibliographies in the annual and quarterly series have, therefore, provided a basic list of references for a wide circle of readers interested in various aspects of Canadian development ...

Let me now turn to the situation in which was founded forty years ago the *Review of Historical Publications Relating to Canada*, published annually, and later in 1920, expanded into the *Canadian Historical Review*, published quarterly. That was a time of expansion in historical study. The influence of the German university was at its height, and methods of teaching history were dominated by the example of the German seminar. Archives were being opened to the student. The impression was growing that not only had something been distorted but also that something had been neglected in the study of the past. The distortions could, it was believed, be corrected by renewed examination of the sources of information. Neglect was another matter. History needed a new emphasis. The historians of the past had tended to dwell chiefly on activities in high places, on rulers, on leaders in politics and in war, on controversies in religion. Not enough attention had been paid to the condition of the people. Now the change had come. By 1896, the first year covered by the *Review*, nearly every educated person was reading, or had read, John Richard Greene's *Short History of the English People*, published in 1874. Green was himself a pioneer in the new views and study of history. Impetus from him led after his death to the founding of the Oxford Historical Society and the *English Historical Review*. In Germany the mark of expert training in history had become the degree of doctor of philosophy, the final product of the seminar. While England went her own way and remained but slightly affected by the example of Germany, the German method was eagerly followed in the United States and the degree of doctor of philosophy became the aim of aspirants for an academic post. Those who could do so went to Germany to study and to bring back the product of research in a thesis, a doctor's dissertation.

There was something in the spirit of the time, the *Zeitgeist*, that led to expansion in the study of history in the English-speaking world. The *English Historical Review* was founded in 1886. In the previous year the American Historical Association was organized and following this came, in 1896, the child of this association, the *American Historical Review*. In 1897 appeared the first volume of the *Review of Historical Publications Relating to Canada*. These three publications are linked in spirit. The *English Historical Review* provided the impetus that led to the founding of the other reviews.

Canadians are influenced by forces operating in both England and in the United States. I always felt it important to keep in touch with historians in the United States. For many years I attended the annual meetings of the American Historical Association and for a time, indeed, sat on the council. I was present at the meeting in New York when it was decided to found the *American Historical Review*, and I remember that the recently founded *English Historical Review* was both admired and criticized by the creators of the new venture. I have pleasant memories of the friends one made at the meetings of the American Historical Association: blithe Herbert Adams, loved by everyone, died all too soon; Morse Stephens, a product of Balliol, was always there, always an Englishman, ardent for Kipling's imperialism, but also ardent for his adopted country and, like Adams, loved by everyone. I was grateful for his tactful support when in 1916, during the war, with a German professor in the chair, I spoke on the growth of nationalism in the British Empire. Morse Stephens is gone and so also is Turner, who threw such new light on the influence of the frontier. Ferguson, Harvard professor from Prince Edward Island, Albert Bushnell Hart, Franklin Jameson, Andrew McLaughlin, and A. Lawrence Lowell are still among the living. At one time Goldwin Smith was president of the association, at another Woodrow Wilson.

It is not without significance that the first volume of the *Review of Historical Publications* covered the publications of 1896, the year in which appeared the *American Historical Review*. I am not conscious of any direct connection, but no doubt contact with scholars in the United States helped to reveal the need for some organ in Canada that should bring adequate criticism to publications related to its history ...

Vital interest in archives had hardly yet reached the universities. In the United States interest in regard to history in the university was already keen in 1896. Harvard had six professors of history and twelve members of the historical staff, Stanford had four professors, Chicago and Cornell each three. In Canada McGill, Queen's, and Toronto each had one professor. While the United States had in 1885 an historical association national in character, it was not until 1923 that the Canadian Historical Association was founded. In the University of Toronto, for fear of appeals to existing party feeling, no history of Canada later than 1815 was studied; that of the United States was wholly neglected; and England and Europe received about the measure found in the ordinary text-book. In truth history was neglected and a not greatly dissimilar situation was found in other Canadian universities. It would be difficult now to name anyone who taught history at McGill and Queen's universities before the coming of Colby some forty years ago and of Shortt, whose subject was economic history. When we compare this with the situation to-day of voluminous and competent writing and teaching of history in Canadian universities, we realize that the study has passed into a new era ...

Notes

1 See Dr. D. McArthur's presidential address to the Canadian Historical Association, 'The Canadian Archives and the Writing of Canadian History,' in the *Report* of the association for 1934.
2 An opportunity for the publication of articles embodying the results of research was provided in the *Proceedings of the Royal Society of Canada* founded in 1882 and also in the *Bulletin des recherches historiques*.

Past Historians and Present History in Canada

GUSTAVE LANCTÔT

(September 1941)
CHR 22, no. 3: 241–53. Excerpt: 241, 251–3.

In the course of the past four centuries, Canada has experienced three distinct periods: the Indian, the French, and the British. Along this retrospective route many stages can be signalized simply by headings which sufficiently describe them: exploration, colonization, fur trade, and warfare; growth of population, and agriculture; military conquest, and the arrival of the Loyalists; constitutional strife, commercial expansion, and Confederation; economic and demographic progression, national evolution, and international independence within the British Commonwealth of Nations.

Now, by singular good fortune, this history of an arresting past possesses archives which are practically complete, permitting us fully to relate, with its many episodes, the slow evolution of a feudal colony into an international state. With the material of the great Canadian achievements so complete, what have historians done and what have they left behind for us to read and use? ...

At the start, Canadian history was of the descriptive order based on explorations and details of the new country and its resources, with a mixture of ethnographical data. It was unavoidably so from lack of facts to relate and also in consequence of the newness of the country. Lescarbot is a typical example of this, the initial type of our history.

Later, explorations being over and the country opened up, physical and economic descriptions came to be superseded by the dominant fact and factor of Indian and Anglo–French wars. Writings on Canada then present but a nomenclature of battles and military exploits. La Potherie can be cited as the representative of this second type of history.

A third type sprang up with the British Conquest. With the exception of two brief periods, war disappeared from our midst and was succeeded by the strife of political reforms and party programmes. From that time Canadian history is fairly well divided into two sections: the wars under the French régime and the political battles under British rule. The country and its resources, the people and their labours disappeared almost completely beneath the ever-mounting flood of military and political narratives. Kingsford is the best example of this tidal wave which sweeps through his ten volumes.

Fortunately, while still in the morass of military and political publications, a new light appeared in the historical sky. Economic studies and investigations of our past commenced to creep in. The change was rather overdue, for Taine's theory of environment had been proclaimed as early as 1865 and Rogers had published in 1888 his *Economic Interpretation of History*. It was Adam Shortt, a Scottish Canadian, who really blazed this new trail. Much water has passed under the bridge since Brymner scorned calendaring the papers of the Canada Land Company and Marmette pronounced the financial papers of New France to be without interest. Today economics and sociology are deemed an essential part of any worthy book of history. The resources of the country and the life of the people have re-entered into our writings under the aegis of scientific history which now obtains in Canada ...

To those literary people, history is nevertheless indebted for the founding of the Archives in 1871, which opened full and wide the door that led to scientific history. For the first time historians were given easy access to an enormous wealth of material, beside which began the accumulating of large collections of original documents, published by historical societies and provincial governments. At the same time European methodology was seeping into the country. The new technique was consistently preached by the *Review of Historical Publications Relating to Canada*, which, founded in 1896, has played such an essential part in raising Canadian history to European standards. Another valuable influence in the same direction was the successive founding of chairs of modern history in the various Canadian universities.

Now, scientific history in Canada was confronted with a bigger task owing to the increasing quantity of accessible sources and the lack of preliminary spade-work in almost every field. The result was that the historian began to abandon the writing of general history to co-operative workers. Collaboration indeed offers the advantage of being able to cover more thoroughly the whole field of history and to entrust each part to a specialist. On the other hand, it carries the disadvantage of breaking the continuity of thought, method, and narrative. Nor does it possess the grandeur of conception, the strength of conviction, or the glowing ardour which permeate the work of a single brain ...

Today, the best of Canadian history has lifted itself above its former `provincialism,' to use an expression of W.L. Grant, and attained the level of European methodology. It has started to revise the interpretation of the Canadian past in a scientific way. In fact, the ground is being cleared of many errors, inaccuracies, and prejudices. There is still much persistent work to be done, but we may entertain the hope that the day is approaching when the same text-book will take its place in the schools of all the provinces.

This reminds us that Canadian history is confronted with peculiar difficulties. Politically, the country is scarcely out of the colonial stage and a great number of its people have not yet acquired that national faith – of biblical mention – capable of moving mountains. Our Canadian citizen, not being integral, often continues to hold a tenacious allegiance to his province, the federation of which is still alive in his mind. Finally, often faltering politically and socially, he submits in many ways to the call of his religious denomination, of his racial ascendancy, or of his political partisanship. Among this heterogeneous and too young a people, there are still lacking that depth of national consciousness and that sense of criticism which would enable them to prefer documentary history to conformist publications. Many are still more interested in British or world history than in the Canadian past and evolution.

This peculiar situation has thrust upon the historians of the country a double task. The first, which is essential, is to inject into history documentary truth and the complex of sociological facts. The second is to infuse into that history a spirit, a faith, and a colour befitting the great achievements narrated and the greater future looming ahead. Such historical writings should help to build up among the opinion-forming minority, at any rate, a sound knowledge of, and a moral pride in, the past, and should help also to strengthen the bond of national unity.

Note

This paper by Dr. Gustave Lanctot, the Dominion Archivist, was read as his presidential address at the last meeting of the Canadian Historical Association. Its French version is being published in the *Report* of the Association for 1941.

Dollard des Ormeaux and the Fight at the Long Sault: A Reinterpretation of Dollard's Exploit

E.R. ADAIR

(June 1932)
CHR 13, no. 2: 121–38. Excerpt: 121, 135–7.

To most people in Canada the story of Dollard des Ormeaux and the fight at the Long Sault is well known ...

... Dollard appears to have been an ambitious young man anxious to redeem his reputation by leading a raid upon small groups of Iroquois as they returned from hunting. His party has been followed day by day, its deeds set down, and the dates upon which they were performed fixed with reasonable certainty. But there still remains the question as to what were the real results for Montreal and for the colony at large of this exploit at the Long Sault. Should Dollard and his men be called the saviours of New France?

There seems no doubt that Dollard knew nothing, when he set out from Montreal, of the two hundred Iroquois up the Ottawa or of the five hundred Iroquois at the mouth of the Richelieu. But Quebec had heard about the latter force and spies and prisoners had magnified reports of its size; consequently, Quebec was fully prepared for an attack and there was not much real danger that even five hundred Iroquois could have done a great deal of damage to the fortified houses that made up that little town.[1] ...

Much the same can be said of Montreal: it certainly was smaller and weaker than Quebec, but with a population of about two hundred fighting men it should have had no real difficulty in repelling two hundred Iroquois. In fact it is extremely doubtful if in either case the Iroquois would have made a real attack on Montreal or Quebec. Such a thing was entirely alien to their habits and they undoubtedly felt how great would be their disadvantage; whereas in their chosen method of warfare, that of swooping down upon an occasional farmer or an isolated house, all the odds were on their side. Their plans, then, for the spring of 1660 may well have included doing as much damage as they could to single houses or incautious *hatitants* and hunters and Hurons, but it is hardly probable that they intended a full-dress siege of either Quebec or Montreal.

Still it may be argued that the self-sacrifice of Dollard and his men, even if it were unpremeditated, did send the Iroquois home defeated and discouraged. Dollier de Casson as a good Montrealer holds this view: he maintains that Montreal as usual served as a bulwark against the Iroquois, that the salvation of New France was the result of the fear inspired by the dauntless seventeen from Montreal.[2] But this opinion is unsupported by contemporary evidence. Marie de l'Incarnation all unconsciously gives us the real key to the situation, for she writes that the Iroquois 'après la défaite [i.e., of Dollard] dont je viens de parler, s'en sont retournés en leurs pays, enflés de leur victoire, quoiqu'elle ne soit pas grande en elle-même. ... Mais c'est le génie des sauvages, quand ils n'auraient pris ou tué que vingt hommes, de s'en retourner sur leurs pas pour en faire montre en leurs pays.'[3] ... The Iroquois returned, therefore, to their own lands not disheartened, but feeling with some justice that they had achieved success. Owing to Dollard's headstrong folly, they had, at one blow, killed or captured sixty of their enemies of whom seventeen were French. This may sound a small number to-day, but it must be remembered that seventeen represented nearly one-tenth of the male population of Montreal. Nor can it be said that the losses the Iroquois suffered in defeating Dollard struck such terror into their hearts that they were more wary in their future attacks. On the contrary, either in revenge for those losses or emboldened by their victory over Dollard, they ravaged New France in the following year as it had never been ravaged before, killing or capturing the French and their Indian allies whenever they could catch them outside their stockades or their fortified houses.[4]

Notes

1 Benjamin Sulte, *Lettres ... de ... Marie de l'Incarnation*, 98–104.
2 Dollier de Casson, *A History of Montreal* (ed. by R. Flenly), 253, 267.
3 Sulte, *Lettres ... de ... Marie de l'incarnation*, 116.
4 See Chapter 1 of the *Jesuit Relations* for 1660–1.

Was Dollard the Saviour of New France?

GUSTAVE LANCTÔT

(June 1932)
CHR 13, no. 2: 138–46. Excerpt: 138–40, 142–3, 146.

In 1660 Dollard and sixteen Frenchmen decided to engage in a military expedition against the Five Nation Indians. Taking post at the Long Sault, they were attacked by several hundred Iroquois and, after a most courageous fight lasting several days were completely annihilated. Whereupon the Indians returned to their villages and did not attempt any raid against New France for the next eight months.

Supported by documents such is the authentic outline of the historical fact of the battle at Long Sault. Even the 'sceptical' Kingsford admitted that much.[1] Naturally to this splendid epic, as with all epics, there have been attached embellishments and exaggerations, mostly due to honest but uncritical interpretation of none too clear sources ...

In 1920, there was printed under the editorship of Mr. E.Z. Massicotte a series of documents relating to Dollard and his companions.[2] In reviewing this book, the present writer took occasion to assert for the first time[3] on the strength of the documents there published 'that, before leaving, Dollard and his companions never contemplated, as currently related, sacrificing themselves in a fight to death in order to stem the coming invasion.' He then went on to say: 'They did not know the existence of such an invasion. Their first idea was only to make raids on the Iroquois ... It is evident that it was only when they realized the strength of the enemy that the heroes decided to die in the attempt to stop them. This does not lessen their glory, but merely throws a new light on it.'[4]

Going still further along lines similar to those in the above quotations, Professor E.R. Adair has now given us an interesting but antagonistic version of the whole Dollard story. His view in brief is that Dollard was not the saviour of New France, as is commonly supposed; that he was, rather, an ambitious young man, anxious to regain a lost reputation, hopelessly unskilled in Indian warfare, and that his death, together with that of his sixteen companions at the hands of the Iroquois horde, did more harm than good to the struggling young French communities of Montreal and Quebec.[5] ...

Coming to facts, the controversial part of the story may, for the present purpose, be considered under two headings: what were the intentions of Dollard and his party, and what were the results of their expedition? ...

The contemporary sources all agree in stating that the expedition saved the colony, as the most powerful invasion yet planned by the enemy was diverted from an unsuspecting and unprepared small colony and then the Iroquois abstained from new raids for eight full months.[6] ...

Thus contemporary sources agree in stating unanimously that the struggle at Long Sault saved the colony from widespread devastation and massacre. This alone would justify calling Dollard the saviour of New France. But another result must be mentioned. Dollard's expedition saved New France from starvation. There was a terrible scarcity of food, as Marie de l'Incarnation declares: 'What is to be feared is famine, for if the enemy comes in the fall, he will devastate the crops; and if he comes in the spring, he will prevent seeding.'[7] ...

... Little wonder that the people of Quebec, on hearing of Dollard's expedition and the retreat of the Indians which liberated them from possible destruction and starvation, sang a *Te Deum* because for the first time 'everybody began to breathe, as for five weeks there had been no rest by day or night but to fortify as well as to watch for one's own safety.'[8] In the ordinary sense of such an expression, Dollard had really saved the colony.

...

In the face of documentary evidence supporting the facts and giving the opinions of the contemporaries, are we to refuse Dollard des Ormeaux the title of saviour of New France simply because in the following years Iroquois came down and killed more Frenchmen? If so, we cannot say that the first Canadian division saved the allies at Ypres, for more Canadians than ever were killed the next year. In the same way, historians could not write that Joan of Arc was the saviour of France, for, when she died at Rouen, one third of France still remained in the hands of the English. Certainly Mr. Adair must know that such an expression is not used in an absolute but in a relative sense. Nobody means in using it that Dollard saved the colony from future Indian attacks, but only from a great immediate danger. In such a relative sense, because the struggle at Long Sault warded off from a famishing and unprepared colony devastating hordes of Iroquois bent on destroying it, Dollard and his seventeen companions are in our opinion entitled to bear, as awarded to them by history and by the grateful colonists, the name of saviours of New France.

Notes

1 William Kingsford, *History of Canada* (Toronto, 1887), I, 261–2.
2 E.Z. Massicotte, *Dollard des Ormeaux et ses companions* (Montreal, 1920).
3 Kingsford's assertion in 1887 was only made in the way of a doubt based on unsupported reasoning.
4 *Canadian Historical Review*, 1920, I, 394.
5 *Montreal Daily Herald*, March 21, 1932. An interesting newspaper discussion by Professor Adair and M.E. Vaillancourt appeared in the *Montreal Gazette* of April 7.
6 Dollier de Casson, *A History of Montreal*, 271.
7 *Lettres de la Mère Marie de l'Incarnation*, 164.
8 *Lettres de la Mère Marie de l'Incarnation*, I, 172.

Women of New France (Three Rivers: 1651–63)

ISABEL FOULCHÉ-DELBOSC

(June 1940)
CHR 21, no. 2: 132–49. Excerpt: 132, 148–9.

Except for three or four heroines of general renown – Madeleine de Verchères, Mademoiselle Mance, Madame de La Peltrie, and Marie de l'Incarnation – we know very little about the women of New France. And necessarily so. The documents most often consulted by historians have to do with matters of political importance rather than with simple household affairs. But there are available sources for the social historian which have as yet been little used and which serve to throw some light upon colonial domestic life. These include the notarial and law-court records of Quebec Province, Montreal, and Three Rivers.

The following essay relies principally upon the material relating to Three Rivers for the period 1651–63 ...

At this period there were no sheep in the colony, no flax, and no hemp. Consequently there were no hand-looms or spinning-wheels. The home industries developed later. Textiles had to be imported from France. From these the women made dresses for themselves and their children as well as shirts and underwear for the men. Men's outer dress – doublets and hose, coats and hats – had to be brought out from France. They were very scarce and costly in the colony. Worn clothing, sold after a man's death, fetched a price which seems excessive in terms of other commodities.[1] The materials used for women's clothing seem to have been chosen for durability rather than colour or beauty. They included: *crézeau* (serge or kersey), *grisette* (cheap gray stuff), *treillis* (sackcloth, buckram), *ras de Châlons* (napless material, shalloon), *toile de Mélis* (sail-cloth).

The scarcity of specie made barter a common practice and there were cases of women exchanging grain or vegetables for manufactured goods which another family had imported. In summer French merchants arrived to trade their goods for furs or money. There is mention of women trading furs for merchandise but this is probably because furs were legal tender, not because the women were in the fur trade. There was one outstanding exception in Jeanne Enard, wife of Christophe Crevier, Sieur de la Meslée, mother of six children and mother-in-law of Pierre Boucher. By her husband's own avowal she was the business head of the family both as regards the fur trade and household management.[2] Another woman, Mathurine Poisson, wife of Jacques Aubuchon, was a recognized merchant and sold imported goods to the colonists. She acted in her own name and had no need for her husband's permission in her dealings.[3]

We can visualize these women going about their daily errands on foot or by boat in the river highway, on snowshoes in the winter, assembling on invitation to witness a marriage contract, turning out in force for baptisms, weddings, and funerals as well as High Mass on Sunday mornings, after which public notices were cried and posted, and auctions held. We can see them gossiping with the neighbours and returning home to cook the midday meal – all very much as if they were at home in France instead of in the heart of the Canadian wilderness surrounded by hostile Iroquois. Through all these documents they appear very human. Sometimes litigious to the point of absurdity, they thus reveal the piquant details of their lives and themselves as well. Some of them stand out with startling clearness. Mme Christophe Crevier, estimable wife and mother, was undoubtedly disagreeable in business relations, a termagant. Mme des Groseilliers, the first advocate of women's rights, attains her moments of grandeur. During those troubled times, it was these women (who else?) who nursed the sick and wounded, cooked for the colony's defenders, cared for the children, acted as midwives. It was they who looked after the household and the family business during their husbands' long absences. We must regret that the records are so meagre of these achievements. It was no light accomplishment to have bequeathed to later generations the traditions of the French household, built up of the thousand and one events of ordinary human living.

These traditions were strongly individualistic and included a keen sense of property. Boundaries had to be maintained; goods or produce damaged had to be paid for; slandered reputations atoned for. For them, the family was the first loyalty. The one collective institution which flourished during the period and which has remained to this day – the guardianship of minors – is essentially a family matter. But in the early years of the colony, before families had many ramifications, we find outsiders devoting their time and energy to the interests of little children with praise-worthy zeal.

This essay has attempted to give a general view of women's life and work in New France during the early critical years when marriage dominated the lives of women and forced all other careers, except that of the religious life, out of existence. The feminine members of the struggling colony had to fulfil their natural destiny as wives and mothers during a longer period of their lives than is required of most women of European stock. Married at twelve or thirteen they continued their career uninterrupted even by major calamities. They became specialists of marriage and motherhood. Few in number as they were, they assumed successfully the task of populating the colony.

Notes

The late Madame Foulché-Delbosc (née Isabel Jones) was a graduate of the University of Toronto and for a time a member of the staff in history at the University of Saskatchewan. She was later associated with her husband in historical work in France. After his death she returned to Canada. She planned a careful study on the women of New France and did much research on the subject. The high quality of the work she would have done is indicated by this article which was found substantially in this form among her papers. We are indebted to her brother-in-law, Professor Morley Ayearst, for drawing it to our attention and preparing it for publication. [CHR EDITOR]

1 The Hertel inventory included 'un manteau de drap garni de boutons d'or' selling for 54 *livres*, and 'un pourpoint, hault de chausses et bas de drap' for

40 *livres*, while a six weeks' old heifer cost only 24 *livres* and even a house and lot in town was sold for 135 *livres*.
2 Testament of Christophe Crevier, Sieur de la Meslée, Dec. 1, 1652. (This date has been added by another hand.)
3 Palais de Justice, Québec, *Greffe Guillaume Audouart*, Sept. 6, 1658, no. 675, and Musée de Québec, *Prévôté des Trois-Rivières*, I, May 8, 1660.

The Historian and Society

CHARLES BEARD

(March 1933)
CHR 14, no. 1: 1–4. Excerpt: 1–2, 3–4.

History, like science and literature, belongs to the republic of letters which knows no political boundaries, tariffs, and embargoes. Historians, to be sure, have their locus in space and time but history as thought transcends these particular considerations. The earth of circumstance clings to the garments of the best writers and thinkers in this field, but the vows of the craft and the unity of all things command them to rise above the temporary and relative.

Indeed it may be said that herein lies a paradox: it is by becoming unmoral that history serves the highest morality. The contention may be illustrated by reference to the course of historical thought in the United States. As long as American historians regarded the war between the states, or the social war, as a conflict between right and wrong, night and day, the powers of good and the powers of evil, neither understanding nor reconciliation was possible. It was by putting aside the moral function of meting out damnation that they entered into the kingdom of comprehension. It was when they sought to assume the position of the physicist or chemist and to see the reality of the struggle as it was that they escaped from the gall of bitterness and bondage of iniquity. By observing the tension as an antagonism of interest and cultures, they gained in understanding and brought healing to the nation.

This indifference to local righteousness may, of course, land the historian in jail upon occasion, especially if not used with discretion. There are, as Henry Adams once remarked, four powerful organs in the modern world for suppressing unwelcome opinions and theories: the state, the church, property, and labour. While the church claimed to guard the truths of geology, biology, physics, and astronomy, many bitter conflicts arose with men of science and some of the latter suffered in spirit and estate as a result of their temerity. The plight of the historian, however, is far more difficult, because he, by refusing to accept face values as final, is likely to collide with powerful political and economic institutions, as well as with the organizations which claim to possess the seals of religion. For the serious in mind, tragedy and tears lurk here; for the light-hearted, irony and cynicism.

From this dilemma there is only one avenue of escape, that is through the narrow way of specialism. The historian may refuse to think. He may become a chronicler; that is, a discreet chronicler. He may choose as his life work the fluctuations in the price of cotton in Alabama between 1850 and 1860. He may get out a new edition of the sayings of Marcus Aurelius. He may annotate Gildas. He may resolve to know more about the manor of Weissnichtwo than any other person on God's footstool. He may particularize on the geographical errors of Froude. In short, he may do many useful things under the head of history.

But when the historian widens the area of his operations in time and space, when he comes to deal with things that are not unequivocal, when he has to use thought, he finds himself in the very middle of universals. If he asks why he puts some items in his chronicle and leaves others out, why cotton fluctuated in price in Alabama, whether Marcus Aurelius spake truly, how Gildas acquired his ideas, what relation the manor of Weissnichtwo in 1215 had to previous and succeeding conditions and to surrounding circumstances, or why anyone should bother about the geographical errors of Froude, then the historian's troubles begin. He then finds himself perplexed by the issues of thought which beset St. Augustine, Bossuet, Gibbon, Hegel, Marx, and Spengler. He confronts the task of making some kind of pattern out of isolated particularities, and the longer and harder he thinks the deeper and wider becomes his pattern. And the more certain he is to alarm or amuse his colleagues and contemporaries ...

Immediately, practical persons, bent on deciding whether tariffs should go up or down or whether branch factories are to be tolerated or taxed, will say: 'All this is irrelevant moonshine without utility for business in hand.' To this the historian may make many answers. He may reply in this vein: 'Will you practical persons kindly define utility, make a list of all things that do not serve utility, and tell us what kind of civilizations and world relations we should have with intangibles, imponderables, and immeasurables ruled out?' That is a pertinent question and answers from practical persons would be interesting, perhaps diverting. Again the historian may, in response to the challenge, declare that practical persons also seem to display facilities for getting mankind into distresses – facilities no less efficient than those of theoretical persons. Finally, a more modest answer may be made: 'Since we have so many provincial judges with a practical turn of mind prepared to mete out praise and damnation, perhaps there is room in the world for a few persons desirous of comprehending without praising or damning.'

Whether we take the price of commodities, the arts, the religious faiths we profess, inventions, the ideas we employ in thinking, the characters used in writing our histories, or the tongue we speak, we are led beyond the boundaries of nations, economic systems, and political jurisdictions. This mandate is inescapable. The greater the tension of thought and the wider the knowledge of fact, the harder we struggle to grasp the unity of all things; the higher our architecture of conception, the more relative and transitory seem the provincialisms that engage the passions of mankind. Thus we are brought to the abyss of totality which Croce has sought to cover with the frail net of history as philosophy.

In the long sweep of time, who shall judge the judges? Paradoxically enough, beyond world history itself there is no higher earthly tribunal and it is that very world history which gives historians all their aches and pains.

Note

The two short papers here printed were read at the forty-seventh annual meeting of the American Historical Association and associated societies which was held in Toronto on December 27–29, 1932. That by Professor Beard [this selection], who is president of the American Historical Association for 1933, was delivered as part of an address at the dinner given to the visiting societies by the University of Toronto. Professor Wrong's paper [the next selection] was read at one of the regular sessions under the title 'The historian's duty to society.'
[CHR Editor]

The Historian and Society

GEORGE M. WRONG

(March 1933)
CHR 14, no. 1: 4–8. Excerpt: 4, 5–6, 7–8.

The historian is both the guardian and the interpreter of the past. He is a treasure-house of human experience. He both collects its records and tells us what they mean. While other animals have memory, man alone builds up a formal story of his life in the past and is governed by its traditions. This gift of memory involves a duty. The historian has no right to falsify or distort the record. He is the guardian of the truth. The society in which he lives is the child of history and has the right to know the truth about its parent. We may be sure that to falsify the past will give a shaky foundation to the convictions and methods of the present. Nature is rigorously truthful and preserves an exact relation between cause and effect. As long ago as a century and a half before Christ Polybius said: 'It is not events that are interesting but their causes.' If the cause is misstated in regard to human society the result will always be tainted by a lie. There are a good many lies to be swept away in regard, for instance, to the American and the French Revolutions and not least, perhaps, in regard to the Great War ...

The historian's duty to society is not easily discharged, for many questions to which we should like to know the answer are really insoluble. What is the historian to say of the origin of race and also, perhaps, of its significance? What is the influence of climate on a nation's history? How comes about what we call the *Zeitgeist*, the spirit of an age? We may only guess; these forces are vital in society, and yet there is nothing about them in the state and the private papers on which the narratives of history are based. I am sometimes amused at being told that 'history teaches' this or that. Who knows what it teaches? I hear it said that such and such an outcome in history was 'inevitable.' Who knows the forces that give it this character? I am told that it is not the duty of the historian to indulge in moral judgments; he is only to tell us what was done. If Napoleon murdered the Bourbon Duc d'Enghien, the only duty of the historian is to tell the story. On the same basis we have no right to condemn British rule in Ireland in the eighteenth century; we may only describe it. We may pass no moral judgment on the treason of Benedict

Arnold. On the other hand, Lord Acton said that 'the great achievement of history is to develop and perfect and arm conscience' and, if so, conscience must pass moral judgments. The historian is the guardian of truth, truth not merely as to specific fact, but truth as expressing constructive standards of conduct. The dead bodies of those whom Napoleon massacred at Jaffa are not more historical realities than are the motives moral or otherwise that inspired the deed ...

I am not speaking to the methods of inquiry of the historian but of his duty to society. Society is a half-blind mass, living on its traditions, not knowing whither it is going, requiring leadership that will tell it the truth. Only the historian can find whether the experiment it pursues has been tried in the past and found good or ill. Yet I am quite sure that, during the past half century, the influence of the historian on society has declined. There is a double cause. The many have other reading than that of serious books. They have copious newspapers in which, with a certain envious longing, the women of the classes less favoured in fortune read of the doings of the more opulent society. They may, too, watch the advertisements for bargains. The men may spend most of the evening's leisure reading about sport in the newspaper; or listening to jazz and vulgar humour on the radio, which has much in its favour but also much to dismay serious minds. Our very variety of interests creates such desultory habits of thought that writers of the type of Macaulay and Lecky and Prescott and Motley, requiring continued attention, are not devoured by this generation as they were in their own. In truth we have now no Macaulays nor Motleys. Speaking broadly the historians tend to write with their fellow historians, rather than the public, in view. They watch each other for mistakes or omissions. Woe to them if they miss reference to a learned book or article that bears on their subject. In vindication they pour out on their pages the contents of notebooks. I have seen a work in which on a single page there were fifteen notes relating to the same volume. It is all very thorough and sound but where does the public come in? They want the truth told so that it will hold their interest. Since the art of arts is to conceal art, they want a finished product, not an exposition of the methods of the workshop. The cook, as M. Jusserand says wittily, peels the potatoes but he does not do it on the dining room table. The historian has the duty to cultivate an attractive style. It is of little use to tell the truth about the past to the east wind. Society asks to know of a past that has complex phases of life like those of the present. It is, perhaps, less interested in politics and war which, after all, have touched directly only limited classes, than in the mode of life, the ambitions and rivalries, the loves and hates, the dress, the speech, the wit and humour of the men of the past. These interests will reveal their views of life and duty and furnish a vital tie with the present.

...

... The historian has no right to go beyond the rigorous implications of his authorities. While he needs imagination to see their significance he is tied to them; he must have evidence for all that he tells us. Is his task difficult? Yes, and in this is its fascination. He needs insight to discern the truth, courage to tell it and defy sentiment. Fear is a permanent curse in a democratic world. The politician fears the whole truth lest it should hurt his party. He fears to defy a current phase of public opinion though he knows it is wrong. The churchman fears the charge that he is drifting from the old accepted beliefs. The patriot is for his country right or wrong. The historian for his part must banish fear. He may have to assault the reputation of popular heroes, to offend their admirers, to denounce the methods that have led to national victory, to wound national pride, to shock religious sentiment, to shatter belief in accepted economic policies and sumptuary laws. All this is a part of his day's work. His reward? To have told the truth and so to lead society to an understanding of its own foundations and of its enduring interests.

DEFINING THE CANADIAN NATION

Canada and the Imperial War Cabinet

GEORGE M. WRONG

(March 1920)
CHR 1, no. 1 (March 1920): 3–25. Excerpt: 3, 5–11, 20.

I. British Protection of Canada

The defence of the British Empire is a perplexing problem. Attempts to solve it provoked the great revolution from which came the republic of the United States. This revolution was even more momentous than the French Revolution. Not only did it determine the form of the political institutions of the greater part of the two continents of America, but it was itself also in large measure the cause of the French Revolution. Royalist France was aflame with eagerness for republican principles, as applied in America, to the hurt of a hated rival in Europe. These principles, however, would not remain on the other side of the ocean from France. They crossed to Europe and in the end helped to make France herself a republic. Thus a problem of the internal government of the British Empire expanded into a world problem, the struggle between democracy and aristocracy, between local liberty and centralized control. Ever since, in 1607, English colonists settled in Virginia it has haunted the politics of the British Empire. After a stormy history of three hundred years it has taken on a new character because of the great war which broke out in 1914.

The British Empire, as now we all see, has become a world-wide Commonwealth of Nations. When once the British over the seas attained to importance as states they could not be controlled and directed by the people of Great Britain and the consequent problem of continued union became one of the most searching which statesmanship could face ...

... For a hundred years after the American Revolution, Canada was protected almost wholly at the expense of the British government. The colonies which remained to Britain were in truth what George III had desired the lost colonies to be, children to be protected by the parent and to give in return affection, trust, and obedience. Their political education could begin only when they were populous enough to take care of themselves.

For half a century after the American Revolution a majority of the people of Canada were of French origin with no tradition of British self-government. The British element, however, multiplied. Perhaps fifty or sixty thousand people, chiefly of English, rather than of Irish or Scottish, origin, driven out from the young republics, because of their loyalty to their king, took refuge in Canada. They were reinforced later by Irish and Scottish elements. While Canada was poor, weak in numbers, without importance compared with the wealth and power of the British Isles, it was easy to adhere to the view of parent and child. What the parent chiefly owed to the daughter state was protection, the protection of the strong for the weak. It was, of course, desirable that the people of the colony should, as far as possible, control their own local affairs. Final authority rested, however, with the mother country. It sent out a governor who was intended really to govern. Each colony had its little legislature, but this ought not to take itself too seriously. It could make laws and vote money. Over its doings, even in respect to these things, the governor kept a watchful eye and could at any time block action by refusing his consent to measures proposed. The legislature must do nothing that touched upon more than the internal interests of the colony and the judge of the import of its actions was to be the governor. It was for him to appoint to office and to dismiss from office. He had no ministers in any true sense of the word. There was no colonial cabinet which he must consult. He took advice from whom he would. Why should he not, since Great Britain was responsible for the well-being of the colony and pledged to protect it from all danger? Of partnership on the part of the colony with Great Britain there was no thought. The strong parent protected a weak child.

By 1850, however, Canada had between three and four million people, a larger population than that of the American colonies at the time of the Revolution. By 1850, too, it had been established, and not without strife and bloodshed, that the legislature of Canada should control completely its internal affairs. For the first time, Canada had a real cabinet. On all purely domestic matters the Governor acted on the advice of his ministers. Outside affairs, however, he attended to himself ...

The Civil War in the United States, lasting from 1861 to 1865, produced a great effect in Canada ...

II. The Growth of National Self-reliance in Canada

War was happily averted, but the menace helped to make the British colonies in North America realize a weakness which was due largely to lack of union. The small provinces on the Atlantic sea-board, Nova Scotia, New Brunswick, and Prince Edward Island, had each a separate government wholly independent of what was then Canada and is now the provinces of Quebec and Ontario. The great West was still a wilderness ruled by the Hudson's Bay Company and outside the pale of Canadian politics. The Civil War made the United States a great military nation. The North was irritated with Great Britain because of the widely extended sympathy of the English ruling class with the aspiration of the South for separation. It was not impossible that one of the aims of the restored Union, with a great army and a consciousness now of strength, would be to insist on a policy which should break any remaining political tie of American States with Europe ...

Fear of dictation from the great republic was not, of course, the only motive which led the scattered colonies to think of union. They needed union to save them from obscurity and isolation. Thus it came about that just at the time in 1864 when the North was planning the supreme effort to end the civil war, when Sherman was making his desolating march from Atlanta to the sea, and Grant was nerving himself for the last heavy blows which brought in the end the unconditional surrender of Lee, delegates from the British provinces were in conference at Quebec on the problem of union. Their conference was fruitful, and out of it came, in 1867, the federation since known as the Dominion of

Canada. Within a few years it included the West as well as the East. By 1873 Canada was a vast country stretching across the American continent and covering an area as great as the United States.

For a time no change was apparent in the relations with Great Britain of this state so potent in promise. The Canadian people had still the colonial mind. They though it incumbent on Great Britain to protect them. They liked to see the British red coats in Canada; and to the petty type of Canadian politician it was an added source of satisfaction that, for the support of these regiments, not a penny came from the Canadian tax-payer. One thing, however, had been settled. The great federation was completely self-governing. The Governor-General, who represented the dignity of the British Crown, no longer made any claim really to govern. He was at Ottawa what the King was at London, the official head of the state with duties chiefly formal and ceremonial. He could act only on the advice of his responsible ministers ...

So far so good; but the most difficult problem remained still unsolved. What should be the relation of Canada to Great Britain? In this problem was wrapped up the larger one of the relations of all other British self-governing states, of Australia, New Zealand and South Africa, to Great Britain. Could the relation remain one of subordination? Could a great state, continental in area, continue to be in a dependent position, its defence paid for by the heavily burdened tax-payer of Great Britain? India paid for its own defence, since the cost of the Indian army came from the exchequer of India. Canada, however, paid nothing for the British fleet and the British army which made her secure from attack. During many years there was slight interest in the question. Canada was creating the great railway systems which should bind together the East and the West and her financial power was so strained to meet the vast cost that, for a time, collapse was feared. In such conditions it would have been impossible, except in a time of dire peril, to persuade the Canadian voter to carry any tangible share of the burden of fleet and army. He had, moreover, no sense of impending danger. Down to 1914 was seemed to the average man in Canada an almost impossible thing. When war had actually touched him there had been a partial awakening. This had happened in 1899 when Canadian regiments were sent to fight in South Africa. The scene of war was, however, remote, and, compared with what we now know, the effort was insignificant. Only in 1914 did the scales fall from the eyes of Canada and she saw the colossal figure of war, naked and menacing, rise up to imperil her own liberty and that of every free people ...

Defining the Canadian Nation

... Now, in the Great War, Canada, for the first time, paid her own way as Britain and France paid their own way. For the first time the Canadian people subscribed for great loans to their own government to carry on the war. Hitherto a debtor nation, Canada became in part a creditor nation. She made vast quantities of munitions of war. Hitherto her manufacturers had not ventured upon some of the more delicate work in, for instance, steel, but now they made complex and difficult products. The young nation was showing itself competent. Its soldiers proved equal to the best. The officers, most of them civilians before the war, quickly acquired skill and enterprise in making war. What was to be the political expression of this national vitality?

III. Changes in the British Cabinet System

...

Long before the war broke out there had been plans for cooperation among the different states of the Empire both in time of peace and in time of war. In 1887 sat for the first time what came to be known as the Imperial Conference. Here representatives of all the self-governing states discussed matters of common interest, chiefly relating to communications and to trade. The great achievement of the Conference on Imperial Defence in 1909 was that it confronted this acute problem and later led to the creation of the Imperial Defence Committee. This Committee provided a means for counsel and cooperation among the various states of the Empire to meet the emergency of war. But in Canada, at least, it was never taken very seriously. The conviction of the unreflecting and uninformed that civilized states had outgrown war and that no great conflict was likely proved particularly strong in Canada as it did among similar classes in the United States. Between 1909 and 1914 there had been hot debates in Canada as to the creation of a Canadian navy or, failing this, a sharing of the burdens of the British navy. Little was done, and when the dark clouds broke in 1914 Canada was unprepared to meet the crisis ...

At the same time other precedents were going by the board. In 1915 the existing British Parliament prolonged its own life beyond the statutory term of five years and, in fact, continued to sit for eight years, until the election of December, 1918. A little later Canada took similar action. Meanwhile even coalition government was proving ineffective since it laboured under the cumbrous methods of the days of peace. The coalition Cabinet formed in Great Britain in May, 1915, contained twenty-two members. It was too large and met too infrequently to direct from day to day the vast energies engaged in the war. It tried the plan of giving to a small War Council of five members the direction of the war. This council was a committee of the larger Cabinet and reported to that body. The members of the smaller body with the Prime Minister as its head were most of them heads of departments. Their burden was too heavy. The summer of 1916, which saw the great offensive on the Somme, brought to Britain depression and disillusion, for it showed that not yet were the allies able to strike effectively at the military power of Germany.

It thus happened that the end of 1916 saw a startling change in British politics. On December 1, Mr. Lloyd George wrote to the Prime Minister, Mr. Asquith, urging that the conduct of the war should be placed in the hands of a small body consisting of four members. So far as the carrying on of the war was concerned this body was really to be the government. It was a bold innovation when Mr. Lloyd George insisted that the Prime Minister, with his many other duties, should not be a member of this committee. This action brought the fall of Mr. Asquith's government. On December 7, Mr. Lloyd George himself became Prime Minister, and Mr. Asquith and many Liberal members retired from the coalition government. On December 9 met for the first time the small War Cabinet now created to direct Britain's effort in the war.

...

... Observers were puzzled by the anomalous British Empire which at one time was a unit under a single sovereign, the King-Emperor, and at another time stood as half a dozen independent units. Not without the firm pressure of Canada's Prime Minister, was her status and that of the other Dominions recognized by other nations. A similar difficulty was met and overcome when Canada insisted upon a separate status in the International Labour Conference, a creation of the Treaty of Peace, and also in the League of Nations. That the British Empire had six votes in the League of Nations was seized upon by anti-British elements in the United States and was one of the chief reasons why the American Senate took objection to the Peace Treaty, without reservations which the President regarded as destructive.

VI. The Future

Such is the story of the Imperial War Cabinet. It is a far cry from the early years of the nineteenth century, when Canada was a small dependent colony, to those days in Paris in 1919 when the Prime Minister of

Canada presided over the British Peace Delegation in its deliberations concerning a new settlement of the world. The title of the Imperial War Cabinet already belongs to the past, and we may hope that it need never be revived. The experiences of war have become, however, the endowment of all the peoples of the British Commonwealth ... But if we forget the past, we shall be wise to remember the future. The states which make up the British Empire form, at last, a real league of nations, among whom war is impossible, who are united on terms of equality, who, while held together by common traditions and loyalties, are free to remain distinct nations with differences of national outlook and national temper. Those who have dreamed of younger Englands in all parts of the world will never see their dream realized. They will see something richer in promise – varied types of British nations within a single commonwealth.

The Growth of Canadian National Feeling

W.S. WALLACE

(June 1920)
CHR 1, no. 2: 136–65. Excerpt: 136, 138–9.

I see in the not remote distance one great nationality, bound, like the shield of Achilles, by the blue rim of Ocean.

THOMAS D'ARCY MCGEE
Speech in the Legislative Assembly of Canada, 1862.

The growth of Canadian national feeling might reasonably be regarded as the central fact in Canadian history. Yet, apart from a pamphlet entitled *Canadian Nationality, Its Growth and Development*, published by William Canniff, the historian of Upper Canada, as long ago as 1875, there has been hitherto – so far as would appear – no attempt to trace in a connected way the process whereby Canadian national feeling has grown to be what it is to-day. The historians of Canada have been legion, but, curiously enough, few of them have thought it worth while to lay stress on this cardinal aspect of Canadian history; and where they have touched on it, they have done so invariably in a casual and incidental way. They have described fully the military campaigns, the political changes, the boundary disputes, the economic and intellectual developments; but they have said little about the main fact which these details merely serve to explain and illustrate – the growth in Canada of a distinctive national feeling.

One of the chief reasons for this neglect is, no doubt, the fact – of which Canadians nowadays are apt to be forgetful – that Canadian national feeling is a phenomenon of very recent growth. Certainly its recognition has not been of long standing. As recently as the Confederation epoch, there were many able and distinguished men in Canada who refused to recognize the existence of what was called at that time 'the new nationality' ...

... To-day, however, he would be a bold man who would deny to Canada the existence of a distinctive national feeling – a national feeling not French-Canadian or British-Canadian, but all-Canadian. Since 1892 Canada has had her own national flag, the union ensign of Canada, the outward and visible sign of an inward and invisible unity. She has travelled so far along the road of autonomy that she is now on the point of creating the germ of a Canadian diplomatic service; and it is announced that she will soon have at Washington a diplomatic envoy of her own. In the Great War the maple leaf badge came to be recognized as the symbol of a strong national spirit which never failed before any task with which it was confronted, and which contributed in a substantial measure to the breaking down of the German defences in the latter half of 1918. Canada's war effort was distinctly a national effort, the extent and quality of which was determined by the national will; and the direct result of this effort has been that Canada has been assigned, not only a place in the Assembly of the League of Nations, but has been pronounced eligible for election to the Council of the League. This means, if it means anything, that Canada has now not only achieved a national consciousness, but has won from the rest of the world – with the apparent exception of the United States – the recognition of this national consciousness.

Canada as a Vassal State

ARCHIBALD MACMECHAN

(December 1920)
CHR 1, no. 4: 347–53. Excerpt: 348, 349–53.

Historically, Canada is a by-product of the United States. The American 'plantations' were never at their ease as long as the power of France was enthroned at Quebec. It was largely through their activity that the Golden Lilies gave place to St. George's Cross; then, as Parkman points out, the road to independence was open. The successful rebellion of the Thirteen Colonies created Ontario, whither were driven the upholders of a lost cause and a sullied flag. And Ontario made the three prairie provinces. The expulsion of the Loyalists also created the province of New Brunswick, and set an ineffaceable mark upon Nova Scotia. At the present time the most progressive, intelligent and desirable immigrants into our West are Americans. What our histories do not teach, and what our people do not realize, is how many Americans, who were anything but Loyalists, settled in Canada, and how strong, from the very beginning, has been the drag towards the United States ...

It is inevitable that the United States should exert a tremendous influence upon Canada. Our domains march together for three thousand miles. The same speech, the same laws, the same religions prevail on both sides of the border, as Goldwin Smith was never weary of preaching. Intercourse between the countries is easy. A standard gauge and common courtesy have made the continent one country for purposes of railway transportation. C.P.R. cars may be seen in Texas, and Omaha and Santa Fé in Cape Breton. Traffic between Canada and the United States is far easier than between the separate colonies of the Australian Commonwealth. Then, our neighbours are many and rich; we are few in the land, and until lately we were very poor. Hundreds of thousands of Canadians have been drawn across the border, because of the better opportunities for making a living, and for making money, under the Stars and Stripes. All these things were inevitable, and tend to make of Canada nine more states not yet brought formally under the control of Washington.

But our spiritual subjection goes deeper. Canada has definitely, if tacitly, declared her position as between American and English ideals. To begin with the individual. The most popular set of caricatures ever designed in this country were Racey's portrayal of the green 'young Englishman' and his mistakes, much as the 'new chum' is represented in Australia. The Englishman's accent, voice, manner, clothes are considered odd, departing from the norm. The American's are not, because they do not strike us as different from our own.

Take the most potent influence at work to-day upon the popular mind, our journalism. Hundreds of thousands of Canadians read nothing but the daily newspaper. Not only is the Canadian newspaper built on American lines, but it is crammed with American 'boiler-plate' of all kinds, American illustrations, American comic supplements. American magazines, some of them distinctly anti-British in tone and tendency, flood our shops and book-stalls. Every new Canadian magazine is on an American model, some of them borrowing an American title and changing only the national adjective. *The Week*, founded on the English model, is dead; and so is *The University Magazine*.

Another potent influence for bringing Canada into spiritual subjection to the United States is the moving-picture show. The films are made for American audiences, naturally, to suit their taste. Then, they come to Canada. We originate none, practically. I dropped into a 'movie' theatre in a small Nova Scotian town. It was filled with noisy, excited children. The point of the plot was the continual thwarting of a villain through the agency of several small boys and girls. They occurred and recurred in a sort of procession, the leader carrying the Stars and Stripes; and whenever they appeared the little Bluenoses cheered like mad.

The case of Capital and Labour in Canada is notorious. Self-determination is a joke. The price of our steel products is fixed in New York, and our Nova Scotia miners obey the orders of a *Vehmgericht* in Indianapolis. The protective tariff has forced many American firms to establish branches in Canada. A large part of our prosperity is due to this exhibition of American enterprise, and not to the initiative of our own business men. Our business methods are American, with the exception of our great banking system.

American influence is seen even more plainly in our universities. The curriculum, text-books, methods of teaching, oversight of students, 'credits,' are borrowed from the United States. Organization and administration are on the American model. Among the students, American ideas prevail. Such matters as Greek letter societies, class organizations, with president, prophet, critic, and 'exercises,' down to the big initial on the football sweater and the curious war-cries known as class and college yells, are borrowed directly from American colleges. Our students did not originate these ideas; they borrowed them. The Dalhousie 'yell,' for example, was introduced by an American teacher of music.

Canadian sport has become more and more American. Our one native game, lacrosse, is dead. Cricket, which flourishes in Australia, is here a sickly exotic. But baseball is everywhere. Our newspapers are filled with reports of the various 'leagues.'

In minor matters, the popularity of such toys as the Teddybear, that curious tribute to the worth of an American president, the spread (by seductive advertising) of the chewing gum habit, the establishment of the automatic chewing gum machine, that monument of progressive civilization, are all to be reckoned with. Our fashions in clothes are decreed for us in New York, whither our tailors resort yearly to ascertain 'what will be worn'; and our youths develop knobbly shoulders, semi-detached trousers with permanent cuffs or hour-glass waists, according to the whim of certain multiples of nine in the commercial metropolis of America. All these are straws showing how the wind blows.

The list of such straws might be extended indefinitely. No Canadian ever invents a new slang term. All our slang is brought in and distributed by the American 'shows,' of one kind or another. We have imported Thanksgiving Day, a heathen festival of autumn, as Goldwin Smith points out, Labour Day, Arbor Day, Mother's Day. As soon as our cousins south of the line decide to celebrate Great-grandmothers' Day we will uncritically adopt it too. Fate has even underlined this tendency by placing our national birthday on the First, beside the American Fourth, of July. Our very coinage bears the impress of our neighbours' customs. Our children call cents 'pennies' (thus showing that the half is at least equal to the whole), and our pretty five cent silver pieces they call 'nickels,' after their ugly American equivalents. The government mint itself has followed the stream of tendency and issued cents the size of the American cent. Our police uniform badges and clubs are American. Our patriotic buttons – an American idea – are made in Newark, New Jersey.

...

But the optimist will have his say, as well. 'Confronting all these facts, and many more which might be alleged, I find that there always has been a viewless force making for national unity, not only strong enough to resist the drag towards absorption in our neighbour state, but to create a national spirit, a national character, a national unity. That spirit is now more potent, that character more clearly defined, that unity more compact than ever before ... For four years Canada lived on the heights of heroism. The national spirit revealed in the fierce storm of war was alive, if latent, before the war; it is alive now. It has the power to shape a national ideal worthy of Canada's part in the great struggle and to lift our people to its height.

Nationalism and Self-Determination

W.P.M. KENNEDY

(March 1921)
CHR 2, no. 1: 6–18. Excerpt: 7–11.

...

II

Seeing then that *truth* consisteth in the right ordering of names in our affirmations, a man that seeketh precise *truth* had need to remember what every name he uses stands for; and to place it accordingly; or else he will find himselfe entangled in words, as a bird in lime-twiggs; the more he struggles the more belimed.

– HOBBES, *Leviathan*, I, 4.

In turning then to consider nationalism and self-determination, an effort must be made at definition. We shall see how difficult is the definition of either – 'inclusive and exclusive,' as the Schoolmen would have said. At the same time some attempt is necessary if we are not to add to the already large confusion of political thought. Indeed this confusion is largely due to the inconstant and fluctuating use of terms. For example, nationalism is used at one time for patriotism, at another for racialism – two social facts which are sometimes incompatible or antagonistic. Nationalism is also sometimes regarded as synonymous with nationality, though it is clear that nationality is frequently used in a semi-legal sense which could not be included under the term nationalism – for example, in a passport or in the returns of the census. It is evident then that if we are to make any progress at all we must try to use clear terms in writing of nationalism and of self-determination.

...

What then is nationalism? It is obviously a kind of 'common spirit' – that to which Aristotle refers in his *Politics*. A further distinction however is necessary, as there are varieties of common spirit; – that of a regiment or university; the community of feeling which belongs to a fraternal society; the brotherhood of labour manifested in guild or trade union, or the cementing ethos of a church or religious foundation. The common spirit which animates such organizations has clearly nothing to do with nationalism. We are compelled to seek in the common spirit of nationalism some distinctive and distinguishing feature. We may seek that feature in history. An examination of the historical phenomena of nationalism will disclose many factors which have contributed to it in different generations and in different continents. We can trace in the development of Aristotle's 'common spirit' many varied forces at work – racial or supposed racial solidarity; a common language; a common religion; common economic backgrounds; a common history or tradition; common political ideals; common political institutions; a common home – often possessing a certain geographical unity. But are any of these factors common factors?

Racial solidarity is not everywhere a feature of nationalism. In Europe it is largely a myth. It is possible to describe feeling between white man and black man or yellow man as racial antagonism; but from the ethnological point of view, there is to-day among the European peoples hardly one which is not of mixed racial origin. Italy, where one of the strongest national movements of modern times arose, is the home of most composite races. Germany is a blend of Teuton and Slav and Celt. Greece represents almost every race in Europe. The greatest modern nation – the United States – is merely re-enacting in race assimilation what has been going on in European states for centuries.

Identity of language – which is popularly confused with identity of race – has undoubtedly contributed to nation-building, but he would be a fool-hardy historian who would call it an essential element. The Scottish people are a nation, though they speak both English and Gaelic. The Belgians are a nation though they speak both French and Flemish. The Swiss are a nation, though actually tri-lingual.

The diversity of tongues does not discount the reality of American nationalism. We can dismiss identity of language along with a common religion. The latter has brought its gifts to the building of nations; but religious varieties have often been most prominent where nationalism has been strongest and most vigorous.

Nor can we explain nationalism by common economic interests. These lie behind much in human history, and examples are not wanting of their influences in nationalist movements. Their influences can be seen indirectly at work in the American Civil War, and more directly we can find them at work in the *Zollverein*, with Prussia at its head, which laid the foundations of the modern German Empire. On the other hand, it would be hard to find common economic interests at work in the fusion of the Thirteen Colonies out of which the American nation was born. Indeed the nation, as an economic unit, largely exists artificially through the influence of protective tariffs.

It would be possible to examine common history and common traditions and to find that they are not the common factors which we have been seeking. The nationalism of the North American continent, for example, owes little to the past ...

Nationalism in its simplest terms seems to demand nothing more than a common spirit, whatever factors may combine to form it, and a common *patria*. This common spirit, too, is not merely on fire – it is glowing with a flame that burns but does not consume the hearts in which it rules. For no embers, however bright, will start a national conflagration. No common-day community spirit has national creative force. The Yorkshireman, the Devon man, the Nova Scotian have common spirits and common homes; but no one would confuse Yorkshiremen, Devonians, Nova Scotians with nations. There are then diversities of common spirits. There is that which can, without offence, be called localism or provincialism, which expresses itself in the everyday activities of a narrow social group in a narrow geographical area; and there is that higher type which we call nationalism, to which Mr. Zimmern applies the test, *Will men die for it?* Yorkshire and Devon and Nova Scotia are fair to see, and to their citizens they bring hallowed ties, precious associations, sacred memories; but before the wider challenge of England and of Canada they are little. The common spirit which we know as nationalism is of such intensity that it consumes the lesser loves as it takes up the gauntlet of defying death. Nationalism then is a common spirit, almost uniformly related to a fatherland; and it is of such consuming force that men will gladly die to preserve it and the *patria*, which is its outward and visible expression.

This conception of nationalism covers most cases; but while appearing to solve one problem it creates another. A moment's thought will show that there may be two or more nationalisms for which men would die. A Scotchman would perhaps be willing to die for Scotland, an Ulsterman for Ulster; both have died for the British Empire. A French Canadian might be willing to die for Quebec, for Canada, or (as many of them have done) for the British Empire. It would seem then as though there might be a nationalism within a nationalism. Or rather there seems to be such a thing as a super-nationalism, in which two or more nationalities may merge without losing their identity – as English, Scotch, Welsh nationalities have merged, distinct but one, in British super-nationalism.

Whatever objections may be levelled against these definitions, I hope that I have made clear what I mean when I speak of nationalism. Patriotism is not meant – for that, after all, is individual devotion to the political state in which a man has been born or to which he has transferred his allegiance. There was abundance of patriotism in the Roman Empire, but little nationalism. Neither do I mean racialism, nor linguistic or religious bonds, nor even local feeling. Nationalism may partake of the character of any or of all of these. Above all that exclusive political fanaticism is excluded which thinks of the world too exclusively in terms of boundaries, in terms of invidious comparisons, or in terms of mere tolerance. Nationalism is a separate and peculiar form of corporate consciousness.

Canada's Relations with the Empire as Seen by the Toronto *Globe*, 1857–1867

F.H. UNDERHILL

(June 1929)
CHR 10, no. 2: 106–28. Excerpt: 106–7, 127–8.

This paper is an attempt to examine the part taken by the Toronto *Globe* in the discussion of the imperial question during the decade before Confederation. The making of the Dominion of Canada is so important an event in the history of the Empire that a study of what British Americans were thinking about the Empire at this time should be a fruitful one. Moreover, the events of the period gave them many an occasion to think about the question. It was the era when Canadian fiscal autonomy was achieved; when the strained atmosphere of the American Civil War raised in an acute form the question of the relative obligations of mother country and colony in the defence of Canada; when, following upon the alarms of the Civil War, the abrogation of Reciprocity compelled Canadians to face the question of their ultimate future as a distinct people on this continent; when they first began to look beyond their own boundaries to the Red River and British Columbia and to agitate for incorporating them into a great British American union; when, finally, they did achieve a union with the older colonies in the East. All these were matters which directly or indirectly affected the relation between colony and Empire, which involved prolonged negotiations between colonial and imperial governments, and which roused on both sides of the Atlantic a discussion that was copious in volume and often vehement and excited in tone.

The *Globe* was the outstanding newspaper in Upper Canada at this time. Its circulation apparently far surpassed that of any of its contemporaries and rivals. And, if one may judge by the frequent extracts from the Upper Canada Reform press quoted in its columns, what the *Globe* thought to-day the whole of the small town and village weeklies of the Reform persuasion in politics would be thinking in their editorials next week. Papers in the larger towns, such as the Hamilton *Times* and the London *Free Press*, did occasionally break away from the *Globe*'s leadership, just as in the legislature individuals or groups frequently rebelled against Brown's imperious mastery of the Reform party. But, in general, the *Globe* seems to have had a remarkably loyal following. It gained an intellectual domination in Upper Canada which has never been equalled since. Its discussions of the imperial question may accordingly be taken as contributing powerfully to mould the opinion of its constituency or as representing what a large part of Upper Canada already thought on the subject.

The first thing that strikes a modern newspaper reader on going through the pre-Confederation *Globe* (or any of the other newspapers of the time) is that the Canadian community was very definitely colonial in its intellectual outlook. The *Globe* was always full of pride in its own land. It never ceased to fight strenuously against the inferiority complex which affected Canadians when they compared themselves as a people with Americans or Englishmen. It never ceased to preach to them the advantages of Canada as a place to live in. But, at the same time, no one can turn over its news columns without realizing that for it the centre of the world was still in Europe. It followed European affairs with a close and tireless interest; and, since it was without the apparatus of Associated Press and special correspondents, and till 1866 without the cable, it relied largely for its information upon the English papers. It lifted articles openly and shamelessly from them in order to give its readers the best guidance on the subject possible. Thus the backwoods farmer of Upper Canada got the benefit, several weeks late, of the news services of the London *Times*. And one need only read the *Globe's* news and editorials upon (say) Napoleon III or the Schleswig-Holstein question to realize that the reader of the 1860s was given a much more intelligent understanding of what was happening in Europe than is given to the newspaper reader of the 1920s.

Still more detailed was the news provided for him on English affairs. The *Globe* followed the ups and downs of parties and individuals at Westminster with almost the same personal interest as it followed similar events at Toronto and Quebec. On English politics it had a definite point of view. It supported steadily the radical cause, and was usually scornful of Whigs and Tories alike. The men it admired most were Cobden and Bright, though it was far from sharing their views about the Empire. It received regular letters from London which consistently gave the radical interpretation of current events. It reproduced articles from the *Daily News* and the *Morning Star* with frequent approval ...

But nationalism to the *Globe* did not mean separatism. The new Confederation was to be a nation within the Empire. Whatever might be the *Globe's* criticisms of particular individuals or groups in England, its imperialism in the end was as strong as its nationalism ...

It will be obvious from the many extracts quoted in this paper that there are two main tendencies running through the *Globe's* discussions of imperial affairs. In the first place, it is sturdily Canadian. It is determined that the Canadian people in all matters which concern them directly shall be free to act as they see fit. It resents criticism and advice from across the Atlantic, and invariably adopts the most effective form of defence by taking the offensive against the critics themselves. It never wearies of putting Englishmen in their place. But, on the other hand, while it asserts Canada's rights with the utmost vigour, it glories in the traditions and power of the Empire. It has no use for the 'Little England' ideas which were prevalent in the mother country. It is proud of the connection with 'the grand old British Empire,' and determined to maintain it 'intact and unimpaired.' One may easily find fault with the *Globe's* conception of the responsibilities that were involved in membership in the Empire, and critics of the time did find fault. But its fundamental faith that the two seeming opposites, Canadian autonomy and imperial unity, were the most reconcilable things in the world, has been justified by later experience ...

Some American Influences upon the Canadian Federation Movement

R.G. TROTTER

(September 1924)
CHR 5, no. 3: 213–27. Excerpt: 213–15.

Much Canadian history can only be read aright with one eye on the United States. Especially is this true of the movement which led to the federation of the British provinces and territories in continental North America, under the British North America Act of 1867. The initial contribution made by the United States to building the Dominion of Canada came very early. It lay in a two-fold failure of the 'patriots of '76.' By failing to draw within the orbit of their revolt the northern fringe of colonies, they marked out the site for the future dominion. Then, by failing to reconcile to their success the party of the imperial connection within their own borders, they provided in the persons of the exiled loyalists, and later the descendants of those loyalists, an element of population with vital traditions, which, though in many respects essentially American, were yet by both conviction and prejudice strongly antirepublican. The United States, having thus unwittingly assumed the rôle of fairy-godmother to the remnant of British Empire in continental North America, has since continued to play the rôle in diverse ways, sometimes obvious, sometimes curious, and as often as not quite unintentional.

...

But when this much is said, it must still be recognized that the makers of Canada's federal constitution were working primarily in the British tradition as already embodied in their own institutions. Accustomed as they were to legislative supremacy and a responsible cabinet of the

British type, they built on that system as a basis. Their work as completed was avowedly intended, not to secure divergence from British institutions and precedents, but rather, following these as closely as might be, to add merely such features as the adoption of a federal system should make necessary ...

And in the fundamental problem common to all federal systems, the allocation of powers to central and local authorities respectively, United States experience prompted the fathers of Canadian federation to avoid, rather than to imitate, the principle of distribution embodied in the American Constitution. For to the colonial spectator of the long sectional conflict in the States that culminated in the war of secession, the root of the difficulty often seemed to lie in the wide extent and sovereign nature of the power of the states. To 'states rights' he was prone to ascribe what frequently, in the early 'sixties, he considered the lamentable failure of the American federal system. This influence wrought powerfully among the provincial leaders who shaped the federation scheme for the provinces.[1] In fact, so strongly convinced were some of union's chief advocates that success could only be insured by placing control at the centre, that they even urged the elimination of the provincial governments.[2] A unitary system, however, was impossible, on account of sectional and racial obstacles; but the centralists succeeded in securing indubitably for the federal authority the paramount power.

Notes

This paper was read by Professor Trotter at the annual meeting of the American Historical Association at Columbus, Ohio, in December, 1923. In contributing it to the *Review*, the author has equipped it with documentary references.

1 For evidence of this fact see *Parliamentary Debates on Confederation* (Quebec, 1865), pp. 33 and *passim*.
2 [*Parliamentary Debates on Confederation* (Quebec, 1865)], pp. 29, 75. The writer is indebted to Mr. Clarence M. Warner of Boston for the privilege of examining an interesting volume that once belonged to John A. Macdonald, first prime minister of the Dominion and a principal leader in the federation movement's culminating stages, entitled *Secret Proceedings and Debates of the Convention Assembled at Philadelphia in the Year 1787 for the Purpose of Forming the Constitution of the United States of America* (Washington, 1836). The work evidently received a careful reading. There is considerable pencilling in the margins, and it is interesting to note that in almost every instance the passages

thus emphasized are arguments for a strong central government. D'Arcy McGee, a leading associate of Macdonald's, put forth in 1865 *Notes on Federal Governments, Past and Present* (Montreal, 1865), in which, as his principal conclusion, he pointed the same moral.

The Struggle for Financial Control in Lower Canada, 1818–1831

D.G. CREIGHTON

(June 1931)
CHR 12, no. 2: 120–44. Excerpt: 120–1, 143–4.

In 1818, for the first time in the history of Lower Canada, Sir John Sherbrooke called upon the legislature to vote the sums necessary for the ordinary annual expenditure of the province. The financial controversy, thus precipitated by the embarrassed and unwary executive, dominated Lower Canadian politics with its furious excesses for over a dozen years. Its pre-eminence was neither fortuitous nor unwarranted: its causes were as profound as its results. In the financial issue, two classes, two civilisations, two ages of economic and social development met and clashed. The last defenders of the French old régime and the early aggressive champions of the English industrial revolution collided inevitably in the financial issue and fought with all the unreasoning fury of complete misunderstanding. The petty disputes of Craig's term, the use of such antiquated and cumbrous machinery as impeachment were forgotten in the fight for the control of the public purse. In the financial issue, the assembly, for the first time, discovered a great constitutional principle which, to a large extent, altered the character of its opposition and transformed an undignified racial animosity into a legitimate constitutional struggle. Over this question, the assembly petitioned, resolved, and fulminated until it had worked itself into a fury which not even the ultimate concessions of the imperial parliament could placate. Five governors and one lieutenant-governor – Sherbrooke, Richmond, Dalhousie, Burton, Kempt, and Aylmer – either failed signally to achieve a solution, or succeeded temporarily only because they were willing to abandon the extreme pretensions of the colonial office. Finally, in 1831, the controversy was settled simply by being placed beyond the possibility of equitable settlement; for the imperial parliament, by its long-delayed but unavailing concession of 1831, had abandoned the strongest guarantee of that financial independence by which alone the executive could continue the struggle for an acceptable compromise.

'I see no subject of quarrel that ought to be considered serious except the finance,' wrote Dalhousie soon after he had assumed office;[1] and time did not alter this conviction.[2] Admittedly, Dalhousie underestimated the profundity and complexity of the opposition which confronted him; and it was not merely 'half-a-dozen seditious demagogues' who foiled his efforts. The animosity between the English and the French, between the rulers and the ruled, between those who enjoyed the profits of office and those who coveted them, had arisen long before Sherbrooke first attempted to enlist the support of the legislature in the financial difficulties of the executive. But, while the disagreement over the finances was not a primary cause of the struggle in Lower Canada, it was, on the other hand, an expression of a fundamental divergence in the attitudes of the French Canadians and their opponents. The French Canadians, a pastoral people dominated by professional groups, were in most essential respects Frenchmen of the *ancien régime*; the British, whether bureaucrats or *commerçants*, were typical products of the age of the industrial revolution and of *laisser-faire*. The nineteenth-century English instinct for expansion, the urge for prosperity, the familiarity with vast commercial and financial projects collided violently with the inherent economic conservatism, the petty prudence, the unadventurous economy of the French. The financial issue could not create a conflict; but, inasmuch as it reflected strongly this basic social antagonism, it deepened the significance of the conflict which already existed. It gave, moreover, to this seemingly petty racial conflict, a greater constitutional importance and a more general interest. By its insistence upon the popular control of the public purse – a principle which three revolutions had already legitimized – the Lower Canadian opposition began to take up its unassuming but natural place in the contemporary liberal movement. The adhesion of Neilson, the support of the English radicals, the sympathies and concessions of the whigs were the gratifying results of this evolution. And the encouragement of these concessions, the stimulus of these new associations and influences, the consciousness of the historic importance and its cause spurred the assembly along to the final stage in its political evolution, the revolutionary proposals of the '30s.

...

VI

Public finance, in a new country where men and politics are largely influenced by material considerations, is the centre towards which the ideals and greeds characteristic of a new world are inevitably focussed. The right to control the government's expenditure, the power to determine the amount and the character of the government's assistance in the race for expansion and the rush for the spoils, is one of the richest and most coveted prizes of a new land. The struggle for these powers intensifies party warfare, as the possession of them helps to create party prestige or contribute to party disaster. In Lower Canada, however, the financial struggle has this additional and special significance: that, in distinction to similar financial rivalries in English-speaking Canada, it was not a quarrel between two ambitious groups who cherished the same dreams of prosperity and who accepted the same economic gospel. It was a contest between two classes, between two ages of economic and social development, between the France which the political revolution had destroyed and the England which the industrial revolution had created. A peasant and professional community, unambitious, parsimonious, and unmoved by the lush economic possibilities of a new land, was confronted by a governing class whose deepest instincts were towards improvement, expansion, and prosperity ...

Notes

1 The Public Archives of Canada, *Dalhousie Papers*, 111, Dalhousie to Kempt, September 23, 1820.
2 The Public Archives of Canada, *Series Q*, vol. 168, pt. 2, Dalhousie to Bathurst, July 5, 1824.

Canadian Migration in the Forties

FRANCES MOREHOUSE

(December 1928)
CHR 9, no. 4: 309–29. Excerpt: 309.

I. 1840–45

The movements of people in the middle of the nineteenth century are a striking example of the way in which economic history cuts across the more or less artificial divisions made by political boundaries. The New World offered relief to the Old in a number of ways and places, and those who needed that relief, and could avail themselves of it, took what offered with small regard for political connotations. There is something grimly humorous in the contrast between the conscious nationalism of the migrations planned by government officials and philanthropists, and the headlong movements which actually took place. Emigrants were not as a rule men who could afford political preferences; they wanted to land and to live wherever work and a living could be found. The United States and British North America were really more or less an economic unit, varied and vast but helpfully complementary in their parts, at the very time when political feeling between them was at its most unhappy climax. The history of migration, especially in the nineteenth century, can not be studied on strictly national lines.

The Beginnings of Nova Scotian Politics, 1758–1766

W.S. MACNUTT

(March 1935)
CHR 16, no. 1: 41–53. Excerpt: 41, 52–3.

It is small wonder that the history of Nova Scotia between the turbulent days of the Acadians and the American Revolution has, until recently, been largely neglected. What was happening there in those years had very little to do with the main currents of development either in Europe or in America. A northern appendage of the American empire, its connections with the continental colonies were of the slightest. A few cargoes of fish to the West Indies, a small Bay of Fundy trade with Boston and other New England ports, an occasional shipment of produce to Great Britain were its sole contributions to imperial commerce. With Quebec it had nothing in common. The people, between ten and fifteen thousand in number, were chiefly of New England stock, the consequence of an immigration from across the bay, a struggling hard-bitten folk, their interests totally occupied in eking from the soil a precarious livelihood. Halifax at this period was the only centre of any real political life. There, a little cluster of officials and merchants disbursed the imperial subsidy, which was still necessary for the maintenance of the public services, much to their own interests. Beneath the shadow of the more opulent and advanced sister colonies to the south, Nova Scotia was the Cinderella of the imperial family, little known and little respected.

...

There should be no review of the beginnings of political life in this isolated community without reference to certain social facts. Of these the most important is the character of the central and dominating Halifax settlement. When Lord Halifax drew up his plan for the colonization of Nova Scotia, the new town was to have two purposes, that of a fortified stronghold and base for operations against the French, and that of a centre of commerce and industry. The first objective had been attained, but largely at the expense of the second. By 1755 practically the whole civilian population of Halifax was engaged in catering to the military and naval forces. Commerce and industry were lost sight of in the midst of the multifold preparations for the expulsion of the French ...

And so the once turbulent and dissatisfied group of merchants and traders crystallized under Francklin's leadership into a colonial artistocracy with estates at Windsor and in other parts of the province. The Halifax cliques united and for many years violent partisanship seems to have been extinguished. As vacancies occurred in the council, Francklin's henchmen were drafted into it. Green, Morris, Bulkely, and Belcher, who had sat under Lawrence, in varying degrees accepted his authority. William Nesbitt, who occupied the curiously paired offices of speaker of the assembly and attorney-general, was his friend and ally. The Gerrish brothers, Binney, Fillis, and the merchants who dominated the assembly were ranged behind him in a harmonious grouping. All were reconciled to his leadership for there seem to have been offices and favours for all. When William Cawthorn, a London merchant with a large trade in the plantations, visited Halifax towards the close of 1766, he found Francklin at the head of a faction which dominated the colony and which, after refusing him a grant of land, virtually drove him out of the country for fear that he would go into business there.[1] It was this faction which, in the opening years of the American Revolution, so bitterly fought Legge; and, when the Loyalists came to Nova Scotia, they found the same group endeavouring to exclude them from office and patronage.

These, then, are the homely beginnings of Nova Scotian politics. The scene is a rustic and provincial one, filled with petty issues and small personalities which are not suggestive of the spacious days of Howe in the century which followed. But the same has been true of nearly all new and frontier settlements. And, even in our own time, the political art is one associated with all sorts of misdemeanours.

Note

1 [Public Record Office, London, Colonial Office papers] C.O. 217, vol. 44. Cawthorn's memorial, Oct. 5, 1766.

THE ENVIRONMENT AND NATURAL RESOURCES

The Assault on the Laurentian Barrier, 1850–1870

A.R.M. LOWER

(December 1929)
CHR 10, no. 4: 294–307. Excerpt: 294–5.

There is no element in the present Dominion of greater significance than the so-called Canadian Shield or Laurentian Barrier. This vast region of lakes, rocks, and forest, which occupies all but a few thousand square miles of eastern Canada and which interposes the most formidable of obstacles between the usable regions of the East and the fertile areas of the West, has determined the direction and rate of the country's growth in the past, and doubtless will continue to be a decisive factor in its expansion in the future.

As one comes up the St. Lawrence, he observes the mountainous shores of the Gulf giving place to the flats of the middle river and the rolling country of the lakes – that is, he passes from the Laurentian formation to a projecting spur of the great continental plain of the interior. If he were to travel by aeroplane, he could almost fly high enough to see, from any point on the line of the river and Great Lakes, the outposts of the Barrier looming up to the northward. It is on this narrow and limited strip of territory between the Barrier and the lakes and river, with a total area rather less than that of England, that the political and social structure of the present provinces of Quebec and Ontario has been projected. The question of questions for these two provinces – and indeed for Manitoba and Saskatchewan also – is the extent to which the million square miles of rock and forest to the north can be utilized for the enlargement of that political and social structure. Only within the present century has the hope that it may become something more than an inhospitable wilderness appeared to have some foundation.

...

When the settlement of the upper St. Lawrence valley began, few people were interested in the country which lay beyond their immediate ken. The surveyors could do no more than keep just ahead of the settlers, and for all available settlers there seemed plenty of room on all sides. It was known that to the northward there were rocks, but no one seems to have realized that the character of the country changed abruptly once those rocks were reached. The wilderness was simply the wilderness, a haunt of Indian and beaver, whether it were the Huron tract or the Hudson Bay country. In due course, no doubt, the forest would fall and farms would appear in the one place as in the other. There was little sense of limitation in the Canada of the first half of the nineteenth century. It had a wide horizon of expansion.

Unfortunately the horizon was not long in proving itself a mirage. By about 1850 most of the available farm lands in the St. Lawrence valley proper were in private hands, and the bold outlines of the Barrier were everywhere revealing themselves.[1] But people were slow to see that their emergence had radically affected what was then the chief concern of the colony, the extension of settlement, and it was not until the extension of settlement had clashed with the only other industry of importance – lumbering – that very much attention was directed to the problem which the existence of the Laurentian plateau presented.

During the initial stages of lumbering the presence of the settler had proved a great boon to the lumberman, for the oats, hay, and other produce raised on the little frontier farms obviated the necessity of bringing in their equivalent from 'The Front,' as the line of the St. Lawrence and the lakes was called.[2] As good soil and pine forests seldom went together, the two industries fitted in very well with each other and accompanied each other further and further into the wilderness.

This was all very well as long as the pineries still stood within areas suitable in the main for agriculture. When exploitation had attained considerable depths within the Shield, the matter assumed a very different complexion. It is true that within the Shield there were occasional fertile valleys, and as long as the settler stuck to these he was welcome. But the settlers as a class had no mind to stick merely to the fertile valleys. The country was before them and, after the age-old manner of settlers, they would possess it. Consequently, there arose a conflict between the two interests which has gone on ever since, and the lumberman soon perceived that there were conditions under which settlement would do more harm than good ...

Notes

1 There was still some good land in northern Grey and Bruce.
2 See Charles Shirreff, *A Few Reasons against Any Change in the System of Our Colonial Lumber Trade* (Quebec, 1831), 5.

Economic Factors in Canadian History

W.A. MACKINTOSH

(May 1923)
CHR 4, no. 1: 12–25. Excerpt: 12–15, 25.

There will be few dissenters from the position that there is need that more attention should be devoted to the geographic and economic factors in Canadian history, and that greater place should be given to the continental aspects of Canadian history. Up to the present the constitutional bias has been strong, and for the obvious reason that the most recent and in many ways the most significant chapter of British constitutional history has been written in Canada. The familiar schoolbook periodization of the history of British North America in terms of succeeding instruments of government is sufficient illustration of this bias of the British constitutionalist. The artless query of a high school pupil, 'Was everybody a member of parliament then?' indicates the false picture which has been too frequently drawn. It is true that of late years more attention has been given to the economic and geographic factors, but in many cases the chapters on constitutional development have not been in the least influenced by the addenda on 'social and economic progress,' or by the introduction on 'physical characteristics.' Constitutional crises lose none of their great importance when viewed as the periodic results of changing conditions, and of the needs and political prepossessions of various elements of the population. History is emphatically not 'past politics'; it is the life of yesterday in the present.

The simplest features of American geography are of primary importance in understanding the developing life of the people of this continent. The initial fact to be noted is that for several reasons, structural and climatic, North America faces Europe. That is to say, by far the greater part of this continent is most easily accessible from the Atlantic coast. This has facilitated, though not accounted for, the success of European rather than Asiatic colonization. The evolution of energetic, industrious, forthfaring peoples under the peculiarly favourable climatic conditions of north-western Europe is the most important element in that success. If then we start with the fact of the European colonization of the Atlantic coast, the structure of American barriers, plains, and waterways takes on a special significance. That structure shaped the course of westward progress; it facilitated or hindered the connection of the frontier with the older settlements and with Europe; it selected to some extent its own settlers; and together with other factors it determined the trend of industrial production.

Structurally, North America, in broad terms, is made up of narrow coastal plains on the Atlantic and the Pacific, the old glaciated Laurentian plateau around Hudson Bay, and a great Central Plain from the Appalachians to the Rockies, with no significant uplift barrier from the Gulf of Mexico to the mouth of the Mackenzie. The presence of the Appalachian barrier to westward movements of population and commerce has given premier importance to the existing gaps in that barrier, of which two, the Mohawk and the St. Lawrence valleys, outrival all others. The partial gaps of Pennsylvania, the Cumberland, and the southwesterly valley of the Shenandoah have all played important parts in American history; but New York to-day is witness to the significance of the Mohawk valley, as is Chicago to that of the St. Lawrence. When the Dutch and French controlled both gateways to the interior, English colonies built solid communities in the coastal and piedmont regions. Meanwhile the French followed the westward path of the St. Lawrence to discover the basic fact of modern Chicago, viz., that the low watershed causes the St. Lawrence there to pivot on the Mississippi, and on that fact France built a grandiose policy not of settlement but of empire: a policy which failed because of the weakness of the initial settlements.

When the forerunners of British settlements began to enter the central valley and speculative ventures such as that of the Ohio Company about 1745 were set on foot, France and Britain inevitably clashed. They clashed on the upper tributaries of the Ohio where France was busily constructing a line of forts to block British progress into the interior. In later years the war took a European name, the Seven Years' War. Hostilities, however, began earlier in America; they had a distinct American objective, and that objective was not Canada – which was scarcely preferable to Guadeloupe – but the Mississippi valley.

From about 1763 on, the rapidly increasing population of the old colonies overflowed into the Mississippi valley. New England, spreading north and west, entered the valley of the St. Lawrence in the Green Mountain state; and because of its geographical relation to Canada, Vermont did not enter the Union until 1791, ignored the Non-intercourse Act, and was an unwilling and half-hearted partner in the War of 1812. New York and Pennsylvania were already expanding along the Mohawk and the upper Ohio valleys and the men of Virginia occupied the valleys of Tennessee and Kentucky. New problems brought new movements, and the 'men of the Western waters' became a significant element in American legislatures.

Later, and with different setting, the same movement into the interior took place in Canada. The American Revolution, the causes of which were not unconnected with the occupation of the west, turned part of the westward movement to the Loyalist settlements of the St. Lawrence valley. At the same time, and later, British immigration augmented the increasing population of the western frontier of Canada. That old West of Canada differed from the settlements of Lower Canada not only in race and religion but in the pioneer problems which it had to face.

In those brilliant introductions to his *Readings in the Economic History of the United States*, the late Professor Callender set forth the basis of colonial economy. 'Progress does not take place unless the colony possesses markets, where it can dispose of its staple products. The history of modern colonization does not show a single case where a settled country has enjoyed any considerable economic prosperity, or made notable social progress without a flourishing commerce with other communities.' The prime requisite of colonial prosperity is the colonial staple. Other factors connected with the staple industry may turn it to advantage or disadvantage, but the staple in itself is the basis of prosperity. The colonies of North America were fortunate in being capable of producing staples which for the most part found ready markets in Europe. Virginia and the other southern colonies found in tobacco, indigo, naval stores, and other products excellent colonial staples, on which the prosperity of the South and southern culture were based. In the north, French furs found ready sale, but the conditions of the industry brought few advantages to the settlement. New England and the Middle Colonies were less favourably endowed. Their products were not dissimilar to those of Europe, and the markets were small and uncertain ...

To Canadians of the present generation political writings of fifty years ago read strangely. Annexation, commercial union, Zollverein, Canada First, Imperial Federation, these have no place in contemporary politics. We are less sensitive on these points. It is difficult to realize that Canadians ever believed in them. The difference is not in Canadians. It is in the economic background. When frustration of Canadian progress was overcome, and a period of expansion resulted, Canadian nationality was assured, and policies which cast doubt upon that nationality fell away. For the first time in Canadian history, powerful and effective western forces made themselves felt. For the first time western problems became capable of solution. The end is not yet; for the West still struggles in time of world-depression with a bulky staple and a long transportation haul. But improvements in transportation have made problems not insoluble. A new factor has arisen in the existence of a manufacturing East. Another is developing in the opening of the Pacific trade; and still another, of unknown significance, will come into play as the forest frontier of the north is attacked in earnest.

Canada is a nation created in defiance of geography, and yet the geographic and economic factors have had a large place in shaping her history. It is not contended that these are the only factors. Others have been often and adequately dealt with. But unless one is to consider Canada merely as a collection of racial types and not as a nation, the basic facts of economic and historical geography can never be ignored. In Canadian history as it is written, there is much of the romance of the individual, sometimes significant and sometimes not. It behooves present-day historians to perceive the romance of a nation in the story of a people facing the prosaic obstacles of a colonial existence, developing national traits, and winning through to nationhood.

Note

The present article contains the substance of two lectures in Canadian economic history given at the School of Historical Research at Ottawa during the summer of 1922. The thesis presented is one which the writer thinks susceptible of proof, but which cannot be taken as proved until further research has established it on a sound basis. Much elaboration and obvious illustration have been omitted in order that the argument might be presented within reasonable compass. As originally given, the lectures purported to show the relation of economic and geographic factors to general history, and to suggest the great need for detailed research in many phases of Canadian economic history. The point of view of the article has been suggested by the writing of Professor F.J. Turner and the late Professor G.S. Callender.

The Extermination of the Buffalo in Western Canada

FRANK G. ROE

(March 1934)
CHR 15, no. 1: 1–23. Excerpt: 1, 10–11.

The extermination of the plains buffalo in the north-western United States and in western Canada (as a wild species roaming in freedom) occurred, broadly, between 1876 and 1883. The 'southern herd,' as it was generally termed, after its virtual separation by the building of the Union Pacific Railway along the valley of the Platte River about 1867, was for all practical purposes extinguished in 1875, after some five seasons of terrific and shockingly wasteful slaughter. Contemporary opinion seems to have felt no uncertainty in ascribing this to the hide-hunters – principally white – in both the northern and southern buffalo range. This is open to serious doubt. Even after allowing for Indian 'wastefulness,' which has been much (and sometimes preposterously) exaggerated, and for the ordinary demands of the fur-trade before the advent of railways, the evidence does not indicate that the buffalo could have been exterminated in any such short time by the meagre red and white population of the territory west of the Mississippi. The Red River hunt was somewhat different; but, even in this case, it was much of the nature of a movement on the buffalo 'flank' so to speak – a movement which pushed the buffalo westward and stripped the territory between Red River and the line approximately of 107° west; which was roughly their eastern boundary at the time of their extermination in Canada.

The dramatic suddenness of the disappearance of the buffalo is possibly the reason why other theories than that of extermination by man have more recently been advanced to account for the event. Perhaps the most remarkable of these is that of decimation by some form of epidemic disease. The purpose of this paper is, first, to present such information concerning disease as I have been able to discover, and then to examine the historical evidence which throws light on the extermination of the buffalo by slaughter ...

II. Historical Evidence of the Extermination

Concerning the final extermination of the plains buffalo as a wild species in Canada, it is interesting to note that when the same thing came to pass in the north-western United States in 1883, the disappointed hide-hunters, who had 'outfitted' as usual in the fall of that year for the expected slaughter, could not bring themselves to believe it. The common explanation of the disappearance was that the great herd had 'gone north into Canada'; and would shortly return in force.[1] Contrary to this opinion, however, the virtual extermination in Canada actually preceded the final slaughter of 1880–83 in the United States.

It may be said that, up to about 1870, there never was any progressive 'extermination' in Canada for robes alone, in the way that there was in the United States. Whether by Indians or by whites (practically all the latter being, almost until the end, Hudson's Bay Company's employees only), the utilization of buffalo embraced almost all the principal uses to which buffalo had ever been put by those Indians who depended upon it almost exclusively; meat being, of course, the first and predominant use. The reasons for this difference between Canada and the United States are in my opinion as follows. Since settlement of the plains was confined at first to the United States, 'extermination' first became a pressing question there, either as a necessary prelude to, or a consequent result from, settlement, or as a semi-political *desideratum* for other reasons. Secondly, the Hudson's Bay Company's deliberate opposition to settlement in western Canada until the latest moment retarded the opening up of 'bulk-transportation' routes, and so deprived the commercial class in Canada of any visible incentive to foster or promote a policy of extermination for the sake of a commodity whose cost of transportation, in larger quantities than their own local uses necessitated, was virtually prohibitive; especially was this the case since the conveyance for immense distances of lighter and more valuable fur-products taxed their facilities to the utmost. The easiest and most natural outlet by land from the Upper Saskatchewan country was over the watershed of the Missouri basin, southward to Fort Benton, Montana. But it was not until about 1870 – speaking broadly[2] – that the determined hostility of the northern (i.e., Canadian) Blackfeet and their confederated tribes was overcome, and passage through their country was made possible.[3] When this was effected, the (buffalo) fur-trade made its appearance; and, as historical students of this era are well aware, it was the introduction of the 'bad men' and other demoralizing elements so characteristic of the development of other sections of the great west, which resulted in the inauguration of the North West Mounted Police in 1874.[4]

Notes

1 W.T. Hornaday, 'The Extermination of the American Bison' (*Smithsonian Reports*, 1887, published 1889), part II, 511–512.
2 Miss Diller gives 1866 as the first year in which American traders came across the line from Fort Benton (Dorothy Diller, 'Early Economic Development of Alberta,' chapters ii, 12; iv, 3). I note that Father Lacombe went east that way in 1869, presumably indicating by then an established route (Katherine Hughes, *Father Lacombe*, Toronto, 1911, 172).
3 Although the Hudson's Bay Company's record toward Indians is generally good, such rhapsodies on the company's 'mission' as those of Lord Strathcona (Beckles Willson, *The Great Company*, Toronto, 1899, introduction, xi–xiii) are idle and preposterous; particularly for the south, where, since about 1840, Hudson's Bay men dared not venture before the mounted police era, and where they foretold disaster to the McDougalls in 1873 (John McDougall, *On Western Trails in the Early Seventies*, Toronto, 1911, 15, 21, etc.). The men who really paved the way for the police in Alberta were Lacombe, Scollen, and the McDougalls.
4 On the Cypress Hills' massacre of Assiniboines by Americans, in 1872, see S.B. Steele, *Forty Years in Canada* (London, 1915), 55; McDougall, *On Western Trails*, 253; John Hawkes, *Saskatchewan and Her People* (1924), I, 145–146. On ruffians of Fort Benton and south Alberta, see McDougall, *On Western Trails*, 75, 128–130, 257–260; Steele, *Forty Years in Canada*, 53–58; Denny MS. (in Provincial Legislative Library, Edmonton), 120, 327; A.O. MacRae, *History of the Province of Alberta* (Calgary, 1912), I, 263; C.M. MacInnes, *In the Shadow of the Rockies* (London, 1930), 66, etc.

NATIVE–EUROPEAN CONTACT

Review of Harold A. Innis, *The Fur Trade in Canada*

W.A. MACKINTOSH

(March 1931)
CHR 12, no. 1: 65–7. Excerpt: 65–7.

The Fur Trade in Canada: An Introduction to Canadian Economic History. By Harold A. Innis. With a preface by R.M. MacIver. New Haven: Yale University Press. 1930. Pp. 444. ($5.00.)

This is the book in Canadian history which most needed writing, and Mr. Innis has written it well. For years Canadian historians have given us glib generalizations on the importance of the fur trade, have speculated about Peter Pond's map, or have written vaguely and ignorantly of the 'romance' of the fur trade. It has remained for Mr. Innis to write, after a long period of laborious and patient research, an authoritative history of the fur trade which will remain for many years the standard work on this subject. It is to be hoped that the fur trade and this interpretation of it cannot now be ignored with impunity by Canadian historians.

Mr. Innis sees his subject as the history of an epoch in which fur as a commodity dominated and shaped the life, at first of the whole of Canada, and then of a diminishing portion. He sees the fur trade, also, as the nexus between the mature mercantile and industrial culture of Europe and the primitive culture of the North American Indians. In the early days of the fur trade the Indians, at least in the north, lived in what has been described as a collectional economy, while western Europe was entering a metropolitan economy. Between these two economies the fur trade provided the contact which brought revolutionary changes and which proved disastrous to the primitive economy.

The book begins by explaining the overshadowing importance of the beaver in the fur trade. Before European settlement, the material culture of the Indians of the Canadian Shield was associated, according to Mr. Clark Wissler, with the white-tailed deer. After the trade with Europe began, the beaver, hitherto relatively unimportant, became the medium through which European commodities profoundly modified Indian culture. Since the beaver was non-migratory, easily discovered, and without adequate defense against fire-arms, it was foredoomed to extinction. Since, further, the fur, desired for making beaver hats, was *castor gras*, that is, beaver fur which had been worn in robes by the Indians until the long guard hairs had been worn off and only the short downy fur suitable for felting was left, the supply in any one area was soon exhausted. These facts, emphasized at certain times and places by advancing settlement, made it inevitable that the fur frontier should recede rapidly, and that, in consequence, transportation should become the chief conditioning factor of the trade.

...

If he had merely set forth the chronicle of the fur trade Mr. Innis would have written an important book. He has, however, gone much further and offered an able and suggestive analysis of the economic processes by which, from the contact of a primitive collectional economy with a mature metropolitan economy, the modern Canada has arisen. Fur was only one (although the most important) of successive staples which bound Canada to British industrialism. In his conclusion, in which he summarizes his analysis, the author sketches briefly the influence of other staples, wheat and the forest products. It was the fur trade, however, which contributed most. The organization built up by the fur trade gave the model, Mr. Innis contends, for the centralized organization of Canadian industry, finance, and transportation, and thus made easy and rapid the assimilation of machine industry when it came. It was fur, and the other staples finding their market in industrialized Britain, which made it inevitable that Canada should remain British.

These broad generalizations are suggestive and illuminating but there is need for caution. It is not demonstrable that the great staples kept Canada British, though it can be clearly shown that they were centripetal forces. Neither is it demonstrable that Canada's unified banking system sprang from a unified fur trade. Influence there no doubt was, but it can be argued that the geographical conditions and the political boundary which produced an attenuated line of settlements was a conditioning factor which would have existed, aside from the influence of the fur trade. Mr. Innis has enriched his work greatly by the aid of anthropology, but in his conclusions he is in some danger of succumbing to the favourite and seductive sin of the anthropologist, sweeping generalization.

These, however, are small faults; and they are the less serious in that they produce instant correctives in the reader's mind. Mr. Innis has made the most distinctive contribution that has been made to Canadian history for a long time, and he has made a notable beginning in the study of the most important subject in economic history to-day – the study of the development of an immature economy in contact with more mature economies.

Social Revolution in Early Eastern Canada

ALFRED GOLDSWORTHY BAILEY

(September 1938)
CHR 19, no. 3: 264–76. Excerpt: 264, 275.

The close relations which are developing between the natural and human sciences[1] have increased the importance of the work of the anthropologist, since he seeks to apply the method of natural science to the study of human affairs. That branch of anthropology, which treats of the evolution of culture, is concerned with the processes of diffusion and invention, and with environmental influences. Diffusion and invention cannot be entirely separated since an individual may manufacture traits in his endeavour to adapt himself to an ever-changing environment, and invention is therefore involved in the diffusion which may cause cultural changes. We need not conern ourselves here with the several ways in which diffusion may occur; we need only recall the fact that the culture of any given group has been blended from diverse sources into a vivid entity which resists the diffusion of traits from other cultures. Thus, when a people migrates into an already inhabited area, a conflict almost inevitably arises between the culture of the immigrants and that of the indigenous population. The result of such a conflict may amount both in intensity and magnitude to nothing less than an economic and social revolution.

The history of Canada might well be treated from this point of view since Canada is an area into which diverse peoples have from time to time migrated. In the course of the conflict between rival cultures some of the constituent groups in the Dominion of Canada have forged ahead, others have merely maintained their place, and still others have fallen behind, several having suffered extinction. The Indians, for example, often failed to survive the shock of the conflict. Sometimes, however, a fusion of Indian and European elements occurred and resulted in new cultural traits which were neither European nor Indian. To the fusion from Indian and French sources have been added throughout succeeding years elements from other immigrant groups. The permutations which have resulted from the process of fusion are distinctively Canadian, and are unique since they have not occurred in precisely the same way elsewhere ...

V

It may be taken as evident that every frontier has two sides, and that the advance of the one is invariably conditioned by the recession of the other.[2] The factors of Indian retreat before European invasion partly determined the nature, extent, and direction of that invasion. Not only were the Indian cultures modified by the thrust of European civilization into the new world, but the latter was modified as a result of the resistance of those cultures. Moreover, European culture became scattered and spare in its passage of the Atlantic, and many of the traits that achieved importation were unsuited to the American environment. Although many household articles were brought by the immigrants, many were of necessity left behind, and often the settlers were almost entirely lacking in the technical equipment which was essential to survival in the new country. The Puritan settlers and the French traders alike were incapable of exploiting the flora and fauna of the eastern woodland without the aid of the Indians' knowledge which was the result of centuries of careful adaptation to the specific environment.[3]

The Puritan had to be shown how to cultivate corn and how to make the implements and utensils which were necessary to grow and prepare it. The French were schooled by the Indians in the methods of hunting, fishing, and gathering edible roots and berries.

Of great significance was the influence of the Indian cultures upon the social and political development of the Canadian dominion. The present boundaries of the Dominion of Canada testify to the pervasive influence of the fur trade with the Indians in the colonial period. It was also the wilderness economy that bred an individualism and impatience of restraint in the Canadians, which renders the revision of the old story of paternalism long overdue ...

Notes

1 See, for example, the article by Principal R.C. Wallace of Queen's University, 'Co-operation in the Natural and Human Sciences' (*Canadian Historical Review*, XIV, Dec., 1933, 371).
2 W.C. MacLeod, *The American Indian Frontier* (London, 1928), preface.
3 For accounts of the English Puritans' relations with the Indians, see H.U. Faulkner, *American Economic History* (New York, 1924), 60; H.W. Schneider, *The Puritan Mind* (New York, 1930), 38; T.J. Wertenbaker, *The First Americans, 1607–1690* (vol. II of *A History of American Life*, ed. Schlesinger and Fox, New York 1927), 83; J.T. Adams, *The Founding of New England* (Boston, 1921), 15–16.

PART TWO

WAR, CENTRALIZATION, AND REACTION, 1940–1965

COMMENTARY

Society and War

As contributions to the *CHR* make clear, the crises of the late 1930s, culminating in the Second World War, deeply affected historical practice. These cataclysmic events raised numerous questions, ranging from practical concerns about how scholars would be able to do their research during war to philosophical considerations regarding the political positions that they should adopt. Many writers advocated reasserting the moral role of history rather than emphasizing specialized research; others expressed concern that wartime engagement would pose threats to intellectual liberty.

Once the war began, G.P. de T. Glazebrook, a member of the *CHR*'s editorial committee, argued that the profession ought to be concerned primarily with Canada's international stature. He argued that the country's separate declaration of war in 1939 demonstrated its position as a world state and the reality of foreign affairs as a theme in Canada's history. He called on his colleagues to contribute to literature on international relations, including topics not directly related to Canada.[1] From a different standpoint, Reginald Trotter argued that even though the war made research difficult, social scientists had to be responsible citizens as well as academic observers; they should explain what was at stake in the crisis and help shape public opinion in efforts at postwar reconstruction.

The editors of the *CHR* noted that Canadian social scientists disagreed on these issues.[2] However, A.R.M. Lower (March 1941) argued that social scientists must be formative agents in a new world order emerging in the wake of the decline of nineteenth-century individualism and liberalism. The task would be different in each country, he thought, but it would have to adhere to the enduring values of Western civilization. In Canada, historians should create a history for a country that did not yet have one. Canada was a 'practical' country that had lost its British moorings, the movie and radio had usurped the church, and the 'masses' were surging into university, and so history must also serve as a moral guide. The United States had successfully built a new civilization, he continued, but Canada, except for the Conquest, which had forced French Canada into self-examination and to strike a line of action for the future, had as yet had no revolution to cut it off from the old world. Canadian historians faced a problem in constructing this history – 'What is Canada?'

In the Western world, the war posed challenges to notions of objectivity that had grounded historical practice since the late nineteenth century. How to explain two world wars in an era of supposed scientific rationality? Numerous contributors to the *CHR* asserted that Canadian historians must enlarge their scope and examine international developments. Because these had economic and social causes, an emphasis on political and state history was not totally adequate.[3] Two contributions criticized the dangerous interwar overshadowing of military and political history. A.E. Prince (March 1944) lamented the dismissal of military history along with the great man approach. And the 1950s began with G.P. de T. Glazebrook's letter (December 1950) to *CHR* editors calling for a re-evaluation of political history. While not downplaying other historical approaches, Glazebrook reminded social historians of the role of the state, especially in an era when it was becoming dominant.

Redefining the Nation

In the aftermath of the Second World War, efforts to reshape the story of Canada's past continued. Directly or indirectly, historians responded to Lower's call to 'create' a Canadian history for the new world order. Among them, a form of political history focused on individuals emerged most strongly. Political biography also caught hold in the United States and Britain; in Canada, Donald Creighton led the way. His *CHR* article 'Sir John Macdonald and Canadian Historians' (March 1948) promoted biography while deriding the pro-Liberal, nationalist, and North American orientation of Canadian historians. Arguing that North America could not be treated as an environmental bloc, he emphasized Canada's separateness within the continent and the enduring strength of British traditions.

In the mid-1950's, J.M.S. Careless and D.C. Masters (March 1954) constructed a framework for explaining Canadian political, economic, and social development that emphasized urban rather than frontier influences. This interpretation challenged the Turnerian frontier theory, which many Canadian historians had adopted during the 1920s and 1930s to explore environmental influences on Canadian society and politics.[4] W.L. Morton had already taken issue in the *CHR* with analyses of the troubles in the Red River valley in 1869–70 by such historians as Chester Martin, A.S. Morton, and G.F.G. Stanley. While they saw the forward movement of the frontier as having forced Canadian political and religious issues on an isolated and primitive society, W.L. Morton (December 1949) posited other factors – primarily the deficiencies of the buffalo hunt and subsistence agriculture.

Margaret Prang's article (March 1965) on the origins of public broadcasting in Canada demonstrated that the state had also played a central role in defining the nature of Canadian culture and national consciousness. As in transportation, so in broadcasting, government policy – creation of the CBC – was 'defensive expansionism,' here in an 'area possessing cultural implications unprecedented in earlier phases of national policy.'[5] In its focus on an aspect of national public policy, her article reflected the preoccupation of many contributors to the *CHR* in the two decades after the Second World War and anticipated future trends in Canadian historical writing.

Nationalism Challenged

The late 1950s and early 1960s constituted a turning point. Those critical of the 'fragmentation' of Canadian historical writing point to the 1970s and 1980s, but several earlier *CHR* contributions attacked nationalist interpretations. In 'Chapleau and the Conservative Party in Quebec' (March 1956), H. Blair Neatby and John T. Saywell argued that national parties and leaders had distracted historians from a crucial development in Canadian *political* history – Quebec's transfer of allegiance from the Conservative to the Liberal Party.

Quebec nationalism also came under critical scrutiny from both within and outside the province. Beginning in the late 1950s and through the 1960s, as Blair Neatby noted in a *CHR* book review, French Canadians 'dedicated their energies to debating the nature and future of their society.'[6] Much of this self-examination turned on the nature of Quebec's economic development and on whether it had been enfeebled by the British Conquest or by later events, such as the reinvigoration of the church. This controversy, in turn, prompted heated debates about the nature of Quebec society and the role played by its supposedly dominant institutions in shaping its social values. The various positions are evident in excerpts presented below from G.F.G. Stanley (March 1958), Michel Brunet (June 1959), and Fernand Ouellet (December 1961). Such articles added a new dimension to the *CHR*, which had always experienced difficulty in attracting contributions from French-language historians because their nationalist interpretations had conflicted with forms of nationalism promoted by English-Canadian *CHR* contributors.

The postwar decades also introduced *CHR* readers to class-based historical analyses. The appearance of S.R. Mealing's 'The Concept of Social Class and the Interpretation of Canadian History' (September 1965) coincided with the publication of John Porter's *The Vertical Mosaic.* Although Porter's book revealed that Canadian historiography had been impoverished by the lack of class analysis,[7] a few *CHR* contributions had wrestled with the issue. In his 1929 presidential address to the Canadian Historical Association, 'Some Neglected Aspects of Canadian History,' A.R.M. Lower had urged more studies of 'the common man.' In the midst of the Great Depression, Frank Underhill's 'The Development of National Political Parties in Canada' offered a materialist analysis of how the country's party system had evolved out of conflicting economic interests.[8]

Perhaps most significant were contributions by H.C. Pentland and F.W. Watt. In his study of the Lachine Strike in 1843 (September 1948), Pentland demonstrated the class-based nature of Canadian society, while Watt's 'The National Policy, the Workingman, and Proletarian Ideas in Canada' (March 1959) treated the cultural expressions of class consciousness in the era following Confederation. As Bryan Palmer has noted in a review of Pentland's book *Labour and Capital* (1981), Pentland and Watt inserted the study of class and culture – as historical processes of relationship and reciprocity, opposition and alternative – into a historiography largely devoid of such perspectives. Their articles were read and reread throughout the late 1960s and 1970s by a new generation of Canadian historians who had found class analyses in other fields of history attractive. As Palmer also asserted, the impact of these works shows that it was more than the importation of Thompsonian theory that had shaped the ideas of Canada's so-called new labour historians.[9]

Notes

1 G.P. de T. Glazebrook, review article, 'Canada and Foreign Affairs,' *CHR* 21 (June 1940): 180
2 Reginald Trotter, review article, 'Canada and Commonwealth Affairs,' *CHR* 22 (Sept. 1941): 302; A.R.M. Lower, 'The Social Scientists in the Postwar World,' *CHR* 22 (March 1941), preamble, p. 1
3 This argument is traced in R. Flenley, 'History and Its Neighbours Today,' *CHR* 34 (Dec. 1953): 324–6.

Commentary 139

4 On the origins and uses of the frontier theory, see Morris Zaslow, 'The Frontier Hypothesis in Recent Historiography,' *CHR* 29 (June 1928): 165–6.
5 Margaret Prang, 'The Origins of Public Broadcasting in Canada,' *CHR* 46 (March 1965): 1.
6 H. Blair Neatby, review of Gérard Bergeron, *Le Canada français: après deux siècles de patience* (Paris: Editions du Seuil, 1967), in *CHR* 50 (March 1965): 95
7 See Margaret Prang and Arthur Lower, 'Sociology and History,' *CHR* 47 (June 1966): 156–61.
8 Frank Underhill, 'The Development of National Political Parties,' *CHR* 16 (Dec. 1935): 368, 387; see also Allana G. Reid, 'The First Poor-Relief System of Canada,' *CHR* 27 (Dec. 1946): 424–31.
9 Bryan D. Palmer, review of H. Clare Pentland, edited with an introduction by Paul Phillips, *Labour and Capital in Canada* (Toronto: James Lorimer, 1981), in *CHR* 64 (June 1982): 227

SOCIETY AND WAR

The Social Sciences in the Post-War World

A.R.M. LOWER

(March 1941)
CHR 22, no. 1: 1–13. Excerpt: 2–7, 9–10.

... The social scientist, both as teacher and writer, like everyone else will be affected by the issue of the present war, – it therefore behooves him to try and discover how. While no one can make a blue-print of the future, there probably will be fairly general agreement about some of the aspects it is likely to wear. Some measure of agreement may also be found among social scientists with regard to the nature of their calling and the way in which it is affected by the society in which they practise it.

It is commonly said that we stand at the end of an era, or indeed at the end of two eras – at the end of nineteenth-century individualism, sometimes called liberalism, and at the end of the longer period of individualism ushered into the world by the Renaissance and Reformation. It seems pretty clear that we stand at the end of nineteenth-century economic anarchy. Whether we stand at the end of Protestantism and free inquiry is another matter, not yet so evident. It is a common mistake to equate freedom with liberalism. Liberalism as a fairly definite philosophy was elaborated during the nineteenth century. It was European rather than Anglo-Saxon in origin and nature (as witness its anticlerical and anti-religious tendencies on the continent) and was derived from our own older tradition – a more vital tradition for us – of legal 'liberties,' of the reign of law. Magna Carta, in other words, is older than the Declaration of the Rights of Man. This medieval tradition has never faltered in England itself and has been carried by Englishmen to the self-governing parts of the English world, where it wages continuous battle with the native influences of the environment ...

It is apparent that in the leading countries of the world, if not in the backwaters, the impulses released so vigorously in the nineteenth century began to run out in the twentieth. These impulses are often dubbed 'capitalism,' far too narrow a word, and people who use that appellation go on to say that the capitalist system or era is coming to a close. The truth would appear to be that something wider and deeper than mere economic change is occurring. The first Great War had much to do with increasing the speed of the change, even if it did not originate it, and this present war will similarly hasten the historic process. That some profound change is occurring, the *malaise* of the last two decades, their indecision, apathy, irresponsibility, their economic cataclysms and political earthquakes, are sufficient testimony. What Hitler did in Germany, essentially, apart from his cruelties, was to end the confusion of purpose, the irresolution, the fumbling, that necessarily attend the senility of a social philosophy. Few of us like the unceremonious way in which he gave it the *coup de grace* and we would hope ourselves to conduct a more dignified funeral, one less difficult for the attendants to bear, but we must admit that his expeditious hustling out of the old order gave him for the moment at least a great advantage over the rest of us, still perplexed as to how to do it.

Having ended the old order, he was able to present his countrymen with a new. It seemed a rather ugly baby at the time and has not increased in favour with God or man since, but no one can deny its strength and self-assurance. Meanwhile, we westerners are still speculating. A new order is struggling to be born among us, but in genetics as in other things we cling to *laissez-faire* ideas, so none of us knows much about what the infant may be like. That is the great problem on our hands at the moment, trying to divine the nature of the future, and as social scientists, perhaps even essaying to act as its midwives.

As a matter of prophecy it at least seems safe to suggest that whatever the result of the war, in the future the individual is going to have to subordinate himself to society more than he has done in the past. If our western world is to be kept afloat it will surely be because of organizing skill, and organizing skill spells the death of our pleasant old social and political anarchy – for all of us except the organizers, anyway. Out of this a two-fold problem emerges: in what kind of hands is the new society to be and how can it be built without losing the enduring values that our civilization has created? There is little hope of getting a really satisfactory answer to these questions yet, though certain guesses may be hazarded. In the first place it would seem futile to look for any universal order: each country will get the kind of régime that the political forces in it necessitate. Canada will certainly not have socialism, fascism, communism, or democracy just because Great Britain and the United States come to have something people may decide to call by one of these names. In fact, if history is any guide, the social process in Canada will lag behind by a generation or so and yet, of course, will not be entirely unaffected by events elsewhere. Our experience will inevitably be different, therefore, from that of either Great Britain or the United States. Our future will probably be organized by a different type of person from those who are doing the same task elsewhere and therefore in a different way. We shall not have the advantage of the mature political wisdom of the English civil service and governing classes, for example, or the semi-revolutionary, informed zeal of the American New Deal. So far the war has shifted power in Canada into the hands of men who represent social régimes preceding those now coming into existence in the other two countries, men who perhaps worship idols whose shrines tend to be deserted in their own temples, and it would seem likely that these men will manage to retain much of this power. The Canadian future, like the future of every other country, will therefore be organized in its own particular way.

The great problem, of course, is how to do the necessary job of organizing without losing the enduring values that western civilization has created. It should not be beyond human ingenuity to put its house in order without sacrificing the spirit of freedom and the well-being that comes from this spirit and from it alone. We can make up our minds to a large measure of control in every area of life, but control and servitude are not necessarily to be equated. Controls accepted with a good heart and out of a sense of duty do not diminish the spirit of freedom. The member of a team is not a slave. But here again, every country will return a separate solution, depending upon its experience ...

The social scientist must recognize this difference between the English and the Canadian scene before he begins making blue-prints of the future, for the type of material he has to work with is very different from that of his English or his American colleagues. It is going to be exceedingly difficult to work out a closely organized Canadian society that shall at the same time have the spirit of freedom, far more so than in England.

We have already seen a vast increase in the edifice of control, both economic and political. The innumerable boards and commissions thrown up by the war go some distance towards establishing its mechanisms. They nearly all rest at the moment on the War Measures Act, a law which bestows complete and absolute power upon the Dominion government. If at the close of the war the Dominion were suddenly to put off the powers it has assumed under this Act, something like anarchy would result ...

II

It is obvious that the nature of the state is a matter of supreme concern to the social scientist, not only as furnishing him with the phenomena that he seeks to describe but also, and perhaps more significantly, determining the conditions under which he describes them. Most social scientists like to think of themselves as detached observers, no more affected by the events and circumstances they are watching than is the astronomer by his stars. This is of course arrant nonsense: we are all part of the society in which we live, attached to it in a dozen ways and affected by it not only through our minds but also our hearts. And we cannot go away somewhere else and describe a society utterly alien to us, for there are very few who have either the opportunity, the ability, or the necessary detached penetration so to do ...

We cannot escape our surroundings: they change, and we with them. The social sciences, in other words, and certainly social scientists, can never be completely detached, unprejudiced observers. Further, most social science must be limited and impermanent: it is the result of a limited observation by an imperfect observer of a limited scene and therefore most writing, historical, economic, sociological, etc., is in the nature of an interim report, to be revised as occasion offers ...

The Canadian historian is especially faced with this conumdrum: What is Canada? What is it he is to describe? Is he to confine himself to the English in the Maritime Provinces, to the French upon the St. Lawrence, to the Loyalists in Upper Canada, or can he bring a multitude of diverse phenomena under some general head? Can there be any such thing as *Canadian history*? Some of us have described economic activities that went on in the past in or about a certain geographical area now called the Dominion of Canada. These activities as often as not have been carried on by persons who have had only a fortuitous connection with the area. They have ransacked a region of natural wealth and have disappeared, leaving not a wrack behind. Their activities in a sense are the stuff of Canadian history in much the same way as were the activities of palm-oil traders on the Niger, who came one day and went the next – part of the history of the aborigines of that country. An area and its exploitation may be described, and that is a useful, if humble, task, but it is questionable if such description is history in the deepest sense ... Our exercises in the description of times past, on the other hand, are in essence efforts to supply a history to a country that as yet has not got one, a kind of ready-made history, awaiting the arrival of a people to purchase it.

...

... Thus, we come by another way to the essential truth that Canadian writing must be for Canadians (or Australian for Australians, for that matter, or all except the widest and greatest, even in the relatively narrow sphere of the social sciences, for the people out of whom it grows), and for that relatively small group among Canadians who are interested not only in what has taken place and is taking place but also in what is about to take place.

This small group is both passive and active. It provides the circle of readers for which its members write. It observes and records. It does more. It creates the scene and it creates the audience. It therefore seems to me that the social scientist in Canada must be more than a mere observer and recorder. He must be more than a mere scientist. He is a member of a group of workmen engaged in a common project. He must be to some extent an artist. Social science in Canada, in other words, is not so much like physical science as it is like medical science, both an art and a science. The social scientist will have something to do with creating and affecting society as well as with describing it.

...

Response to Lower, 'The Social Sciences ...'

H.A. INNIS

(March 1941)
CHR 22, no. 1: 118–20. Excerpt: 118–20.

Social scientists who participated in active service in the last war have little excuse for forgetting either the lessons of the war or of the peace. They have no excuse for ignoring the contributions of Adam Smith and his successors as to the significance of division of labour. The social scientist will do well, and he cannot do better than, to follow the advice of his masters and specialize on his own interests. In other words he can make his most effective contribution to the maintenance of morale on the home front, to the advancement of his interests, and to the solution of problems of democracy by showing confidence in the traditions of his subject and minding his own business. He must either do this or throw in his hand to the enemy.

At no time has the task been more difficult or more urgent. In a young country with its insistence on nationalism, in a period of depression and war with its insistence on activity and intervention of the state, the scholar is under tremendous handicaps. But if he believes in democracy he must believe in the significance of contributions by individuals. It is the scholar, more than any other, who must demonstrate to his colleagues and his students the necessity of continuous, active, mental alertness in facing the difficulties of his work particularly in the social sciences. He must face the necessity of giving his life to the pursuit of truth and realize that he cannot hope to make contributions of significance with less than twenty to twenty-five years of his life and before he reaches an age of at least fifty. To fail in this is to believe that democracy cannot survive. He owes this to the traditions of scholarship, of universities, and of western civilization. In this task he will be harassed by obstacles of every conceivable type,[1] but he has the consolation that success in withstanding them will mark the success of democracy. At least this much should be understood after one war which made enormous demands on scholarship, after an interlude in which an interest in scholarship was threatened and undermined continuously by the widening influence of the press and the radio, and in a second war in which every effort must be concentrated on maintaining the morale of the home front.

Note

1 The range of historical research fluctuates widely and at the present time has narrowed appreciably. Extension of governmental activities leads to the withdrawal of social scientists from research work of a fundamental character. While it definitely improves the standard of government work, and generally the standards of living of those absorbed, it lowers the standard of intellectual achievements in academic work. It may widen the range of the individual and strengthen his contributions to academic work, if and when he returns, but it would be difficult to point to sustained work of profound importance achieved under these circumstances. The individual becomes accustomed to governmental requirements and the academic profession becomes a standing surplus reserve labour pool to meet the varying demands of governments. Universities are required to provide employment for the periods incidental to governmental vagaries. These disturbances have far-reaching serious implications. Gaps are filled temporarily by cheap and unskilled labour in most cases drawn from graduate schools. Graduates are hampered in their efforts to secure degrees and irregular employment creates the unemployable. The social scientist reaches the stage when he cannot work independently.

The difficulties created by governments for academic work are intensified by repercussions in other fields. Because governments demand social scientists, industrial and financial organizations are compelled also to employ them for purposes of self-defence. The energies of both business and government are dissipated in a struggle which is only slightly concerned with the advance of the social sciences.

All this is not to belittle the importance of the social scientists to government work in war and peace. Their position is difficult and thankless. They are distrusted, if not looked upon with contempt, by those on active service, and they are under suspicion in the serried ranks of the civil service. They need every possible support. The scholar can best support them by showing an increasing concern with scholarship.

The Need for a Wider Study of Military History

A.E. PRINCE

(March 1944)
CHR 25, no. 1: 20–8. Excerpt: 20–2.

This is a frank essay in the apologetics of military history, an argumentative vindication of the history of war; it is no shame-faced 'apology.' Undoubtedly there has been in the last generation or two a most salutary broadening of the interests of the historian; 'he now casts his net wider,' as Gooch says, 'and embraces the whole opulent record of civilization. The influence of nature, the pressure of economic factors, the origin and transformation of ideas, the contribution of science and art, religion and philosophy, literature and law, the material conditions of life, the fortunes of the masses – such problems now claim his attention in no less degree' than 'the growth of nations, the achievements of men of action, the rise and fall of parties,' which, to Dr. Gooch, still 'remain amongst the most engrossing themes of the historian.' But, especially on this side of the Atlantic, the cult of 'the New History' has distorted the vision of too many of its devotees, particularly those intellectuals who put on a profound air of having mastered all science and art and learned all the answers to the riddles of life!

These ultra-modernists have a withering scorn for the old classic historians and their subject matter, patronizingly praising their 'style' but airily dismissing their works as 'drum-and-trumpet history,' outmoded 'tales of backstairs Court intrigues,' 'feudal, mediaeval' supernaturalism, 'Great-Man nonsense,' and the like ...

A strong case can be put for the view that the perversions of the New History movement in the liberal democracies must bear no small responsibility for our present international troubles. For one thing the problems of war and the study of the art of war have been despised or ignored. This trend was fostered by the optimistic belief of the nineteenth century that the 'Era of the Great Peace' had been ushered in, that mankind was on the march, steadily upward and onward ... Sensitiveness to social and economic backwardness led to the intelligentsia concentrating on the study and solution of social and economic problems. The economic interpretation was raised aloft as the master-key. The graph of progress showed a steady upward curve of evolution.

Swords, outside museums and their use in cutting officers' wedding cakes, had been turned into ploughshares; the kingdom of Utopia, of perfectionism, of millenarianism was at hand – or at least in infra-red sight. The belief that Great Power wars were outmoded led to an evaporation of interest in the history of war.

These glowing assumptions were, however, rudely jolted by the shock of events from 1911 onwards, with Italy's Libyan War and the Balkan Wars providing a prelude for the World Wars beginning in 1914. As Edward Grey perceived, the lights all over Europe (and the globe) were going out, not to be lit again for at least a generation. Democracy and the principles of parliamentary and party government were challenged in mortal defiance by arrogant militant autocracy. The victory of 1918 brought no adequate settlement, and was indeed followed by a confusion of tendencies and ideas, which at least demonstrated that 'man does not live by bread alone,' by economic activation. Political, militaristic, and other factors came to bulk large – greed for prestige and territorial aggrandizement, the clash of forms of government, personal ambitions of psychopathic ex-corporals and ex-*daimios*, racial ideologies of master races, and even the desire to 'live dangerously' (the cult of guns rather than butter). New creeds arose, Soviet communism and many varieties of fascism. The Carlylean 'Great-Man' theory of history attained a new and sometimes sinister vogue, e.g. the leadership principle in Fuehrer Hitler, Duce Mussolini, and Caudillo Franco. Even the idea of peaceful continuous evolution was brought into question. 'History is quite as much cataclysmic as evolutionary,' wrote the military historian Sir Charles Oman, 'it is not a mere logical stream of events, but a series of happenings, affected in the most inscrutable fashion by incalculable things – natural phenomena, the appearance of outstanding personalities, new inventions and discoveries, not infrequently a mere chance of War.' ...

In Defence of Political History

G.P. DE T. GLAZEBROOK

(December 1950)
CHR 31, no. 4: 443–5 (Notes and Comments).

To the Editors of the Canadian Historical Review:
An eminent historian recently remarked with regret that political history had been unduly overshadowed by other approaches, such as social, economic, and so on.

While acceptance of the multiplicity of causes is common ground for all serious students of history, there have been few modern writers who have felt that they could handle more than one theme, or, at most, have not chosen their own focus on a period or area. Like the industrial system, history became divided into fields for specialists. With all its inherent advantages, the system of specialization could – and to some extent, did – develop disadvantages. It is a great deal easier to know more and more about less and less than to maintain a philosophical and balanced view of the march of humanity; and a temptation, not always resisted, to regard a particular 'field' as an end in itself rather than as one thread, the significance of which depends on its proper position in a complicated pattern.

The broader and more varied study of history, which became marked from about the middle of the nineteenth century, was in part a revolt against the 'political' history which was then standard, and in part simply the result of utilizing the technique of specialization. It is not my purpose to question in general the wisdom or effectiveness of the change, but to suggest that there were two serious miscalculations.

The first arose from a failure fully to appreciate that the revolt was not against political history as such, but against the ways in which it was taught and written. Too often the older histories were the record not of states but of governments. It is not necessary to call yourself a 'social historian' to remember that a state is made up of individuals, or that the thoughts, problems, and activities of private citizens as well as holders of public office must be given some attention. The method of learning by rote – one now too quickly dismissed – was applied to history as well as to literature and Greek prepositions with the result that less than a century ago children thought of English history in the form of rhymes tying together the names and dates of the kings of England. It was not useless information, but it meant very little in itself, and consequently the system was properly criticized.

The second miscalculation indicates an unconscious negation of the very purpose of the new and broader approach. Apart from those happy fanatics who see single and beautifully simple causes, historians were not seeking to rule out particular historical themes, but rather to isolate individual ones to the end that they could be more accurately examined. It was not, then, intended to represent the rise and fall of the bubonic plague, the invention of the bicycle, or the progress of the Masonic Order as the sole explanation of the story of the human race; but rather to look at each in detail and assess its effect on, and place in, the larger scene. Filled with enthusiasm for the new régime, however, medical historians, engineering historians, or institutional historians might forget that the object of the operation was not to replace one narrow approach with another but to broaden the whole by demonstrating the diversity of human life.

Curiously enough, the very period in which historians were going through the development suggested above was that in which the state as such was becoming more dominant than it had ever been. Broadly speaking, this increased significance has taken three complementary forms. In the first place, small political units became less common. The German Empire, the Kingdom of Italy, and the Dual Monarchy of Austria–Hungary covered most of the continent of southern Europe. In the East Japan followed the fashion. The United States remained united by process of civil war; and to the north the British provinces were joined into a single state. The national state was a significant phenomenon of the late nineteenth and early twentieth century. The historian cannot ignore the steel production of the Rhineland nor the technological advances that made possible the new economic imperialism; but equally he should not ignore the great national powers themselves.

Secondly, the modern state so increased its functions as to become almost unrecognizable. The 'welfare state' is new only in degree. Bismarck used social security as a bulwark against political socialism, and the United Kingdom moved steadily from its original Poor Laws to the protection of its citizens against unemployment, old age, and ill health. A government which could control prices and production, negotiate agreements between employers and employees, and perform all the other functions that have been added to it, cannot be thought of as distant and as narrowly 'political.' In some recent cases states have been admittedly totalitarian. A citizen, therefore, may not only have the traditional obligations, such as military service, payment of taxes, conformity to the civil and criminal law: he may expect benefits in case of illness, old age, or unemployment. In some cases he may not speak, write, paint, or compose music except according to the view of the state.

Thirdly, attention may be drawn to the role of the state as the protagonist of an ideology. The position, of course, is not a new one and may be found in some form in any period. The best modern example, and the one affording the most striking parallel with the contemporary world, is the Jacobin régime in France. A single party controlling a great state sought to extend its power and influence in Europe and beyond in such a way that no distinction could be drawn between the promotion of ideas and the political expansion of the state, between the defence of an ideology and its imposition on a reluctant world. There is little need to remind ourselves how militant ideologies have affected the world in the last generation, and how they continue to do so.

I have no desire to suggest that political history, or any other approach, should suppress the others. It does seem useful, however, to look back from the Great Leviathan of the twentieth century at least to note how not unsimilar issues were faced in the past. You may, if you like, call the writ of habeas corpus a part of legal history, control of the press a part of literary history, and torture a result of technological skill. To the individual affected, however, these distinctions are unreal. To him the government has or has not the authority to treat him as it chooses. The rule of law, the right of free expression of ideas, government as the servant of the people – these are basic freedoms which have been and are threatened, and without which all other freedoms are vain.

Yours very truly,
G. DE T. GLAZEBROOK
Ottawa, Canada.

REDEFINING THE NATION

Sir John Macdonald and Canadian Historians

D.G. CREIGHTON

(March 1948)
CHR 29, no. 1: 1–13. Excerpt: 1–5.

I

John Alexander Macdonald was born on January 11, 1815, and died on June 6, 1891. Of the seventy-six years of his long life, well over half – forty-seven in all – were passed amid the agitations of Canadian politics. He was elected to parliament in 1844, when he was not yet thirty; he became a minister of the Crown in 1847, when he had just turned thirty-two. For over ten years under the system of the dual premiership which obtained in the old Province of Canada, he was one of the two principal leaders of government; and for nineteen years he was prime minister of the new Dominion. It is an astonishing record – astonishing, and, as a whole, unique. It is true that Mr. Mackenzie King has been prime minister of the Dominion of Canada for a longer period than Sir John Macdonald. But Macdonald's career of leadership stretches back beyond Confederation; and his record as a whole, in both the Province and the Dominion, is unsurpassed and probably unsurpassable.

The very length and variety of a career which spanned so much of Canada's history and touched so many of its activities pose a question which is, perhaps, of general interest to Canadian historians. What have we done with the man who lived for nearly fifty years at the centre of Canada's political affairs and who dominated them for over twenty-five? What have we done with the five hundred volumes of his papers which lie in the Archives at Ottawa, with the monumental mass of government documents, parliamentary debates, newspapers, periodicals, pamphlets, memoirs, and autobiographies which record his multifarious activities in neutral, complimentary, or abusive terms? It seems a fair question to ask – a reasonable test to apply to Canadian historiography. How do Canadian historians measure up to it? It may be that, in an effort to answer this question, we shall come upon certain qualities, or characteristic features, of Canadian historical writing which are worthy of critical reflection.

There are, to begin with, two curious and unexpected facts to be noticed about the biographical literature on Macdonald. In the first place, there is not very much of it; and in the second place, what there is is not new, but relatively old. In the years immediately preceding and following Macdonald's death, when his career was at its end and his reputation at its apogee, there appeared several biographies of him, written with little concern for form, and in a spirit of uncritical laudation, of which the best, by long odds, because at least it was based upon the documents, was Sir Joseph Pope's two-volume study. These were followed, after a long interval, by Sir George Parkin's volume in the original 'Makers of Canada' series; and this in turn, after a further and longer interval, by Mr. W.S. Wallace's short biographical sketch. There the procession ended. It ended, curiously and incomprehensibly, in the middle nineteen-twenties, at the very moment when historical scholarship in Canada was already launched upon a sustained and comprehensive attack on the problems of Canadian history. And it has not been resumed. The thirty years from 1918 to 1948 have witnessed a minor revolution in the study of Canadian history; but they have added very little to the biographical literature on Sir John Macdonald.

This is not to say, of course, that the work of these years has contributed nothing to our knowledge of Macdonald's career, or to our understanding of his personality. Within limits, it has done both. During the last twenty years the Macdonald Papers in Ottawa have been raided by a small company of scholars for all sorts of purposes, and in pursuit of all kinds of themes – national and regional, political, constitutional, military, and economic. But the interest of these scholars in Macdonald has been secondary, not primary, and sometimes even accidental. They have, so to speak, walked all round Macdonald without troubling to look at him. They have taken him for granted, mainly because they were preoccupied with other matters, partly because they assumed that they knew all about him anyway. Almost nothing has been done to examine, correct, or justify the traditional picture of Macdonald – the picture, half legend and folk-lore, of the easy-going, pleasure-loving, and none too scrupulous opportunist, who survived a half-century of political conflict by means of a dubious series of compromises, appeasements, and reconciliations.

Now there may be a single, simple, and sufficient explanation for these calm assumptions and this evident neglect. Canadian history, even when it is regarded as a part of the history of either the British Empire or the North American continent, is possibly a parochial, not to say limited, theme. It attracts a few enthusiastic scholars; but their number will never be very large; and, though their work has acquired a certain popularity at the present moment, both publishers and public have not shown a great deal of interest in it in the past, and may possibly show as little in the future. All this may be enough, and more than enough, to account for the slow and uneven progress of Canadian historical research, for the unaccountable gaps and lamentable omissions in Canadian historical literature. Possibly, and yet the explanation seems somehow unsatisfactory. It explains too much or too little. It has little light to throw upon the direction and the character of the work which has actually been produced. Perhaps it is worthwhile to pursue the matter a little further, to approach a little more closely the problem of Canadian history and Canadian historical biography in general, and of the biography of Macdonald in particular.

II

Biography is a distinct and special branch of historical writing. Of all branches it is perhaps most closely related to the art of the novel, and this in both a legitimate and an illegitimate sense. In a biography, as in a novel, the phases of historical development, the conflict of historical forces, are seen, not in generalities and abstractions, but concretely, in terms of a central, main character, a set of subordinate chracters, and a series of particular situations. A biography may achieve the vividness and actuality of a novel; but, with even greater ease and frequency, it may degenerate into the trivial, or dull, improbability of fiction and propaganda. The complex facts may be cheerfuly disregarded for the sake of dramatic simplicity, or they may be deliberately perverted for the purpose of political justification. And all too frequently, therefore, historical characters come to be divided into two broad classes; those who look like appropriate figures for melodrama, and those who appear to be required subjects for political panegyric. On the one hand, there is the light-hearted, fictional biography with its gaudy jacket which has been written with a keen eye, not so much for facts, as for sales; and on the other, there is the solemn work of commemoration, usually in two fat funereal volumes, which looks, as Lytton Strachey observed, as if it had been composed by the undertaker, as the final item of his job. These are the two extremes of historical biography in English; and in the late nineteenth and twentieth centuries fashionable practice has tended to alternate between them in certain fairly well-marked cycles or periods.

Canada has never passed through these alternating phases. It would have been better if it had. But in this, as in so many other aspects of our literary development, our experience has been almost entirely vicarious ... But we still seem to lack, what the fictional biography might at least have taught us, a lively interest in character and personality. Canadian biographies have a formal, official air, as if they had been written out of the materials of a newspaper morgue, or from the resources of a library largely composed of Blue Books and Sessional Papers. In all too many cases, the subject remains an important Public Personage – in capitals – dwarfed by the circumstances of his 'Times,' which are portrayed in great chunks of descriptive material, pitilessly detailed, and among which he drags out an embarrassed and attenuated documentary existence, like an unsubstantial *papier maché* figure made up of old dispatches and newspaper files. It seems difficult for us even to make our characters recognizably different; and as one reads through a small shelf-full of Canadian biographies, one is aware of a growing and uncomfortable sensation that one is reading about one and the same man ... Now this abstract and inhuman method of presentation, which may be called the Procedure Appropriate for the Portrayal of Public Personages, is damaging enough to most historical characters, but completely fatal to Macdonald. It is a nineteenth and twentieth-century historical technique; and Macdonald, though his entire political career lies within the reign of Queen Victoria, was never an exemplary and typical Victorian statesman. In some important ways at least, his affinities seem to lie rather with the eighteenth and early nineteenth century than with his own age.

...

III

A second reason is to be found surely in the strong partisan tone of a good deal of Canadian historical writing. Macdonald was a Conservative; and throughout Canadian historiography there is easily discernible a stiff strain of Liberalism with a capital L. It would not be very difficult, and it might be amusing, to compile a list of Canadian historians and political scientists who have been editors of Liberal newspapers, cabinet ministers in Liberal administrations, deputy ministers, heads of boards, and members of Royal Commissions appointed by Liberal Governments. In respect of the latter of these gentlemen, it is not necessarily implied that appointment, in their case, was a kind of public recognition of strict party fidelity; but, in the state in which Canadian politics were and perhaps still are, the evidence is, to say the least, suggestive. The list would not be a very short one; and it might be supplemented by a further list of historians and political scientists who have, so to speak, shared the Liberal table and contributed to the growth of the Liberal interpretation of Canadian history.

Toronto vs Montreal:
The Struggle for Financial Hegemony, 1860–1875

D.C. MASTERS

(December 1941)
CHR 22, no. 4: 133–46. Excerpt: 133, 134–5.

The development of urban rivalry between Toronto and Montreal has been a factor of great significance in Canadian history. Not only has it exerted a profound influence upon the economic structure of Canada; it has been an important element in many political controversies such as the struggle between Upper and Lower Canada over customs duties before the union of 1840, George Brown's 'rep. by pop.' agitation, the controversy attending the collapse of the Conservative government in 1873, and the long series of issues between Ontario and the Dominion government.

Toronto was a potential rival to Montreal from the time of the French period when its strategic advantages as a trading post had already become apparent.[1] Its emergence as an actual rival resulted from the development of commercial interests which profited by the construction of the St. Lawrence Canals in the forties, but which also developed an extensive trade with New York – a trade that was much encouraged by the American Drawback Act of 1845 and the Reciprocity Treaty of 1854. By the time of Confederation, Montreal and Toronto were obvious, and indeed frankly admitted, rivals for the control of the Canadian hinterland ...

Rivalry between Montreal and Toronto was to some extent a projection of the older rivalry between Montreal and New York. Considerable attention has been devoted to the struggle between Montreal and New York for control of the American North-West.[2] By 1870 that struggle had, to a great extent, been decided in favour of New York, and Montreal was left largely dependent on the potentialities of a purely Canadian hinterland. In this area it was also challenged by New York. Toronto was, so to speak, at the point of intersection between the line of Montreal expansion moving in a westerly direction and the line of New York dominance moving north-west. Toronto was in danger of coming completely within the orbit of one or the other. That it emerged into semi-independence was a result of the pull and tug of divergent forces. This dualism is still reflected in the Toronto financial world and in Toronto psychology. Even a casual examination reveals the existence of two distinct groups, the one (the old line element) closely identified with Montreal, and the other, chiefly mining interests, associated more closely with New York.

The study of the urban development and consequent rivalry of Toronto and Montreal can better be understood if related to the views of Professor N.S.B. Gras.[3] Both cities, in their deveopment, have exhibited all the characteristic features originally described in his analysis of the growth of metropolitan centres. Mr. Gras has attributed the development of the economy of the Western World to the dominance of certain great metropolitan centres. These emerged during the period of the commercial revolution and evolved from earlier mediaeval towns. Mr. Gras cites London and Paris as early metropolitan centres; but he extends his analysis to the New World where the rise of such cities as New York, Boston, Montreal, and New Orleans supports his thesis. In his view metropolitan development must be considered in terms not only of the rise of cities, but also of the development of metropolitan areas in which the cities are the focal points. 'Metropolitan economy is the organization of producers and consumers mutually dependent for goods and services, wherein their wants are supplied by a system of exchange concentrated in a large city which is the focus of local trade and the centre through which normal economic relations with the outside are maintained.' The focal city dominates the trade within its immediate hinterland and also controls the trade between its own and other metropolitan areas.

In its rise to metropolitan dominance the city proceeds through four characteristic stages. During the first the city performs the essential function of creating a well-organized marketing system for the whole metropolitan area. This involves the establishment of wholesaling, storage, and exchange facilities and the gradual specialization of function within those categories. The general organization of the market is followed by a second stage – the increased development of manufactures either in the metropolis itself or in the hinterland. The third stage is marked by an active programme of transporation developments. Measures are taken to avoid traffic congestion within the city, and vigorous efforts are made to secure new and better means of communication within the hinterland and beyond it with other metropolitan areas. The final stage of metropolitan development is the construction of a mature financial system 'to care for both the extended and the hinterland trade, the inter-metropolitan commerce and extra-metropolitan commerce.' In this stage by the control of banks, investment houses, and insurance companies the metropolis performs the functions of mobilizing capital within itself, radiating capital when required to various points of the hinterland, and facilitating the movement of capital between itself and other metropolitan areas.

This analysis may be applied with advantage to the cases of Montreal and Toronto. The clear emergence, in the sixties and seventies, of the struggle between them shows the operation of all the features of development described by Mr. Gras. Both were competing for control of the market in the Ontario hinterland. Subsequently that struggle was to be projected toward the North-West.

Notes

1 H.A. Innis, 'Toronto and the Toronto Board of Trade' (*Commerce Journal*, University of Toronto, March, 1939).
2 See D.G. Creighton, *The Commercial Empire of the St. Lawrence* (Toronto, 1937); Samuel McKee, Jr., 'Canada's Bid for the Traffic of the Middle West' (*Canadian Historical Association, Report of Annual Meeting*, 1940).
3 See N.S.B. Gras, *An Introduction to Economic History* (New York, 1922).

Agriculture in the Red River Colony

W.L. MORTON

(December 1949)
CHR 30, no. 4: 305–21. Excerpt: 305–6, 307.

The Red River troubles of 1869–70 have usually been explained as a result of the impact of external forces on an isolated and primitive society. That the forward movement of the Canadian-American frontier in the eighteen-sixties and the sudden intrusion of Canadian political and religious issues precipitated those troubles has been demonstrated by Professors Martin, Morton, and Stanley.[1] That internal causes of disintegration were also at work is perhaps an hypothesis which invites further examination.

The proposition is here advanced that by 1870 the three customary sources of food in Red River – the buffalo hunt, the fisheries, and agriculture[2] – were in a critical condition. They could no longer feed the native population in exceptionally bad times, as had been demonstrated in the 'grasshopper year' of 1868, when everyone experienced distress.[3] In good years they were not capable of supplying the needs of any considerable addition to the population, or of furnishing any sizable export surplus. Nor did the future promise better times; the hunt was approaching its end with the extermination of the buffalo herds, and agriculture was incapable of expansion within the established framework of Red River farming. If this proposition should prove reasonably demonstrable, it would further appear that a crisis in the affairs of Red River was rapidly approaching in the eighteen-sixties, and would have occurred even if there had been no land rush to destroy the old order.

It is first to be noted that of the three sources of food, two – the buffalo hunt and the fisheries – belonged to the nomadic hunting economy of the fur trade. They were organized developments of the fur traders' practice of employing hunters to bring in game. These food supplies, in the nature of things, could support only a scanty population.[4] The third, agriculture, was the begining of a new, sedentary economy. Selkirk's settlement at Red River in 1812 marked the first attempt at systematic field culture, as distinguished from the sporadic horticulture of the fur-trade posts.[5]

In the Red River colony, however, agriculture did not thrust aside the nomadic economy. Its initial difficulties, the adversities of climate and season,⁶ the opposition, ending in violence, of the North West Company, and the shortcomings and mistakes of the colonists themselves,⁷ resulted in a hybrid economy, at once nomadic and sedentary. In the early years of crop failure and violence, the buffalo hunt at Pembina, or the fisheries of Lake Winnipeg were the recourse of the Selkirk colonists, as they were of the native Métis. The grasshopper plague of 1818–20 was followed by the great flood of 1826. Not until 1827 did a series of good crop years begin, and agriculture become established in Red River.⁸ The introduction of cattle in 1822 and 1823 had only a limited success,⁹ as had that of sheep in 1833.¹⁰ The severity of the winters and the attacks of wolves ensured that no pastoral economy developed in Red River.

The consequence of the slow establishment of agriculture in Red River over fifteen uncertain years was the fusion of the new agricultural economy with the old hunting economy of the fur trade. During those years the organized Red River buffalo hunt took form, and became the major occupation of the larger part of the population of the colony ...

The result of this interdependence of the hunt and the farm was an economy which resembled not so much any contemporary one as the then vanishing economy of the Mandans on the upper Missouri and their extinct predecessors of the great river valleys of the high plains to the southwest of Red River ... The comparison is admittedly not to be pushed too far; the Red River settlers were, in varying degrees, the representatives, if isolated, of the dynamic society of western Europe. They had outrun, but would not escape, the Industrial Revolution. The resemblance, nevertheless, if not exact, was fundamental.

Notes

1 Chester Martin, 'The Red River Settlement,' *Canada and Its Provinces*, XIX (Toronto, 1914); A.S. Morton, *The History of the Canadian West to 1870–71* (Toronto, [1939]); G.F.G. Stanley, *The Birth of Western Canada* (Toronto, 1936).
2 J.J. Hargrave, *Red River* (Montreal, 1871), 447.
3 *Ibid.*, 457.
4 E.g., John Tanner's *Mémoires de trente années dans les deserts de l'Amérique du Nord*, I–II (Blossville's translation, Paris, 1835), I. 65. 'After a stay of three months, game became scarce, and we all began to suffer from hunger. The chief of our

band, named the Little Assiniboine, proposed that we should change our camp, and fixed a day for removal; but in waiting our distress became extreme' (author's translation). The frequent short rations and not infrequent near-starvation of the fur traders might be abundantly documented.

5 E.g., *United Kingdom, Report from the Committee Appointed to Enquire into the State and Condition of the Countries Adjoining the Hudson's Bay and of the Trade Carried on There, 1749, passim*; Edward Umfreville, *The Present State of Hudson's Bay Territory* (London, 1790), 126 and 152; D.W. Harmon, *A Journal of Voyages and Travels in the Interior of North America* (Toronto, 1904); E. coues (ed.), *New Light on the North-West; The Journals of Alexander Henry the Younger and David Thompson*, I–II (New York, 1899), 188–9, 197, 211, 228, 242, 252, 267, 280, 291.

6 Drought and grubs ruined the crops of 1813: [Public Archives of Canada, Ottawa], Selkirk Papers, Miles Macdonnell to Selkirk, July 17, 1813; see also M. Giraud, *Le métis canadien* (Paris, 1945), 89. In 1814 and 1815 returns were fair, Morton, *Canadian West*, 565 and 572, but in 1816 the colony was broken up by the Nor-Westers. The year 1817 was one of storms and early frost, and in 1818 came the locusts: *ibid.*, 644.

7 Morton, *Canadian West*, 565, quotes Macdonnell as writing of the first two bands of colonists: 'None of them cared for settling on lands.' Highland agriculture was just emerging from mediaeval, not to say pre-historic, conditions: cf. Henry Hamilton, *The Industrial Revolution in Scotland* (Oxford, 1932), 5. The genuine settlers, those from Kildonan, were, as the historian Gunn noted, stockmen rather than agriculturalists: D. Gunn and C.R. Tuttle, *History of Manitoba* (Ottawa, 1880), 144. No plough was in use in the settlement until 1823: *ibid.*, 242–3.

8 See *Lettres de Monseigneur Joseph-Norbert Provencher, Premier Evêque de Saint-Boniface: Bulletin de la Société Historique de Saint-Boniface*, III (Saint-Boniface, 1913), 20, 40, 45, 79, 87, 93, 97, 107, 114, 119 for comment on the crops of 1818–20 and 1822–7.

9 See Alexander Ross, *The Red River Settlement* (London, 1856), 150–1, and Gunn and Turtle, *Manitoba*, 271–2, for details of the failure of the Tallow Company, an attempt at large scale cattle raising.

10 See Morton, *Canadian West*, 643, for details of the introduction of sheep. The first stock of the colony, brought in with the colonists, or purchased locally, had perished in the struggle with the Nor-Westers.

The Origins of Public Broadcasting in Canada

MARGARET PRANG

(March 1965)
CHR 46, no. 1: 1–31. Excerpt: 1–4, 30–1.

The decisive role played by the federal government in the first fifty years of the Canadian endeavour to create a nation around a transcontinental system of transportation has been the subject of frequent comment. Although some historians have tended to overemphasize the distinctiveness of the role of government intervention in Canadian economic life, it is still true that state initiative has played a larger part in the nation's economic growth than is the case in most countries in the Americas and western Europe. Two conditions have been primarily responsible for the extent of state intervention in Canada: the inability or reluctance of private enterprise to take the business risks imposed by the vast extent and small population of the country, and the willingness of influential groups of Canadians to use the power of the dominion government in the search for national security in the face of economic and political threats from the United States. The establishment of a system of public broadcasting in Canada occurred mainly because these two conditions once more prevailed; in response, the federal government again resorted to 'defensive expansionism,'[1] this time in an area possessing cultural implications unprecedented in earlier phases of national policy.

I

While the Canadian economic structure was being built and maintained precariously against the southward pull of the American giant there were always Canadians, from the time of the short-lived Canada First movement onwards, who declared that railways and tariffs were not an end in themselves, but rather the material basis for the growth of a uniquely Canadian culture. Yet by the end of World War I, when a degree of economic stability had been achieved, there was little evidence of that northern flowering for which a new generation of nationalists looked. Only in the painting of the Group of Seven was there an art that could be considered 'Canadian'; the defenders of the painters of primeval rock and jack pine often exaggerated the *Canadian* qualities of the Group of Seven, but many Canadians in the 'twenties still failed to recognize the new painting either as art or as Canadian, and concurred in the judgment of Toronto *Saturday Night* that its 'harsh, uncompromising style ... is alien to the Canadian temperament.'[2]

Despite the meagre cultural achievements of Canadians the postwar generation of nationalists, especially young intellectuals, were firm in the conviction that the political community, whose independent existence had been recognized by the rest of the world at the Peace Conference and in the League of Nations, was the bearer of a distinctly Canadian way of life which would soon find adequate artistic and intellectual expression. To hasten that day a group of young professors at the University of Toronto and their friends established a new national journal of opinion, the *Canadian Forum*, with the purpose of discussing international affairs from a Canadian viewpoint and evaluating Canadian domestic developments, both political and cultural. The founding of the Canadian League in 1924 for the study of national issues was, with its branches in several cities across the country, a manifestation of the same spirit among professional and business men. Throughout the first postwar decade national organizations were born with a frequency unprecedented in Canadian history, while old ones took on fresh vitality. Among the host of national bodies formed were the Canadian Chambers of Commerce, the Native Sons of Canada, the Canadian Teachers' Federation, the Canadian Institute of International Affairs, the Canadian Federation of University Women's Clubs, the Canadian Authors' Association, the first national organization of university students – the Student Christian Movement – and the creation of the United Church of Canada. All were in some measure an expression of the rising national sentiment. So too was the rapid growth of Canadian Clubs, which increased in number from 53 in 1926 to 120 before the end of 1927.[3] Some thirty years later, writing about this period from a position in the federal cabinet, Brooke Claxton who had played a prominent role in several of these endeavours observed that 'every kind of organization, national and local, cultural and religious, political and commercial, was at a peak of activity hardly equalled since ... All these were manifestations of the growth of national feeling – it was nationwide, spontaneous, inevitable. It cut across political, racial and social lines; indeed, it was curiously a-political.'[4] Thus, in the 1920s proportionately more Canadians than in any decade since Confederation had some knowledge of their counterparts in other regions of the country and were committed to organizations or undertakings professing to serve national needs or aspirations.[5]

Ironically, just when an increasing number of Canadians were involved in the activities of flourishing nation-wide enterprises a revolution in communications, possibly as far reaching in its consequences as the change from wood and wind to iron and steam which had done so much to bring about Confederation itself, was threatening the clearer delineation of a Canadian identity. The advent of radio broadcasting, as a potential medium of communication with every home on the continent, added a new and alarming dimension to Canada's relations with the United States. Never before had the 'undefended boundary' presented such an open door to cultural annexation.

By 1930 the whole settled area of Canada was within regular range of American radio stations, while only about 60 per cent of the total Canadian population was able to hear Canadian programmes on any regular basis. Of some seventy Canadian stations only three (in Montreal, Toronto, and Winnipeg) were as powerful as 5,000 watts. The total broadcasting power of all stations in Canada amounted to under 35,000 watts, compared to the 675,000-watt power of American stations regularly and easily heard in Canada. There was a national Canadian network of limited scope: wire service was provided by the C.N.R. and the C.P.R., and time was purchased from local commercial broadcasters across the nation. This arrangement provided an average of one hour's coast-to-coast broadcasting per day during the winter and half an hour in the summer. There were only three continuing regular sponsors of live, national broadcasts, the Canadian National Railways, the Canadian Pacific Railway, and the Imperial Oil Company, although other companies sponsored coast-to-coast broadcasts less frequently. Except for the stations operated by universities, by the government of Manitoba, or by a few radio societies, all Canadian stations were financed by commercial advertising and the distribution of broadcasting power reflected the distribution of consumers' markets. One-half of the total power in Canada was concentrated in Toronto and Montreal and several of these stations devoted a high proportion of their time to relaying American programmes sponsored by American commercial interests doing business in Canada; the Maritime provinces had only 5 per cent and British Columbia 4 per cent of the broadcasting power in Canada. Although there were ten transmitters in British Columbia, eight of them in the lower mainland and Victoria, their total power was only 1,320 watts. Most of the interior of the province and the Peace River country were outside the range of any Canadian station and formed part of the territory of a powerful station in Seattle. Not only were Canadian stations weak in power, but by an agreement between Canada and the United States, based primarily on population rather than on the area served, they had access to only six clear channels, shared eleven others with American stations, and were frequently drowned out by their more powerful neighbours. Although Canadians had produced some programmes of high quality there was general consent in Canada that the standard of Canadian programmes of all kinds was inferior; Canada could not compete either with Amos n' Andy or the Chicago Symphony, and even when they could get Canadian programmes most Canadians preferred American broadcasts. The net result was that at the end of the 'twenties at least 80 per cent of the programmes listened to by Canadians were of American origin.[6]

Under these conditions the Liberal government of Mackenzie King was faced with mounting discontent from many quarters over the content and reception of radio programmes in Canada ...

Although the Minister of Marine and Fisheries, P.J.A. Cardin, tried to defend the decisions of his department, he admitted the substance of opposition criticism by granting that it had become impossible for the government 'to exercise the discretionary power ... given by the law ... for ... the moment the minister in charge exercises his discretion the matter becomes a political football ... all over Canada.' Cardin indicated that the government was favorably inclined toward the establishment of a Crown company, similar to the British Broadcasting Corporation, to place the control of broadcasting beyond political influence. Since the government did not possess the information needed to establish a new policy, it proposed to appoint a royal commission to advise parliament on the future control, organization, and financing of broadcasting.[7] ...

... The Canadian Radio Broadcasting Commission was a full-time three-man commission appointed directly by the government and responsible both for the determination of policy and for the actual management of the national system. This body bore no resemblance to the much larger, voluntary Board of Governors advocated by the Aird Commission and the Radio League, which was intended to have only general oversight over policy, leaving the management of broadcasting to professional staff. Further, the act provided for a $2.00 licence fee rather than the $3.00 fee required by the Radio League scheme. In 1932 few Canadians realized what was to become painfully clear in the ensuing four years – that the commission was too dependent on the government and that the financial provisions were so limited that the national network was only partially constituted. Local private stations were therefore allowed to proliferate to an extent unforeseen either by the Aird Commission or the Radio League ...

V

Thus a traditional 'Canadian' solution had been accepted in response to a new version of the classical Canadian dilemma. Regional and racial divisions had yielded to a national unity, long in the process of growth, but brought to fresh consciousness by a new American threat. The federal government had once more given leadership in the design of another protective policy. As in earlier Canadian enterprises there was no commitment to public ownership in principle, but once convinced that the choice was between 'the State or the United States,' most Canadians of the 'thirties had a ready answer. For some the choice was made easier by the realization that in the market conditions of the time the financial stakes were not worth a major battle, or that their material interest would be best served by government action to maintain the east–west communications axis. Strictly economic factors similar to those which involved the government in the building of the C.P.R. played a part. The decisive force was national feeling. Thus the radio policy of the 1930s was proof that Canadians had created a national identity and were prepared to use a new medium of communication to protect and nourish it.

Notes

The Institute of Economic and Social Research of the University of British Columbia provided financial assistance which enabled me to consult the R.B. Bennett Papers in the Bonar Law–Bennett Library, University of New Brunswick. I am grateful also to Mr. Graham Spry of London, England, for his many helpful comments, and to Mrs. H.A. Dyde of Edmonton for the use of documents in her possession.

1 The term is from Hugh G.J. Aitken, 'Defensive Expansionism: The State and Economic Growth in Canada,' in Aitken, ed., *The State and Economic Growth* (New York, 1959).
2 *Saturday Night*, May 17, 1924.
3 *Canadian Annual Review*, 1927–28, p. 672.

4 Cited in E.A. Corbett, *We Have with Us Tonight* (Toronto, 1957), p. 104.
5 For a general comment on the importance of institutional associations in the functioning of the Canadian federal system see J.A. Corry, 'Constitutional Trends and Federalism,' in A.R.M. Lower, F.R. Scott, et al., *Evolving Canadian Federalism* (Durham, N.C., 1958), p. 109f.
6 University of British Columbia Library, Alan Plaunt Papers, Graham Spry to H.M. Tory, Oct. 29, 1930, and pamphlet *The Canadian Radio League* (Ottawa, 1931); *Report of the Royal Commission on Radio Broadcasting* (Ottawa, 1929); Graham Spry, 'A Case for Nationalized Radio Broadcasting,' *Queen's Quarterly*, XXXVIII (winter, 1931), 151–69.
7 Canada, House of Commons, *Debates*, June 1, 1928, p. 3662.

NATIONALISM CHALLENGED

Chapleau and the Conservative Party in Quebec

H. BLAIR NEATBY AND JOHN T. SAYWELL

(March 1956)
CHR 37, no. 1: 1–22. Excerpt: 1, 22.

Until the 1890s Quebec was considered a Conservative province; since the 1890s it has been a Liberal stronghold. This transfer of political allegiance has long been recognized as one of the most significant developments in Canadian political history. And yet historians have never satisfactorily explained why the change occurred. Possibly Canadians have been too concerned with national parties and national leaders, and so have concentrated on Laurier's assumption of national leadership and his policy as a national figure. It is apparently assumed that French Canadian voters deserted the Conservatives in 1896 because Laurier was a French Canadian, although he had become leader of the national party in 1887; or because Louis Riel was hanged, although the execution took place in 1885. In concentrating on Laurier's victory, the role of regional and provincial leaders and the interaction of provincial and national politics has been overlooked or drastically simplified.

In 1896 the Conservatives lost Quebec. They lost Quebec because the party was divided and leaderless as it had seldom been before, at a time when both unity and leadership were essential. Chapleau might have provided the leadership and saved Quebec for the party in 1896 as he had done in the past, but he made no effort to do so. A study of Chapleau's career gives some insight into the complexities of Canadian politics, and also provides a partial explanation for the transition from the Macdonald era to the Laurier era in Canada ...

Chapleau died a few months after his departure from Spencer Wood in 1898, at the age of fifty-eight. In spite of his talent and ambition he had failed to dominate Quebec as Cartier had done. Yet his career is significant in the history of his province and his country. He had consistently fought against the ultra-clerical faction and had probably saved the Quebec Conservative party from becoming a narrow Roman Catholic party. His failure to unite his party might be attributed to his temperament, to his instinctive preference for destroying the Castor faction rather than compromise, but he was not entirely to blame. The Castors were no less determined to destroy him. Nor would it be just to describe him as no more than an ambitious or self-seeking politician. He was an ambitious man, it is true, but in two national crises, the execution of Riel and the Manitoba school question, he refused to seek personal power at the expense of the interests of his compatriots and the nation. His career illustrates the dilemma of a national politician representing a minority group. It helps to explain why Quebec became a Liberal province. And it should be a warning to historians that to speak exclusively of national parties and national leaders is to superimpose on a pattern of great variety and intricate design another of the utmost simplicity which, while simplifying Canadian political history, may at times tend to distort it.

Note

The authors would like to thank the Canadian Social Science Research Council and the Humanities Research Council who supported other studies of which this article is a by-product.

Review of Guy Frégault, *La Guerre de la Conquête*

G.F.G. STANLEY

(March 1958)
CHR 39, no. 1: 67–9.

During the seventeenth and eighteenth centuries the major problem of North American history was that of the co-existence of French Canada and English America, cheek by jowl, upon the same continent. To this problem there appeared to be no solution save the judgment of the sword. Just two hundred years ago, the war which followed was entering its last phase. 1758! the year of Louisbourg, Carillon, and Fort Frontenac, with the capitulations of Quebec and Montreal but a year and two to go. And yet how very remote these events appear to Canadians of the present generation. This very fact makes the appearance of a comprehensive study of this most decisive war in North American history a timely event, and one all the more significant because it is penned by an author who is rightly regarded as one of French Canada's foremost historians.

This book, which deals with the causes, events, and results of the Seven Years' War in North America, is rich in documentation. In this respect it follows the pattern which we have learned to expect from M. Frégault, whose earlier works on Vaudreuil and François Bigot have established him as the leading authority in this period of our history. He has consulted the transcripts from the archives of France and Great Britain which are to be found in Ottawa and Washington. He has also made extensive use of contemporary newspapers and pamphlets, many of them published in the Thirteen Colonies.

Let it be clear from the outset that M. Frégault has not written a treatise on strategy or an essay on tactics. He expressly disclaims any intention of so doing. After all, this has been done by previous writers. What M. Frégault has in mind is to analyse the motives, policies, and personalities of the war. That is not to say that the author does not discuss military manoeuvres. He does, and at times in considerable detail. But his main purpose is to establish the thesis that the Seven Years' War (he prefers The War of the Conquest as being a more accurate title) was the death blow to French Canada as a living society. The surrender of Canada in 1763 was more than a military defeat. It was a political, economic, social, and cultural annihilation. French Canada came to its bitter end, never to rise again. Those Canadians to whom Quebec is a living reality will be disposed to agree with Canon Groulx's remark that M. Frégault's book has 'something of the tone and doubtful savour of a funeral oration.'

Upon this thesis there will be no unanimity of opinion on the part of historians in Canada, be they French- or English-speaking. Nevertheless, writing as he does with such obvious sincerity and conviction, the author cannot but present a strong argument. Even so, this reader, for one, without in any way seeking to minimize the crippling effects of the War of the Conquest upon the emerging, national society of French Canada, is unable to accept M. Frégault's conclusion that the conquest was that society's death warrant. That French Canada did receive a terrific shock in 1763 will readily be admitted; but French Canada did not succumb. Its strength was to be found in its deep roots on this continent. Its survival was not dependent upon an umbilical cord holding it to its mother, France. Canada was no puling colonial babe. As a matter of fact, M. Frégault himself points out the extent to which Canada – French by tradition and North American by geography – had developed its own sense of national identity by the middle of the eighteenth century. If the colonial Englishman had become an American, the colonial Frenchman had certainly become a Canadian. It was the strength of this national consciousness which made survival possible. French Canada would never have continued in being without it; and without such continuance, M. Frégault would have written his books in English rather than in French.

The British Conquest: Canadian Social Scientists and the Fate of the *Canadiens*

MICHEL BRUNET

(June 1959)
CHR 40, no. 2: 93–107. Excerpt: 93–4, 101–7.

Social scientists have the task of describing how human societies are built, how they develop, how they are arrested in their development, how they disintegrate, how they vanish. Such an undertaking is not an easy one. It requires long research, and much hard and fresh thinking about man's behaviour. Unfortunately, social sciences are still in their infancy. This field of knowledge has always been and is still neglected. For centuries, most social scientists were mere defenders of the *status quo*. They were entrusted with the job of vindicating the ruling classes to which they belonged or whose servants they were. Only a few thinkers did sincerely try to meditate upon the motives and interests which influence human history. Some reformers did unmask the false dogmas upon which the social order of their time rested. They were looked at with scorn, fear, or hostility in official and academic circles. One always takes the risk of being persecuted or ignored when one dares to question the social and political conceptions of the dominant minority.

We are now in the second half of the twentieth century. In the natural sciences, man has freed himself of all the fallacies which formerly impeded the extension of his knowledge of material things. Every day new frontiers of learning are opened to man's inquiry. But in the social sciences there has been little progress because too many social scientists have satisfied themselves with repeating the commonplaces, platitudes, and watchwords of past generations. They have not gone beyond the romantic period of the nineteenth century. Their vocabulary is a Victorian one. Others have spent their time writing long and dull monographic studies on minor topics and have missed the fundamental questions of their craft. Were they afraid to challenge the social creeds of their time and to contest the validity of their forefathers' ideology? Was the power of the ruling class so overwhelming that they have felt compelled to keep silent? Perhaps the majority have been the unconscious victims of social conformity.

In any case, the result is that we live in a world we do not understand. We are almost powerless to meet the problems of our industrialized and urbanized society. Social scientists must reconsider their frame of reference if they want to make a real, scientific, attempt to explain the political, economic, and social evolution of the Atlantic world from the Renaissance to our confused contemporary age. A new approach is needed, and the need is urgent.

There are many proofs of the social scientists' failures and shortcomings. It is not my intention to draw up an inventory. I shall confine myself to an historical and sociological problem which I have long studied: what has actually been the historical evolution of the French-Canadian collectivity since the British Conquest and occupation of the St. Lawrence valley, and how have four generations of social scientists interpreted this historical fact?

With the help of France, and under the direction of their natural leaders, the *Canadiens* had organized a colonial society in North America. They had the legitimate ambition of developing alone and for their own profit the St. Lawrence valley. For a century and a half, they succeeded in maintaining their separateness and their collective freedom.

Being too weak to keep for themselves the northern half of the continent, the *Canadiens* were defeated, conquered, and occupied. Many of their leaders, having realized that their interests as a ruling class were in jeopardy under a foreign domination, decided to emigrate. The mass of the people could not follow them, and had no choice but to submit to the British invaders who now ruled the colony. French Canada could no longer rely on its mother country whose support it vitally needed to grow normally. A colonial nation is always the offspring of a metropolis devoted to its progress. Deprived of this help, the *Canadiens* were left to their own resources which were very limited. Their new lay leaders had no influence in politics and business. Their priests became their principal spokesmen, yet the collaboration of the clergy was necessary to the British authorities and they skilfully managed to keep it. As a collectivity, the *Canadiens* were doomed to an anaemic survival. One must never forget that to survive is not to live.

...

French Canadians themselves have been unable, for two centuries, to understand the actual causes of their ordeal as a collectivity. The first spokesmen of French Canada, after the Conquest, were obliged to collaborate with the British authorities under whose thumb they now had to live. They developed the habit of flattering their conquerors with the hope of gaining their protection. They gradually adopted all the commonplaces, watchwords, and slogans of their British masters about the rights of Englishmen and the exceptional merits of the British constitution. They spoke with scorn of the French régime knowing very well that such a language pleased the government and the British merchants. Indeed, the *Canadiens* who were responsible for dealing with the British administration and *bourgeoisie* were not free to act or think differently. They had to conciliate the invaders who occupied their country. The result was that after one generation, the leaders of French Canada had almost assimilated all the official thinking of their British rulers.

The Church did much to contribute to the dissemination of this British propaganda. One must always remember that the ecclesiastical administrators, whose influence was now very great in a society deprived of its natural lay leaders, became the most faithful supporters of the british domination immediately after the Conquest. By granting the Church a few privileges, the conquerors skilfully secured their devotion. The French Revolution strengthened this bond. The priesthood and all church-going *Canadiens* came to the conclusion that God himself had favoured the British Conquest of Canada in order to protect the Catholic Church of this country and the *nation canadienne* from the abuses and horrors of this wicked revolution. The British did their best to propagate this providential interpretation of their coming to the St. Lawrence valley. The French royalist priests whom the London government encouraged to immigrate to Canada from 1792 to 1802 were very useful to this end. Many generations of *Canadiens* have asked themselves with alarm what would have been their fate if they had been members of the French Empire during the revolutionary era. Even today, this question still troubles some conservative minded French-Canadian leaders who have not yet rejected the legends their forefathers believed in.

...

Social scientists of French Canada have not been more clear-sighted than its politicians. Men of action are not bound to analyse the social and political evolution of the collectivity. They have other problems to face and to solve. However, historians, political scientists, and sociologists have the task of giving a true picture of the society they study. With the exception of François Xavier-Garneau who partly realized what had been the consequences of the British Conquest for the *Canadiens* as a people,[1] French-Canadian historians have, in general, adopted with only a few slight differences the historical interpretation of the American and English-Canadian scholars.[2] This fact is a striking one and it has never been adequately pointed out. It indicates that the French-Canadian upper classes have been engaged, since the Conquest, in a process of assimilation to English Canada. The assimilation of one people by another always begins with its leaders. But one has also to take into consideration that the teaching of social sciences has long been and is still neglected in French-Canadian universities. Laval University, founded in 1852, and the University of Montreal, a mere branch of Laval from 1876 to 1920, have never had the intellectual traditions and the financial resources required to become genuine institutions of higher learning. The situation has somewhat improved during the last ten years but there are still too few French-Canadian scholars carrying on fresh investigations in the social sciences ...

Social scientists from both French and English Canada, and foreign students of French-Canadian history, have all failed to describe the actual situation of the *Canadiens* as a people because their frame of reference was inadequate. They have never seriously asked themselves how a society forms itself – especially a colonial society – and under what conditions it comes to maturity. How can it be arrested in its development and reduced to a status of mere survival? Why does a society disappear? These are the essential questions a social scientist must bring forward and answer to fulfil his responsibility as a scholar. Unfortunately, the social sciences have not yet shaken off the limitations of amateurism and romanticism. Social scientists are too often literary men who become students of society by accident, and their approach is often that of the novelist.

...

The era of amateurism and romanticism is over. It is time to put Parkman aside. Social scientists should leave to the politicians and preachers the job of making pep-talks about the grandeur and virtues of British liberty, free enterprise, rugged individualism, and similar topics. They must approach the study of society with more scientific methods. They must state with candour and lucidity all the problems and challenges of our times ...

Can we say that social scientists have up to now been equal to their task in dealing with this sociological problem? Was not their approach to it quite unsatisfactory? Their wishful thinking and their romanticism have impeded their examination of the fundamental facts that have determined the historical and sociological evolution of Canada. They have never perceived the true nature of the relations which have existed, since the Conquest, between *Canadiens* and Canadians. They do not even have the excuse of having promoted 'national unity.' A true and fruitful partnership between French and English Canadians cannot be based upon a common misunderstanding of Canadian history and Canadian society. Empty words about democracy, self-government, *bonne entente*, and the riches which a bilingual and bicultural state is supposed to enjoy have too often deceived the social scientists of Canada. They have first the obligation to analyse the facts without troubling themselves with the vested interests they will hurt or the unfavourable reactions of the influential people they will scandalize. For the good of Canada, and Atlantic civilization itself, they have the opportunity, by studying with a fresh approach our own historical and social problems, to make a worthy contribution to the progress of the social sciences.

Notes

The Gray Lecture delivered at the University of Toronto, October 31, 1958.

1 See François-Xavier Garneau, *Histoire du Canada* (4 vols., Québec, 1845–52), III, 296, 303–4; IV, 313.
2 See Michel Bibaud, *Histoire du Canada sous la domination française* (Montréal, 1843), 414; and *Histoire du Canada et des Canadiens sous la domination anglaise* (Montréal, 1844), 5; G.-H. Macaulay, *Passé, présent et avenir du Canada* (Montréal, 1859), 6; Philippe Aubert de Gaspé, *Les Anciens Canadiens* (Québec, 1863), 202; *Les Ursulines de Québec depuis leur établissement jusqu'à nos jours* (Québec, 1863–6), III, 349; J.-S. Raymond, 'Enseignements des événements contemporains,' *Revue canadienne*, VIII (1871), 55; Benjamin Sulte, *Histoire des Canadiens-Français* (Montréal, 1882–4), VII, 134; L.-F.-G. Baby, 'L'exode des classes dirigeantes à la cession du Canada,' *The Canadian Antiquarian and Numismatic Journal*, 3rd series, II (1899), 127; Desrosiers et Fournet, *La Race française en Amérique* (Montréal, 1910), 292; Thomas Chapais, *Cours d'histoire du Canada* (Québec, 1919–40), I, 3–5; Lionel Groulx, *Lendemains de conquête* (Montréal, 1920), 182, 183, 216, 232–3, 235; Gustave Lanctôt, 'Situation politique de l'Eglise canadienne sous le régime français,' *Rapports de la Société canadienne d'histoire de l'Eglise catholique*, VIII (1940–1), 56.

Le Nationalisme canadien-français: De ses origines à l'insurrection de 1837

FERNAND OUELLET

(December 1964)
CHR 45, no. 4: 277–92. Excerpt: 277–81, 291–2.

Considéré à la lumière de l'historiographie traditionnelle et même de la néo-nationaliste, le problème des origines du nationalisme canadien-français serait des plus faciles à résoudre. En effet, les historiens nationalistes du Québec ont eu la conviction que le cadre national est indispensable à toute existence collective. C'est pourquoi ils ont affirmé, sans l'ombre d'un doute, que la naissance du nationalisme canadien-français datait des origines de la Nouvelle-France. Cette thèse, assez peu contestée jusqu'à une époque récente mais fort contestable, nous la trouvons exposée en toute netteté dans le livre de M. Guy Frégault, *La Civilisation de la Nouvelle-France*. Les habitants de la vallée laurentienne, affirme cet historien, avaient, à partir du XVIIe siècle, pris conscience « de leur individualité ethnique » et, un siècle plus tard, ils avaient vraiment « une conscience nationale »[1]. On comprend la portée décisive de cette interprétation. Voilà esquissés en leurs fondements essentiels le *drame de la conquête* et ses conséquences tragiques.

Pour la plupart des historiens nationalistes, c'est, au lendemain même de 1760, la lutte pour la survivance qui s'amorce et ne s'arrêtera plus désormais; pour d'autres, la conquête inaugurait l'ère des grandes déchéances et des compromis stérilisants. La vision du chanoine Groulx, qui prend appui sur les victoires passées et sur les enracinements antérieurs, s'ouvre sur la bataille de la survivance et sur les non moins glorieuses luttes constitutionnelles. « Comme celle d'hier, écrit-il, l'histoire du peuple canadien [après 1760] restera un appel à la tension volontaire, au continuel dépassement[2]. » Par contre la perception[3] de M. Michel Brunet, qui s'inscrit en faux contre les « glorioles d'autrefois », débouche sur la représentation du cataclysme de la conquête qui, en décapitant, prétend-il, la nation canadienne-française de sa bourgeoisie, aurait voué cette jeune nation à l'infériorité et à la dégénérescence. Dans l'esprit de Brunet et de Séguin, il n'y a pas eu que la décapitation sociale pour réduire les Canadiens français à un état de servitude; le drame de la conquête, en coupant toute attache avec l'ancienne mère-patrie, a eu un effet traumatisant sur cet être fragile qu'était encogre la nation canadienne. Si on n'était en présence d'un pur symbolisme, on aurait néanmoins raison de s'interroger sur les causes de l'excessive vulnérabilité d'une adolescente si peu vigoureuse. Donc, entre les positions réconfortantes du chanoine Groulx et le pessimisme de M. Michel Brunet, on note, malgré des divergences appréciables, un point de départ commun : à savoir, l'existence avant 1760 d'une nation canadienne-française. Toute leur interprétation de l'histoire canadienne découle logiquement de cette constatation première et de la conception particulière qu'ils se font du caractère de cette nationalité.

Ces interprétations ont certes eu le mérite d'accrocher les sensibilités et, par ce biais, de rejoindre les intelligences. Mais correspondent-elles à la réalité ? Leur contenu émotif serait-il le garant de leur véracité ? Bien avant nous, d'autres historiens en ont douté. Nous pouvons dire que nos recherches nous permettent de partager cette inquiétude.

Le nationalisme canadien-français au XVIIe siècle : un mythe ou une projection ?

Cette affirmation de la présence en Nouvelle-France d'une nation repose sur un dossier des plus minces et, semble-t-il, fort peu convaincant. Elle tient, croyons-nous, davantage à la conscience de l'historien qu'à l'évidence de la preuve. Que la société canadienne du temps n'ait pas été un pur reflet de celle de la métropole, qu'elle ait manifesté une certaine originalité, on l'admettra d'autant plus volontiers que les circonstances locales ont puissamment agi sur la mise en place des structures sociales. D'ailleurs les sociétés coloniales, même si on leur impose des modèles tout faits et même quand elles se livrent à l'imitation, ne sont jamais une réplique fidèle de la mère-patrie. Les conditions géographiques et économiques et les libres choix des hommes nécessitent une adaptation des modèles. Qu'en conséquence les Canadiens du régime français aient développé une mentalité différente à beaucoup d'égards de celle des métropolitains et qu'il en ait résulté des incompréhensions voire même, des oppositions tenaces, cela ne débouche pas nécessairement sur l'existence d'un sentiment national. En d'autres circonstances et à une époque plus récente, tout cela aurait pu servir à fonder une conscience nationale; mais telle n'est pas la situation sous le régime français.

La population de la Nouvelle-France n'est pas encore éveillée aux valeurs nationales. Ses croyances, ses aspirations, ses intérêts, même ses faiblesses ne la poussent pas en cette direction. Sur le plan économique, la dépendance à l'égard de la France est totale. Le commerce des fourrures et les investissements militaires lient entièrement la colonie à la métropole. Le mercantilisme constitue même la philosophie acceptée sans restrictions de ces rapports économiques. On devrait même s'étonner, si on ne connaissait au préalable l'anémie de la bourgeoisie locale, que des pressions répétées n'aient pas été faites en vue d'obtenir un assouplissement du système colonial. Cette petite bourgeoisie éprouve bien une quelconque frustration à la vue de la toute-puissance des marchands métropolitains qui dominent les échanges entre la France et le Canada; mais elle n'a ni la force de s'affirmer ni l'énergie de protester. Aucun effort sérieux n'est fait pour faire valoir les intérêts de la colonie, encore moins les intérêts de la nation, contre ceux de la métropole.

Ce n'est pas seulement du point de vue économique que la Nouvelle-France est tributaire de la mère-patrie; elle en a même un besoin constant sur le plan militaire. Les rivalités commerciales avec la Nouvelle-

Angleterre et les confits européens dessinent sur la vallée du Saint-Laurent un danger presque permanent. On ne doit donc pas s'étonner si la colonie a toujours apprécie à son juste prix la protection que lui devait la métropole. Car il ne s'agit pas d'une simple garantie, variable au gré des événements; l'appui militaire de la France est une composante essentielle du système colonial et des croyances qui le supportent.

Mais, au niveau politique et social, les rapports sont encore plus intimes et profonds. C'est autour de l'idéal monarchique que se réalise toujours la synthèse des valeurs qui rallient l'ensemble des individus. Ce sentiment n'a d'ailleurs pas en lui-même une teinte nationale. La fidélité au monarque, en raisons de ses fondements religieux et politiques, s'impose au delà même des adhésions nationales. L'habitant de la Nouvelle-France participe au plus haut point à ce monde de valeurs, d'autant plus que sa situation ne lui laisse entrevoir aucune autre option. Ses structures sociales et ses croyances en cette matière, sans être un reflet exact de celles de la mère-patrie, en émanent jusqu'à un certain point.

Malgré les affinités profondes et l'attachement qui lient l'homme de la vallée laurentienne à la France, il porte en lui des adhésions propres à assourdir le choc qu'aurait pu provoquer la mutation de régime. L'habitant de la Nouvelle-France, parce que son univers implique l'indispensable présence d'une métropole et d'une monarchie, a les moyens de s'adapter rapidement à la situation nouvelle. Au surplus les scandales de la fin du régime français et un profond besoin d'ordre et de paix facilitent beaucoup la transition. L'attitude lucide et compréhensive des commandants militaires agit dans le même sens. Il ne faudrait cependant pas croire que le changement d'allégeance liquide tout le passé sans laisser de traces. Des craintes subsistent chez les paysans, en particulier celle de la déportation, crainte qu'on retrouve encore en 1775[4]. Mais, dans l'ensemble, la conquête n'a pas été la source d'un traumatisme qui expliquerait tous les maux dont aura à souffrir par la suite la société canadienne-française. C'est que les structures économiques, politiques, sociales et juridiques restent bien en place, au moins jusqu'en 1791. De sorte que la conquête n'engendre aucun changement essentiel dans la vie de l'habitant de la vallée laurentienne. Elle a même, en liquidant les profiteurs de l'ancien système, clarifié bien des situations et soulagé nombre de commerçants. Le mémoire présenté en 1765 par les commerçants canadiens-français[5] prouve non seulement la permanence en leur conscience des valeurs anciennes mais aussi le caractère tout-à-fait sain de leurs réactions face au nouveau régime et aux tâches qui s'imposaient. Au lendemain de 1760, l'homme de la Nouvelle-France n'est pas un être dont les ressorts psychologiques sont brisés et dont l'unique issue serait l'asservissement. Des perspectives fructueuses s'ouvrent à lui, des choix multiples sont inscrits dans les défis qui se posent à son attention. Son destin est donc lié à la qualité de ses réponses.

Dans ces conditions, on s'explique mal pourquoi la conquête aurait déclenché, ou la fameuse lutte pour la survivance, ou bien, la dégénérescence de la société canadienne-française. Entre 1760 et 1791, il existera des conflits mais ceux-ci n'ont aucun caractère national. Ils sont proprement sociaux et opposent les gouverneurs, les fonctionnaires et les seigneurs, de toutes origines, aux classes commerçantes. A cette époque, le clivage fondamental n'était pas encore ethnique mais social. Le professeur Creighton l'a bien montré[6]. Cependant, pour le professeur Lower, ces affrontements, sans être nationalistes, ont un caractère plus global[7]. Ils ont leur source dans les conceptions différentes que Canadiens français et Britanniques se faisaient de la vie individuelle et collective. Les variantes culturelles seraient déjà l'occasion de mésententes susceptibles de déboucher, dès que les circonstances seront propices, sur un nationalisme conscient. Ces deux points de vue qui se complètent, constituent, selon nous, une approche valable mais, à certains égards, incomplète du problème des origines du nationalisme canadien-français.

En réalité, l'interpretation nationaliste ne vit pas que d'abstractions et de projections; elle s'appuie sur des faits, dont, sans le vouloir, elle exagère et déforme la signification. Ainsi, la politique exprimée dans la Proclamation royale de 1763 serait l'incident majeur qui aurait stimulé les réflexes défensifs des élites de la nation canadienne-française. Dès lors, le clergé et les seigneurs auraient assumé le leadership de la masse dans la bataille de la survivance et forcé, grâce à l'appui de bons gouverneurs, les dirigeants de Londres à réviser leurs positions. Cette conception fait d'abord erreur sur la signification réelle de la politique adoptée en 1763; elle confond traditionalisme et nationalisme et se méprend singulièrement sur la conjoncture de l'époque.

...

Ainsi, l'idéologie nationaliste, création de la bourgeoisie des professions libérales, était aussi le fruit d'une intériorisation par cette élite des malheurs de la société rurale canadienne-française. La volonté d'affirmation qui en résulte se fait par conséquent dans le sens de la tradition et à l'encontre du capitalisme qu'il soit commercial, financier ou industriel.

Quant au clergé, il ne commencera à accéder au nationalisme que vers les années 1830. Il appartiendra à Mgr Lartigue, premier évêque de Montréal, de libérer le nationalisme de ses attaches libérales et d'en faire le moteur en vue de l'édification d'une société théocratique et cléricale.

...

Tels sont les principaux facteurs qui rendent compte de l'évolution du nationalisme canadien-français depuis ses premières manifestations au début du siècle jusqu'à l'explosion de 1837. A mesure que les malaises économiques s'enracinent, que le capitalisme cherche à étendre son emprise, à mesure que s'inscrivent les pressions démographiques, les tensions sociales et les conflits politiques, le nationalisme canadien-français, stimulé par les mouvements européens, pénètre davantage dans les consciences. Jusqu'en 1830, la crise nationaliste n'aboutit cependant pas à une remise en question des structures coloniales comme telles; elle débouche plutôt sur une réforme des institutions parlementaires qui s'inspirerait d'une interprétation beaucoup plus libérale des traditions britanniques. C'est que les nationalistes croient pouvoir réaliser tous leurs objectifs en demeurant des *réformistes*. Néanmoins, à partir de la crise de l'Union en 1822, au coeur même de la querelle pour le contrôle des subsides, le nationalisme tend à se libérer peu à peu de ces solidarités passées. Le *parti canadien* devient le *parti patriote* et, dès lors, un esprit républicain inavoué chemine sous le masque réformiste. On prend maintenant conscience que la nationalité canadienne-française ne pourra pas s'épanouir sous l'écran protecteur des institutions britanniques. Les chefs politiques réalisent que l'accession des professions au pouvoir politique et au leadership social sera impossible aussi longtemps que le vieux système colonial restera en vigueur. Aussi les constructions politiques des *patriotes* s'inspirent-elles après 1830 du modèle américain. C'est pourquoi on revendique l'extension du principe électif à tous les niveaux où cette pratique paraît applicable. En même temps, l'opposition aux réformes économiques, sociales et juridiques se durcit. L'obstruction politique, pratiquée dans le passé avec tant de succès, acquiert un caractère systématique. On rêve maintenant d'une république canadienne-française, établie grâce à la collaboration forcée de Londres et ne conservant que de vagues rapports avec l'Angleterre. Mais, les plus violents et les plus réalistes songent à la révolution armée comme seul moyen d'obtenir l'indépendance. La Banque du Peuple, fondée en 1835, se donne comme but secondaire le financement d'une éventuelle prise d'armes. Il est certain que l'intensification des conflits conduisait après 1834 à un dénouement tragique. L'intransigeance et l'agressivité des adversaires atteint alors un sommet. Il suffisait de l'aggravation de l'une ou l'autre composante de la crise pour qu'une explosion se produise.

A cet égard, l'année 1837 présageait mal. La récolte de l'année précédente avait été des plus mauvaises et rien ne laissait entrevoir une amélioration prochaine. Pour comble de malheur, une crise financière déferle sur l'Angleterre et les Etats-Unis et rebondit en Canada. L'inquiétude et l'agitation gagnent toutes les classes de la société. C'est au milieu de cette détresse génerale, pondérée dans une certaine mesure par la résistance du commerce du bois et de la construction navale, qu'arrive la nouvelle de l'adoption des fameuses résolutions de Russell. Un défi était lancé aux patriotes. Ces derniers ne pouvaient pas ne pas le relever.

L'échec lamentable des insurrections de 1837–38 n'est pas le résultat d'un hasard malheureux. Il ne doit pas non plus être imputé en premier à la seule opposition des clercs. C'est un facteur d'explication mais ce n'est certes pas le plus important. Ainsi, la conduite contradictoire d'un Papineau eut une portée aussi décisive sur l'issue du mouvement que les fulminations d'un Mgr Lartigue. En réalité, les insurrections étaient trop liées aux intérêts immédiats de certains groupes et individus pour réussir. Elles tenaient surtout trop à des malaises passagers, dont la solution réelle était ailleurs. L'indépendance du Bas-Canada n'aurait en rien résolu le défi de la révolution des techniques agricoles. En coupant le Québec des marchés impériaux, elle aurait plutôt accentué le sous-développement économique et laissé le champ libre à la théocratie et à la féodalité. L'idéal libéral et démocratique n'aurait certainement pas résisté à une pareille évolution.

Notes

1 Guy Frégault, *La Civilisaiton de la Nouvelle-France* (Montréal, 1944), p. 267 ss.
2 Lionel Groulx, *Histoire du Canada français* (Montréal, 1951), II, 265.
3 Michel Brunet, « La Conquête anglaise et la déchéance de la bourgeoisie canadienne », *Amérique française*, XIII, 19–84; *Canadians et Canadiens* (Montréal, 1955).
4 Adam Shortt et Arthur Doughty, éds., *Documents Relating to the Constitutional History of Canada*, 1759–1791 (Ottawa, 1907), p. 437.
5 Archives publiques du Canada, Q 2, p. 434, Mémoire du 1er mai 1765.
6 D.G. Creighton, *The Empire of the St. Lawrence* (Toronto, 1956).
7 A.R.M. Lower, *Colony to Nation* (Toronto, 1946).

The Concept of Social Class and the Interpretation of Canadian History

S.R. MEALING

(September 1965)
CHR 46, no. 3: 201–18. Excerpt: 201, 207–10.

Students of the social sciences generally accept two propositions: that a society characteristically has a class structure, either of the classic Marxian pattern or something more complex, and that this class structure is of a fundamental importance in determining what happens in a society. Historians as a group are not formally committed to or against these propositions, although as individuals not very many historians would be likely to reject either of them outright ...

What I have said so far refers to historians in general. The historians of Canada have not responded differently, although they have probably responded less. They have made practically no ideological response to the idea of class. A very few attempts have been made to write Canadian history in terms of class conflict. They have received, and would appear to have deserved, a rather chilly reception.

It is a more serious omission that Canadians have written very little lower-class history. Professor Lower, urging more of it in 1929, observed that 'the study of the common or common-place man, if overdone, would no doubt make for common-place history ...'[1] If he was right, Canadian historians have largely avoided at least one way of being commonplace. We know more, or have written more, about our military history than about the lives of most of the civilian population. We have only the most general and obvious knowledge of the social composition of the nineteenth-century migrations. There are fewer useful articles dealing with the Irish immigrants in Montreal than there are books about those in Boston.[2] We have no adequate history of trade unions, or of charities, or of social welfare. What Canadian historians have written about, say, the Winnipeg general strike does not compare with what American historians have written about, say, the Sacco–Vanzetti case. How many Canadian undergraduates – how many Canadian historians – are as likely to know the terms of the Ontario Factory Act of 1884 as they are to know those of Shaftesbury's pioneer measure in Great Britain? Comparisons with American or with British achievements are of course unfair, considering how much more of our 'normal' party political history for the critical decade of the nineteen-'thirties remains to be written. Yet the relevance of a class issue has been shown in one of the most purely political and personal of animosities.³ Nor is this sort of omission one that we are very actively repairing. The past dozen years of the *Canadian Historical Review* yield a couple of articles on organized labour, a couple on poor relief, and a couple on socialist politics.⁴ Companion journals cannot be said to have been remedying the deficiency; over the same period the *Canadian Journal of Economics and Political Science* has carried three articles of this kind dealing with the nineteenth century.⁵ Outside observers, whether outside history or outside Canada, may reasonably think that we are neglecting an area of some importance ...

The general interpretation of the period from Confederation to the Conservatives' decline is probably more settled, and more recently buttressed by research, than that of any other period in our history. That interpretation leaves one to assume that class differences were of little importance in the long arguments over the tariff or railways, and that they need not be considered much in explaining Canadian attitudes towards the United States. Confederation itself was apparently the one major nineteenth-century instance of constitution-making in which class played no significant role; and no historian of Confederation has been class-conscious enough to remark on this exception to what would otherwise be a rule. The historians who have arrived at this general interpretation are, I think, generally correct. The interpretation is internally consistent and does answer most of the questions that historians have felt like asking. It is also not closed, and more likely to be enriched than damaged by consideration of such things as the increasingly popular organization of political parties.⁶

The practitioners of some other disciplines may suspect that it has been reached by ignoring the idea of class at the outset, not by excluding it after full consideration. The suspicion can hardly be called groundless, although it will not disturb historians very much. The proof of the pudding, after all, lies in the eating, not in the recipe. Nevertheless, we cannot claim to know what this pudding would taste like if the idea of class were added to its ingredients.

The themes which are commonly thought especially to invite recourse to the formal concept of social class are all comparatively recent in Canada: the complexities of an industrial society, the politics of social welfare, the emergence of organized labour, and so on. In dealing with topics that thus particularly invite it, historians have sometimes demonstrated not merely a formal but a sophisticated understanding of the concept.[7] Oddly enough, however, such explicit recourse as Canadian historians have had to the idea of class relates chiefly to the period before Confederation ...

Notes

1 'Some Neglected Aspects of Canadian History,' *Canadian Historical Association* (C.H.A.), *Report*, 1929, p. 66.
2 There seem to be two: G.R.C. Keep, 'The Irish Adjustment in Montreal,' *Canadian Historical Review* (*C.H.R.*), XXXI (1950), 39–46; J.I. Cooper, 'The Social Structure of Montreal in the 1850's,' C.H.A., *Report*, 1956, pp. 63–73.
3 D.G. Creighton, 'George Brown, Sir John A. Macdonald, and the Workingman,' *C.H.R.*, XXIV (1943), 362–76.
4 F.W. Watt, 'The National Policy, the Workingman, and Proletarian Ideas in Victorian Canada,' *ibid.*, XL (1959), 1–26; Bernard Ostry, 'Conservatives, Liberals, and Labour in the 1870's,' *ibid.*, XLI (1960), 93–127; J.I. Cooper, 'The Quebec Ship Labourers' Benevolent Society,' *ibid.*, XXX (1949), 336–43; G.E. Hart, 'The Halifax Poor Man's Friend Society, 1820–27: An Early Social Experiment,' *ibid.*, XXXIV (1953), 109–23; K.W. McNaught, 'J.S. Woodsworth and a Political Party for Labour, 1896–1921,' *ibid.*, XX (1949), 123–43; G.L. Caplan, 'The Failure of Canadian Socialism: The Ontario Experience, 1932–45,' *ibid.*, XLIV (1963), 93–121.
5 Eugene Forsey, 'A Note on the Dominion Factory Bills of the Eighteen-Eighties,' *Canadian Journal of Economics and Political Science* (*C.J.E.P.S.*), XII (1947), 580–84; Elisabeth Wallace, 'The Origin of the Social Welfare State in Canada, 1867–1900,' *ibid.*, XVI (1950), 383–93; Bernard Ostry, 'Conservatives, Liberals and Labour in the 1880's' *ibid.*, XXVII (1961), 141–61.
6 On this, see R.W. Cox, 'The Quebec Provincial Election of 1886,' unpublished M.A. thesis, McGill University, 1948.
7 For example J. Eayrs, *In Defence of Canada: From the Great War to the Great Depression* (Toronto, 1964), pp. 41–61; K.W. McNaught, *A Prophet in Politics: A Biography of J.S. Woodsworth* (Toronto, 1959).

The Lachine Strike of 1843[1]

H.C. PENTLAND

(September 1948)
CHR 29, no. 3: 255–77. Excerpt: 255–7, 276–7.

Historians have paid considerable attention to the English capital that made possible Canada's canal and railway building in the eighteen-forties and fifties, and some attention, too, to the Scottish contractors who supervised the work. But there has been almost complete neglect of the real builders of Canadian public works, the thousands of labouring men, mainly Irish, who toiled with pick and shovel at a time when the application of power machinery to construction had scarcely begun. The omission is due, in part, to a lack of source material. Nevertheless, documents bearing on the subject do exist, and some of the matters which they reveal are presented below.

The history of Irish employment on Canadian canals involves the history of a long series of strikes which in bitterness, or even in terms of the number of men involved, have scarcely been equalled in Canadian history. The present paper deals with one of these, the Lachine strike of January to March, 1843.[2] It is better documented than most strikes of the period, and the reasons for this relative abundance of material may be of interest. One of the first results of the Lachine strike was that troops were called out and stationed along the works. This procedure roused once again a long-standing dispute between civil and military authorities in Canada over the use of troops for civil purposes. Senior military officers opposed this use of the army on several grounds: troops were for defence from invasion, and could not be suitably disposed when tied down by local disturbances; detachments used in strikes were likely to be placed in embarrassing situations, in which whatever was done, was wrong; there was fear of the effect on the discipline of underpaid soldiers of mingling with strikers; finally, but not least, the officers were indignant at the obstinate refusal of civil authorities to provide and pay for police services, so long as they could depend on the military in emergencies.

In the present instance, the military authorities were concerned enough to undertake an inquiry into the causes of the strike. It was hoped that the inquiry would bring to light remedies which would obviate the use of troops in the future. The opinions collected provide a symposium of public, or at least official, thinking on labour relations in 1843. For this reason, the Lachine strike is of unusual historical value, and in this article the opinions of the 'Industrial Relations experts' of 1843 are therefore presented at some length, following a discussion of the background and course of the strike itself.

The canals and railways of the eighteen-forties and fifties were features of a transitional period in Canadian history. These new transportation facilities permitted integration of the Canadian economy, linked it more closely to the outside world, and led it in the direction of industrial capitalism. Similarly, the group behaviour of the canal labourers constitutes a curious intermediary stage between the behaviour of labour in the raw period before 1837, and in the period succeeding the construction boom. It is scarcely too sweeping a generalization to say that 'labour' and the 'labour problem,' in their modern connotations, had not been thought of before 1837.[3] There were, of course, many labourers and craftsmen in Canada, and even some timid and abortive attempts at guild-like organization; but the frontier was open, relations of employer and employee were either of a man-to-man or feudal character, while markets for the produce seldom existed in the fixed impersonal sense of the economist. Turning to later decades, we can see definite stirrings of Canadian labour in the eighteen-fifties, with the birth of a good many unions of a local but 'modern' type. By the eighteen-sixties, these were coalescing into national and international unions. In the eighteen-seventies came the first Canadian labour 'movement' (the Nine Hour Movement), which was remarkably widespread, and important enough to receive a good deal of attention from national politicians.

The canal builders of the forties, then, stood between pre-capitalist and capitalist labour. Almost for the first time in Canada, free labourers were concentrated into large groups at close quarters, divorced from any but the most indirect relations with their employers. But industrial capitalist production did not yet exist: the pace was set by foremen rather than machines; and canal building was scarcely an ordinary industrial pursuit.

...

The opinions on labour relations presented in this paper are thought to give a fair picture of Canadian opinion in the eighteen-forties. It should be borne in mind that there was in this instance a good deal of public sympathy for the labourers – probably more than was usual in such cases. Racial and political groupings, turning on the isolation of the merchant class in Montreal, help account for this. ...

Aside from this unlettered opinion of wage-earners and habitants, there seem to have been two groups: the merchants-employers, represented by Henry Mason, Norman Bethune, and the Montreal magistrates; and the governing class, rooted in feudal England, with General Hope, Captain Wetherall, and Charles Atherton for its spokesmen.

It is clear that neither of these groups thought of the labourers as human beings in their own image, but considered them rather as machines for doing work. In the employers' case, the result was a feeling of rage that the machine did not run according to specifications; both the working class and the employing class in Canada were as yet naive, undisciplined, and irritating to the other. This mechanical approach, however, may have assisted members of the governing class to remain detached in their appraisal of industrial difficulties. Particularly was this possible because the governing class had little higher opinion of the employers than of the employed. The rise of the large railway corporation in the eighteen-fifties was to destroy this attitude of impartial superiority; but government officials seem to have been able, in the eighteen-forties, to discuss industrial relations with a calm that is almost academic.

While the canal contractors and canal labourers were the forerunners of the modern Canadian capitalist and working classes, the bureaucrats were representative of an old order about to be swept away. The public works, which they strove so hard to build, helped destroy that order, in favour of new economic and political groups. The eighteen-forties was thus a decade of transition, marking the rise of wage-labour on a large scale, and of a milieu that would forge labour into a self-conscious independent force.

Notes

1 Material on the Lachine strike is found in the Public Archives of Canada, Provincial Secretary's Correspondence, Canada East, 1843; and C Series, vol. 60. References to the Beauharnois strike are from Sessional Papers, Appendix (T), 1843. Other references are specific.
2 As will appear below, there were two strikes. However the view taken here is that the second may be regarded as a continuation of the first.
3 The large and carefully organized labour force of the fur traders, particularly

of the North West Company, may seem to be an exception. The view taken here is that the relation of these employees to their employers is best described as 'feudal.' Certainly these men were 'exploited' by the Company; but on the other hand they were cared for in a paternalistic fashion. It may be noted too that they worked usually in small groups, and were led to develop all sorts of rivalries and local loyalties. These observations hold with less force for the employees of the timber and lumber trades. However, these workers exhibited a much higher turnover of labour, and the market was an uncertain one.

The National Policy, the Workingman, and Proletarian Ideas in Victorian Canada

F.W. WATT

(March 1959)
CHR 40, no. 1: 1–26. Excerpt: 1–2, 25–6.

Historical accounts of Victorian Canada have largely overlooked the existence of a small but active radical labour press in the last quarter of the nineteenth century. As a consequence they have failed to recognize in the era following Confederation many radical ideas and attitudes which in this country are usually thought of as stemming from the Russian Revolution or the Great Depression; they have ignored the influence of current American and English radical thought at that time; and they have neglected evidences of class-conscious social ideals among some working men which run contrary to the nation-building aspirations of the main political parties.

Victorian Canadians, with their difficult job of nation building to carry out, could not afford the luxury of radically conflicting social ideologies. As early as 1879 the majority had found a symbol for their material and political aspirations in that National Policy which soon became a generally acceptable programme of economic nationalism – east–west expansion, large-scale immigration, and state-encouraged 'free enterprise.' Theoretical discussions of economic and political ideas were rare among political leaders, and the National Policy itself was pragmatic rather than ideological. In time all serious opposition to the National

Policy within Canada's major political tradition ceased. However, the growth of industrial urbanism encouraged by the National Policy carried along with it a potential threat to the course of nation building and economic nationalism. The rise in numbers, strength, and organization of the working class, though not immediately of much political significance, fostered radical ideas which challenged the assumptions of the established social philosophy. From radical writers and especially from the small labour press, it is possible to infer a tradition of radicalism surprising in its extent and development. Though now virtually forgotten, it foreshadowed the more familiar radicalism which grew into prominence in the twentieth century, after the National Policy had largely done its work.

...

From the evidence of the labour press, the intellectual developments of a quarter of a century since the *Ontario Workman* of 1875 had carried the proletarian ideology a long way. In those early days labour was concerned with immediate problems, of hours and wages mainly, and acquiesced in the capitalistic order of growing industrial urbanism. In the eighties, with the growth in size and strength of the working class, some members began to entertain ideas of basically altering the system which was fostering it, and eagerly drew on a bewildering variety of subversive doctrines for the means to carry out their intentions. The radicals remained the obscure 'lunatic fringe' of society, but their analysis of current social developments towards 'collectivism' (however impractical and distasteful their proposals at the time) was often better informed than that of more respectable citizens, as later years proved.

By the nineties some radicals were becoming less eclectic and both more consistent and more dogmatic. Here were prophetic hints of the early twentieth century, when left-wing sects and cults burgeoned forth throughout Canada, as radicals still failed to achieve responsible status, prestige or respectability in society.[1] Only later, in the international calamity of the Great Depression, by which time the material and political aims of the National Policy had largely been fulfilled, had proletarian ideals grown powerful and acceptable enough to enter prominently into the national political debate. By then it was evident that few of the problems of the workingman had been solved by the National Policy which had helped to spawn him. But the success of that policy seemed to ensure that their recurrence and their working out, whenever that might be, should take place within the framework of the nation of Canada.

Notes

The author wishes to thank the Committee to administer the Rockefeller Grant at the University of Toronto.

1 See S.D. Clark, *Church and Sect in Canada* (Toronto, 1948), where the sociology of religions is treated; in some respects the situation of minority political and religious groups in this period may be considered analogous.

PART THREE

THE RENEWAL OF DIVERSITY, 1966 TO THE PRESENT

PART THREE

THE RELEVANCE OF OUR CONCLUSIONS TO THE PRESENT

COMMENTARY

Limited Identities

While English-Canadian politicians were celebrating Canadian nationalism during the Centennial year of 1967, Canadian historians were considering the limitations of nationalism as a historical approach. Ramsay Cook's article in the autumn 1967 issue of *International Journal*, 'Canadian Centennial Cerebrations,' provided the metaphor that would come to dominate the field for years – 'limited identities.' Cook suggested that historians, instead of deploring the lack of a Canadian identity, should try to understand and explain regional, ethnic, and class identities. He also noted, 'except for our overheated nationalist intellectuals Canadians find this situation quite satisfactory.'[1]

Within a couple of years, studies on the theme appeared in the *CHR*, perhaps in response to J.M.S. Careless's call in March 1969 for such studies in 'Limited Identities in Canada.' More probably, it reflected changes already under way in historical practice in Canada, as well as in the United States, where consensus history was being dismantled. The early 1970s saw not only a revival of the kind of diversity typical of interwar historiography, but efforts to explode myths about Canadian society and tear down some time-worn icons.[2]

Family and demographic history, and the introduction of the computer for quantitative analysis, created intellectual and methodological difficulties for historians conditioned 'to approach historical research as a very subjective dialogue between an individual historian's trained intuition and his primary literary sources.'[3] Accordingly, *CHR* contributions such as Michael Katz's 'The People of a Canadian City: 1851-2,' (December 1972) were important not merely because of their subject matter – a focus on 'ordinary' people instead of élites – but because they introduced methods and sources used by social historians.

The *CHR*'s increasing focus on regional history was a result partly of the population boom of the late 1960s and early 1970s, which led to creation of new universities and expansion of history departments across Canada. David Sutherland (March 1978) attempted to revise the image of businessmen in Canada. Challenging the traditional view of them as architects of nationhood or agents of continental assimilation, Sutherland showed that Halifax's merchant community had consciously tried to build a northern regional economy distinct from that of the United

States. In the same issue Ernest Forbes described the history of the uneasy relationship between the Maritime and prairie regions.

In the 1980s and 1990s, the best 'regional' studies came from historical geographers who were attuned to environmental approaches as well as to scholarship in intellectual history and political economy. Cole Harris's 'Industry and the Good Life around Idaho Peak' (September 1985) employed an Innisian framework to demonstrate how the convergence of capital and labour in the Slocan Valley created close juxtapositions of people from different ethnic backgrounds. He suggested that this phenomenon had not only complicated regional and class definitions in British Columbia but imparted a shrillness to the province's political debate. Rusty Bitterman, Robert A. MacKinnon, and Graeme Wynn (March 1993) contrasted the mid-nineteenth-century Nova Scotia countryside and its social and political instability with its traditional image as a stable, pastoral society.

Quebec and Nationalism

The year 1970 was one of great turbulence, culminating in the October crisis in Quebec and the imposition of the federal War Measures Act. The turmoil was mirrored in the *CHR*. In September, the journal had published one of its longest book reviews – Fernand Ouellet's assessment of Michel Brunet's *Les Canadiens après le Conquête* (1969). Ouellet argued that the work demonstrated that the Montreal school's interpretations of Quebec's history reflected not national consciousness but cleavage along ethnic lines.[4] In the next issue, Brian Young (December 1970) showed that one of Brunet's recurrent themes – unity among French- and English-Canadian political élites, the Roman Catholic church, and English business leaders in Montreal – was incorrect. His analysis suggested that the electoral defeat of George-Etienne Cartier in 1872 revealed the existence of shifting political alliances. Jean-Pierre Wallot (March 1971) examined the popular influence of the Roman Catholic church in early-nineteenth-century Quebec and found it as weak as it had been under the French regime. T.J.A. LeGoff (March 1974) reviewed the historiographical controversy over whether or not an agricultural crisis in early-nineteenth-century rural Quebec had fuelled the nationalism underlying the rebellions of 1837–8.

Through the 1980s and 1990s, *CHR* editors attempted to incorporate Quebec history by publishing lengthy review articles.[5] They devoted the March 1992 issue, for instance, to historiographical and interpretive writing on Quebec. In a highly controversial article, Ronald Rudin (March 1992) suggested that the newer, 'revisionist' generation of Quebec historians, in their efforts to demonstrate that Quebec was a 'normal' society, had been wrong to discount the legacy of the province's traditional institutions. He proposed introduction of comparisons and parallels with Irish historiography. Rudin's article was the basis of his even more hotly debated book *Writing History in Twentieth-Century Quebec*, which was the subject of a *CHR* Forum in the December 1999 issue.

Class Consciousness

Although articles in working-class history were scarce in the *CHR* throughout the 1970s and 1980s, the journal offered glimpses into class and social conflict in the Canadian past. Desmond Morton's timely 'Aid to the Civil Power' (December 1970) showed that throughout the late nineteenth century the Canadian militia, officially created for national defence, was regularly called in to meet threats to the public order in the form of riots and strikes – forty-eight times between 1876 and 1914. In 'The Shiners' War: Social Violence in the Ottawa Valley' (March 1973), Michael Cross described the conflict between Irish timberers and French Canadians in 1835 over jobs and wages but also emphasized that in that region the lower classes expected internal violence and the wealthier classes viewed it with equanimity.

By 1977, the new generation of Canadian working-class historians had their own outlet for articles, *Labour/Le Travailleur* (later renamed *Le Travail*), but in that same year, the *CHR* published a major article by two members of this group – Craig Heron and Bryan D. Palmer's 'Through the Prism of the Strike' (December 1977). It revised previous portrayals of early twentieth-century southern Ontario by revealing large-scale industrial conflict there, which also suggested the existence of class consciousness. Kenneth McNaught's 'E.P. Thompson vs Harold Logan' (June 1981) traced the development of the so-called new Canadian labour history, finding its roots in younger historians' frustration with the 'mind-numbing' history of trade unionism and in a new emphasis within the historical profession throughout western Europe (including Britain) and the United States that combined social history with Marxist and other egalitarian critiques of advanced capitalism and imperialism.

In the 1980s, Canadian working-class and social historians came under attack for ignoring national and political issues. The notion that the state was ever absent from working-class history is questionable, but the publication of such influential books as *The Great Arch: English State Formation as Cultural Revolution* (1985), by Philip Corrigan and Derek Sayer, underlined the links between culture and politics. Informed by such works and by a persistent commitment to Marxist theory, working-class historians displayed renewed interest in political culture and the state. One example was Sean T. Cadigan's *CHR* article, 'Paternalism and Politics: Sir Francis Bond Head, the Orange Order, and the Election of 1836' (September 1991). Here, Cadigan showed that paternalism, rooted in Upper Canada's social formation, continued to shape politics and contributed to the Reformers' loss of the election.

The Return of Native History

Beginning in the late 1960s, Native history made a reappearance in the *CHR*, after decades of absence. Its profile in the journal seemed to rise along with the increasing number of court cases dealing with treaties and land claims.[6] In 'The French Presence in Huronia,' Bruce Trigger (September 1968) criticized the fact that few studies of early seventeenth-century Canada had sufficiently credited the decisive role of the country's Native peoples. Both Trigger and, later, Cornelius Jaenen – in 'Amerindian Views of French Culture in the Seventeenth Century' (September 1974) – pointed out that a full explanation of the contact experience necessitated understanding of both cultures; each writer suggested how this could be accomplished. A historiographical piece on Native history by Bruce Trigger (September 1980) traced the multifaceted reasons for the rise, decline, and resurgence of interest in Native history in Canada through the nineteenth and twentieth centuries. The revival of Native history served to reinvigorate interest in the history of the fur trade and Native–European relations, as well as a reconsideration of the Métis and Louis Riel.[7]

Gender Politics

Women's history was relatively absent from the *CHR* until the 1980s. March 1981 saw publication of Ruth Roach Pierson's 'The Bind of the Double Standard: VD Control and the CWAC in World War II.' In 1982, while the *CHR* was introducing new areas of specialization via historiographical essays, Eliane Leslau Silverman (December 1982) called for examination of gender and class and urged incorporation of women's history into the mainstream of Canadian historical writing. Informed by massive international literature, Joy Parr (December 1987), in 'The Skilled Emigrant and Her Kin,' combined feminist and gender history, as well as labour and economic approaches. Her study showed how gender shaped the kinds of jobs that women sought and the social relationships that they established. A special issue of the *CHR* in 1991 on women's history reflected the research of established historians and younger scholars. It included Veronica Strong-Boag's article on the everyday lives of middle-class women in suburbia and Karen Dubinsky and Franca Iacovetta's analysis of a 1911 murder case in Sault Ste Marie's Italian community that drew international attention to a woman who murdered her husband in order to defend herself from abuse and forced prostitution.

Much as these and other *CHR* publications demonstrated the strength of Canadian feminist historiography, women's and gender historians found themselves criticized as contributing to the fragmentation of the Canadian nation. In 'Gender History and Historical Practice,' written for the 75th anniversary issue of the *CHR*, Joy Parr (September 1995), expressed dismay that older colleagues had attacked gender history, cultural studies, and the 'new' social history by making such claims. She noted that 'scholarship is to open rather than extinguish questions, to discomfit rather than enshrine both settled certainties and the collective practices they sustain.'[8] Asserting that the best history recognized temporariness and impermanence, she explained that the interpretive possibility engaged by gender history was that 'manliness and womanliness are socially constituted and continually reconstrued in specific historical conjunctures' and that this process goes down to the body itself.[9] In effect, gender history historicized the biological foundations of sexual difference; in so doing, it represented another challenge to universal assumptions about human nature.

Cultural History

If social, labour, and women's historians had been frustrated by their small number among *CHR* contributors, intellectual and cultural historians had stronger reasons for dissatisfaction. In 1966, Carl Berger despaired over the state of Canadian intellectual history. He observed that it required 'penetrating analysis of ideas and painstaking attention to their inner coherence,' which had been characteristic of recent work in American history. Instead of 'genuine essays in thought,' there were 'chronicles of opinion or the bibliographical essays which sometimes pass as histories of the mind in Canada.'[10] An exception lay in the historical writing on religion, perhaps because of its close links with pre-Confederation political history and with late-nineteenth- and early-twentieth-century reform movements. The *CHR* third issue of 1968 published fine examples of these approaches, including articles by J.M. Bliss (September 1968) and Richard Allen (September 1968).

By the 1970s, although intellectual history was starting to blossom, this was not reflected in the *CHR*. In effect, its practitioners were caught in the cross-fire between political and social historians. The former generally dismissed their work as consisting of philosophical wanderings, and the latter, for dealing with élites and lacking in materialist grounding. These attitudes seemed to confirm English-Canadian historians' relative hostility to theoretical approaches – a legacy of moral philosophy, traced so well by A.B. McKillop in *A Disciplined Intelligence* (1979). In French-Canadian historiography, in contrast, the *Revue d'histoire de l'Amérique française* had from its beginnings published methodological pieces. Indeed, in 1947, Richard Saunders reviewed Marcel Trudel's *L'Influence de Voltaire au Canada* (1945) in the *CHR*, applauding it as the best example of Canadian intellectual history and of major importance to Canadian historiography. Saunders noted that interest in the history of ideas in French Canada had been 'closely linked with the concern for the cultural survival of French Canadians.'[11] In the *CHR*, articles by A.I. Silver (March 1969 and December 1976) explored the myriad cultural reasons for the lack of French-Canadian expansionist ideas towards the west and the ideas of imperialism and mission that shaped French- and English-Canadian ideological conflicts in the late nineteenth and early twentieth centuries.

The late 1980s and the 1990s saw the resurgence of cultural history throughout Britain, Europe, and the United States, as it brought together the approaches of the history of ideas, social history, anthropology, semiotics, and critical theory. Keith Walden (September 1989), for example, applied the influential work of T.J. Jackson Lears on cultural hegemony and Dominick LaCapra and Clifford Geertz's studies of texts. By analysing grocery-store window displays, Walden explored what it meant to be 'modern' in late-nineteenth and early-twentieth-century English Canada. These trends in cultural history carried over to other areas of Canadian history. For example, Tina Loo examined language, discourse, hegemony, and power in 'Dan Cranmer's Potlatch: Law as Coercion, Symbol and Rhetoric in British Columbia,' in the June 1992 issue of the *CHR*.

Notes

1 Ramsay Cook, 'Canadian Centennial Cerebrations,' *International Journal* 22 (autumn 1967): 659–63.
2 See, for example, S.W. Horrall, 'Sir John A. Macdonald and the Mounted Police Force for the Northwest Territories,' *CHR* 53 (June 1972): 179, 199, which deconstructed the myth of the peaceful settlement of the Canadian frontier.
3 David Gagan and Herbert Mays, 'Historical Demography and Canadian Social History: Families and Land in Peel County, Ontario,' *CHR* 54 (March 1973): 27–8.
4 Fernand Ouellet, review of *Les canadiens après la Conquête (1759–1775): de la Révolution canadienne à la Révolution américaine* (Montreal: Fides, 1969), in *CHR* 51 (Sept. 1970): 312–13, 315–16
5 See B. Vigod, 'Canadian Books in French, 1982: The Study of Postwar Ideologies,' *CHR* 64 (June 1983): 257; Michael D. Behiels, 'Recent Contributions to the History of Twentieth-Century Quebec,' *CHR* 68 (Sept. 1987): 393–4
6 See, for instance, W.J. Eccles, 'Sovereignty-Association, 1500–1873,' *CHR* 65 (Dec. 1984): 475
7 See the *CHR* issue of March 1988.
8 Joy Parr, 'Gender History and Historical Practice,' *CHR* 76 (Sept. 1995): 354–5
9 Ibid., 355
10 Carl Berger, review of Norman Shrive, *Charles Mair, Literary Nationalist* (Toronto: University of Toronto Press, 1965), in *CHR* 47 (Dec. 1966); 367–9
11 Richard Saunders, review of Marcel Trudel, *L'influence de Voltaire au Canada, Tome I, 1760–1850; Tome II, 1850–1900* (Montreal: Edition Fides, 1945), in *CHR* 28 (Sept. 1947): 316

LIMITED IDENTITIES

The People of a Canadian City: 1851–2

MICHAEL KATZ

(December 1972)
CHR 53, no. 4: 402–26. Excerpt: 402–4, 406.

On an average day in 1851 about 14,000 people awoke in Hamilton, Ontario. Most of them were quite unremarkable and thoroughly ordinary. In fact, there is no reason why the historian reading books, pamphlets, newspapers, or even, diaries and letters should ever encounter more than seven hundred of them. The rest, at least ninety-five out of every hundred, remain invisible. Insofar as most written history is concerned, they might just as well have never lived.

One consequence of their invisibility has been that history, as it is usually written, represents the record of the articulate and prominent. We assume too easily, for example, that the speeches of politicians reflected the feelings and conditions of ordinary people. Another consequence is that we lack a foundation on which to construct historical interpretations. It was, after all, the activities, interactions, and movements of these invisible men and women that formed the very stuff of past societies. Without a knowledge of how they lived, worked, behaved, and arranged themselves in relation to each other our understanding of any place and point in time must be partial, to say the least. A third consequence is that we apply contemporary assumptions to past society. We use our everyday experience of modern social relationships to make models which we apply to the past. We believe, for instance, that we are more sophisticated than our ancestors about sex, marriage, and the spacing of children. As a result, we imagine that they must have married younger than we do today and reproduced as fast as nature would allow. Both of these assumptions, as it happens, are generally quite untrue.

The problem, of course, is evidence. How are we to write with meaning of the life of an ordinary labourer, shoemaker, or clerk in a nineteenth-century city? Or trace the most common patterns between important social features such as occupation, wealth, religion, ethnicity, family size, and school attendance? Those questions may be answered more directly and in a more straightforward manner than we have often imagined, as I hope to make clear in the rest of this essay. My purpose is twofold: first, to show the range of questions about ordinary nineteenth-century people that may be asked and answered, and second, to sketch what, at this juncture, I take to be the primary social and demographic patterns within a mid-nineteenth century Canadian city. The two great themes of nineteenth-century urban history, I shall argue, are transiency and inequality; I shall devote a section of this paper to each and, as well, to the nature of the family and household. For differences in family and household structure reflected, in part, the broad economic distinctions within urban society.

...

The manuscript census is the most valuable source of information about people within nineteenth-century cities. Its value is enhanced by its arrangement because it provides a list of features not only for each individual but for each household as well. For individuals the census from 1851 onward lists, among other items, name, age, birthplace, religion, occupation, school attendance, and birth or death within the year. It provides a residential location for each household and a description of the kind of house occupied; it permits the differentiation of relatives from non-relatives and the rough delineation of the relationships of household members to each other. In some cases it provides information about the business of the household head by listing other property, such as a store or shop owned, and number of people employed. Assessment rolls supplement the manuscript census with detailed economic information, usually about each adult member of the workforce. The assessment lists income over a certain level, real property, personal property, and some other economic characteristics. As well, it lists the occupation of each person assessed, the owner of the dwelling, and hence, whether the individual was an owner or renter of property. (In some instances a man who rents one house or store owns another; in other cases individuals own property around the city. These bits of information about individuals may be gathered together to present a more complete economic profile.) Published city directories corroborate the information from other sources and provide, additionally, the exact residential address of people and, in the case of proprietors, the address of their business if outside the home. Directories include, additionally, listings of people in various important political, financial, and voluntary positions within the city. Many other sources which list information about ordinary people supplement the census, assessment, and directory. Newspapers are the richest of these; mined systematically they yield an enormous load of information about the activities of people within the city. There are marriage records, church records, records of voluntary societies and educational institutions, cemetery records and listings of other sorts as well. Each of these sources may be studied by itself and the patterns it presents analysed and compared with those found in other places. It is most exciting and rewarding, however, to join records together. By finding the same individuals listed in different records it is possible to build up rich and well-documented portraits of the lives of even the most ordinary of people.[1] ...

The population, this evidence suggests, contained two major groupings of people. The first consisted of relatively permanent residents who persisted within the city for at least several years. This group comprised between a third and two-fifths of the population. The remainder were transients, people passing through the city, remaining for periods lasting between a few months and a few years.

Many of the transients were heads of household, not, as we might suspect, primarily young men drifting around the countryside. The age distribution among the transient heads of household closely resembled that among the more permanent. If anything, the transients on the average were very slightly older. Nor, as one might expect, were the transients all people of little skill and low status. The percentage of labourers among the transients (15 per cent) was only slightly higher than among the more permanent residents. Indeed, there were many people with skilled or entrepreneurial jobs who moved from place to place; the transients included twenty-four merchants, fifty-eight clerks, seven lawyers, fifty-one shoemakers, twenty-eight tailors, and so on.

Although the transients approximated the rest of the population in age and occupation, they differed in one critical respect: wealth. Within every occupational category, the people who remained within the city were wealthier.[2] Thus, it was the *poorer* merchants, shoemakers, lawyers and, even, the poorer labourers who migrated most frequently. All of this points to the coexistence of two social structures within nineteenth-century society: one relatively fixed, consisting of people successful at their work, even if that work was labouring; the other a floating social structure composed of failures, people poorer and less successful at their work, even if that work was professional, drifting from place to place in search of success.[3] ...

Notes

The research on which this essay is based has been entirely supported by The Ontario Institute for Studies in Education. The project is officially titled 'The Study and Teaching of Canadian Social History' (The Canadian Social History Project, for short).

1 Record-linkage is one of the central technical problems of all studies similar to the one described here. For a discussion of the problem, and of our approach to it, see Ian Winchester, 'The Linkage of Historical Records by Man and Computer: Techniques and Problems,' *Journal of Interdisciplinary History*, 1, 1, autumn 1970, 107–24. The hand-linkage of the 1851 census, 1852 assessment, and 1853 directory was done by Mr John Tiller, who also has done most of the coding of the 1851 census and assessment. I should like to acknowledge Mr Tiller's continued and invaluable participation in this project.
2 The mean assessed wealth of all the people engaged in commerce was £96; of the transients in commerce, £63; of resident professionals, £71; of transient ones, £21; of resident artisans, £25; of migrants, £13; of resident labourers, £9; of migrant ones, £7.
3 The existence of a similar phenomenon – a division of success within trades – is clearly revealed by Henry Mayhew's description of the organization of various trades in London in the middle of the nineteenth century. An example is the distinction between the 'honorable' and 'dishonorable' parts of the tailoring trade. See, E.P. Thompson and Eileen Yeo, *The Unknown Mayhew* (London 1971), pp. 181–277, on tailors.

Halifax Merchants and the Pursuit of Development, 1783–1850

DAVID SUTHERLAND

(March 1978)
CHR 59, no. 1: 1–17. Excerpt: 1–3, 17.

The image of the businessman in Canadian history is in a state of flux. Once viewed as the architect of nationhood, more recently he has tended to be portrayed as the agent of continental assimilation.[1] Until now, assessment of entrepreneurial performance has largely concentrated on activities within central Canada. This paper seeks to broaden the geographic scope of the inquiry by analysing the eighteenth- and early nineteenth-century development strategy of the merchant community in Halifax, Nova Scotia. The inquiry seeks to establish the extent to which this east-coast business élite consciously attempted and in fact succeeded in building a northern regional economy distinct from that of the United States. The analysis focuses on the period between the end of the American Revolution and the coming of free trade.[2]

Any assessment of Halifax's function must begin with acknowledgment of its distinctive geographic characteristics. Although endowed with a large, secure, ice-free harbour and situated adjacent to the major transatlantic shipping lanes, the port suffers one crucial liability. Unlike the ports of the St. Lawrence, Halifax lacks river access to the adjoining hinterland. It is trapped on the Atlantic coast, shut off from the resources of the interior by a barrier of rock, swamp, and scrub forest. Communication by sea is interrupted by storms and ice during winter. During the rest of the year, Maritime coastal waters have traditionally played host to an international fishing and commercial fleet competing all too vigorously for control of regional resources and markets. Geography and the presence of external rivals meant that, through the first quarter century after its founding in 1749, Halifax functioned as an isolated imperial garrison, having only minimal commercial contact with the neighbouring region.[3]

The Revolutionary War contributed decisively to a redefinition of Halifax's identity. Loyalist merchants, crowding into the Nova Scotia capital early in the 1780s, became the focus of a lobby demanding implementation of a comprehensive regional development strategy, one that envisioned the Maritimes being transformed into 'new' New

England, playing the role of supply base and market for the British Caribbean. Those based in Halifax saw their port emerging as a second Boston, thriving on the West Indies carrying trade and functioning as chief commercial entrepôt within the Maritimes.[4] Implementation of this development programme demanded the elimination of competition from 'old' New England, a task colonial lobbyists believed could be accomplished through the application of mercantilist restrictions against American business enterprise. Their aspirations received at least partial support from the British government. While conceding American access to the inshore fisheries of British America under the Treaty of Paris, the London authorities did introduce imperial Orders-in-Council barring American vessels from British Caribbean ports.[5] Thus emboldened, Halifax entrepreneurs embarked during the 1780s on an effort to build their port into a regional commercial metropolis.

...

In an effort to preserve both their metropolitan ambitions and a separate regional identity in an era of free trade, Halifax entrepreneurs opted for promotion of ever greater integration between the Maritime and St Lawrence colonies. In time, that aspiration would come to be associated with a desire to combine commercial with industrial development.[6] Thus it can be seen that the Halifax merchants were moving on a course parallel with their Montreal and Quebec counterparts. Through the first half of the nineteenth century they were leaning toward a joint effort to build a separate northern economic 'empire,' founded initially on commercial enterprise, but with the potential to diversify into industrialization. Ironically, this pursuit of British American integration ultimately led to the destruction of the metropolitan ambitions and separate regional identity which Halifax entrepreneurs had pursued since late in the eighteenth century.[7]

Notes

1 For classic statements of the opposing point of view, see Donald Grant Creighton, *The Empire of the St. Lawrence* (Toronto 1956); R. Tom Naylor, *The History of Canadian Business, 1867–1914*, 2 vols. (Toronto 1975).
2 General studies dealing with Maritime regional economic development include Harold Adams Innis, *The Cod Fisheries: The History of an International Economy* (Toronto 1940); Gerald Sandford Graham, *Sea Power and British North America, 1783–1820: A Study in British Colonial Policy* (Cambridge, Mass. 1941); Andrew Hill Clark, *Acadia: The Geography of Early Nova Scotia to 1760* (Madison,

Wisc. 1968); Robin F. Neill, 'National Policy and Regional Development: A Footnote to the Deutsch Report on Maritime Union,' *Journal of Canadian Studies*, IX, 1974, 12–20.
3 Ian Brookes, 'The Physical Geography of the Atlantic Provinces,' in *The Atlantic Provinces*, ed. Alan G. Macpherson (Toronto 1972), 1–45; John Warkentin, 'The Atlantic Region,' in R. Cole Harris and John Warkentin, *Canada before Confederation* (Toronto 1974), 169–231; Arthur Hill Clark, 'Contributions of Its Southern Neighbours to the Underdevelopment of the Maritime Provinces Area, 1710–1867,' in *The Influence of the United States on Canadian Development: Eleven Case Studies*, ed. Richard A. Preston (Durham, NC 1972), 164–84.
4 William Stewart MacNutt, *The Atlantic Provinces: The Emergence of Colonial Society, 1712–1857* (Toronto 1965), 86–111; Harold Hampden Robertson, 'The Commercial Relationship between Nova Scotia and the British West Indies, 1788–1822: The Twilight of Mercantilism in the British Empire' (unpublished MA thesis, Dalhousie University, 1975), 1–28.
5 Innis, *Cod Fisheries*, 220, 227–8; Graham, *Sea Power*, 19–55; Alfred Le Roy Burt, *The United States, Great Britain and British North America from the Revolution to the Establishment of Peace after the War of 1812* (New Haven 1940), 42–70.
6 Abraham Gesner, *The Industrial Resources of Nova Scotia* (Halifax 1849).
7 The impact of development strategy on the politics of Confederation and Halifax response to the National Policy is discussed in Delphin A. Muise, 'The Federal Election of 1867 in Nova Scotia: An Economic Interpretation,' Nova Scotia Historical Society, *Collections*, XXXVI, 1968, 327–51; and Thomas William Acheson, 'The National Policy and the Industrialization of the Maritimes, 1880–1910,' *Acadiensis*, 1, 2, 1972, 3–28.

Never the Twain Did Meet: Prairie–Maritime Relations, 1910–27

ERNEST R. FORBES

(March 1978)
CHR 59, no. 1: 18–37. Excerpt: 18–20, 37.

In their preoccupation with Central Canada, Prairie and Maritime historians have had little to say of their regions' relations with each other. Yet, especially in the early decades of the twentieth century, these were significant. The three Maritime and the three Prairie provinces had important interests in common. As provinces with relatively small populations and narrow tax bases, each had a stake in breaking from the rigid per capita subsidy formula imposed at Confederation and guarded thereafter by gargantuan Ontario. Distant from the principal centres of population and acutely concerned with the maintenance of a cheap and efficient service for railway users, each had to fight demands for greater profits or reduced deficits on the railways. Nevertheless, in the interregional jockeying in the formation of national policy on these and other issues, the Prairies and Maritimes seldom appeared as allies. Where they seemed to have the most in common, they were often in sharpest conflict. In 1917 a Westerner attacked the low rates on the Intercolonial. Five years later a Maritimer led the opposition to the maintenance of the Crow's Nest Pass rates. The Maritimers fought the Prairie subsidy claims of 1918 and Westerners opposed the implementation of the Duncan Commission recommendations of 1926. Successive bids for co-operation between the two regions failed. An incipient Prairie–Maritime alignment in the Progressive party was still-born; attempts to forge a common front between Progressive and Maritime Rights members of parliament quickly aborted. These failures can be traced to three principal sources: a genuine divergence of interest on the tariff, a narrowness in vision on the part of their leaders, and the astuteness of metropolitan leaders in playing off one region against the other. The following is an attempt to explain the conflict and failures in co-operation which highlighted contacts between the two regions.

In both the Prairies and Maritimes, regional consciousness was largely a product of the people's difficulties in defending economic interests. The anger of Prairie farmers at high freight rates, suspected grain marketing 'rip-offs,' and adverse tariff policies is well known. So too are their efforts at economic and political organization – an organization employing a rhetoric which associated the progressive reform ideology of the day with the region and identified the forces of reaction with the East.[1] The Maritime experience was not entirely dissimilar. Although divided politically and economically throughout most of their three hundred years of history, Maritime residents by the early twentieth century were beginning to grope towards some form of unity. While Westerners united to demand a political influence and status which they had not yet achieved, Maritimers were uniting to retain an influence and status which they were rapidly losing. Their region's decline was apparent in losses in representation at Ottawa, in a reduced share of federal subsidies, and in tariff and freight rate changes disastrous to their economy.² The rise of one region while the other was declining was itself a factor which discouraged interregional co-operation. To the Maritimers it often seemed that the gains of the Prairies were made directly at their expense. To the Prairie residents, the Maritimers' efforts to check their declining influence often appeared as blatant attempts to maintain 'special privilege' – the *bête noire* of Western reform rhetoric.

...

This was not true, however, of the transportation and subsidy issues. Here the broad goals of both regions were basically similar. Yet, despite all their talk of co-operation, neither region proposed a transportation or subsidy policy which comprehended the needs of the other. Such a failure suggests a chronic narrowness of vision on the part of the leadership. But the problem went deeper. For more than two decades Maritime and Prairie regional spokesmen had expressed their transportation and subsidy problems in terms of injustices inflicted upon their regions alone. As these rationales were popularized they hardened into ideologies.³ Even when Prairie and Maritime leaders perceived basic problems in common, as they sometimes did, they could not seriously advocate joint solutions without facing the politically difficult, if not impossible task of radically revising the established ideologies. None seem to have tried to do so.

In the development of conflicting regional ideologies and interregional conflict lay still another factor – the hard-to-measure role of the representatives of metropolitan interests in playing off one portion of the hinterland against the other. This is not to suggest any conscious, long-term policy of inciting conflict but rather the *ad hoc* actions of federal politicians and railway leaders in breaking up or heading off coalitions of interest against their policies. The federal government's handling of the subsidy through special deals with individual provinces or regions facilitated divide-and-rule tactics by the centrally-dominated parties. The rigid rate structure imposed by the Railway Act and maintained by the Board of Railway Commissioners enable railway leaders to project the potential gains of one region as barriers to the aspirations of the other. Finance Minister Robb followed a similar strategy in resisting the recommendations of the Duncan Commission. Indeed, given their genuine differences in interest, and the ability of metropolitan leaders to play off one region against the other, one might well wonder if co-operation between such distant portions of the hinterland could reasonably have been expected.

Limited Identities

Notes

This paper is essentially a study of Prairie–Maritime relations at the diplomatic level – that of politicians and newspapermen who claimed to speak for their respective regions. Other important aspects of Prairie–Maritime relations, such as their contacts in harvest excursions, are currently being examined by other scholars. While potential conflict between Prairie and Maritime interests and attitudes may be traced back to the previous century – at Confederation, for example, some Maritime politicians were keenly apprehensive of the costs of Western development – direct confrontation between the two regions did not emerge until the second decade of the twentieth century.

1 W.L. Morton, *The Progressive Party in Canada* (Toronto 1950); P.F. Sharp, *Agrarian Revolt in Western Canada* (Minneapolis 1948); J.H. Thompson, 'The Harvests of War: The Prairie West, 1914–1918' (PhD thesis, Queen's University, 1975); Gerald Friesen, 'The Western Canada Identity,' Canadian Historical Association, *Historical Papers*, 1973, 13–19.

2 E.R. Forbes, 'The Origins of the Maritime Rights Movement,' *Acadiensis*, autumn 1975, 54–66; K.A. McKirdy, 'Regionalism: Canada and Australia' (PhD thesis, University of Toronto, 1959); C.D. Howell, 'Nova Scotia's Protest Tradition and the Search for a Meaningful Federalism,' in David Bercuson, ed., *Canada and the Burden of Unity* (Toronto 1977); G.A. Rawlyk, 'Nova Scotia Regional Protest, 1867–1967,' *Queen's Quarterly*, spring 1968, 105–23. The author's major study on this topic, *The Maritime Rights Movement, 1919–1927: A Study in Canadian Regionalism*, will be published in the spring of 1978 by McGill-Queen's University Press. [It appeared in 1979.]

3 H.J. Darling, 'Transport Policy in Canada: The Struggle of Ideologies versus Realities,' in K.W. Studnicki-Gizbert, ed., *Issues in Canadian Transport Policy* (Toronto 1974), 9.

Industry and the Good Life around Idaho Peak

COLE HARRIS

(September 1985)
CHR 66, no. 3: 315–43. Excerpt: 315, 339–43.

Capital and labour began to penetrate the recesses of Canadian space early in the sixteenth century and, in various forms, have continued to do so ever since. Settlement, most of them ephemeral, have suddenly appeared in the wilderness, their locations dependent on transportation technology and resource availability, their economies tied to distant markets, their populations migratory and largely male, and their rhythms of work and leisure bound to technologies of resource procurement. When modern British Columbia was being settled the well-established pattern continued: first in association with the fur trades, then with the gold rushes, and, in the last decades of the nineteenth century, with fishing, logging, and hardrock mining. All these activities relocated capital and labour close to new resources, far from markets, and, often, where no one had ever lived before.

In British Columbia the late nineteenth-century influx of capital and labour, accompanied by a pretested industrial technology, fuelled by largely unregulated speculation, and cushioned neither by agriculture nor the past, had a particular intensity. Camps, probably the most common form of settlement in the province, burst into existence, generated other settlements by their momentum, and then flickered and died, leaving a residue of people, settlements, and derelict landscapes. Such, generally, is the story of the Slocan valley in the Kootenay district of southeastern British Columbia. In 1890 the valley was virtually unknown. Five years later it was served by spur lines of two transcontinental railways, and by 1910 when a forest fire burned out many railway trestles and mine buildings the Slocan valley was already a quiet backwater in the wake of a mining boom. In the twenty years since the first discoveries, some 28 million ounces of silver and 200 million pounds of lead, with a gross value of nearly $30 million, had been shipped from the Slocan (Figure 1).

...

Much of what happened around Idaho Peak had been anticipated, not only in the American Cordillera, but long before when European

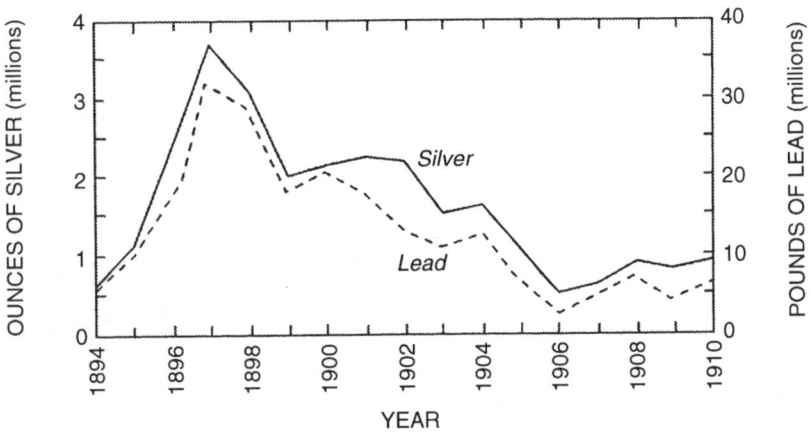

Figure 1: Silver and lead production in the Slocan, 1894–1910

capital and labour first penetrated North American middle latitudes. The sixteenth-century Basque whaling stations on the Labrador Coast, the shore installations of the migratory dry fisheries in the seventeenth and eighteenth centuries, and the fur posts on Hudson Bay and in the hinterland of the St Lawrence, like the mines on Idaho Peak, were temporary, male workplaces in wilderness.[1] All were connected by lines of credit to distant sources of capital, and by ties of family and culture to distant sources of labour. All were dominated by specialized economies and techniques, and by the transportation problem. All were vulnerable to international fluctuations in price and to local depletion of stocks. Often there was no alternative employment. When whales were hunted out off bleak shores, furbearers trapped out from areas of granite and muskeg, pine cut from sandy soils, or mines worked out on Idaho Peak, workplaces were abandoned. Perhaps there were regional, if not local, multipliers. Staple trades would encourage urban growth, initially nearer the source of capital than the resource, but eventually at points of regional accumulation. The closer the nucleation to the resource, the more vulnerable it would be.[2]

...

Staple trades, as Harold Innis insisted, were the initial, and long the most vigorous, motors of the Canadian economy.[3] In all of them specialized strategies of resource extraction were abruptly superimposed on uninhabited or sparsely inhabited land. Because the strategies were different in each of the staple trades, each created characteristic spatial patterns, settlements, and landscapes; but all removed the buffers of tradition and custom that in older societies tended to moderate the relationship between capital and labour. In these trades, wages were free labour's common return from the resources of a new land. Men worked under a foreman in isolated workplaces where tasks were specialized and standardized.[4] Social relations were sharply, often brutally, hierarchical. Labour was detached from its social context; only at the end of the nineteenth century would unions attempt to interpose between employer and employee. Long before the mechanized factory, the staple trades separated place of work from place of residence – not by a walk through the brick streets of an industrial city, but often by a seasonal migration of hundreds or thousands of miles.[5] In the western hardrock mines the separation was such that place of residence, and with it family and home, often disappeared, and life became a bachelor journey through a succession of mining camps.[6]

The weak commercial economies that developed around the edge, as it were, of staple trades in settings where people could live but not participate vigorously in an export economy often outlived their staple trade progenitors. In the long run these economies (that Innis hardly considered) nurtured much of the early Canadian population. The societies associated with them were relatively detached from local and external capital, and also, in new settings, from traditional, landed power. If the staple trades abstracted capital, specialized technique, and labour from former contexts, these societies abstracted the sentiment of the family and relatively subsistent economies. They tended to turn around their own internal momentum, and their social range was not very great. For all the boosterism of the early years, by 1910 New Denver was quickly slipping into a truncated, early twentieth-century version of this pattern. In an earlier Canada such economies depended on mixed farming, but Idaho Peak, like most of British Columbia, barely permitted this option. Although some people in New Denver depended directly on the mines, most lived on the modest trade of a declining service economy, on institutional employment (school, post office, hospital, churches), and on odd jobs – just enough employment to open a niche somewhat apart from a staple trade. With neither space nor time to expand, this niche was filled by a village that soon exported most of its young.

Over the years lives were being reassembled in Canada in settlements somewhat like those around Idaho Peak. The community of memory and custom that underlay societies where people had lived together for many generations was absent. Rather, the process of migration had extracted relatively mobile components of such communities – particularly individuals and nuclear families – and new settlements had juxtaposed people of different background in, often, highly specialized work environments.

In the mines, as in all staple trades, technique tended to override culture. From outside the men were miners; even from inside, common work, a measure of common interest, and friendship soon cut across cultural backgrounds, if not as quickly or as completely as the union would have wished. Although men of similar ethnicity congregated when they could – sometimes providing most of the labour at a given mine – little of the larger culture from which they had come was at hand. Ethnicity as an implicit way of life was being succeeded by work. Languages other than English (or various dialects of English) would survive for a time if there were enough men to speak them. National days would be boisterously observed, and a man's sense of his own ethnicity would tend to become explicit. But the context of life was not established by ethnicity: men worked in the mines, slept in company-built bunkhouses, ate food prepared by a cook, cursed bosses, and drifted through much of a continent looking for jobs. In such circumstances ethnicity became increasingly symbolic, an identification rather than a way of life, and eventually expressed by a few essential markers – to the point, around Idaho Peak, where 'whiteness,' a concept that overrode all the local texture of ethnicity, could become the essential criterion of acceptability.

In places like New Denver, where families settled down, there was more opportunity for cultural replication, but even there different backgrounds were not reproduced and assimilation was rapid. Detached minorities had no cultural support. English-speaking people of British background, the majority, came from many different regional traditions in the British Isles and eastern North America, none of which could be sustained in a small, new settlement dependent on a different economic base and composed of diverse people. Everyone left a good deal behind; details, but never the whole composition, of former cultures survived. In New Denver, as elsewhere, selection reflected the requirements and limitations of the economy and the prevailing background of immigrants. Had there been time for generations to pass and relatively contiguous space for expansion, as often there had been in eastern North America, the new mixture could well have expanded into a regional, North American culture.

Around Idaho Peak there was neither time nor space. Settlement began in 1891, soon ran out of resources, and had nowhere nearby to go. On a continental scale it was insignificant. But Idaho Peak was a patch of New World wilderness that, like many another, was suddenly penetrated by capital and labour, and it has something to say about the process. It reveals the characteristic stamp of Cordilleran mining camps and, more broadly, of staple trades in wilderness. It provides examples of the sequestered economies that often emerged, somewhat inadvertently, in their train. These two basic constituents of the economic geography of early Canada were frames within which a good deal of the country's demographic, social, and ethnic character evolved. In the East they were often separated. Around Idaho Peak they converged – creating the close juxtapositions of different backgrounds and experiences that so complicate regional and class definition in British Columbia and impart such shrillness to the province's political debate. Idaho Peak concentrated two basic New World economies within one or other of which a great many early Canadians assembled the detached elements of Old World lives. More than fifty years ago Innis identified part of the pattern, and I suspect that his essential ideas about early Canada are more expandable than the last generation of Canadian studies has conceded.

Notes

1 As *The Historical Atlas of Canada*, volume 1 (forthcoming) should make clear. [*Historical Atlas of Canada, Vol. 1: From the Beginning to 1800*, R. Cole Harris, editor; Geoffrey J. Matthews, cartographer/designer (Toronto 1987).] The pattern also emerges clearly in works such as C. Grant Head, *Eighteenth Century Newfoundland: A Geographer's Perspective* (Toronto 1976); and Graeme Wynn, *Timber Colony: A Historical Geography of Early 19th Century New Brunswick* (Toronto 1981).
2 I.M. Robinson, 'New Industrial Towns in Canada's Resource Frontier,' Department of Geography, Research paper No. 73, University of Chicago, 1962; R.A. Lucas, *Minetown, Milltown and Railtown: Life in Canadian Communities of Single Industry* (Toronto 1971); J.H. Bradbury, 'Towards an Alternative Theory of Resource-Based Town Development in Canada,' *Economic Geography*, LV, 1979, 147–66.
3 The term 'staple trade,' well-established in the literature since the early work of Harold Innis, is perhaps misleading. Only the fur trade was a trade per se; fishing, lumbering, and mining were resource industries that produced export staples.

4 Often long before they were mechanized, as in the early fishery.
5 Such migrations, of course, were not confined to the European outreach to the New World, or to staple trades. See Olwen H. Hufton, *The Poor of Eighteenth-Century France, 1750–1789* (Oxford 1974), chap. 3.
6 I have argued some of these matters in other contexts: 'The Simplification of Europe Overseas,' *Annals, Association of American Geographers*, LXVII, Dec. 1977, 469–83; and 'European Beginnings in the Northwestern Atlantic: A Comparative View,' in D. Hall and D.G. Allen, eds., *Seventeenth Century Massachusetts*, forthcoming.

Of Inequality and Interdependence in the Nova Scotian Countryside, 1850–70

RUSTY BITTERMAN, ROBERT A. MACKINNON, AND GRAEME WYNN

(March 1993)
CHR 74, no. 1: 1–43. Excerpt: 1–5, 35–7, 41.

In 1929 historian Lawrence J. Burpee proclaimed his return 'from a visit into the past of Nova Scotia.' Writing at the end of a difficult decade for the three Maritime provinces – a decade marked by radical economic changes, widespread discontent, vigorous claims for regional 'rights,' and a massive hemorrhage of population from the region – he had no doubts about what he had seen. Carried back into the previous century by a handful of recently published books, he had glimpsed the good years, 'when the wooden sailing ship dominated ... life ... [in] the colony.' In those days, he argued, a large fleet of schooners, barques, brigs, and brigantines, built and sailed by skilful Maritimers, had scudded across the world's oceans, 'making the name of *Bluenose* familiar to thousands of alien communities,' and returning profits to their home ports. More than this, they had brought to mid nineteenth-century Nova Scotia 'a degree of prosperity which she had never enjoyed before, and which, from some points of view, at least, she has never enjoyed since.' This, wrote Burpee, was the province's 'Golden era.'[1]

Ten years later, archivist and historian D.C. Harvey – convinced that Maritimers had been 'floundering in the Slough of Despond for more than fifty years' – also looked backward to discover that mid nineteenth-century Nova Scotians were 'alert, hopeful, ambitious ... [and] eager to know the extent and variety of their intellectual and economic resources.' In Harvey's mind, these were the 'spacious days' of the province, and they were well worth recalling in hope of recovering their spirit.[2]

From such promising material, historical alchemy quickly transmuted the Maritime past. The 'Golden era' of Burpee's text became the 'Golden Age' of his title in *Queen's Quarterly*. D.C. Harvey looked forward, optimistically, to 'an age more golden' than even the most spacious early days of Nova Scotia. And within a year the Royal Commission on Dominion–Provincial Relations reinforced the growing conviction that prosperity and happiness marked the mid nineteenth-century Maritimes by describing the pre-Confederation decades as the 'Golden Age' of the region.[3]

Included within this conceptualization, and fundamental to it, was a laudatory vision of rural life in earlier times. These studies, and others that followed in their wake, emphasized the self-sufficiency and independence of farm households and farm communities in the mid nineteenth century. At their core lay the assumption that easy access to land assured the well-being of countryfolk and sustained an essentially egalitarian rural social structure.[4] Real poverty, wrote one of the region's leading historians of conditions in the 1850s, was an urban ill, 'found only in the more squalid slums of the seaports.' Even where the land was of marginal quality, 'the country could always produce food.' This, to be sure, was still a region of pioneers, 'but pioneering was yielding a modest competence'; free trade, Reciprocity, and the renewed productivity of the fishery had broadened prosperity and created a general sense of well-being across the provinces.[5] Happy and honest, independent and industrious, turning their hands to a range of tasks, sheltered from the ills of the world, and providing for their own and succeeding generations, the farmers of this Maritime Golden Age were veritable yeomen, their image – surely unwittingly but nonetheless perceptibly – shaded by association with the classical poets' descriptions of the first and best age of the world.[6]

The need for reconsideration is clear. Any review of recent historical writing on the Maritimes reveals the dearth of detailed work on the rural scene. In the absence of new inquiries, addressed to new questions and informed by the insights and approaches of studies in agricultural history elsewhere, old concepts have survived, neither challenged nor confirmed, to assume the authority of convention. Knowing little of the shape and structure of rural communities in the nineteenth-century Maritimes, and less of how farm families responded to the changes that were a constant facet of life in the region through these years, scholars essaying syntheses have, perforce, fallen back on sweeping conceptualizations of rural change – from subsistence to commercial, peasant to capitalist, tradition-bound to modern, or stratified European to egalitarian North American – to carry their narratives across the broad, sketchily charted terrain of the Maritimes' rural past.[7] Fuller understanding has been hampered by the general failure of recent Maritime scholarship to ask fundamental questions about how the rural majority of the region's people lived; how they shaped their material, social, and political worlds; and how their life-chances were affected by the timing and location of their settlement in the provinces.

...

A Golden Age?

Examined systematically, rather than through the lens of nostalgic memory, the settlements of Hardwood Hill and Middle River are revealed as anything but simple, secure, homogeneous communities of independent households practising subsistence agriculture. Inequalities of material condition, social position, and economic prospects marked these complex places. Wealth and poverty, comfort and suffering, plenty and want not only existed side by side, they were intimately interconnected. The prosperity of the well-to-do rested on the availability of labour to attend those tasks it was beyond the capacity of individual households to manage. The survival of the poor depended on the returns of off-farm work. Position and power were the privileges of wealth. Subservience and dependence were the implications of poverty. More than this, patterns of affluence and adversity were generally perpetuated through the years. Large, productive farms yielded surpluses for export, and profits for reinvestment in mills, shipbuilding, and land, each of which offered prospects of further returns on capital.[8] 'Casual' labour was chronically uncertain; it supplemented meagre incomes, but little more. Title to one's land provided security and the collateral with which to raise a mortgage for improvements on investment. Squatters on the crown domain were forever subject to the threat of eviction and the loss of such toeholds as they had gained in the new world.

...

Day by day, the consequences of their position bore in upon rural Nova Scotians in these stratified communities. They were revealed by substantial differences in the material circumstances of settlers, in the prospects of their children, in the type and terms of their work, in their standing in their settlement, and in their power to shape their lives. They were, moreover, clear products of the past. The picture was drawn in more or less bold strokes across the colony, but everywhere its essential lines were the same. In the fragmented, agricultural ecumene of Nova Scotia, where settlement filled countless small pockets of cultivable land in the century or so before Confederation, early arrival conferred enormous advantages.[9] In narrow valleys and on more gentle upland slopes, where large variations in the quality of soil and site were characteristic, first-comers had the pick of land. Depending on the pace of settlement and the details of local geography, those who arrived slightly later might find land and resources adequate to their needs; but those who followed were pressed to the margins. Remote locations, inferior soils, and short summers were their characteristic lot.

...

Spawned by the economic and social disruptions associated with the transition to a new industrial order in the Maritime provinces, the picture of an idyllic pre-Confederation past always owed more to nostalgic memory than to fact. Like all such recollection, it offered a highly selective view of the past to satisfy present needs. In times of high unemployment and advancing urbanization, memories of poverty, struggle, and dependence were poor salves to hardship and despair. By contrast, comfort and hope lay in bucolic visions of seedtime and harvest, and the roll of the seasons; to look back to a time when provincial sailors crossed the world's oceans and ordinary people were in command of their destinies was to make room for optimism. If life was thus once, might it not be so again?

Notes

A Queen's Fellowship from the Social Sciences and Humanities Research Council of Canada (SSHRC) and Maggee and Hugh John Flemming scholarships from the University of New Brunswick supported Bittermann's work on Middle River. The Hardwood Hill case study is drawn from Wynn's larger investigations of pre-Confederation Pictou County and the historical geography of the Maritime provinces, supported by SSHRC, to which MacKinnon contributed as a research assistant while developing his own study of Nova Scotian agriculture. Written by

Wynn, in time provided by a Canada Council Killam Fellowship, this paper draws much from the meticulous work of Bittermann and MacKinnon; it has also been shaped by continuing discussion, among us, about the patterns of rural life in nineteenth- and early twentieth-century Maritime Canada.

1 Lawrence J. Burpee, 'The Golden Age of Nova Scotia,' *Queen's Quarterly* 36 (1929): 380–94, reviewing F.W. Wallace, *In the Wake of the Wind Ships* (Toronto: Musson Book Company 1927), R.C. McKay, *Some Famous Sailing Ships and Their Builder Donald McKay* (New York: Putman 1928), C.H.J. Snider, *Under the Red Jack* (Toronto: Musson Book Company 1928), A. MacMechan, *There Go the Ships* (Toronto: McClelland and Stewart 1928), and W.R. Mackenzie, *Ballads and Sea Songs of Nova Scotia* (Cambridge, Mass.: Harvard University Press 1928)
2 D.C. Harvey, 'The Spacious Days of Nova Scotia,' *Dalhousie Review* 19 (1939): 132–42. For a general overview of economic development in the Maritimes after Confederation see G. Wynn, 'The Maritimes: The Geography of Fragmentation and Underdevelopment,' in L.D. McCann, ed. *Heartland and Hinterland: A Geography of Canada* (Scarborough, Ont.: Prentice Hall 1987), 174–246. For the 1920s see especially E.R. Forbes, *The Maritime Rights Movement: A Study in Canadian Regionalism, 1867–1927* (Montreal: McGill-Queen's University Press 1979), and J.G. Reid, *Six Crucial Decades: Times of Change in the History of the Maritimes* (Halifax: Nimbus Publishing 1987), 161–92.
3 *Report of the Royal Commission on Dominion–Provincial Relations, vol. 1: Canada: 1867–1939* (Ottawa: King's Printer 1940), 24
4 An extensive literature illustrates this point. Clearly it has strong Turnerian overtones; so A.R.M. Lower wrote in 'The Origins of Democracy in Canada,' Canadian Historical Association (CHA), *Report*, 1930, 65–70, that 'society in a new country is almost necessarily egalitarian and democratic.' See also J.L. McDougall, 'The Frontier School and Canadian History,' CHR, *Report*, 1929, 121–5, and M.S. Cross, *The Frontier Thesis and the Canadas: The Debate on the Impact of the Canadian Environment* (Toronto: Copp Clark 1970). Similarly, D.C. Creighton found it 'not unnatural that the domestic life of the inhabitants [of the lower provinces] should be characterized by a hardy, self-reliant simplicity'; *British North America at Confederation* (Ottawa: King's Printer 1939), 27. And A.L. Burt, *A Short History of Canada for Americans* (Minneapolis: University of Minnesota Press 1942), 137–8, concluded that farming in British North America 'was not a business' but an exercise in subsistence.

On another tack, and following the romantic, anti-modernist rhetoric of Nova Scotian tourism in the 1930s which saw Cape Breton, in particular, as a haven of simple, innocent folk, scholars portrayed the region's Scottish settlers as concerned only 'to provide for their own needs' and content to ignore 'appeals to efficiency and progress.' The best example of this ethnic essentialism is N. MacNeil, *The Highland Heart in Nova Scotia* (New York: Charles Scribner's Sons 1948); for the extension of the argument see, for example, R.L. Gentilcore, 'The Agricultural Background of Settlement in Eastern Nova Scotia,' *Annals of the Association of American Geographers* 46 (1956): 378–404. I. Mackay effectively reviews and interprets these developments in 'Tartanism Triumphant: The Construction of Scottishness in Nova Scotia, 1933–1954,' *Acadiensis* 21, 2 (1992): 5–47. See also A. MacNeil, 'A Reconsideration of the State of Agriculture in Eastern Nova Scotia, 1791–1861' (MA thesis, Queen's University 1985), and his 'Cultural Stereotypes and Highland Farming in Eastern Nova Scotia, 1827–1851,' *Histoire sociale/Social History* 19 (1986): 39–56.

Andrew MacPhail's *The Master's Wife* (Toronto: McClelland and Stewart 1977) and the stories of L.M. Montgomery indicate the pervasiveness of such pastoral views. Their echoes persisted well into the 1960s; to take a single, influential example, sociologist S.D. Clark clung to a belief in the fundamental egalitarianism of the Canadian frontier despite his own description of marked differences in status and material circumstances among inhabitants of early Canadian communities. R.C. Helmes-Hayes, 'The Image of Inequality in S.D. Clark's Writings on Pioneer Canadian Society,' *Canadian Journal of Sociology* 13 (1988): 211–33, provides a fuller treatment of this paradox; for examples from Clark see *The Developing Canadian Community* (Toronto: University of Toronto Press 1968), 65 and 78, and *Canadian Society in Historical Perspective* (Toronto: McGraw Hill-Ryerson 1976), 56. Gwendolyn Davies also remarks on this phenomenon in 'The Song Fishermen: A Regional Poetry Celebration,' and 'The "Home Place" in Modern Maritime Literature,' in her *Studies in Maritime Literary History, 1760–1930* (Fredericton: Acadiensis Press 1991), 163–73 and 192–9.

5 W.S. MacNutt, *The Atlantic Provinces: The Emergence of Colonial Society* (Toronto: McClelland and Stewart 1965), 249–50, 267. Recent work has begun to challenge these views: see D.A. McNabb, 'Land and Families in Horton Township, Nova Scotia, 1760–1830' (MA thesis, University of British Columbia 1986), and S.J. Hornsby, *Nineteenth-Century Cape Breton Island* (Montreal: McGill-Queen's University Press 1992).

6 P.H. Johnston, 'In Praise of Husbandry,' *Agricultural History* 2 (1937): 80–95; R.H. Abbott, 'The Agricultural Press Views the Yeoman: 1829–1859,' *Agricultural History* 41 (1968): 35–48; R.C. Loehr, 'Self-Sufficiency on the Farm,' *Agricultural History* 26 (1952): 37–41; B. Moore, *Social Origins of Dictatorship and Democracy: Lord and Peasant in the Making of the Modern World* (Boston: Beacon Press 1966), 491

7 More extended comments on 'The Condition of Nineteenth-Century Rural

History in the Maritimes' can be found in K.R. Bittermann, 'Middle River: The Social Structure of Agriculture in a Nineteenth-Century Cape Breton Community' (MA thesis, University of New Brunswick 1987), 1–40. See also R. MacKinnon, 'The Historical Geography of Agriculture in Nova Scotia, 1851–1951' (PhD thesis, University of British Columbia 1991). The impressive literature on early American agriculture and rural life, much of which is pertinent to understanding the Maritimes, can be approached through J.T. Lemon, 'Agriculture and Society in Early America,' *Agricultural History Review* 35 (1987): 76–94, and through R.B. Sheridan, 'The Domestic Economy,' and J.T. Lemon, 'Spatial Order: Households in Local Communities and Regions,' in J.P. Greene and J.R. Pole, eds., *Colonial British America: Essays in the New History of the Early Modern Era* (Baltimore: Johns Hopkins University Press 1984), 43–85 and 86–122. P. Benes, ed., *The Farm*, Annual Proceedings of the Dublin Seminar for New England Folklife 1986 (Boston: Boston University 1988), contains a useful bibliography of New England farm studies.

8 R. Bittermann, 'The Hierarchy of the Soil: Land and Labour in a Nineteenth Century Cape Breton Community,' *Acadiensis* 18, 1 (autumn 1988): 33–55, deals with these patterns of reinvestment, and makes the point that half the livestock surplus of Middle River in 1860 came from 20 per cent of farms.

9 This theme is implicit in MacNabb, 'Land and Families,' and is also an element in the interpretation offered in G. Wynn, '"A Share of the Necessaries of Life": Remarks on Migration, Development and Dependency in Atlantic Canada,' in B. Fleming, ed., *Beyond Anger and Longing: Community and Development in Atlantic Canada* (Fredericton: Acadiensis Press 1988), 17–52.

QUEBEC AND NATIONALISM

The Defeat of George-Etienne Cartier in Montreal-East in 1872

BRIAN J. YOUNG

(December 1970)
CHR 51, no. 4: 386–406. Excerpt: 386–72, 405–6.

One of Michel Brunet's recurring themes is what he has called 'the Great Compromise of Canadian history.'[1] This was the alliance between the French and English political élites, the Roman Catholic church and the English business leaders of Montreal and Toronto. Formed in 1854, the Great Compromise made Confederation possible and was a dominant factor in Canadian political life until the mid twentieth century. In the Brunet thesis French-Canadian political leaders from Cartier to St. Laurent in concert with church and business leaders forced centralization and unification on to a docile French-Canadian populace.[2]

If this theme of unanimity, conspiracy, and exploitation by Canada's élite is as predominant as Brunet has implied, it should be clearly evident in the career of George-Etienne Cartier. As the heir of Lafontaine and leader of the Bleus, Cartier was the ally of first Hincks and then Macdonald and Galt. His efforts to protect the Protestant minority in Lower Canada, his influence in the Grand Trunk, and his vigorous promotion of Montreal's economic growth brought him the friendship of such English-Canadian élitists as Hugh Allan, William Molson, and C.J. Brydges. With his social conservatism, his preference for the *status quo*, and his support for traditional rural life, Cartier and the Bleus received strong assistance from the church. Confederation, at least initially, was a great victory for Cartier and the forces of the Great Compromise. After 1867 Cartier and his political friends dominated the newly-formed Quebec government, had strong influence in the Macdonald administration, and controlled Quebec patronage and appointments at both levels. Montreal emerged from Confederation with its position as the entrepôt of the St Lawrence system strengthened. As well, French-Canadian national and religious rights were protected in the province of Quebec.

However, by 1872 cracks in the Great Compromise were evident. The breakdown in the alliance is quite apparent by an examintion of Cartier's own riding in the general election of 1872. In 1871 Montreal-East with 46,291 people was the most populous of the city's three ridings. Despite an overall growth of 25 per cent between 1861 and 1871, the riding remained largely Catholic and French-speaking; the number of residents of British extraction declined to 3645 by 1871. Montreal-East was primarily a workingman's riding with a heavy predominance of labourers, clerks, shoemakers, and shipbuilders. The census of 1871 summarized the occupations as commercial, 3209; domestic, 1300; industrial, 7609; professional, 1137. Of the 9019 adult illiterates in Montreal, 4970 lived in Montreal-East.[3]

Cartier's riding, like the rest of the city, was experiencing the tensions of rapid expansion. The city's population grew 56.5 per cent in the decade 1851–61 and another 18.7 per cent from 1961–71. This rapid increase was due to an influx of rural people; in 1872 Montreal was the only area in the province where deaths exceeded births. Housing was poor and the population density almost doubled in twenty years from 11,195 people per square mile in 1851 to 20,800 in 1871.[4] The growing number of displaced rural workers in Montreal-East, the increasing homogeneity of the riding as Catholic and French, the high level of illiteracy, and the industrial and urban problems engendered by these developments posed special difficulties for Cartier and his allies. Not surprisingly in view of his own outlook and commercial connections, Cartier minimized the class and industrial problems of his riding by means of the traditional sources of power: the church, patronage, French-Canadian national societies, the traditional party structure, and the active support of English employers. However, even by 1867 industrial and nationalist tensions in Montreal-East were combining to threaten his position as *le chef.*

...

Apologists for Cartier have described his defeat as a caprice of the popular will. John Boyd, for example, argued that in 1872 Cartier simply reaped the harvest of his years of leadership. Others have emphasized the role of religion. *Le Nouveau Monde,* not surprisingly, explained his defeat as retribution for challenging the spiritual authority of the Bishop of Montreal. In this interpretation, Cartier's failure to disallow the New Brunswick schools legislation was the decisive issue. In John A. Macdonald's opinion Cartier brought about his defeat by 'sheer obstinacy.' He had alienated the British element 'on account of some petty detail of administration' and had mishandled the railway question.[5] Donald Creighton has stressed the role of Allan and the railway issue as 'an apparently irresistible political force directed against Cartier.' Once Allan and Cartier did come to terms, it was too late 'to allay the popular storm.'[6] Finally, it has been argued that Jetté owed his victory primarily to the Institut Canadien and the Rouge remnants. *La Minerve* supported this view in its post-election analysis.

French Canada was under stress in 1872. Having committed themselves to confederation many French Canadians saw the Riel affair and the New Brunswick schools question as disquieting reminders of their minority status. Yet the election was not simply a mandate against confederation. Montreal's social problems, Cartier's struggle with Bourget, the continuing emigration, and the railway question were all election issues that either predated or were peripheral to confederation.

...

Whether or not it was the Bishop of Montreal, the English business community, the liberals, or Cartier himself who was primarily responsible for the defeat, it is clear that the Great Compromise did not exist in any unified sense in 1872. In contrast to Professor Brunet's depiction of the Cartier era as one of unity among the élite, an examination of electoral conditions in Montreal-East shows a riding and a city alive with industrial, religious, and nationalist tensions in which shifting alliances, complex power struggles, and old-fashioned pragmatism seem more characteristic than the monolith of the Great Compromise.

Notes

1 Michel Brunet, 'The French Canadians' Search for a Fatherland,' in Peter Russell, ed., *Nationalism in Canada* (Toronto 1966), p. 51

2 Michel Brunet, *Quebec: Canada Anglais* (Montreal 1968), p. 169
3 *Personal Census: 1861*, 1; *Census of Canada 1870-71*, I, II, and v
4 *Census of Canada 1870-71*, v, 33
5 Quoted in Joseph Pope, *Memoirs of the Right Honourable Sir John Alexander Macdonald, First Prime Minister of the Dominion of Canada* (Ottawa 1894), pp. 155-6
6 *John A. Macdonald: The Old Chieftain* (Toronto 1955), pp. 131, 142

Religion and French-Canadian Mores in the Early Nineteenth Century

JEAN-PIERRE WALLOT

(March 1971)
CHR 52, no. 1: 51-90. Excerpt: 51-2, 77, 80-1, 90.

A devout, obedient, pastoral, and God-fearing people, entrenched behind parish and family life, endowed with the noble mission of permeating materialistic Anglo-Saxon America with spiritual values; or a traditional, semi-feudal, ignorant, priest-ridden, and backward people, impervious to change and sealed to the outside world for two centuries until a grudging acceptance of industrialization unleashed the 'Quiet Revolution.' Thus, in the one guise or the other, emerges French Canada through much of our historiography.[1] Both are gross distortions which stem partly from the scarcity of scholarly monographs based on painstaking and little-rewarding research, partly from their usefulness as a mythical rationalization of the Canadian duality or as a self-righteous example of the sociological model of the 'folk-society.' Recent studies, however, have revealed new material and fewer clichés about the French-Canadians' outlook on life and religion, about their social classes and values, about the impact of the Atlantic world on them in the realms of politics, commerce, and ideas, about short-term and long-range changes in their society, under the French and British regimes.

...

The Canadian faithful did not live up to the hallowed myth which was later painted in pious colours by folkloric pride and religious historians. On the whole, one can detect a great continuity with the French regime.[2] In any event, at the beginning of the nineteenth century, the *Canadiens* were religious to the extent that they partook of a general

Christian conception of man's destiny, and that they usually went to church on Sundays, when there was a priest: the latter was not only a religious, but a social event, an occasion to meet neighbours, discuss crops and politics. A systematic perusal of travellers' accounts, of the clerical correspondence, and of numerous other sources reveals that French Canadians were as much superstitious as pious. Was not the bishop forced to condemn publicly so-called healers?[3] The Canadian men, recorded John Lambert, were less religious than women and did not kneel any more at the foot of crosses along the roads.[4] Like peasants elsewhere, the habitants were hard-hearted, disobedient, and independent, very close with their cash as far as religion was concerned, always trying to evade, in an incredible number of ways, the payment of the tithes and necessary repairs to the churches or prebyteries.[5] Most of the time, the priests had to bestow many gifts to their parishes, while the ungrateful habitants, if and when they paid their tithes, brought their worst wheat.[6] To that one must add secular and religious ignorance, although the church invested a lot of energy in the editing of thousands of books of prayers and catechisms.[7]

...

The picture comes more clearly into focus by adding the French Canadians' undeniable propensity for merriment, drinking, dancing, and the rest,[8] the result partly of their French heredity, partly of their relative affluence and of the long inactive winter months,[9] partly of the economic and social changes.[10] It may also be sharpened by a greater awareness among priests, capitalists, and political leaders of the ills of the times. The French Canadians who had sojourned in the western territories seemed the wildest: they brought debauchery to the parishes where they chose to settle down.[11] Naturally, there were good, pious, and exemplary families. But the point is they did not seem to be very numerous. On the contrary, the bishop was constantly admonishing, threatening, or punishing parishes (by recalling the priests) for not providing enough for the subsistence and lodging of their curés; for staging 'horrible' charivaris and orgies, particularly on the occasion of parish celebrations in honour of their patron saint – another occasion of feasting.[12] Some habitants seemed to be professional patron saint or marriage celebrators, going merrily from one parish to another in a seemingly endless spree, crashing – 'en survenants' – local ceremonies and parties, and debauching the local population. Finally, the bishop had to suppress most religious holidays, to the great satisfaction of the Protestant British merchants who were horrified (and perhaps a little bit jealous) at such a loss of time in merriment instead of hard work.[13] The Bishop's journal of pastoral visits mournfully lists the main sins among the population: irreligion, leaving the church during sermons, drunkenness, public disorders and scandals, dances, adultery, incest, fornication.[14]

...

Conclusion

We may safely conclude that at the turn of the nineteenth century, the Catholic Church was *not* a strong, prosperous, and triumphant institution at the head of a quasi-theocratic society; the clergy was *not* very influential or dominant, except in strict matters of faith and dogma, when and if they arose; the faithful were *not* exceptionally religious and virtuous. The church was fighting hard simply to subsist outside the control of the state and not to let the countryside become dechristianized. It could not rely upon the aristocratic or the professional classes. The other layers in society were more or less indifferent to its plight, if they even knew anything about it.[15] Attendance at mass on Sundays and holidays was generally high among the people, when they had a church and a priest not too far away. Their view of life and death was Christian. But the quality of their religious life, in fact their whole moral outlook and social manners, appear no more than normal (at best) in a society of farmers and labourers of some affluence and little education[16] in a time of economic restructuring and social change ...

Notes

Except for the notes, this article comprises the text of the Gray Lecture given at the University of Toronto on 3 April 1970, its scope limited by the restrictive format of a single lecture. The main conclusions derive from research in various collections of documents held in the Public Archives of Canada [PAC], the Archives de l'Archevêché de Québec [AAQ], the Archives de la province de Québec [AAQ], and the Quebec Diocesan Archives [QDA]. Although the illustrative documentation presented here concentrates on the 1800s, the main points are generally valid for the period 1791–1815. An overview of the history of the Catholic church and of its institutional evolution, after 1760, may be reaped from the following studies: L. Lemieux, *L'Establissement de la première province ecclésiastique au Canada 1783–1844* [*L'Establissement*] (Montreal 1968); A. Gosselin, *L'Eglise du Canada après la Conquête, 1760–1789* (2 vols., Quebec 1916–17); J.S. Moir, ed., *Church and State in Canada 1627–1867* (Toronto 1967); Mgr. Têtu and C.-O. Gagnon, eds., *Mandements, lettres pastorales et circulaires des évêques de Québec*

[*Mandements*] (6 vols., Quebec 1887–90; P. Hurtubise, 'Chronique d'histoire religieuse,' *Eglise de Théologie*, I, 1970, 395–402. For summaries of the bishops' correspondence during the years 1791–1815, see the *Rapports de l'Archiviste de la province de Québec* [RAPQ] (Quebec 1927–8, 1928–9, 1930–1, 1932–3).

1 For better examples of these contradictory views, see L. Groulx, *Histoire du Canada français depuis la découverte* [*Histoire*] (4 vols., Montreal 1950–2), and D.G. Creighton, *Dominion of the North: A History of Canada* (Boston 1944).
2 See, in particular, W.J. Eccles, *The Canadian Frontier, 1534–1760* (New York 1969), chap. 5.
3 Eg, Mgr Plessis's mandement to the parish St-Pierre, Ile d'Orléans, 17 March 1808, APQ, gr.coll., livres de mandements, par. St-Pierre. On superstition, see also Lambert, *Travels*, I, 179, passim; *Mandements*, II, 457–8, passim.
4 Lambert, *Travels*, I, II ff, 179; II, 12. 'They are religious from education and habit, more than from principle. They observe its ... formalities, not because they are necessary to their salvation, but because it gratifies their vanity and superstition' (ibid., I, 154).
5 See note 115. '... they [French Canadians] love money ...' (ibid., 155)
6 ... le blé de dîme ... est généralement le plus mauvais ...' (Letter from Rev. Clément, in *Letters from the Curates of the Respective Parishes of Lower-Canada* ... ([Quebec 1823], 85–6). More often than not, the faithful relied on the priests' generosity to get the necessary sacred vases, ornaments, candeliers, for their churches. Sometimes, they even tried to dump on their curé the burden of the cost of repairs to the church or the presbytery (e.g., APQ, pet.coll., Rev. Chouinard's Papers, notes dated 23 Dec. 1798 and 1 Nov. 1799). In the course of many years, the Rev. Panet endowed the vestry of Lislet with more than 3000 french livres in gifts of all kinds. But he was accused of being rich and hiding his money! (APQ, gr.coll., Rev. J. Panet's Papers). See also note 8.
7 From 1765 to 1791, the church had 19,000 catechisms printed (M. Tremaine, *A Bibliography of Canadian Imprints* [Toronto 1952], nos 59, 76, 255, 373 A and B, 700, 701). By 1810, 40,000 catechisms had been published since 1760 (Hare and Wallot, *Imprimés*, nos 54, 134, 135, 136, 192, and 244). Unless the printers and the church deliberately set out to lose money, one must conclude that the French Canadians' ignorance, at that time, has been exaggerated by the historiography (J. Hare, 'Les imprimés, le vocabulaire et la diffusion des idées,' paper presented to the first colloquium of GRISCAF, Montreal, September 1969, to be published in *Annales historiques de la Révolution française*). The bishop admitted that children sometimes learned the words without understanding their meaning: '... néanmoins je ne crois pas

qu'on puisse faire un catéchisme assez simple, pour que les enfants l'entendent sans explication' (Mgr Panet to Mgr Plessis, Rivière Ouelle, 17 May 1813, AAQ, cartable: évêques de Québec, 4: 40).

8 'They are fond of dancing and entertainments, at particular seasons and festivals, on which occasions, they eat, drink, and dance in constant sucession. When their long fast in Lent is concluded, they have their 'jours gras,' or days of feasting. Then it is that every production of their farm is presented for the gratification of their appetites; immense turkey-pies; huge joints of pork, beef, and mutton; spacious tureens of soup, or thick-milk; besides fish, fowl, and a plentiful supply of fruit-pies decorate the board. Perhaps fifty or a hundred sit down to dinner; rum is drank by the half-pint; often without water; the tables groan with their load, and the room resounds with jollity and merriment. No sooner, however, does the clash of the knives and forks cease, than the violin strikes up, and the dances commence ... to the discordant scrapings of a couple of vile fidlers ...' (Lambert, *Travels*, I, 174–5; also Gray, *Letters*, pp. 260 ff).

9 'They possess every necessary of life in abundance, and, when inclined, may enjoy many of its luxuries. They have no taxes to pay ...' (Lambert, *Travels*, I, 180, 154–5, 282; Gray, *Letters*, pp. 249 ff, 321–2).

10 On economic and social change, see D.G. Creighton, *The Empire of the St. Lawrence* (2nd ed., Toronto 1956), chaps. V, VI, and VII; F. Ouellet, *Histoire économique et sociale du Québec, 1760–1850* (Montreal 1966), chaps. VI, VII, and VIII; G. Paquet and J.-P. Wallot, 'La restructuration de l'économie et de la société canadienne au tournant du XIXe siècle: une hypothèse,' paper for the Vth International Congress of Economic History (Leningrad, August 1970), mimeo, 100 pages, to be published; also Ossenberg, 'The Conquest Revisited,' p. 206 ff.

11 Ossenberg, 'The Conquest Revisited,' p. 207; Gray, *Letters*, p. 219; Observations on Canada, c. 1800, 413

12 See notes 115 and 116; AAQ, registre des lettres, 6: 2, 41, 65, 69; *Mandements*, III, 39, 55, 73, 90; Lambert, *Travels*, I, 322. Plessis has learned with 'douleur' that the habitants of Laprairie had staged an unprecedented 'affreux et horrible charivari ... soit pour la duré, soit pour les injures, obscénités, impiétés de toute espèce ... les travestissements, mascarades, profanations des cérémonies, ornements et chants funèbres de l'Eglise ...' The Bishop compared them with the Israelites 'devenus tout à coup idolâtres et se livrant à des danses et à des jeux insensés autour d'une veau d'or.' Had not God punished them by exterminating 23,000 of those sinners 'le même jour'! The parishioners would have to make public penance (Plessis's mandement to the habitants of La Prairie-de-la-Magdeleine, Quebec, 3 Dec. 1807, AAQ, registre G, 125r; also ibid., 127r).

13 In the countryside, particularly in summer, religious holidays had become 'pour la plupart, des jours de débauche et de licence.' They were suppressed little by little 'pour l'honneur de la religion' and were finally unified in a single day by Mgr Plessis (Mgr Plessis to Rev. Boiret, Maskinongé, 4 July 1807, AAQ, registre des lettres, 4: 248; suppression of the feast of St Joachim, 11 July 1804, account books of Pointe-Claire; Plessis's mandement of 10 Dec. 1810 suppressing patron saints' holidays, APQ, gr.coll., Fréchet-Desaultels Papers; *Mandements*, III, 42; AAQ, registre G, 167v.; Lambert, *Travels*, I, 322–3; also note 123).

14 AAQ, cahiers des visites pastorales, e.g., years 1806, 1809, 1811

15 '... depuis la Conquête jusque vers 1840, elle [the Catholic Church] avait été dépourvue de tout, condamnée à la stagnation, humiliée sans cesse par le Gouvernement; et l'on oublie qu'a certains moments elle a été sérieusement menacée dans son existence même' (Trudel, 'La Servitude,' p. 64).

16 Lambert. *Travels*, I, 180 ff; Gray, *Letters*, p. 321

[For reference]

115 E.g., AAQ, registre G, 139r, 140r, 141r, 143r, 147v, 166r, 167v, 169r, 181r, 182r, 195r; *Mandements*, II, 523 ff. 'Les services que vous avez rendus à la paroisse de St-Antoine pendant plus de 50 ans, ne devraient pas vous attirer tant de tracasseries pour le tiers des dîmes. Je vous exhorte à les regarder comme une part de la croix de Jésus-Christ ...' (Mgr Hubert to Rev. Noël, 3 Aug. 1792, AAQ, copies de lettres, 5: 143).

116 Rev. Beaumont narrowly missed being the victim of 'la haine et la vengeance de quelques *malheureux*, de quelques *scélérats* à qui il n'est devenu odieux que par son zèle à s'élever contre les désordres dont ils sont les auteurs' (Mgr Denaut to Mgr Hubert, Longueuil, 12 Oct. 1796, AAQ, copies de lettres, 5: 479–80).

The Agricultural Crisis in Lower Canada, 1802–12: A Review of a Controversy

T.J.A. LEGOFF

(March 1974)
CHR 55, no. 1: 1–31. Excerpt: 1–2, 30–1.

Historians for some time now have been aware that basic changes were taking place in the economy of Lower Canada in the first two decades of the nineteenth century. These changes in one way or another drastically reshaped a society which had up to then retained most of the economic structure of the pre-Conquest period. They are considered to have played a significant part in setting off and keeping alive the political conflicts which developed during these years, in which a new French-Canadian professional group, backed by the bulk of the Canadiens, fought for power against the alliance of English merchants and placemen in a struggle which finally exploded in the 1837–8 rising and the troubles of the 1840s. These economic transformations can be grouped under three heads. One is the decline of the northwest fur trade through Montreal, the St Lawrence and the Great Lakes system. Another is the growth of the timber trade after 1807, when Great Britain, finding difficulty in obtaining timber from the Baltic because of Napoleon's Continental System, turned to Canada for its ship and other timber. Finally, there was the opening of the British market to Canadian and North American agricultural produce after the British entry into war with France in 1793.[1] Yet if historians agree that these were the principal transformations in the Lower Canadian economy, they are far from sure what the impact was of each of these changes.

This is especially true of the third phenomenon mentioned above: the change in the market for agricultural produce. In recent years a rather bitter polemic has been carried on by Fernand Ouellet on the one hand and by Gilles Paquet and J.P. Wallot on the other over what happened to Lower Canadian agriculture at the turn of the century. Unfortunately, the debate over this question has been carried on in a rather confused fashion. Moreover, both parties to the discussion clearly believe that the answer to the question 'What happened to Lower Canadian agriculture between 1800 and 1820?' has a larger political significance. This was not initially clear when Paquet and Wallot launched an attack on Ouellet's *Histoire économique et sociale du Québec* in 1967[2] but it has been made plain in a more recent article.[3] As for Ouellet, there was never any question that he saw more than purely economic consequences in the agricultural difficulties of Lower Canada at the turn of the century. At this time, he held, French-Canadian agriculture began a long decline which, if its effect became more intense in the 1820s and 1830s, nevertheless had begun as early as 1803. It was then that Lower Canadian agriculture failed to modernize and compete on international markets. This failure of the only sector of the economy in the hands of the French Canadians to grow and expand coincided with the rise of the first French-Canadian nationalism, born of economic and cultural despair, but dressed up by the French-Canadian professional bourgeoisie in the swaddling clothes of a liberal ideology which really masked a conservative social ideal.[4] By taking issue with Ouellet's view of French-Canadian agriculture, Paquet and Wallot clearly intended to lay part of the groundwork for a larger interpretation of the political conflicts of the period.[5] ...

In the meantime, we can only go on the material available to us, and it ought to be evident that many of the figures and models advanced in this article are rather artificial, and it would be unwise to put more weight on them than they will bear. Taken at their lowest, they are merely an attempt, in a fairly rough-and-ready fashion, to test what the existing data produced by the two sides in this controversy can tell us. They do seem to prove that, if there may not have been a thoroughgoing disaster in Lower Canadian agriculture after 1802, there was certainly no boom either. After 1802 the agricultural sector was less and less able to meet internal demand as population rose faster than production. It was this overall population growth, rather than a shift of the labour force away from the agricultural sector, which drove up prices, making exports less possible. Insofar as Lower Canada did continue to export after 1802, it seems that this was because the habitants cut back on their consumption. It would appear at least plausible that the farmers fell back on the more productive but much less remunerative lesser grains to feed themselves and their animals, and ultimately on potatoes and on an increase in livestock. But even such cutbacks could not assure that grain would be available on domestic markets at the price levels of former days.

...

What this limited analysis means for the larger question of the economic and social background to the first French-Canadian nationalism is not completely clear. No doubt it is difficult to associate the long-term maturing of an ideology and class-consciousness with a short period of economic history, and it is probably true, as Paquet and Wallot point out, that manifestations of national or political consciousness among the French majority had already occurred in Lower Canada before the 1790s; perhaps it is too restrictive to make this nationalism the child of economic distress. At the same time, it is hard to see how the interpretation can be reversed and how this nationalism can be made a by-product of agricultural prosperity, especially if there was no such prosperity ...

Notes

1 The classic treatments are D.G. Creighton, *The Commercial Empire of the St. Lawrence, 1760–1850* (Toronto 1937), and F. Ouellet, *Histoire économique et sociale du Québec 1790–1850* (Montreal/Paris 1966).

2 G. Paquet and J.-P. Wallot, 'Aperçu sur le commerce international et les prix domestiques dans le Bas-Canada (1793–1812),' *Revue d'histoire de l'Amérique française (RHAF)*, XXI, 1967, 447–73.
3 G. Paquet and J.-P. Wallot, 'Crise agricole et tensions socio-ethniques dans le Bas-Canada, 1802–1812; éléments pour un ré-interprétation, *RHAF*, XXVI, 1972, 185–237.
4 Ouellet, *Histoire économique*, 169–74, 180–8, 196–212.
5 Paquet and Wallot, 'Crise agricole,' 234–7.

Revisionism and the Search for a Normal Society: A Critique of Recent Quebec Historical Writing

RONALD RUDIN

(March 1992)
CHR 73, no. 1: 30–61. Excerpt: 30–3, 51–2, 55–6, 59–60.

Over the past thirty years most political initiatives from Quebec have had the effect of accentuating the distinctiveness of the province. Focusing largely upon linguistic and constitutional issues, Quebec was proclaimed to have been a 'province pas comme les autres,' or more recently a 'distinct society.' Curiously, at the same time that its politicians were seeking recognition of some sort of special status, the work of Quebec's historians was indicating that this was in various ways a 'normal' society whose past could largely be understood in the context of such processes as urbanization and industrialization that were common to most of the Western world. In the historians' conception, linguistic or cultural concerns took a back seat to an emphasis on Quebec's adherence to a general pattern of economic and social development that barely differed from that followed by other Western societies. While these two ways of looking at Quebec might appear at first glance to be at odds with one another, they were in fact promoted by Quebeckers who came out of very similar backgrounds and who shared a certain common perspective.

The new political masters of the post-Duplessis era were largely cut from the same cloth as the young historians who were coming to fill the recently created posts in Quebec's expanding universities. Both groups were made up of highly educated professionals who had been either trained outside Quebec or, at the very least, exposed to ways of approaching issues that were unknown to their predecessors. The technocrats who came to run the government had been well instructed to adhere to the model of the welfare state. They worked to make Quebec more like the rest of the Western world by pushing the Catholic church aside and by providing the services required by a modern industrial society. In practical terms, however, this 'normalization' of Quebec could not be achieved within the Canadian political system as constituted at the start of the 1960s. Accordingly, Quebeckers were forced to seek a distinctive place within the federation in order to achieve the identification with the surrounding world they so badly desired; they wanted no more for Quebec than the institutions of a 'normal' society, but circumstances forced them to play upon Quebec's distinctiveness to achieve that end.

The bright, young Quebeckers of the 1960s who chose to become historians were similarly exposed to a way of thinking that led them to construct a Quebec, albeit a Quebec in the past, that also looked very much like the rest of the Western world. While the technocrats were being exposed to Keynes, the historians were absorbing the materialist and structuralist preconceptions of the modern social sciences. Some were Marxist, some were influenced by the *Annales* school, and still others were steeped in the quantitative methods that had been refined in the United States. All of them, however, accepted the premise that there were certain paths that all societies followed and that material factors were the motor behind social change. There was little room in this conception for forces such as Catholicism, which could only serve to make Quebec stand out within the North American context. As Gérard Bouchard has put it, Quebec was to be shown to operate 'sur l'heure améri-caine et occidentale. Le Québec est donc une société industrielle, capitaliste et libérale, aussi développé, aussi moderne que les autres.'[1]

This drive for normalcy ultimately pushed the technocrats to toy with notions of special status, but for the historians, freed of such practical political concerns, it simply led to a rejection of a model of Quebec history that had dominated since the middle of the nineteenth century. This model, held by such politically diverse historians as François-Xavier Garneau in the last century, Abbé Groulx in the early twentieth century, and Michel Brunet and Fernand Ouellet in the decades following the Second World War, asserted Quebec's distinctiveness. More specifically, these historians stressed the manner in which Quebec's evolution had been governed by the distinctive values that its people (more specifically its French-speaking people) had held.

...

Historians from Garneau to Ouellet dwelt upon the values of Quebeckers, in the process pushing aside the role of structural factors. By the 1970s, however, a new generation, thoroughly convinced of the primacy of economic forces, was beginning to leave its mark. These historians, hereafter referred to as revisionists, included such individuals as Paul-André Linteau, Jean-Claude Robert, Jacques Rouillard, and Normand Séguin; from the English side of the fence one might also include such historians as Brian Young and Allan Greer, who easily integrated into the intellectual milieu of the revisionists given their capacity to work in French (which earlier English-speaking historians of Quebec did not always have) and their own predisposition to focus on structural factors.

These historians, French- and English-speakers alike, were largely born in the late 1940s and reached university in the late 1960s, before taking up teaching positions in the following decade.[2] In general terms, they rejected the guiding role of the church, the importance of ethnic conflict, and the emphasis upon rural values that had long dominated the literature. They even dispensed with the Conquest as the pivotal event in Quebec history, observing that most political, economic, and social structures were unaffected by what some earlier historians had interpreted as a cataclysm. Freed of their predecessors' need to explain the significance of the Conquest, these revisionists tended to focus on the nineteenth and twentieth centuries to find a Quebec that was urbanizing, industrializing, and profoundly divided by class conflicts as were most other Western societies of the time. As Linteau put it, 'Les gens de ma génération se sont beaucoup préoccupés d'étudier les structures; leur histoire a fait une plus large place aux grands schemas d'interprétation et aux perspectives théoriques.'[3]

It is difficult to be overly critical of this new approach, particularly given the poverty of the one that had dominated for so long and which had focused on the uniqueness of the Quebec experience. Indeed, most reviews of recent Quebec historiography (including two by this author[4]) have generally praised the thrust of revisionism. It was clearly a distortion to maintain that Quebec was a backward, priest-ridden society in which the state did little, French-speaking businessmen were all but non-existent, and ethnic and liguistic battles prevailed to the virtual exclusion of class conflict. Nevertheless, it now seems reasonable to ask whether the pendulum has swung too far in the other direction. In trying to make Quebec seem like other Western societies, have the revisionists placed too much emphasis on structural factors to the exclusion of values that cannot always be linked easily to the prevailing economic and social circumstances?

...

Role of the State

In addition to dismissing the significance of *agriculturalisme* and *messianisme*, revisionist historians have also rejected the importance of Michel Brunet's third 'pensée dominante,' *anti-étatisme*. To Brunet and most other historians writing up to the 1960s, there was something in the French-Canadian psyche that made them ill-disposed towards using the state as a tool for the development of the province. In part this was the legacy of an all-powerful church that preached against the creation of a strong state that might invade its domain. At the same time, there was allegedly a distrust of the state that emerged following the Conquest, since government was somehow tainted as an alien institution.

With the building up of the infrastructure of the Quebec state in the 1960s and 1970s, however, there was tangible evidence that Quebeckers, at least in the late twentieth century, were in the mainstream of Western developments; and revisionist historians looked to the past to find that the Quiet Revolution simply built on an enthusiasm for the role of the state that was always present, if not always easily perceived. Historians such as Marcel Hamelin and Brian Young pointed to the involvement of the Quebec government in various economic ventures in the early years after Confederation, while Paul-André Linteau and the current author discussed the role of municipal governments in building up the local economic base.[5] The cumulative impact of these works was to suggest that government in Quebec was comparable to that elsewhere in Canada. Indeed, Linteau, Durocher, and Robert asserted that the development of the state prior to the 1960s was only impeded by a certain 'insuffisance des ressources financières.'[6] This assertion is supported by the fact that throughout the twentieth century there was scarcely any difference between Canada's two most populous provinces in terms of the percentage of provincial wealth committed to the financing of provincial and municipal government.[7] ...

... In Ireland, as in Quebec, the writing of history was dominated by a nationalist interpretation until well into the twentieth century.[8] ...

In opposition to this traditional historiography, a revisionist alternative emerged in Ireland that was first visible in the 1930s, but which really gained momentum in the 1960s and 1970s as the techniques of the social sciences were brought to bear upon issues that had been discussed for centuries. The revisionists distinguished themselves by de-emphasizing Irish–English conflict in general and political issues in particular, to focus upon the role of larger market forces ...

As was the case in Quebec, both the bureaucrats who went to Dublin and the historians who went to the universities shared an interest in making Ireland appear much like other Western states ... However, there is some evidence of the emergence in Irish historiography of a post-revisionist school of thought capable of melding the traditional and revisionist points of view ...

Revisionists in Quebec have appeared reluctant to admit to the unique aspects of the province's past that might conflict with its newfound image as a modern, vibrant, pluralistic society. Since the start of the Quiet Revolution, the Catholic church has been pushed aside, the Quebec state has become a force to be reckoned with, French-speaking entrepreneurs have built empires that extend well beyond Canada, and some efforts have been made to integrate Quebeckers, regardless of their ethnic, linguistic, or religious backgrounds, into public institutions that had previously been open only to French-speaking Catholics. These various developments placed Quebec in the mainstream of the Western experience. In such an environment, it was only natural for historians to emphasize those aspects of the past that similarly stressed the identification of Quebec with the larger world. It would have been illogical, for instance, for Quebec historians to have dwelt upon a past that was marked by the power of the clergy and the slowness of urbanization at the same time that Quebeckers were increasingly viewing themselves as secular and modern. Similarly, an emphasis on conflict between the French-speaking majority and the various ethnic and linguistic minorities would have clashed with the new self-image of Quebeckers as a people open to outsiders.

Quebec historians need to be less reluctant to face up to aspects of the past that might not fit particularly well with the current image of French-speakers, and the Irish case suggests that some change may be in the offing. Revisionism, the Irish experience, coincided with the concern of the Irish to project an image both to themselves and to others as a people capable of managing their own affairs. Post-revisionism has now begun to emerge out of a sense of self-confidence that has allowed the Irish to explore issues that were earlier perceived as too sensitive. In Quebec, revisionism similarly emerged with the Quiet Revolution and the effort on the part of historians to produce a self-image that was appropriate for a people who were trying to convince both themselves and others that they were able to make it in the world.

In the post–Meech Lake environment of the early 1990s, Quebeckers in general and Quebec historians in particular might be prepared to face up to aspects of their past that were heretofore denied ...

Notes

This article would not have been possible without the financial assistance of the Social Sciences and Humanities Research Council and the comments of the *CHR* readers and of my colleagues Graham Carr, Daniel Salée, and Robert Tittler.

1 Gérard Bouchard, 'Sur les mutations de l'historiographie québécoise: les chemins de la maturité,' in Fernand Dumont, éd, *La société québécoise après 30 ans de changements* (Quebec 1990), 262
2 Paul-André Linteau, 'La nouvelle histoire du Québec vue de l'intérieur,' *Liberté* 35 (1983): 35
3 Ibid., 46
4 Ronald Rudin, 'History from Quebec, 1981,' *Canadian Historical Review* 63 (1982): 34–45; 'Recent Trends in Quebec Historiography,' *Queen's Quarterly* 92 (1985): 80–93
5 Marcel Hamelin, *Les premières années du parlementarisme québécois* (Quebec 1974); Brian Young, *Promoters and Politicians* (Toronto 1978); [Paul-André Linteau, *Maisonneuve ou Comment les promoteurs fabriquent un ville* (Montréal: Boréal express, 1981); published in English as *The Promoter's City: Building the Industrial Town of Maisonneuve, 1883–1918*, trans. Robert Chodos (Toronto: J. Lorimer, 1985]); Ronald Rudin, 'Boosting the French Canadian Town,' *Urban History Review*, 1982: 1–10
6 [Paul-André Linteau, René Durocher, and Jean-Claude Robert, *Histoire du Québec contemporain*, 2nd ed. (Montréal, 1989)], II, 637. Such a point of view is also advanced by [Terry Copp, *Anatomy of Poverty: The Condition of the Working Class in Montreal* (Toronto: McClelland and Stewart, 1974)], when he suggests

that only financial difficulties prevented Quebec governments from dealing with the problems raised by urban life.
7 In this regard see James Iain Gow, *Histoire de l'administration publique québécoise, 1867–1970* (Montreal 1986).
8 Since this is essentially an article on Quebec historiography, the comments regarding the Irish situation are brief and hardly amount to a thorough discussion of recent trends in Irish historiography.

CLASS CONSCIOUSNESS

Aid to the Civil Power:
The Canadian Militia in Support of Social Order, 1867–1914

DESMOND MORTON

(December 1970)
CHR 51, no. 4: 407–25. Excerpt: 407–10, 422–5.

Throughout the nineteenth century, Canadian militia was regularly called into service to meet threats to public order. In the absence of effective local or provincial police forces, the militia was frequently the only available support for a magistrate confronted by rioting Orangemen or defiant strikers. Officially created for the more glorious responsibility of national defence, the Canadian militia found a much more regular employment as an auxiliary police.

...

In the decades after Confederation, there were many calls on the Canadian troops. In the records of the Department of National Defence there is a list of forty-eight separate occasions between 1876 and 1914 when militia were called to the aid of the civil power.[1] Included in the list are five occasions when troops were called out to prevent Orange–Catholic riots and thirty-three different interventions in strikes. On two occasions, militiamen were summoned to prevent illegal prize-fights and at St Andrews, New Brunswick in 1879, troops were needed to guard a hanging. Called on in 1909 to justify the existence of the national force, Laurier's minister of militia, Sir Frederick Borden, claimed that: 'The principal object is perhaps the upholding of the Civil power in the different parts of the Dominion.'[2]

The frequent service of the militia against disturbers of the peace, real or alleged, provides a perspective for a relatively unconsidered aspect of Canadian history, the problem of social order and its defence. How was the militia called into service? How did it function? How was its role regarded by the rest of Canada and by the troops themselves?

Although militiamen were used repeatedly in a police role in the years before Confederation, successive governments in Canada were also able to rely on regular troops from the British garrison to cope with civil disturbances of any magnitude. The withdrawal of British troops from central Canada between 1869 and 1871 left the dominion largely on its own. Apart from a small British garrison at Halifax, the ultimate defence of the government was reduced to the volunteer militia acting under the Militia Act of 1869. Under Section 27 of the Act, when the senior local militia officer received a requisition in writing from the 'Mayor, Warden, or other Head of the Municipality in which such riot takes place, or by any two Magistrates therein ...' he was obliged to call out as many men as he thought necessary to deal with the trouble. Officers and men were committed to obey the summons, and the Act provided relatively stiff penalties for those who failed to appear: a fine of forty dollars for officers and twenty dollars for men in the ranks. This was double the penalty for 'insolent or disorderly behaviour' to a superior officer and four times the fine for illegal absence from an ordinary parade.

The provisions of the Militia Act were amplified by the *Regulations and Orders for the Militia*. These warned militia officers that they had no discretion about providing aid and directed that militia being sent to support the civil power 'must invariably have the requisite quantity of ammunition served out to them before going on duty.' The most detailed instructions governed the circumstances when troops might have to open fire on a crowd. Officers commanding were to 'take the most effectual means, in conjunction with the magistrates under whose orders they may be placed,' to warn any hostile crowd that their men, if ordered to fire, would shoot to kill. 'It is to be observed,' the *Regulations* gently noted, 'that to fire over the heads of a crowd engaged in an illegal pursuit would have the effect of favouring the most daring and the guilty, and might have the effect of sacrificing the less daring and even the innocent.'[4]

Although the Act and the *Regulations* compelled the militia to turn out, the burden of paying the full cost of the troops was left to the requisitioning municipality. It was the personal responsibility of the commanding officer of the militia to collect the money, if necessary taking the municipality to court. No other aspect of the 1868 Militia Act was to cause as much complaint or as prolonged parliamentary discussion. Refusals to pay were common. In the bitter circumstances of a riot or strike, municipal councils and magistrates were often at loggerheads. In large areas of Canada, there were no municipalities to sue.[5] On occasion, partisan considerations affected both the decision to call out troops and to pay for them. In 1872 militia had been summoned to keep order during Sir George-Etienne Cartier's election campaign in Montreal East. Three years later, the men were still waiting for their pay. The Montreal city council insisted that there had been no breach of the peace and no proper authority for the militia to be ordered out.[6] In 1878 the General Officer Commanding the Militia reported that militia sent to a Cape Breton coal strike had lost patience after two years and were planning to sue their captain for their overdue pay.[7] In 1882 militia were again called to the Cape Breton mines and again had a long wait for their money. The elderly staff officer who had been suing on their behalf died in the middle of the case.[8] Perhaps recognizing that it had pressed the loyalty of its volunteers to the limit, in 1886 the federal government grudgingly paid $1472 to the troops called out in Nova Scotia four years before.

It was Canada's federal structure which ostensibly made any remedy of the situation so difficult. As with many other sections of the Militia Act, provision for aid of the civil power had been transferred whole from the statutes of the old province of Canada. However, as the minister responsible, Sir George-Etienne Cartier, must have realized, the new constitution inserted some serious ambiguities. Although the dominion government was responsible for the organization and discipline of the militia, both municipal institutions and the maintenance of order were under provincial jurisdiction. That meant that the militia department had no direct means of enforcing payment from local authorities. In 1883, after years of experience and pressure from politically influential militia officers, the government offered a tiny concession. Henceforth, pay, allowances, and transportation expenses might be advanced on the authority of the governor-in-council but this in no way relieved the municipality of its liability – or the militia officer of his responsibility for collecting the money.[10] Until 1904, when the Department of Militia and

Defence finally assumed responsibility for any litigation, the commanding officer himself had to retain counsel, deposit fees, and, after much time and effort, await a judgment. Since technicalities which mattered little at a moment of crisis could bulk very large in judicial retrospect, there was every possibility that the officer would leave the court, as one critic of the system observed, 'a sadder but wiser man.'[11]

One assumed benefit of placing the full cost on the municipality was that it would discourage frivolous appeals for assistance and that local councils would not regard the militia as a cheap alternative to organizing their own police. In fact, the safeguard was illusory. With militia privates entitled to a pay of only fifty cents a day and their subsistence, it was cheaper to obtain troops than to hire special constables, and the prestige of the militia uniform was much greater. In 1890, when a strike occurred at the Dunsmuir mines at Wellington on Vancouver Island, the company persuaded magistrates at Victoria, eighty miles away, to requisition troops ...

In 1904 the Militia Act was subjected to its first major revision since 1883. At last the government accepted responsibility for recovering the cost of aid to the civil power from the municipalities ...

The Militia Act of 1904 established that henceforth a municipality which requested troops would have to put down a substantial deposit and that the balance owing would be paid directly to the crown ... From 1895 to 1904 militia were called out eleven times, for a total period of seventy-one days. From 1905 to 1914 there were seventeen requisitions, for a total of 1232 days.[12]

There is no mystery in the change. Canada was embarked on her own era of labour strife. Almost every instance of aid to the civil power involved a strike. Almost invariably the troops were needed to protect non-strikers or imported strikebreakers from those who had stopped work ...

Some important questions remain. In the face of legal and financial disincentives, even the opposition of their own employers, why were militiamen so apparently willing to serve? Some parts of the answer cannot yet be given. There is potentially interesting research to be done in discovering the social composition of the Canadian militia, perhaps through attestation records ...

In the postwar years aid to the civil power remained a military responsibility, but even in an era of unrest and change the occasions for military intervention grew fewer ...

Normally muffled in the national rhetoric, the reality of class conflict in Canadian society emerges from the study of aid to the civil power.

'Remember that you are not going there to fight unions,' Col. W.D. Gordon told the Montreal militiamen as they set off to the docks in 1903, 'but to protect the freedom of all citizens without any distinction whatsoever.'[13] There was no such impartiality in the mind of Lt-Col. Septimus Denison during the Hamilton Street Railway strike on the night of 24 November 1906. When the Riot Act had been read, cavalrymen from Toronto charged the crowd, with Denison riding behind, shouting 'Give it to them boys.'

Notes

1 Directorate of History, Canadian Forces Headquarters (D. Hist.), 'Statement of Aid to Civil Power,' file 934.009 (D 404). For a list of occasions between 1867 and 1887, see *The Department of Militia and Defence under the Honourable Sir Adolphe Caron K.C.M.C. and the Military Force of Canada* (Ottawa 1887), p. 20. (Among the cases omitted from both lists was the Caraquet affray of January–February 1875.)
2 Quoted in *Canadian Annual Review*, 1999, p. 278
3 31 Vic. c. 40, ss. 27, 80 and 81. (The penalty for officers was subsequently increased to $100. 49 Vic. c. 41, s. 107.)
4 *Regulations and Orders for the Militia of the Dominion of Canada*, 1883, para. 651, 654.
5 In 1879 the Militia Act was amended to authorize the Lieutenant Governor of Manitoba to call out militia in his own province if troops were needed in the neighbouring North-West Territories. In that event alone the dominion government would assume the full cost (41 Vic. c. 35, ss. 2 and 3).
6 Canada, House of Commons, *Debates*, 30 March 1875, pp. 991–2
7 Canada, Department of Militia and Defence, *Report*, 1876, p. 43; 1878, p. xlviii
8 Murray Dodd, MP to Hon. Adolphe Caron, 14 May, 1884 and minutes, Public Archives of Canada (PAC), Caron Papers, file 3937
9 Deputy Minister of Militia to Acting Deputy Minister of Finance, 27 June 1886, Case A-589 and notes, ibid.
10 46 Vic., c. II, s. 27
11 Lt-Col. Henry R. Smith, 'Military Aid of the Civil Power,' in Canadian Military Institute, *Selected Papers*, x, 1900, 87
12 'Statement of Aid to Civil Power.'
13 Ernest-J. Chambers, *Histoire du 65ème Regiment, Carabiniers Mont-Royal* (Montreal 1906), p. 141

The Shiners' War: Social Violence in the Ottawa Valley in the 1830s

MICHAEL S. CROSS

(March 1973)
CHR 54, no. 1: 1–26. Excerpt: 1–3, 13, 23–6.

By late May of 1835, unrest in Bytown had reached unprecedented proportions. All winter the people of the town, the entrepôt of the Ottawa timber trade, had been bracing themselves, awaiting the annual visitation, the annual affliction, of the raftsmen who came each spring from high up the Valley to roister and riot in the streets of Bytown. Like the freshets in the streams, the raftsmen and social disorder arrived each April and May. But never before had their coming brought such organized violence as it did in 1835. For the Irish timberers now had a leader, and a purpose. Peter Aylen, run-away sailor, timber king, ambitious schemer, had set himself at the head of the Irish masses, had moulded them into a powerful weapon. He had given them a purpose: to drive the French Canadians off the river and thus guarantee jobs and high wages in the timber camps to the Irish.

Confident in their numbers, Aylen and his followers swaggered the streets of Bytown, brawling and drinking on the sidewalks, savagely beating anyone who dared challenge them. The town suffered under this reign of terror for weeks. The Irish mob, glorying in the name of the Shiners, seemed in complete control. But this was a stratified society; there was a class line beyond which even the Shiners went at their peril. While French-Canadian labourers were being abused, the gentry of the community shook their heads in disgust and grumbled about the Irish misbehaviour. When a respectable lawyer, Daniel McMartin of Perth, was assaulted by Peter Aylen, however, the forces of social order sprang into action. Aylen was promptly arrested.

The rule of the gentility in the town, and the aspirations of the Shiners, had come into direct conflict.[1] In 1835 the forces of order and disorder were in fine balance. The authorities were able to hold Aylen by incarcerating him in the sturdy garrison cells and then sending him overland, under heavy guard, to the district jail at Perth. However, in Bytown itself the furious raftsmen were in almost complete control. They paraded the streets, screaming threats at the magistrates, boasting they would burn down Chitty's Hotel, where the injured lawyer McMartin was in residence. Only the reading of the Riot Act and the calling-out of the garrison prevented the destruction of the hotel. Thwarted in their research for revenge on McMartin, the Irish turned to thoughts of rescuing Peter Aylen. From one unkempt raftsman to another, the rumour spread that their leader was to be sent to Perth by boat, along the Rideau Canal. Operating on this erroneous assumption, several hundred Shiners swarmed aboard a steam anchored at Bytown. Furious at their failure to find Aylen, they smashed the interior of the boat and beat several crewmen who had attempted to resist them.[2]

...

The origins of the Shiner movement are obscure, as is its pattern of organization. Even the source of the name is difficult to determine. The Shiners were Irish immigrants who, for the most part, worked in timber camps and river drives. The name has variously been described as a corruption of the French 'chêneur,' or cutter of oak; as a self-designation meaning they were to 'shine' above others; as a nickname derived from the shiny silk hats worn by greenhorns arriving at Bytown; or as coming from the newly-minted half-crown coins with which timberers were paid. When the Shiners emerged is similarly uncertain. The date usually credited is 1828, when a St Patrick's Day brawl at Bytown resulted in the death of an Englishman, Thomas Ford.

However, even if the beginning of Shinerism is placed so early, it was not an organized force until the middle 1830s. 'At first,' a contemporary remarked, 'these ruffians acted independently of one another, and without concert – jeering and insulting the defenceless and unprotected, and occasionally "pounding an enemy."'[3]

The Shiners' War, the period of wide-scale, organized violence, extended into the 1840s, but was at its peak from 1835 to 1837. The emergence of a leader precipitated the outbursts of these years. The leader was the self-styled 'King of the Shiners,' Peter Aylen. Aylen came to Canada from Ireland as a sailor. He jumped ship at Quebec, changed his name, and disappeared into the forests of the Ottawa. Entering the timber trade in 1816, he rapidly became a wealthy merchant.[4] By the time of the Shiners' War, Aylen owned property in Bytown, Nepean Township, and Horton Township, and had large timber operations on the Madawaska, Bonnechere, and Gatineau rivers.[5] He clearly was no hungry ne'er-do-well, but rather one of the wealthiest men in the district. Presumably economic motivations were not central for him. His actions seem explainable only by one of two causes: a genuine desire to aid his Irish countrymen; or a drive for personal power. As a study of the Shiner movement will show, his often cynical manipulation of his followers belies any unselfish motives on Aylen's part ...

The completion of the Rideau Canal in 1832 created an employment crisis in the Ottawa country. Hundreds of Irish were unemployed. Lacking skills and experience, they found it difficult to get work in the timber camps where French Canadians held most of the jobs. But it was also a time of vicious competition among the timber operators, struggling to exploit the best accessible tracts. Some operators began to employ Irishmen to improve their competitive position by intimidation. As the Hawkesbury timber merchant, George Hamilton, complained to the government in 1835, some employers were importing 'bravoes & ruffians' to drive their rivals out of disputed territories.[6] Peter Aylen was one such employer. Another was Walter Beckwith who ruled with an iron hand at Westmeath, near Pembroke. Beckwith boasted he would employ none but Shiners, and they repaid his support by brutally suppressing anyone who questioned Beckwith's right to take timber freely from crown and private lands. On one of the few occasions when the authorities attempted to intervene, in 1835, the problems of maintaining order in this region were again demonstrated. When magistrates arrived to arrest Beckwith for trespassing and illegal timbering, he simply scuttled across the river to Lower Canada, to return and resume his sway when the officers had left.[7]

By 1835 Aylen was prepared to use the Shiners for broader purposes – to seize effective control of Bytown and its region. The first shots of the Shiners' War were fired on 5 January 1835 with the daring daylight murder of a Mr McStravick on a street in Lower Bytown. The murderer, a lumberer named Curry, was arrested but like so many after him he escaped custody and fled to the United States.[8] Sporadic violence continued through the winter in Bytown; tension built up in the village, as stories came from up river, stories of beatings and mutilations and killings. But not even the combined prayers of all the respectable citizens of Bytown could hold back the seasons. Spring came to the Ottawa, and with it the rafts.

While Bytown became the centre of the disorders, they spread the length of the Valley. Aylen quickened the pace of his anti-French campaign, determined to win a rapid, total victory ...

The Shiners' War was over. As late as 1845, communities on the Ottawa were troubled by gangs who called themselves Shiners.[9] But the organization which had marked the years 1835–7 was gone, and the troubles were only those caused by drunken and restless men anywhere. The old leaders had left: they had grown rich and respectable, like Aylen and his right-hand man, Andrew Leamy; or they were dead, like Martin Hennessey, laid low by a blow on the head in a Bytown brawl.[10] And the Shiners had enjoyed only a very partial success. The Irish did win jobs in the timber camps. But the grander purposes, of punishing the community which rejected them, of seizing power over that community, ultimately failed.

Yet, success or failure, the Shiners' War is worth attention for what it says about the sources and nature of social violence in British North America, and for what it says about the community's response to such disorder. The Shiner movement emerged for two major reasons. One was the pattern of violence and disorder imported from Britain. As the experience of so many communities in the colonies demonstrated, the ocean voyage did not wash away old ethnic and religious hatreds, did not bleach out Orange or Green. Indeed, it often reinforced them. The insecurity of a new physical environment tended to cause people to cling even more tenaciously, in their initial period of adjustment, to certain traditional values and means of self-identification. Ethnic and religious bonds could often be tightened by the migration experience. This was especially so in areas such as the Ottawa frontier where many competing groups were thrown together, without the bonds of adequate social institutions. Lacking such institutional buffers, the groups were left to rub together, to find their security in greater emphasis on their group identities.

This points to the second major cause of the Shiner outburst. The community of Bytown and Carleton County failed to absorb the Irish and to give them a legitimate place within that community. They were denied economic security; they were the last hired and first fired. Few social organizations made any attempt to reach them, not even the Catholic church. They were rejected by a community which nursed strong anti-Irish prejudices.[11] Members of the 'better' classes of Irishmen cast in their lot with the Scots and English gentility, rather than show any interest in the welfare of the Irish masses.[12] The Shiners were outsiders, outside the community-at-large. They formed their own pseudo-community, one at war with the general community. It was a community in that its members shared common sentiments, shared the same animosities. It was a community in that it had social coherence, it was organized with its own leadership. However, the qualifying 'pseudo' is necessary, for it lacked a basic requirement of a true community. Its members could not live out their lives within it; they remained dependent upon a larger, outside community for their economic livelihood and for the basic social institutions. Since, in 1835–7, they could not conquer the community-at-large, the Shiners would sooner or later have to come to terms with it.

The initial violence of the Shiners was characteristic of that prevalent in British North America. It often had a 'recreational' character, a simple relief from the frustrations of poverty.[13] And it was largely confined to conflict among the lower orders, rather than to attacks on other classes. For the Irish, the French Canadians were not only rivals for jobs. They were also a weak and identifiable group who could be abused with relative impunity. The Irish, underprivileged themselves, climbed at least a little way up the social ladder by standing on those below them ...

Whatever its impetus, internal violence within the lower class was expected and viewed with relative equanimity by the gentler classes of society. The lower orders were assumed to be brutal, prone to violence and disorder, and so long as they exercised their passions on one another, this was simply a fact of life. This was especially true of the Irish. Until the 1830s, then, there was relatively little excitement over evidence of this brutal passion.[14]

When such violence took on an organized nature, and began to threaten the established order or to turn to physical intimidation of the upper classes, it was treated much more seriously ...

The Shiners hardened society's resistance against them when they moved from group criminality to insurrection. A similar pattern was evident elsewhere in British North America. The revolutionary activity of 1837 profoundly affected the way in which the upper classes looked at violence; it demonstrated the potential threat to their position. There was a similar preoccupation in the thought of Lord Durham, Lord Sydenham, and Robert Baldwin to establish adequate local governmental institutions as a way to control the violent potential in society. Such feelings were strengthened further by the troubles surrounding the Rebellion Losses Act in 1849, when again the politics of violence became apparent. The governor general, Lord Elgin, expressed a not-untypical reaction: 'I confess I did not before know how thin is the crust of order which cover the anarchical elements that turn and toss beneath our feet.'[15] It was no coincidence that the 1850s saw the establishment of police forces in many municipalities, and a much less tolerant attitude towards casual violence.

...

Notes

1 On the gentry of Bytown and the surrounding Carleton County, see Michael S. Cross, 'The Age of Gentility: The Creation of an Aristocracy in the Ottawa Valley,' Canadian Historical Association, *Historical Papers*, 1967. Later class conflict in the area is described in Michael S. Cross, 'Stony Monday, 1849: The Rebellion Losses Riots in Bytown,' *Ontario History*, LXIII, 3, Sept. 1971.
2 The events are described in Public Archives of Canada (PAC), Upper Canada Sundries, vol. 152, George Hamilton to Lt-Col. Rowan, 1 June 1835; ibid., G.W. Baker to Rowan, 15 June 1835; *Bathurst Courier*, 5 June 1835.
3 Toronto *Globe*, 25 Dec. 1856, 'Chaudière Letters'
4 On Aylen, see ibid.; J.L. Gourlay, *History of the Ottawa Valley* (Ottawa 1896), pp. 52–3; Miller Stewart, 'The King of the Shiners,' in *Flamboyant Canadians*, ed. Ellen Stafford (Toronto 1964)
5 *Bytown Gazette*, 8, 29 Sept., 6 Oct. 1836
6 Upper Canada Sundries, vol. 152, Hamilton to Rowan, 1 June 1835
7 Ibid., vol. 158, Baker to Rowan, 20 Oct. 1835
8 Ibid.
9 On the complaints of the citizens of Carillon, see PAC, Canada State Book D, 8 Sept. 1845, p. 533.
10 [William Pittman Lett, *Recollections of Bytown and Its Old Inhabitants* (Ottawa 1874)], p. 23
11 The prejudice in nineteenth-century England is well described in L. Perry Curtis, Jr, *Apes and Angels: The Irishman in Victorian Caricature* (Washington 1971). For examples in Upper Canadian literature see [John Mactaggart, *Three Years in Canada: An account* ... (London 1829)], II, 242–54; John M'Gregor, *British America* (2 vols., Edinburgh 1833), II, 540; Samuel Strickland, *Twenty-Seven Years in Canada West* (2 vols., London 1853), II, 205.
12 This was true in many areas of the colonies, not only in Bytown. See the comments of Mactaggart, *Three Years in Canada*, II, 254.
13 On recreational violence, see Charles Tilly, 'Collective Violence in European Perspective,' in *Violence in America: Historical and Comparative Perspectives*, ed. Hugh Davis Graham and Ted Robert Gurr (New York 1969), p. 15.
14 J. Jerald Bellomo 'Upper Canadian Attitudes towards Crime and Punishment (1832–1851),' *Ontario History*, LXIV, 1, March 1972, p. 4-3.
15 Sir Arthur G. Doughty, ed., *The Elgin–Grey Papers, 1846–1852* (4 vols., Ottawa 1937), I, Elgin to Grey, 30 April 1849, p. 350

Through the Prism of the Strike: Industrial Conflict in Southern Ontario, 1901–14

CRAIG HERON and BRYAN D. PALMER

(December 1977)
CHR 58, no. 4: 423–59. Excerpt: 424–6, 429–30, 457.

... To go beyond such generalized condemnation and probe deeper into the contours and context of industrial strife, we have examined strike activity between 1901 and 1914 in ten southern Ontario cities that were emerging as major industrial centres.[1] In Berlin, Brantford, Guelph, Hamilton, London, Niagara Falls, Oshawa, Peterborough, St. Catharines, and Toronto, the 'toilers' and the 'greedy, grasping, and gloating galoots' clashed frequently after the turn of the century. Through an examination of this conflict, in which the strike looms large, we can learn much about class relationships in these early years of a maturing central Canadian capitalism.[2]

What emerges clearly from even the most superficial glance at strike activity in the years 1901–14 is the magnitude of the conflict between labour and capital. Stuart Marshall Jamieson's portrayal of the 'relative placidity of labour relations' in Ontario during these years seems strangely misplaced:[3] the ten cities under discussion experienced the trauma of 421 strikes and lockouts in this fourteen-year period and approximately 60,000 working men and women participated in these battles.

The pattern of this strike activity buttresses the classic contention that industrial unrest follows closely upon the heels of economic cycles of contraction and expansion. In the boom years prior to 1904 an unusually tight labour market brought about a sharp increase in the incidence of strikes. As years of economic retrenchment, 1904 and 1905 saw the pace of unrest slacken; a resurgence of strikes in 1906 and the early months of 1907 told of the return of more prosperous times. But with the economic downturn of 1908 strike activity came to a virtual standstill, and the severe depression year, 1908, witnessed the least number of conflicts in the entire period. Only in 1910 did the number of strikes begin to rise again significantly, reaching a peak in the early part of 1913. The prewar recession quickly stifled the growing conflict, however, and by 1914 strikes were once again quite uncommon. Strikes,

Table 1
The contours of strike activity, 1901–14

	Number of strikes	Number of strikers
City		
Berlin	13	552
Brantford	14	715
Guelph	24	1020
Hamiton	92	11249
London	38	1650
Niagara Falls	6	1356
Oshawa	1	263
Peterborough	11	302
St Catharines	24	2346
Toronto	198	38903
TOTALS	421	58356
Industry		
Building	110	23654
Metal	106	11216
Clothing	48	8675
Woodworking	33	3345
Food, liquor, and tobacco	31	2184
Miscellaneous	27	1779
Unskilled	24	3758
General transport	14	2377
Printing and allied	11	591
Leather	9	259
Textile	8	518
TOTALS	421	58356

SOURCE: *Labour Gazette*, 1901–14

then, were commonly resorted to in times of prosperity when concessions were more easily wrung from recalcitrant employers, and were more sparingly employed in years of recession, most prominently 1908 and 1913–14, when labour's chances of even the most marginal victories were slim indeed.[4]

Finally, the contours of industrial strife in these years reveal important patterns of geographical and industrial concentration. Predictably, the geographical locus of strike activity coincided with the concentration of population. Toronto and Hamilton, the largest urban centres under consideration, far outstripped the other cities in terms of the number of strikes and workers involved: Toronto sustained 198 strikes or lockouts in the years 1901–14, in which 38,903 workers participated, while Hamilton experienced 92 such conflicts, involving 11,249 working men and women. Oshawa, in contrast, saw only 263 workers strike on a single occasion in the entire period, in February 1903. Workers in the building and metal trades were clearly in the vanguard of this industrial upheaval, leading fully half of the total number of strikes in the ten cities. Trailing them, but playing a major role, were workers in the clothing, food, liquor and tobacco, and woodworking trades. More generally, it was the skilled that provided the cutting edge of opposition: unskilled labour participated in less than 6 per cent of the total number of strikes in the ten southern Ontario cities. In the following pages, therefore, it will be the craftsman who will be prominently in the foreground. From these broad contours we must turn to the context of industrial conflict if we are to capture an understanding of the forces precipitating the many strikes and lockouts of the period.

Perhaps the fundamental feature of the context of industrial strife in southern Ontario between 1901 and 1914 was the accelerating pace of industrial capitalist development. After more than thirty years of economic expansion, the first decade and a half of the twentieth century saw the pace of industrialization quickened and pushed to new heights ...

The disruptive impact of technology and mechanized production on the skilled crafts of the late nineteenth century in advanced capitalist countries is an often told tale, although the Canadian experience has only just begun to receive attention.[5] What has recently been stressed, however, is the other side of the historical coin: the degree to which skilled workers retained much of their craft status, pride, and economic security through a thorough organization and control of the productive process. Gregory S. Kealey has recently demonstrated the lasting power of iron molders and printers in the face of the mechanization of Toronto's skilled trades,[6] while David Montgomery's study of craft workers in the late nineteenth century in the United States regards skilled workers' control of the productive process as the touchstone of their self-conception of manhood: ... Craft workers, as Benson Soffer has argued, cultivated a rich and varied collection of shop floor control mechanisms throughout the course of the nineteenth century. Such devices, assuring skilled workers a degree of autonomy at the work place, exercised a tenuous hold over work relationships in many nineteenth-century trades.[7] Underpinning these mechanisms was a resilient consciousness of price and self-confidence in their social worth that would carry these workers through many struggles.

Yet, even granting the significant degrees of control over the work processes exercised by many craftsmen to the end of the nineteenth century, by the early twentieth century technology had made real strides in diluting skill and transforming the workers' status on the shop floor. Complementing this propensity of modern machinery, moreover, was another development. Aware of the impediments that the autonomy of the skilled worker had raised against productivity and authority, employers turned to an array of managerial innovations and efficiency schemes after the turn of the century. Ranging from the employment of autocratic foremen, pledged to drive men and women harder and faster, to the utilization of complex systems of task simplification, job standardization, time and motion study, cost accountancy, and piece and bonus systems of wage payment, this amalgam of tactics became known as 'scientific management.' This pervasive thrust for efficiency, coupled with the impact of mechanization, constituted a concerted assault upon the control mechanisms and customs of the trade embedded within the consciousness and shop practices of the skilled worker.[8]

...

While the episodic quality of strikes poses problems for wide-ranging generalization, our examination of the contours and context of industrial conflict in the years 1901–14 suggests some conclusions. Skilled workers continued to use the strike to maintain shop-floor control rooted in nineteenth-century work practices, as well as to combat twentieth-century developments in work-shop organization and managerial innovation. At the same time their employers launched a concerted offensive against the institution that harboured and perpetuated much of the craftsman's autonomy, the trade union. By 1914 there was no definite resolution of the conflict between these forces. The cyclical depressions that began in 1908 and 1913 weakened organized labour as an adversary, but each time strikes resumed with the first signs of the return of prosperity. A tight labour market during the war restored strength lost in the prewar slump, and many scenes of the pre-1914 conflict were repeated in the next five or six years, with perhaps even greater intensity.[9]

From this perspective it would seem that the strike was *not* simply a battle over the division of the economic pie. Like Edward Shorter and Charles Tilly, whose massive compilation of data on strikes in France also stresses the role of craftsmen in pre–World War I industrial conflict, we have come to regard the strike as an implicitly political event, a clash over the distribution of power on the shop or factory floor flowing directly from the desire and ability of working people to act collectively.[10] ...

Notes

We are grateful for the critical comments on earlier drafts of this paper made by R.C. Brown, Michael Cross, Russell Hann, Gregory S. Kealey, Ian McKay, and Edward Shorter. While we have made efforts to incorporate suggested revisions, some of our critics are likely to remain unappeased. They bear no responsibility for the shortcomings of the paper. Bryan Palmer would also like to acknowledge the assistance of the Canada Council and the 1973 London Labour History Project.

1. The basic source for much of what follows was the *Labour Gazette*. Because this publication provides only an introduction to the many strikes and lockouts of the period, and an often inadequate one at that, we have also turned to numerous local labour newspapers, the regional *Industrial Banner*, and the standard sources on Canadian trade union history and strike activity: Charles Lipton, *The Trade Union Movement of Canada, 1827–1959* (Montreal 1968), 98–161; H.A. Logan, *Trade Unions in Canada* (Toronto 1948); Stuart Marshall Jamieson, *Times of Trouble: Labour Unrest and Industrial Conflict in Canada, 1900–1966* (Ottawa 1968), 62–157. Finally, because strikes involving national or provincial transportation networks often involved cities outside of the regional concerns of this study, we did not include them in our quantitative analysis of the contours of strike activity. Where such strikes illuminated issues of particular relevance, however, we have included them in our impressionistic discussion of the context of industrial conflict.
2. On the importance of the historical study of strike activity see Michelle Perrot, *Les ouvriers en grève: France 1871–1890*, I & II (Paris 1974): Peter N. Stearns, 'Measuring the Evolution of Strike Movements,' *International Review of Social History*, XIX, 1974, 1–27; Edward Shorter and Charles Tilly, *Strikes in France, 1830–1968* (London 1974); K.G.J.C. Knowles, *Strikes – A Study in Industrial Conflict* (Oxford 1952). Peter Stearns has outlined the main features of mature industrial society: the regularization and intensification of work; new forms of supervision; reduction of working time; reduction of personal initiative on the job; and a new infusion of technological change. As we shall see, such features were to play a prominent role in the evolution of industrial unrest in this period. See Peter Stearns, *Lives of Labour: Work in a Maturing Industrial Society* (London 1975), 343.

3 Jamieson, *Times of Trouble*, 85
4 Thirty-one strikes occurred in 1901, 48 in 1902, 53 in 1903, 35 in 1904, 24 in 1905, 47 in 1906, 43 in 1907, 7 in 1908, 10 in 1909, 20 in 1910, 24 in 1911, 30 in 1912, 36 in 1913, and 12 in 1914.
5 See Gregory S. Kealey, 'Artisans Respond to Industrialism: Shoemakers, Shoe Factories, and the Knights of St. Crispin in Toronto,' Canadian Historical Association *Papers*, 1973, 137–58. David Brody, 'Steelworkers in America: The Non-Union Era' (Cambridge 1960), 27–29; Robert Ozanne, *A Century of Labour Management Relations at McCormick and International Harvester* (Madison 1967); George E. Barnett, *Chapters on Machinery and Labour* (Carbondale 1969); Robert A. Christie, *Empire in Wood: A History of the Carpenters' Union* (Ithaca 1956), 80–2; Gregory S. Kealey, ed., *Canada Investigates Industrialism: The Royal Commission on the Relations of Labour and Capital, 1889* (Toronto 1973).
6 Gregory S. Kealey, '"The Honest Workingman" and Workers' Control: The Experience of Toronto Skilled Workers, 1860–1892,' *Labour/Le Travailleur*, I, 1976, 32–68. For a discussion of the experience of skilled workers in Halifax see Ian McKay, 'The Working Class of Metropolitan Halifax, 1850–1889' (honours thesis, Dalhousie University, 1975), 53–67.
7 Benson Soffer, 'A Theory of Trade Union Development: The Role of the "Autonomous Workman,"' *Labor History*, I, 1960, 141–63
8 This paragraph draws on material in Bryan Palmer, 'Class, Conception and Conflict: The Thrust for Efficiency, Managerial Views of Labour and Working Class Rebellion, 1903–1922,' *Review of Radical Political Economy*, VII, 1975, 31–49; David Montgomery, 'The "New Unionism" and the Transformation in Workers' Consciousness, 1909–1922,' *Journal of Social History*, VII, 1974, 509–29.
9 For example, a massive strike of 1500–2000 machinists in Hamilton's munitions plants in 1916. PAC, RG 27, vol. 304, Strike no 27A
10 Shorter and Tilly, *Strikes in France*. Cf Charles Tilly, Louise Tilly, Richard Tilly, *The Rebellious Century, 1830–1930* (Cambridge 1975); and a brilliant local study, Peter Friedlander, *The Emergence of U.A.W. Local 229, Hamtramck, Michigan: A Study in Class and Culture* (Pittsburgh 1975). Our conclusions, then, stand counterposed to those of Peter Stearns, who regards the main impetus behind strikes as the struggle for economic gain, realized in higher wages. See Stearns, *Revolutionary Syndicalism and French Labor: A Cause without Rebels* (New Brunswick [NJ] 1971).

E.P. Thompson vs Harold Logan:
Writing about Labour and the Left in the 1970s

KENNETH MCNAUGHT

(June 1981)
CHR 62, no. 2: 141–68. Excerpt: 141–3, 167–8.

Over the past ten years or so many younger historians have cast critical eyes on the rather slender accumulation of writing on Canadian labour organization, strikes, and 'industrial relations' which they were asked to consult as graduate students. They were not favourably impressed. The existing literature, they observed, concerned itself almost entirely with endeavours to organize labour, and the evolution of governmental and business responses to such efforts. Moreover, most of the literature expressed an establishment point of view; it was 'élitist,' ignoring the real experience of the working class and minimizing the 'aberrant' manifestations of proletarian radicalism. The Young Turks deplored equally the meliorist mentality which permeated discussion of political action on the left. In the social–economic sphere, formal mainstream unionism and collective bargaining had received the lion's share of attention. Conventional wisdom endorsed either social democracy or Liberal reformism as the most legitimate and promising political expressions of labour's interests. In short, the received version was myopic, biased, and managerial ...

In their critical assessment of all this, many graduate students in the 1960s and early 70s were attracted by one or more expressions of that diaphanous phenomenon, the New Left. They read and took to heart the critics of liberal corporate capitalism. They found particularly congenial those who concluded that the *dirigiste* and repressive nature of the system had achieved such a degree of sophisticated social manipulation and 'hegemony' that direct action was required. The complicity of Canadian élites in support of American-dominated western capitalism led the young rebels to contemplate means of obstructing and even reversing the course of events as they perceived them. Unhappy, also, with the expansive, prosperous complacency of Canada's sixties they identified themselves, not infrequently, with foreign movements of protest and revolution – with the campaigns for nuclear disarmament, with left-wing nationalist movements in the beleaguered regions of European and American imperial power, with volatile American movements for racial equality, participatory democracy, and ending the intervention in Vietnam. Nor was their excitement merely vicarious. Particularly in protesting against the Vietnam war and the lack of student participation in the governance of universities they took part in 'confronting' and sometimes disrupting university administration, conducting 'occupations,' teach-ins, and guerilla theatre, and achieving some changes in the atmosphere and structure of universities.

The writing of the past decade has been influenced not only by the political–social ambience of the sixties but also by a shift of emphasis within the historical fraternities of western Europe, Britain, and the United States. A marked stress on social history worked together with Marxist and other egalitarian critiques of advanced capitalism and imperialism to define new questions to be asked of Canadian history. The trends from abroad brought with them implicit guidelines – both for those attracted to the left and those who wished primarily to flesh out the somewhat skeletal academic version of our past.[1] A general stimulus came from the French *Annales* school, from the work of Antonio Gramsci and from the German neo-Marxists, which stressed the cultural underpinnings of capitalism and employed modern, complex conceptions of the state. More direct influences were those of 'empirical' Marxism evident in British historical analysis. E.P. Thompson, E.J. Hobsbawm, Raymond Williams, G. Stedman Jones, and others, produced a torrent of writing which suggested new approaches, new questions to be asked about Canadian society and labour. Particularly appealing was the British effort to rediscover the positive characteristics of working-class life, apart from trade unionism, and to apply a neo-Marxist, fluid concept of class and the evolution of class consciousness. Students fed on the notion of a nearly inevitable *embourgeoisement* of the lower orders in Canada found exciting the British depiction of a working-class culture underlying the changing expression of class consciousness and buttressing resistance to the discipline of industrial capitalism. Congenial also was the British stress on locality and lost causes. When applied to Canadian labour history these analytical thrusts led to a positive interaction with the more general trend to study the roles of regionalism, urbanization, and 'limited identities.'

... The heat has not subsided,[2] but neither has there emerged a clear antithesis, let alone a synthesis. The cannonading from the left has served principally to achieve those goals which the captains of artillery most vigorously rejected at the beginning of the campaign. The class-conscious researchers have filled in some serious gaps in our social history and they have also tempted others to concern themselves profitably with the regional and local contexts of labour history. Nevertheless, while our knowledge of the conditions of life and labour has been noticeably extended, no thesis has emerged with a convincing new explanation of our labour structure, of governmental labour policy, nor of the nature and role of the political left. On the contrary, most of the recent writing strengthens older notions: that the most effective workers' response to an ever tightening industrial discipline was unionization; that the slow evolution of effective unionization reflected differences of region, culture, and industrial context; that, while gross inequalities and exploitation produced the fears and goals of the workers, the forms and policies of unionization were determined by leaders – a great many of whom became 'collaborators'; that violence has been provoked and employed more often by the state than by the workers; that despite clear evidence of various perceptions of class membership and class conflict, the dominant expressions of such perceptions have been the non-revolutionary strike and efforts to influence governmental policy through pressuring the major parties and/or supporting a democratic socialist party. Efforts to depict, or simply to assert, a free-standing working-class culture in the past (let alone the present) have failed to provide a credible new principle of historical interpretation, while the picture of a complex society in which progressivism, unionism, socialism, and political capitalism have been consistently interactive has been more definitely etched.

...

Notes

1 A perceptive article on recent trends in social history is Laurence Stone, 'The Revival of Narrative: Reflections on a New Old History,' *Past and Present*, no. 85, 1979. A very critical treatment of sociological history, particularly interesting because it touches on recurring tension between Marxist and social history and on the appearance of such tension in much writing about what might be called the common woman, is Tony Judt, 'A Clown in Regal Purple: Social History and the Historians,' *History Workshop*, spring 1979.
2 See, e.g., Bryan Palmer's article in reply to Terry Morley, 'Working Class Canada: Recent Historical Writing,' *Queen's Quarterly*, winter 1979–80.

Paternalism and Politics: Sir Francis Bond Head, the Orange Order, and the Election of 1836

SEAN T. CADIGAN

(September 1991)
CHR 72, no. 2: 319–47. Excerpt: 319–23.

Lord Durham offered the first assessment of Sir Francis Bond Head's role in Upper Canadian politics. His *Report* suggested that Head mistook the debate between Tories and Reformers for one over the maintenance of the imperial connection. On the basis of this belief, the lieutenant-governor acted in ways that polarized Upper Canadian politics on the issue of loyalty to bring about a favourable resolution for the Tory faction.[1] Subsequent work variously characterized Head as a fool, as a self-defined political cavalier, or as a thug who rigged elections through violence and intimidation in the cause of Upper Canadian loyalism versus American republicanism.[2] Recent work still leaves Head as a 'posturing, vainglorious individual devoid of political experience and common sense,' muddying the clear waters leading to constitutional reform by use of the loyalty issue.[3]

...

It would be a mistake to see Head's success in 1836 as a simple function of his own political personality. Tory success in the election of that year lay in the lieutenant-governor's role as a nexus between the different orders of Upper Canadian society – between the high-ranking Tories and their lower-ranking Orange allies. In the shaping of that nexus, personality proved crucial, but Head's political aptitude lay in his role as an astute respondent to a society in which order rested on paternal accommodations within a hierarchical edifice. The lieutenant-governor welded together different Tory and Orange reactions to a diverse yet growing Reform movement. Head's election campaign, particularly in its reliance on Orange intimidation, taught Reformers a lesson that William Lyon Mackenzie had received a decade earlier when the sons of York's Tory elite destroyed his printing equipment: in Upper Canada, the rule of law did not govern the process of political change. Tories continued to accept political violence as a legitimate means of dealing with dissent. The only important difference between Mackenzie's experience in 1826 and the electoral riots of 1836 is that in 1836 Upper Canada's Tory elite let the Orangemen do their dirty work.[4]

The general election of 1836, and Sir Francis Bond Head's role in it, must be understood in terms of the ongoing conflict between Tories and Reformers. This represented but one facet of a paternal order in the throes of dissolution. Social development demanded government through rationalized and bureaucratized institutions which left little room for personal accommodations. Yet in the mid-1830s this transformation was still in its infancy. Paternalism remained vital in political relationships, defining the actions Tories and Reformers took against each other. The strategies of both groups in 1836 were rooted in the paternalism of previous political practice. Tories reduced the Reformers to a small minority in the Assembly in 1836 because, under Head, they better understood the necessity of accommodation inherent in the control of Upper Canadian society. At a point of transition nearing paternalism's decline, Tories under Head's leadership resorted naturally to time-proven political tactics.

Head's political paternalism was an ideology rooted in Upper Canada's social formation. As Bryan Palmer has argued, in a society which predated the social controls of a powerful state infrastructure, Upper Canadian government rested on mutual albeit unequal accommodations between the colony's local elites and those Upper Canadians below them.[5] Paternalism in Upper Canada was the ideological expression of such pervasive accommodations. To stem the tide of American republicanism, British authorities tried to structure Upper Canadian society along the lines of an earlier household-dominated social formation in Great Britain. When Loyalist and other immigrants arrived in Upper Canada, they fell under the direction of British officials who were intent on ensuring that this new society had a patriarchal structure and hierarchy which would counterbalance the democratic impulses of the new American republic. Loyalty to the paternal authority of the British monarch became a defining characteristic of early Upper Canadian political culture.[6] To ensure that Upper Canadian society would approximate the hierarchical structure of English society, British authorities gave Loyalists land grants, seed, equipment, and other aid according to their previous status in the American colonies. Upper Canada thus acquired the basis of its own elite.[7]

Paternalism, within the particular context of Upper Canada, was an ideology well-suited to a colony in which most people could aspire to some ownership of the means of production through household production in agriculture or craft.⁸ The mutuality, unequal though it might have been, that H.C. Pentland saw as essential to masters' cultivation of their hired labour's loyalty within pre-industrial Canada's nascent labour market, bound all social layers together during a period of rapid development.⁹ In a society of households, patriarchal mastery proved a powerful source of ideological cohesion. The image of the master encouraged identification between the different status groups of Upper Canadian society, from labourers and squatters through mechanics, yeomen, merchants, and professionals, to Executive Councillors.¹⁰

...

There was nothing bucolic about Upper Canadian society. Household production in agriculture took place alongside the transitive influence of mercantile activity, staple production, and craft production.¹¹ The result, especially after 1812, was the rapid growth and change of Upper Canadian society as available land beckoned immigrants and trade, stimulating the growth of urban service centres and manufacturing to supply Upper Canada's agricultural population. Paternal accommodations between the Upper Canadian elites and the 'lower orders' were attempts to tape together the bursting seams of a rapidly developing society. As Upper Canadian society matured, new visions of political reformers challenged the rule of the Tory compacts. After the War of 1812, reformers' discontents intensified, stemming initially from their exclusion from the hierarchy of patronage which radiated from the government at York. The military–administrative elites of British and Loyalist gentry stock opposed attempts by merchants, mechanics, more prosperous farmers, and professionals to break into their preserves of political power. Throughout the 1820s and 1830s, members of this new social group coalesced into an eclectic Reform campaign for limited political democracy, the separation of church and state, and reform in education, public health, and public morality. Reformers desired a greater role in the colony's government that corresponded to their importance in economic growth. Members of the Tory compacts were reluctant to relinquish their political control. They continued to cherish the idea that the Upper Canadian social order could rest on deference to their rank within a rigid hierarchy based on ownership or control of land and public office.¹² ...

Notes

The author wishes to acknowledge the financial support of an SSHRC Queen's

Fellowship and an Ontario Graduate Scholarship. In addition, thanks to Bryan D. Palmer, who supervised the research for this article, and G.S. Kealey, Linda Kealey, and Allan Greer for their advice on earlier drafts.

1 Gerald M. Craig, ed., *Lord Durham's Report* (1839) (Toronto 1963), 85–81
2 Subsequent characterizations are found in Chester New, *Lord Durham's Mission to Canada* (1929), ed. H.W. McCready (Toronto 1963), 32–7; Aileen Dunham, *Political Unrest in Upper Canada 1815–1836* (1927) (Toronto 1963), 165–76; Gerald M. Craig, *Upper Canada: The Formative Years 1784–1841* (Toronto 1963), 232–9; Donald Creighton, *Dominion of the North* (Toronto 1944), 238; and Stanley B. Ryerson, Unequal Union (Toronto 1975), 116.
3 Colin Read, *The Rising in Upper Canada, 1837–8: The Duncombe Revolt and After* (Toronto 1982), 57–65
4 Paul Romney, 'From the Types Riot to the Rebellion: Elite Ideology, Anti-legal Sentiment, Political Violence, and the Rule of Law in Upper Canada,' *Ontario History* 79, 2 (June 1987): 115–40
5 Bryan D. Palmer, *Working-Class Experience* (Toronto and Vancouver 1983), v, 12–59
6 Jane Errington, *The Lion, the Eagle, and Upper Canada: A Developing Colonial Ideology* (Kingston and Montreal 1987), 24
7 For a more detailed explanation of this theme see Janice Potter, 'Patriarchy and Paternalism: The Case of the Eastern Ontario Loyalist Women,' *Ontario History* 81, 1 (March 1989): 3–24. Potter demonstrates that British officials went out of their way to ensure that Loyalist women particularly were restructured back into traditional subordinate family roles after having assumed direction of the family as husbands fled to British-held territory during the American Revolution.
8 Leo A. Johnson, 'Independent Commodity Production: Mode of Production or Capitalist Class Formation?' *Studies in Political Economy* 6 (autumn 1981): 93–112
9 H. Clare Pentland, *Labour and Capital in Canada 1750–1860*, ed. Paul Philips (Toronto 1981), 24–60
10 Peter A. Russell, 'Attitudes to Social Mobility in Upper Canada (1815–1840)' (PhD thesis, Carleton University, 1981), 152–90, 359–72
11 Bryan D. Palmer, 'Social Formation and Class Formation in North America, 1800–1900,' in David Levine, ed., *Proletarianization and Family History* (London 1984), 235–40
12 The best analysis of the Reform movement's emergence as a cohesive, province-wide movement remains Graeme Patterson, 'Studies in Elections and Public Opinion in Upper Canada' (PhD thesis, University of Toronto,

1969). See also Stanley Ryerson, *Unequal Union*, 109–20; Craig, *Upper Canada*, 114–23; Read, *Rising*, 16–24; T. Cook, 'John Beverley Robinson and the Conservative Blueprint for the Upper Canadian Community,' *Ontario History* 64 (1972): 79–85; L.F. Gates, 'The Decided Policy of William Lyon Mackenzie,' *Canadian Historical Review* 40 (1959): 185–208.

THE RETURN OF NATIVE HISTORY

The French Presence in Huronia: The Structure of Franco–Huron Relations in the First Half of the Seventeenth Century

BRUCE G. TRIGGER

(June 1968)
CHR 49, no. 2: 107–41. Excerpt: 107–9.

Few studies of Canadian history in the first half of the seventeenth century credit sufficiently the decisive role played at that time by the country's native peoples. The success of European colonizers, traders, and missionaries depended to a greater degree than most of them cared to admit on their ability to understand and accommodate themselves not only to native customs but also to a network of political and economic relationships that was not of their own making. Traders and missionaries often were forced to treat Algonkians and Iroquoians as their equals and sometimes they had to acknowledge that the Indians had the upper hand. If the Europeans were astonished and revolted by many of the customs of these Indians (often, however, no more barbarous than their own), they also admired their political and economic sagacity.[1] Indeed, one Jesuit was of the opinion that the Huron were more intelligent than the rural inhabitants of his own country.[2] If the missionary or fur trader felt compelled to understand the customs of the Indians, the modern historian should feel no less obliged to do so.

In order to appreciate the role that the Indians played in the history of Canada in the first half of the seventeenth century, it is necessary to study their customs and behaviour and the things they valued. Because their way of life differed from that of the Europeans, the fur traders and missionaries who interacted with them frequently became amateur anthropologists, and some of them became very good ones. For some tribes the documentation amassed by these early contacts is extensive and of high quality. For no tribe is this truer than for the Huron.[3] From the detailed picture of Huronia that emerges from these studies, it is possible to ascertain the motives that prompted the behaviour of particular Indians, or groups of Indians, in a manner no less detailed than our explanations of those which governed the behaviour of their European contemporaries ...

Two explanations have been used by anthropologists and historians to justify the existing cleavage between their respective studies. One of these maintains that when Europeans arrived in eastern North America, the native tribes were engaged in a struggle, the origins and significance of which are lost in the mists of time and therefore wholly the concern of ethnohistorians. Because of this, there is no reason for the historian to try to work out in detail the causes of the conflicts and alliances that existed at that time.[4] Very often, however, the struggle between different groups is painted in crude, almost racist, terms (and in complete contradiction to the facts) as one between Algonkian- and Iroquoian-speaking peoples, the former being an indigenous population, mainly hunters, the latter a series of invading tribes growing corn and living in large villages. It should be noted that such a simplistic explanation of European history, even for the earliest periods, would now be laughed out of court by any competent historian. The alternative hypothesis suggests that European contact altered the life of the Indian, and above all the relationships among the different tribes, so quickly and completely that a knowledge of aboriginal conditions is not necessary to understand events after 1600.[5] From an *a priori* point of view, this theory seems most unlikely. Old relationships have a habit of influencing events, even when economic and political conditions are being rapidly altered. Future studies must describe in detail how aboriginal cultures were disrupted or altered by their contact with the Europeans, rather than assume that interaction between Indians and Europeans can be explained as a set of relationships that has little or no reference to the native culture ...

Notes

A shorter version of this paper was presented at the Seventeenth Conference on Iroquois Research held at Sagamore, New York, Oct. 21–23, 1966. This paper is based in part on research carried out with the assistance of Miss A. Elaine Clark during the academic year 1965–66. Miss Clark's assistance was made possible through a research grant provided by the French Canada Studies Programme of McGill University.

1 See, e.g., Samuel de Champlain's comment on the sagacity of the Indians in trade (H.P. Biggar, ed., *The Works of Samuel de Champlain* [6 vols.; Toronto, 1922–36], II, 171), and Jean de Brébeuf, Gabriel Lalemant, and Francesco Bressani on the efficacy of Huron law (R.G. Thwaites, ed., *The Jesuit Relations and Allied Documents* [73 vols.; Cleveland, 1896–1901], X, 215; XXVIII, 49–51; XXXVIII, 277).
2 Thwaites, ed., *Relations*, XVIII, 21. A similar statement is made by Paul Ragueneau (XXIX, 281)
3 P.F.X. Charlevoix, *Histoire et description générale de la Nouvelle France avec le journal historique d'un voyage fait par ordre du roi dans l'Amérique septentrionale*; 3 vols. (Paris 1744); later references are to Charlevoix, *History and General Description of New France*, ed. J.G. Shea, 6 vols. (New York 1866–72).
4 F. Parkman, *The Jesuits in North America in the Seventeenth Century* (Centenary Edition, Boston, 1927), pp. 3, 4, 435, 436; G.E. Ellis, 'Indians of North America,' in J. Winsor, ed., *Narrative and Critical History of America* (8 vols.; Boston and New York, 1884–89), I, 283
5 G.T. Hunt, *The Wars of the Iroquois: A Study in Intertribal Relations* (Madison, 1940), pp. 4, 19

Amerindian Views of French Culture in the Seventeenth Century

CORNELIUS JAENEN

(September 1974)
CHR 55, no. 3: 261–91. Excerpt: 261–4, 291.

Our historiography has been more concerned with French and Canadian views of the Amerindians than with aboriginal opinions and evaluations of the French culture with which they came into contact during the seventeenth century.[1] Yet, the most elementary canons of historical interpretation require that the values and belief systems of both parties concerned in the contact experience be considered. In general, it has been assumed by historians that not only did Frenchmen consider their civilization superior to the aboriginal cultures of North America but also that the native tribesmen viewed French culture with awe and admiration, that they often attempted to imitate the Europeans, and usually aspired to elevate themselves to the superior level of the white man. This interpretation was firmly established in European and Canadian literature by Charlevoix, Raynal, Chateaubriand, and Bossange.[2]

Not until the mid-nineteenth century was there any notable departure from this accepted approach to French–Amerindian relations. While it is true and a few earlier French writers had been critical of the ideas and ideals of their compatriots in comparison with native behaviour, such critical observations were invariably motivated by desires for political and social reforms, by religious toleration, or by scepticism which related to France more than to North America. Clodoré, Abbeville, de Léry, Boyer, Sagard, and Lescarbot made guarded criticisms of French behaviour and institutions employing Amerindian examples to strengthen their arguments.[3] Maximilien Bibaud was the first French-Canadian to depict the Amerindians in a consistently favourable light. He was fully conscious, moreover, that the aborigines had resisted francization and, in the majority, had rejected conversion.[4] Napoléon Legendre pleaded eloquently in 1884 for an impartial and just treatment of Amerindian history, but his was still a voice of one crying in the wilderness.[5]

...

To delineate Amerindian views of French culture and civilization at the time of contact in the seventeenth century is extremely difficult because, first of all, an understanding of both French culture and Amerindian cultures is necessary ...

Secondly, past events must not only be identified but also be interpreted in the manner seen by each of the participants involved. As the archaeologists have contributed much to an understanding of Amerindian cultures, so the ethno-historians and anthropologists have contributed to an understanding of the moral assumptions and value systems involved ... The inability to understand behaviour and thought as conceived by the various Amerindian cultures was the greatest barrier to French appreciation of native civilization, and it remains a formidable challenge to the modern historian who attempts to explain and evaluate the contact experience.

The Amerindians, as a non-literate society, left few documents to assist in reconstructing their views and concepts. The majority of documentary sources are European and, therefore, although designated as primary sources, are interpretations as well as records of events. On the other hand, it can be argued that the recorders were also participants and that this gave them a distinctive advantage over today's social scientists who are deprived of the experience of being eye-witnesses and participants ...

These initial contacts strengthened the Europocentric view of history. In the seventeenth century Europeans invariably assumed that Europe was the centre of the world and of civilization, that its cultures were the oldest, that America was a new continent and that its peoples were necessarily recent immigrants. The literature of the period of exploration was dominated by the theme of a New World populated by peoples of different languages and cultures who conducted European explorers and 'discoverers' on tours along well-known and well-travelled water routes and trails to the various centres of aboriginal population. The conceptual frameworks of Europeans – whether Spaniards, French or English, or whether Catholics or Protestants – were remarkably indistinguishable whenever the circumstances of contact were similar. Explorers were fed, sheltered, offered the other amenities of social life, and provided with multilingual guides. In this context Europeans tended to see themselves and their activities as being at the centre of the historical stage.

The French did distinguish, nevertheless, cultural differences among the tribes or 'nations' they contacted, although contemporary literature is remarkable for the absence of differentiation on the basis of 'race' or pigmentation. On the basis of differences in language and in observable customs and beliefs there was an awareness of the great cultural diversity of the native peoples. It may be postulated, therefore, that the views of Micmacs or Montagnais would differ from the views of the Huron or Iroquois. There are a few indications of differing reactions but these can usually be associated with the context of contact rather than with conceptual variations.

...

In the past Canadian historiography has taken little account of these primordial facts concerning initial European–Amerindian relations. Our knowledge of both the facts and fantasies of this cultural contact is now sufficiently advanced to make a revision of interpretations both imperative and credible. There is no longer place for the uncritical assumption that the Europocentric evaluations and comparisons of the French seventeenth-century contemporary sources represented accurately the social realities of the time, much less Amerindian views of events and values. The corrective considerations and the long overdue reappraisal suggested herein can only have the beneficial and stimulating consequence for Canadian historical writing of challenging description, exposition, and evaluation which depict the Amerindians as part of an American environment to be overcome and subdued to European purposes and policies, which relegate the aborigines to the background and stage-setting of national history, or which represent them as awe-stricken inferiors overwhelmed by the impact of a superior civilization which they aspired to acquire but which their own inadequacies denied them as an elusive and unattainable objective.

Notes

This is the revised version of a paper read at the seventh annual Northern Great Plains History Conference, University of Manitoba, 20 Oct. 1972.

1 This orientation is illustrated in the following important writings: Henri Baudet, *Paradise on Earth: Some Thoughts on European Images of Non-European Man* (New Haven 1965); Gilbert Chinard, *L'Amérique et le rêve exotique dans la littérature française au XVIIe et au XVIIIe siècle* (Paris 1913); René Gonnard, *La légende du bon sauvage* (Paris 1946); George R. Healy, 'The French Jesuits and the Idea of the Noble Savage,' *William and Mary Quarterly*, xv, no 2, April 1958, 143–67; Douglas Leechman, 'The Indian in Literature,' *Queen's Quarterly*, L, no. 2, summer 1943, 155–63; Roy Harvey Pearce, *The Savages of America. A Study of the Indian and the Idea of Civilization* (Baltimore 1953); Donald Boyd Smith, 'French Canadian Historians' Images of the Indian in the "Heroic Period" of New France, 1534–1663' (unpublished master's thesis, Université Laval 1969)
2 D. Dainville, pseudonym (Adolphe Bossange), *Beautés de l'histoire du Canada ou époques remarquables, traits intéressans, moeurs, usages, coutumes des habitans du Canada, tant indigènes que colons, depuis sa découverte jusqu'à ce jour* (Paris 1821); F.-X. Charlevoix, *Histoire et description générale de la Nouvelle-France avec le journal historique d'un Voyage fait par ordre du Roi dans l'Amérique septentrionale*, 3 vols. (Paris 1744); F.R. Chateaubriand, *Le génie du Christianisme* (Paris 1802); J.F.X. Lafitau, *Moeurs des Sauvages amériquains comparés aux moeurs des premiers temps* (Paris 1724); G.-T. Raynal, *Histoire philosophique et politique des établissements et du commerce dans les deux Indes* (Genève 1780)
3 Claude d'Abbeville, *Histoire de la Mission des Père Capucins en l'Isle de Maragnan*

et terres circonvoisines (Paris 1614); Paul Boyer, *Véritable Relation de tout ce qui s'est fait et passé au voyage que Monsieur Bretigny fit à l'Amérique Occidentale* (Paris 1654); J. de Clodoré, *Relation de ce qui s'est passé dans les Isles de Terre ferme de l'Amérique* (Paris 1671); Jean de Léry, *Histoire d'un Voyage fait en le Terre du Brésil, autrement dite Amérique* (La Rochelle 1578); Marc Lescarbot, *Histoire de la Nouvelle France* (Paris 1609); Gabriel Sagard-Théodat, *Le Grand Voyage du Pays des Hurons* (Paris 1632)

4 Maximilien Bibaud, *Biographie des Sagamos Illustres de l'Amérique septrentionale* (Montreal 1848)

5 Napoléon Legendre, 'Les races indigènes de l'Amérique devant l'histoire,' *Mémoires de la Société Royale du Canada*, II, 1884, sec. i, 25-30

The Historians' Indian: Native Americans in Canadian Historical Writing from Charlevoix to the Present

BRUCE G. TRIGGER

(September 1986)
CHR 67, no. 3: 315-42. Excerpt: 315-16, 318, 320-4, 340-1.

Since 1971 several important studies have chronicled the treatment of native peoples in Canadian historical writing.[1] During the same period there has been a growing interest in the history of native peoples as their descendants begin once more to play a greater role in national life. The range of topics being investigated and the understanding of the general outlines of native history have increased as historians, anthropologists, archaeologists, geographers, and economists have combined their professional skills in the pursuit of ethnohistorical research. There is also evidence of a new concern to integrate the findings of ethnohistorians into the broader framework of national history. Now is an opportune time to survey current trends in the study of native history ...

Indians as Allies

In histories of Canada written prior to the 1840s Indians played a prominent role and were treated respectfully. This reflected the actual significance of native people, who as trappers and traders were important to the Canadian economy and who, with the exception of the Iroquois prior to 1701 and the Micmac in the late eighteenth century, were allies of successive French and British governments in their struggles against the English colonists and later the Americans to the south ...

The Antiquated Indian

After the War of 1812–14 the usefulness of Indians as military allies against the Americans declined rapidly. Few native people lived in southern Ontario and Quebec and those that did were increasingly isolated on reserves. Indians thus ceased to be a living presence in the lives of most Euro-Canadians, including those who wrote accounts of Canadian history. This new reality is evident in François-Xavier Garneau's *Histoire du Canada*.[2] This book was written explicitly to be a history of the French-Canadian nation and sought to glorify the struggle of a people to survive and maintain their cultural identity in the face of the British threat. Because of this, native peoples were accorded a more restricted and negative role than they had been previously.

...

English-Canadian writers began to produce their own patriotic versions of Canadian history, beginning with John McMullen's *The History of Canada* in 1855.[3] In these books the French régime was described in detail as a heroic prologue to the development of a British nation. In contrast, Indians were viewed as marginal to the history of European settlement and were accorded even less attention than in nationalistic French-Canadian histories. They were generally portrayed as primitive and animal-like. Particular emphasis was placed on their cruelty, dirtiness, laziness, and lack of religion, while their love of freedom, which Heriot and Smith had praised, was now dismissed as being wild and primeval in nature.[4] Indians were frequently asserted to be incapable of becoming civilized and hence doomed to perish with the spread of European civilization ...

Yet there was considerable inconsistency in the way that English-Canadian historians treated native people. They frequently castigated their American colleagues for exaggerating the cruelty and treacherousness of Indians.[5] Canadian historians also relished comparing the brutal treatment of native people by the Americans with the 'generous' treatment they had received from Euro-Canadians ...

These interpretations of Canadian history required great self-deception or hypocrisy, on the part of writers whose governments were treating their former allies with much the same mixture of repression and economic neglect as American governments were treating defeated enemies ...

After 1900 the attention paid to native people declined still further as English-Canadian historians, who were now increasingly professional academics, abandoned a romantic concern with the French régime and began to pay more attention to constitutional history.[6] At the same time French-Canadian historical writing continued in its accustomed vein. Indians were assigned an ever smaller role even in general histories, where they were normally confined to introductory chapters describing the natural environment and early European settlement. To the extent that they were mentioned at all, their negative image as being a primitive and static people who were doomed to disappear tended to persist.[7] Canadian history, like that of the United States, had as its theme the achievements of Europeans; native people, who were seen as possessing no history of their own, remained the concern of anthropologists. The increasing remoteness of native people from the daily lives of most Canadians made it easier for historians to ignore the role that they had played in Canada's past.

...

Only in the 1930s, when it became evident that native people were not going to die out or disappear through total assimilation, did growing numbers of American anthropologists become interested in studying changes in native cultures since European contact.[8] Yet they continued ethnocentrically to conceptualize these changes as a process of acculturation, which implied that over time native peoples naturally came to behave more like Euro-Americans. Not until the 1950s did these studies acquire sufficiently particularistic and historical features to emerge as a new branch of anthropology called ethnohistory.[9] By that time anthropologists had ceased to study only factors bringing about acculturation and had begun to investigate the ways by which many native Americans had also resisted acculturation and struggled to preserve their cultures over the centuries.[10]

Native American history became popular among historians as well as anthropologists in the United States during the 1960s. At that time the traditional study of American political history gave way to a radical and centrifugal social and cultural history that was focused on specific classes, genders, and racial and ethnic groups.[11] Studies of American Indian history and of changing Euro-American perceptions of native people took their place alongside those of immigrants, workers, blacks, and women, and history and the generalizing social sciences drew closer together. Yet the study of native history in Canada is not merely a belated reflection of academic trends to the south.[12] Canadians have made distinctive and important contributions to the study of ethnohistory. Moreover, serious investigations of native history began with the social sciences earlier in Canada than in the United States.

In Canada the first social scientist to pay significant attention to the historical role of native people was Harold Innis, in his book *The Fur Trade in Canada*.[13] For this and for many other innovative contributions to the understanding of Canadian history and the historical significance of technology, Innis still deserves respect and admiration ...
...

Conclusions

In *The Children of Aataentsic* I sought to demonstrate that it was possible to write the history of a native group primarily using written documentation that was of European origin. In doing so, I tried in part to answer the concerns of ethnohistorians, such as Edward Spicer, who feared that in using such data it might never be possible to understand native history from the inside.[14] I believe that I succeeded in writing a history that is specifically centred on a single native group – the Huron – rather than the French, Dutch, or English colonists, or even on the theme of relations between Europeans and Indians that was ethnohistory's heritage from earlier studies of acculturation. I did this by relying more heavily than most ethnohistorical studies previously had done on archaeology as a secondary source of information that is not biased by European transmission as well as by using the concept of 'interest group' to overcome the lack of detailed information about individual Huron and to secure comparable treatment of the internal diversity of Indian and French behaviour. Although I dealt mainly with the Huron prior to 1660, I am convinced that it is worthwhile to trace the history of specific native groups from prehistoric times to the present. Such studies not only are interesting as ends in themselves to native and Euro-Canadian readers but also provide the building blocks from which a detailed picture of native history can be constructed on a national and continental scale ...

Notes

This paper is a revised version of the first of two Seagram Lectures delivered to the Department of History, University of Toronto, 3 February 1986. I thank those attending for their comments and Nobuhiro Kishigami for his discussions of ethnohistory.

1 J.W. St G. Walker, 'The Indian in Canadian Historical Writing,' Canadian Historical Association, *Historical Papers*, 1971, 21–47; D.B. Smith, *Le Sauvage: The Native People in Quebec Historical Writing on the Heroic Period (1534–1663) of New France* (Ottawa 1974); Walker, 'The Indian in Canadian Historical Writing, 1972–1982,' in I.A.L. Getty and A.S. Lussier, eds., *As Long as the Sun Shines and Water Flows: A Reader in Canadian Native Studies* (Vancouver 1983), 340–57
2 François-Xavier Garneau, *Histoire du Canada depuis sa découverte jusqu'à nos jours*, 3 vols. (Quebec 1845–8); later references are to Andrew Bell's translation, Garneau, *History of Canada from the Time of Its Discovery to the Union Year (1840–1)*, 3 vols. (Montreal 1860).
3 J.M. McMullen, *The History of Canada from Its First Discovery to the Present Time* (Brockville 1855)
4 J.C. Hopkins, *The Story of the Dominion* (Toronto 1901), 44
5 Hopkins, *Story of the Dominion*, 43
6 Carl Berger, *The Writing of Canadian History: Aspects of English-Canadian Historical Writing, 1900 to 1970* (Toronto 1976), 183
7 Walker, 'The Indian in Canadian Historical Writing'
8 Robert Redfield, Ralph Linton, and M.J. Herskovits, 'Outline for the Study of Acculturation,' *American Anthropologist*, XXXVIII, 1936, 149–52; Linton, ed., *Acculturation in Seven American Indian Tribes* (New York 1940)
9 E.H. Spicer, ed., *Perspectives in American Indian Culture Change* (Chicago 1961); Spicer, *Cycles of Conquest; The Impact of Spain, Mexico, and the United States on the Indians of the Southwest, 1533–1960* (Tucson 1962)
10 R.F. Berkhofer, Jr., *The White Man's Indian: Images of the American Indian from Columbus to the Present* (New York 1978; Vintage Book edition 1979), 67–8
11 Thomas Bender, 'Making History Whole Again,' *New York Times Book Review*, 6 Oct. 1985, 1, 42–3
12 Cf W.J. Eccles, 'Forty Years Back,' *William and Mary Quarterly*, XLI, 1984, 410–21, esp 420.
13 Harold Innis, *The Fur Trade in Canada* (New Haven 1930); and ed. (Toronto 1956)
14 Spicer, *Cycles of Conquest*, 289

GENDER POLITICS

Writing Canadian Women's History, 1970–82:
An Historiographical Analysis

ELIANE LESLAU SILVERMAN

(December 1982)
CHR 63, no. 4: 513–33. Excerpt: 513–14, 531–33.

When analysing recent scholarship the historian seems doomed to begin by commenting on the growth in a new field which arises with seeming inevitability in response to previous paucity. Immigrants, labourers, farmers – the cast drifts in from the wings and the audience points, 'There! Look! Did you see that?' The spectators are recent PhDs and their professors coming to the theatre with different pasts and different expectations. They look about, gossip with colleagues at intermission, and rise from their seats to return to their craft – describing and analysing the characters – some vindicated in old prejudices, others excited by new perceptions.

Would that one could begin differently! Alas, women's history in Canada is no exception. A burgeoning field, historians began to write it seriously about 1970. No longer limiting themselves to grandiose hagiography or to demeaning triviality, they proposed in good faith that to study women's past was worthy of their best efforts. A voluminous, rigorous, and often lively literature is emerging.[1] ...

So far, however, they have composed a body of literature that runs parallel to the historical current, not swirling within it but flowing through a nearby gully. The landscapes are similar; the sources, the rhythms, and the channel it cuts quite different. Certainly, the population in women's history is a newly discovered one; more importantly, the female majority it describes is different in important ways that we will analyse later from the males who appear in mainstream history. Some historians have attempted, in fact, to place women within that current with the result, indeed, of broadening it. The fur traders of the early nineteenth century, so significant for the economy, had women introduced into their midst by Sylvia Van Kirk.[2] She argued that the traders married Indian women *à la façon du pays*; these women not only provided their men physical comforts, language lessons, and children, but also served as a liaison in the back country between trappers, traders, and native tribes ...

How to retrieve women's lives from the silence? Very often historians write on subjects merely because they are accessible. Old history, new history, and *mentalité* history can make women visible as individuals and as masses. Historians will want to focus on subjects with adequate records: institutions, political events, and intellectual history. The data must be pulled together and quantified. How did changing birth rates and mortality influence life cycles and reform activities? Did health and sickness cause women to move in and out of the home, in and out of the public eye? Who belonged to reform societies? How much money did women earn? ...

Women's historians must also be prepared to be far more daring than they have been, more prepared to ask new questions, to speculate even from fragmentary data, to be suggestive as well as definitive. There are elusive questions to raise, even if the answers remain tentative. Popular culture, for instance: we need a body of literature on women in the urban cultural institutions that profoundly affected women's lives as they moved into the cities. The apartment house changed women's lives, as did altered housing design. Commercial machine-made products entered the home just as it was being touted as a refuge from the frenzy of industrialization. Did women teach adaptation to the machine in the household? Who controlled the purchasing of household technology? Transit systems brought women into the centres of cities, to department stores in male downtown districts; the housewives' isolation broke down. How did the theatre, vaudeville, and movie houses influence manners and habits? Or eating in restaurants? What happened when women found themselves in public places? The profession must be bold enough to address subjects which produce few records such as attitudes and states of mind. Group culture and individual wills are agents of change as important as demographic development or economic forces.

There are still more elusive problems to be confronted boldly and innovatively. Did women construct mythic hero figures, like the frontierswoman perhaps, which might bring them into a national ethos, or might keep them out? The role of hero images in Canadian ego formation remains a virtually unexplored territory; so is the effect of cultural gender images on women's behaviour. Women's realities were often at odds with idealizations; how do prescription and reality conflict? Was the famous issue of middle-class morality as meaningful for women as men thought, shielding their wives? Did women really bring civilization, or were wives sought when men's search for morality was already in place?[3] Contentious though it is, psychohistory at least poses some of these questions, reminding us to check out age cohorts, or madness brought on by frontier isolation, or women's child-rearing modes during the two world wars when men were away. Psychohistorical method might also address issues in leadership and power, covert or overt. We need many more biographical studies.

The matter of chronology and timing presents another puzzle for historians. Male intellectuals of the 1920s bemoaned work as routinized and boring, finding that conventional work patterns militated against personal freedom. Yet at just that moment, many women found, to the contrary, that work liberated them. When part-time work was despised by men, women accepted it as better than no work at all. The economic crisis of the Depression affected men and women differently; for the latter the lowest paid jobs were available, and even the low pay of domestic service was preferable to unemployment.[4] In the work world, business acumen and ambition were lauded in men while most women were only expected to master becoming invaluable to a man. Deference on the job and in the home dominated women's lives for a century-and-a-half after it had lost its meaning for men. Domestic servants certainly deferred to the women who hired them, wives to husbands, and mothers often to their children.

Which brings me to the subject of family history. It is not necessarily women's history, though women are half of it, any more than military history is men's history. Certainly, historians must study the interaction of the two, with the focus now on women, not on the family as a neuter unit. They may find that the family depended for its existence on the subordination of women. Women and the family were in tension with each other, with women both organizing its social order and subordinated to it. As in politics, as in the law, health care, and the industrial workplace, as in cities and suburbs, so too in the family did men and women perceive and occupy separate realms, separate and in conflict.

Women's history makes women the subjects of a new body of literature. They do not exist in it as the 'other' – subsidiary, auxiliary, objectified – but come to centre stage of the historical experience. Canadian history becomes not at all what we expected. It becomes the story of the female majority living in perpetual tension with the institutions that contained them ...

Notes

I thank the University of Calgary Research Grants Committee for making possible the invaluable and delightful help of Jill Cousins. I offer heartfelt thanks to Sheldon Silverman for his critique and support. I also acknowledge the help of Rhys Williams of the University of Calgary Library.

1 In the last dozen years almost 200 articles and books in women's history have appeared. Of these I will be analysing only a limited number which illustrate the methods and the themes and exemplify certain issues.
2 'Women and the Fur Trade,' *Beaver*, winter 1972, 4–12. See also her expansion of the data in *Many Tender Ties: Women in Fur Trade Society in Western Canada, 1700–1850* (Winnipeg 1980). Also see Jennifer S.H. Brown, *Strangers in Blood: Fur Trade Company Families in Indian Country* (Vancouver 1980).
3 Laurie Alberts, 'Petticoats and Pickaxes.' *Alaska Journal*, VII, 3, 1977, 146–59
4 Marie Lavigne and Jennifer Stoddart, 'Les travailleuses Montréalaises entre les deux guerres,' *Labour/Le Travailleur* II (1997), 175

The Skilled Emigrant and Her Kin: Gender, Culture, and Labour Recruitment

JOY PARR

(December 1987)
CHR 68, no. 4: 529–51. Excerpt: 529–31, 550.

Emigration is generally understood as a gendered process, beginning for men with a solitary experiment in distant lands, for women with a long interlude between two worlds while they wait for word that it is safe to follow. For men the journey is seen as a response to international differentials in the labour market, for women as a way to begin or consolidate a married life. Emigration usually seems to cast men in active roles and women in adaptive roles, men being part of a structured system, and women living out the consequences of subjective choices.[1] These characterizations probably miss the mark, even for emigration within marriage. As descriptions of female migration outside marriage (and probably also within it for all but women of independent wealth), these depictions omit several essentials.

Single female emigrants have not been uncommon historically. Typically they left home in early adulthood, at a marriageable age, although, as Charlotte Macdonald reminds us, the fact that emigration and marriage have similar locations in many life cycles does not establish that young women, any more than young men, left home in order to marry. Most working-class women understood that marriage, either before or after emigration, would not end their experience with wage work. Female emigrants had their eye on the job market, both short and long term.[2] In Canada even young women recruited for their domestic skills often remained for many years in the labour force before marriage.[3] In the twentieth century, emigration frequently has been a flight from marriage rather than a strategy to pursue it, a way either to evade or escape conjugality.[4]

Emigration is a sex-selective process experienced differently by women and men. It is also part of a wider social existence in which gender is perceptible only as it is confounded by time, class, and place. Emigration can be the product of sex imbalances; it also forms them, both in the old country and the new. By its sex-selectivity, emigration creates social groupings in which women and men are present in radically unequal numbers ...

This paper considers the relationships among gender solidarities, wage work, and the reconstitution of family in a community to which many women emigrated when preference or circumstance led them to lives without men. It deals with the particular case of approximately 700 British hosiery workers, principally from the east midlands, whom Penman's Company, then the largest Canadian knit-goods firm, assisted to emigrate to Paris, Ontario, population 4000,[5] between 1907 and 1928 ...

The Penman's emigrants were selected because they were accomplished hosiery workers. The contradictions between being female and being financially independent did not exist for the recruiter while he was recruiting them. Rather, he assiduously searched out skilled female wage earners for the very combination of attributes that complicated their lives at home. He was looking for female wage earners simply because they were wage earners, promising steady long-term employment; but his offer presented these emigrants with a social possibility as alluring as the expected hike in pay.

...

The lives of the female skilled workers and their kin in Paris were formed by a series of common transatlantic experiences passed down as family lore and neighborhood reminiscence to daughters and granddaughters. The women from the east midlands were recruited for their workplace proficiencies with hosiery machinery and knitted fabric and their community traditions of life-long female wage work. In English hosiery districts these traditions were embattled. They were fortified by manufacturers' preferences for experienced, lower-waged women employees and long-standing community acceptance of the jointly constituted household rather than the individually garnered, male-breadwinner wage. They were challenged by the male-dominated hosiery unions who claimed wage-earning wives were complicit in pay cuts and who feared long-serving female employees as competitors with men for the declining pool of skilled jobs in the knit-goods industry. For all parties to the convention, life-long female wage work existed in awkward contradiction to the prevailing social ideology governing gender roles. For skilled women workers, emigration mitigated these conflicts by offering steady and well-paid employment and anonymous distance from the domestic tensions their English circumstances had conditioned. Emigration brought together women experienced in wage work, selected because of their workplace skills, and congregated them in a community where their prospects as wage earners were brighter than their likely fortunes as wives. Among the female emigrants and their kin, the economic and emotional reasons for leaving Britain were recounted as of a piece. Emigration, by offering women in one generation a way to evade or escape conjugality, opened a social possibility that wage work rather than marriage would be the continuity in an adult woman's life. In the community in which women were at both a numerical and an economic advantage, life after emigration was characterized by stronger bonds between women, weakened links with male kin, a more comfortable social acknowledgement of variously constituted female-headed households, and a greater willingness, at least within the emigrant community, to use group pressure to reinforce marital relations that would facilitate life-long female wage work.

Notes

I am grateful to Shula Marks, Alice Kessler-Harris, and the members of the Queen's University Seminar in National and International Development for thoughtful commentaries on this paper.

1 Sheila Allen, *New Minorities, Old Conflicts: Asian and West Indian Migrants in Britain* (New York 1971), 29; Mirjana Morokvasic, 'Why Women Emigrate? Towards Understanding of the Sex-Selectivity of the Migratory Movements of Labour,' *Studi Emigrazione* 20 (June 1983): 133; Elizabeth Ewen, *Immigrant Women in the Land of Dollars* (New York 1985), chap. 3
2 Charlotte J. Macdonald, 'Ellen Silk and Her Sisters: Female Emigration to the New World,' in London Feminist History Group, *The Sexual Dynamics of History* (London 1983), 82–5
3 Varpu Lindstrom-Best, '"I Won't Be a Slave": Finnish Domestics in Canada,' 36, 44–50, and Marilyn Barber, 'Sunny Ontario for British Girls,' 55–71, in Jean Burnet, ed., *Looking into My Sister's Eyes: An Exploration in Women's History* (Toronto 1986)
4 Annie Phizacklea makes this point, based on the unpublished work of Mirjana Morokvasic, in her introduction to *One Way Ticket, Migration and Female Labour* (London 1983), 7.
5 Census of Canada, 1911, 1921

Gender History and Historical Practice

JOY PARR

(September 1995)
CHR 76, no. 3: 354–76. Excerpt: 356, 360, 362, 363, 371–2, 375.

Historians have a long-standing fascination with claims based in nature, with arguments that certain political systems and military organizations were *naturally* superior, that certain classes or races were *born* to rule. It has been an indispensable and honourable part of the historian's work to take human activities presumed eternal, or inevitable, or natural, and to trace the processes by which they have been made and changed through time. This task has included attempts to understand why and how universal and absolute truths have been invoked, how certainty is made out of uncertainty, and to what historical effect. Yet lately this historical inquiry into the construction of the ahistorical, the search to understand how, by whom, and in whose interest some parts of the contemporary are established as beyond temporality, rather than being accepted as integral to the historian's work, has been called corrosive of the historical project, and the historical subject, itself. Highlighting the partialness of our understanding of the past, and the artifices through which certain beliefs and practices have been selected and elevated as absolutes and universals, has been called dangerous.

...

Perhaps our colleagues in preceding generations made their peers uncomfortable when they worked to understand the social processes by which human beliefs in religious freedom and democratic liberty were forged or constructed. Perhaps the historicizing of these truths was once taken as an affront to their worth as ideas, as a reproach to those who wrote their histories. But this is no longer the case. The writing hand has moved on. Surely our forming hypotheses about the historicity of race, gender, and the power of the state are within this tradition, and confirm rather than deny the worth of the historical project, of the historian's work.

The topical space where this generational battle has been engaged has significance. This work is not new, and the unease it causes does not seem to be rooted in the widening of the historical landscape. So long as the cultural and women's historians were off in distant precincts, pushing out the perimeter, all was well. There is something about the return of cultural and women's historians to the metropolis, and the fact that these historians return with theories and methodologies that appear to bind together the study of nationality, race, gender, ethnicity, and the power of the state, which seems to be causing the problem. When insights from cultural and feminist studies make historical the once firmly forged fractures between the political and the social, make historical the once presumed natural markings of national, racial, ethnic, and sexual difference and the truths that sustain hierarchies of power, then alarm bells sound.

...

Why Gender History?

Disputes within historical practice, over how much of what is human changes through time (is historically constructed) and how stable and unified are people's perceptions of themselves and the world around them within time, are central to gender history, and account for its existence distinct from women's history. The premise of women's history was that hierarchical social, economic, and political context rather than biology, history rather than nature, created woman. This insight, that the characterization 'natural' had the power to make specific historical differences seem eternal and unchangeable, had become commonplace among North American historians of women before many on this continent had read Foucault.[1] Early on, studies of the social relationships that had crafted womanliness began to reveal the historical moorings that anchored other distinctions, between the public and the private, between activity counted as inside and outside the market, that had not seemed to be strictly or solely 'about women.' In time it became apparent that questions framed to be about women alone could entail their answers in their asking. A question posed about 'women' called forth responses selectively. These responses always to some degree isolated woman from the social relationships which created her, and presumed that woman existed in certain ways. 'Tell me about woman' always to some degree meant 'Tell me about someone who will be recognizable to me as a woman.'

...

From this position it followed that gender could not be taken *ex ante* as the primary form of identity, although in certain historical conjunctures it might emerge to be so. Both the character and the precedence of gender relations need to be put as historical questions. As gender history is practised, 'in historical context, the social positions women and men occupy are specified in multidimensional terms, and femininity and masculinity are not cultural universals but vary with other forms of power and markers of difference.'[2] This emphasis on social positions as multidimensional and specific rather than universal or totalizing is at the core of poststructuralist theory.[3] In historical studies, these understandings about the simultaneity and heterogeneity of identities were nurtured within a monographic research tradition that emphasizes context, contingency, and specificity. Thus, analyses in gender history and poststructuralist theory have proceeded together, 'if not always hand-in-hand.'[4]

...

Gender History and Keats's Negative Capability

The poet John Keats recommended 'not knowing' as a habit of mind through which to learn. This stance, the willingness to wait, attentive and deliberating, seeking but not foreclosing the search for an answer, he called negative capability.[5] Gender history is practised from this stance, and has tended and is intended to make the question 'What is *this* about?' less constrained in the asking. It has offered a healthy reminder that the discursive field of which the 'this' is a part is best not assumed in the question, that these constituting elements need rather to be located and their influence appraised. It is our task 'to brush history against the grain.'[6] From the moment the archives boxes are opened this habit of mind alerts the researcher to be self-checking: 'What am I expecting?' 'What has my eye been taught to see?' 'What is here, that my specification of the problem might lead me to dismiss?' ...

Conclusion

The implications of gender history for historical practice are not resolved. This, too, is a story that *is not finished*. The ways in which gender history makes a departure at the level of evidence and analysis are clear enough. This is work that begins by acknowledging diversity and instability rather than searching out unity and solidity. The recognition that gender was made by history rather than nature began a cascade of temporality. If gender was made in circumstance, it was likely to vary within time as well as across time, for the circumstances that framed gender were not always the same, and did not always form gender alone.

Thus were identities in fact severalties, multiple, evokable, scrutable, but settled in contingency rather than certainty. Knowing this means not 'knowing what was,' but knowing what was brought to the fore and forced into congruence, both seeking the circumstance which made this precedence and symmetry plausible and reckoning the contradictions which could be its undoing. This knowing is less agnostic than pantheistic, seeking explanation by inclusion rather than excision. And like all historical knowledge, this knowing is interim, expectant, augmentable, recombinant.

Notes

1 Kathleen Canning, 'Feminist History after the Linguistic Turn: Historicizing Discourse and Experience,' *Signs* 19 (1994): 370
2 Editorial, *Gender and History* 6 (April 1994): 3
3 Chris Weedon, *Feminist Practice and Poststructuralist Theory* (Oxford: Basil Blackwell, 1987), 19–42.
4 Canning, 'Feminist History after the Linguistic Turn,' 371
5 John Keats, *Letters*, ed. Maurice Buxton Forman (London 1935), 71–2
6 Walter Benjamin, 'Theses on the Philosophy of History,' in *Illuminations*, ed. Hannah Arendt, trans. Harry Zohn (New York: Schocken 1968), 257

CULTURAL HISTORY

The Methodist Church and World War I

J.M. BLISS

(September 1968)
CHR 49, no. 3: 213–33. Excerpt: 213–16, 230–1, 233.

The quantity and quality of English Canadians' participation in World War I was largely a function of their militant idealism. That idealism was encouraged and sustained by the nation's Christian churches, which, like the churches of every belligerent nation, mobilized all of their spiritual resources for battle. No churchmen in Canada worked harder at hammering their ploughshares into swords than 'the people called Methodists.' Yet, at the same time as they were preaching a crusade against the German anti-Christ, Methodists in Canada refused to idealize the social order at home. During the war years the Methodist Church's historic concern for social redemption blossomed into a comprehensive programme of social reconstruction. By 1918 the Methodist Church of Canada had become the most radical religious denomination in North America. More clearly than any other group in Canada, the Methodists of 1914–1918 synthesized militarism with a radical social critique.

Few Canadian Methodists worried about war in the spring of 1914. Those who did tended to share the attitude of Dr. W.B. Creighton, editor of the prestigious and widely read *Christian Guardian*, who felt that arms makers were the chief impediments to a peaceful world order. Rather than increase taxes in a militarist cause, Dr. Creighton felt that Canada should withdraw from the arms race and press on Britain her desire for 'a broader and more Christian internationalism.'[1] ...

In the autumn of 1914, however, church leaders abandoned their critical acquiescence in war in favour of an unquestioning belief in the righteousness of the conflict and the church's duty to play a positive role in achieving victory ...

All of the allied nations were absolved from blame as Methodist writers, assisted by government-sponsored pamphlets, uncovered Germany's responsibility for the outbreak of war and explained the militarism inherent in German civilization. The Old Testament provided a useful interpretive framework: the German Sennacherib had descended out of the night on Hezekiah (Belgium); alternatively, Germany's envy of Britain and France led to war as surely as Haman's jealousy for Mordecai the Israelite led him to try to slay the Hebrews. It was comforting to realize that Haman had been hanged and that the people of Sennacherib had been smitten 'an hundred four-score and five thousand' by the angel of the Lord.[2] By the summer of 1915 the wave of atrocity stories had convinced Methodists that the Germans did not fight like other nations. Like most Canadians, Methodists eventually believed they were fighting a people that inoculated its captives with tuberculosis, decorated its dwellings with human skin, crucified Canadian soldiers, and enforced a national policy of compulsory polygamy on its virgins.[3] Analysts who had at first argued that a basically Christian people had been misled by the Kaiser's worship of Woden now decided that Christianity had been extinguished among the whole German people so that German religion had become the exact antithesis of Christianity.[4] Methodist leaders nevertheless insisted on some form of humanitarian concern for the German people until well into 1917.[5]

Despite the accumulated evidence that this was a war worth fighting for, Christians were faced with the special problem of reconciling their support for war with those statements of Jesus which seemed to deny the use of violence in any circumstances ...

The church supported the war because it believed the cause was just. Methodists, like most English-speaking Canadians, were 'taken in' by the atrocity stories. World War II has surely taught historians to have more tolerance for people who believed atrocity stories in the earlier war. At the same time historians must ignore some of the lessons of the two wars. Most Canadians of his generation would have agreed with Dr.

Chown's later statement that in 1914 'war appeared to be something legitimate, noble and even sublime.'⁶ ...

Paradoxically, the pacifism at the heart of the Christian gospel was largely responsible for the extremism of Methodism's defence of Canadian liberty. No Methodist could fight a war that Jesus would not have supported. Therefore Methodists could fight only a holy war. If men were not dying for Christ their deaths would have appeared to be meaningless. The despair and sorrow would have mounted with the casualties until the church would have damned the war completely. In its crusading zeal the Methodist Church acquiesced in suppressions of basic liberties; to its own people it eventually denied the right of conscience. The amount of damage that would have been done to the nation's collective morale if its religious institutions had stood in critical judgment of the war is impossible to calculate.

...

It may be generally true that when Canadian historians come to study the wartime experience in depth they will find that these were vital years in Canada's social and intellectual development as well as in its rise to nationhood. The new sense of identity fostered among English Canadians by the war was more than simple patriotism. It was an expression of revived ideals of service to a common principle, participation in commutal activity, and membership in an organic whole. Nationalists and social reformers alike had protested against the fragmentation of community life and the destruction of spiritual values caused by rapid economic growth before the war. Because they aspired to the same end – the achievement of some form of organic unity in society – many nationalists and social reformers could unite in hailing the wartime experience as marking the birth of a new society. Indeed, as the Methodist experience demonstrates, it was both possible and consistent for the same individuals to combine militant nationalism with a determination to reconstruct Canadian society. As nationalists, as socialists, above all as Christian idealists, Methodists in 1918 were ready to participate in the creation of a peacetime community as unified and egalitarian as the wartime society . It is surprising how many other Canadians shared their determination.⁷ Somewhere in the 1920s, though, the new society got lost.

Notes

1 *Christian Guardian,* Jan. 28, April 15, 1914.
2 *Ibid.,* Nov. 18, 1914; Jan. 13, 1915.

3 *Ibid.*, Oct. 10, 1917; Sept. 11, Oct. 23, 1918.
4 *Ibid.*, Feb. 10, 1915; Nov. 1, 1916.
5 By 1918 Methodists were ready to hang the Kaiser and make Germany pay the total costs of the war. At no time had they supported any of the peace proposals.
6 [S.D.] Chown Papers [United Church Archives, Toronto], undated address (postwar), 'What Does the Bible Teach About War?'
7 Significant expressions of this idealism can be found in the Farmers' platform of 1918, the Liberal party platform of 1919, the collection of essays *The New Era in Canada* (Toronto, 1917), W.L.M. King, *Industry and Humanity* (Toronto, 1918), Stephen Leacock, *The Unsolved Riddle of Social Justice* (Toronto, 1920), and C.W. Gordon ('Ralph Connor'), *To Him That Hath* (Toronto, 1921).

The Social Gospel in Canada, 1890–1928

RICHARD ALLEN

(September 1968)
CHR 49, no. 3: 381–99. Excerpt: 383–5.

...

It has been argued that the social gospel in Canada was an indigenous development.[1] Although it is possible that a Canadian social gospel might have developed simply in response to domestic urban and industrial problems, it did not in fact happen that way. To be sure, the earliest expressions of the social gospel in Canada may still lie in sources untouched by historians' hands. And in those sources, the rise of the social gospel may be obscured by the gradual nature of its separation from older forms of Christian social expression characterized by a concern for church–state relations, education, political corruption, and personal and social vice. But almost all evidence regarding the emergence of the social gospel from this tradition points to currents of thought and action which were sweeping the western world, none of which originated in Canada. To trace this 'North Atlantic triangle' of culture and religion underlying the social gospel at large and its transmission to and development within Canada is a worthy but massive project. In this paper, only a description of some of its salient features can be attempted.

The inspiration of the pioneers of the social gospel in Canada and the origin of some of its prominent institutions reveal the extent of its indebtedness. W.A. Douglass in the 1880s expressed his disagreement with individualistic methods of social regeneration by tirelessly campaigning for Henry George's panacea of the single tax.[2] Salem Bland, later to become the philosopher and mentor of the movement, was an omnivorous reader, and in the decade of the 1890s when he seems to have first formulated a social gospel outlook, was especially influenced by Carlyle, Tennyson, Emerson, Channing and Thoreau, by the historical critics of scripture, and by Albert Ritschl, the great German theologian whose optimistic theology played a great role in the emergence of a social gospel theology. At least as significant for Bland was the literature of evolution.[3] The notes for his first socialist lecture, 'Four Steps and a Vision,' acknowledge various works of Darwin, Drummond's *Ascent of Man*, and Kidd's *Social Evolution*, as well as *Fabian Essays*, Arnold Toynbee, Edward Bellamy, and Henry George.[5] Canadians had attended the three great interdenominational conferences in the United States on social problems in 1887, 1889, and 1893, and one follow-up conference had been held in Montreal in the latter year.[6] Institutional vehicles and expressions of the social gospel such as the Brotherhoods, institutional churches, settlements and labour churches derived ultimately from British models, although American mediation and modification took place in some instances. This pattern of influence continued throughout the life of the social gospel in Canada.

The optimism of the social gospel drew on more than a generalized sense of progress, and even on more than the influence of evolutionary concepts. One of the more significant religious developments of the nineteenth century was the expansion of evangelicalism – expressed variously in German pietism, the Methodism of the English-speaking world, the missionary movement, and American revivalism. As against the reformed tradition of Calvinism, evangelicalism stressed free will, an immanent God, religious emotion, and a restrictive personal and social morality which made its followers formidably austere. Among its doctrines was a belief in the possibility of personal perfection beyond the temptation of sin. In the course of the nineteenth century it made an immense impact on all Christian traditions, especially in North America. As evangelicalism became more diffused in the latter half of the century and awareness of the social problem arose, the individualism of the evangelical way seemed to many to be less and less appropriate.[6] The demand 'save this man, now' became 'save this society, now,' and the slogan 'the evangelization of the world in our generation' became 'the Christianization of the world in our generation.'[7] The sense of an immanent God working in the movement of revival and awakening was easily transferred to social movements, and hence to the whole evolution of society. Thus Josiah Strong in the United States could speak of the 'great social awakening,' and many could come to view secular social action as a religious rite ...

The pressures of the last years of depression in the early 1890s precipiated a quickening interest in new forms of social thought and action among a growing group of Christian ministers and laymen ...

Notes

1 [Stewart Crysdale, *The Industrial Struggle and Protestant Ethics in Canada: A Survey of Changing Power Structures and Christian Social Ethics* (Toronto, 1961)], p. 22.
2 C.D.W. Goodwin, *Canadian Economic Thought* (Durham, N.C., 1961), pp. 32–8; *Toronto World*, 7 Feb. 1898; *Grain Growers' Guide*, 21 Nov. 1917, pp. 32–3.
3 United Church Archives, Toronto (UCA), reading lists in the Bland Papers.
4 Bland Papers.
5 C.H. Hopkins, *The Rise of the Social Gospel in American Protestantism, 1865–1915* (New Haven, 1940), pp. 110–15.
6 For an expression of this transition, see the introduction to General William Booth, *In Darkest England and the Way Out* (London: International Headquarters of the Salvation Army, 1890).
7 The distinction was between bringing the message and creating the social reality. For an illuminating discussion of this process, see Donald B. Meyer, *The Protestant Search for Political Realism, 1919–1941* (Los Angeles and Berkeley, 1960), chap. 1.

French Canada and the Prairie Frontier, 1870–1890

A.I. SILVER

(March 1969)
CHR 50, no. 1: 11–36. Excerpt: 27–9, 31–2.

...

In the quarter-century after the Manitoba Act, then, when English Canada was looking to the prairies as the land of promise, the key to Canada's future, and when thousands of Ontarians were pouring onto the plains, three main trends of opinion tended to keep French Canadians away from the region: a disbelief in the material value of prairie land; a fear that to go there was to expose oneself and one's national identity to danger; and a conviction that Quebec alone was the French-Canadian *patrie* so that to go west was to expatriate oneself. The letters of Taché's agents, reporting on their contacts in Quebec, seem to indicate that the first of these reasons was most important with farmers, the actual potential settlers, while the educated, the community leaders, were most concerned with the problem of expatriation and depopulation of Quebec.

Running through all these attitudes is a strain of pessimism, defeatism, or demoralization. One *fears* bankruptcy, harassment, loss of identity, or exile. This frame of mind differs markedly from what has been typically represented as the frontier mentality. The frontiersman is supposed to be fearless, optimistic, independent, expansive. His boundless enthusiasm and self-confidence impel him to enterprise, often recklessly. Essential to the frontier hypothesis is the idea that these characteristics are 'forest-born,' are the result of the impact of the physical environment in changing the personality of the man who comes to the frontier.[1] In this, the frontier hypothesis may well be psychologically questionable, for psychologists appear agreed that personality is established with virtual permanence by the time adulthood is reached.[2] ...

Societies which have produced frontiersmen or colonizers seem always to have been characterized by a certain mobility or dislocation of their parts ...

Again and again we see that great colonizing movements are preceded by a period of mobilization – a period, moreover, in which some obstacle, whether military or economic, is met and surmounted. The Israelites spent forty years in the desert before they could settle Canaan – long enough for the slave generation do die off and a new breed of desert-born strong men to take over. The colonizing activities of the ancient Greeks followed a similar period of migratory wandering.[3] So it was with mediaeval colonizers. The Vikings spent centuries in their Scandinavian homelands, forced into lives of mobility by the scarcity of arable land, before beginning their great settling movement.[4] Norway was an *Aufmarschgebiet* that prepared the settlement of Vikings in Ireland. Ireland prepared the settlement of Iceland, and Iceland that of Greenland.[5]

French Canada in 1870 was far from the condition of any of the great colonizing societies. It was not a society in movement and, rather than having overcome some obstacle, it considered itself conquered, had failed in 1837–8 to liberate itself, and had finally settled for a compromise with the conquerors, politically in Confederation, economically by a withdrawal from competition with the English. Not movement, but stasis, enforced by the very nature of the task of 'survival,' was the keynote of French-Canadian society. The conquest cut off prospects of French-Canadian growth by immigration, giving both conquerors and conquered the idea that the *Canadien* population was fully formed. So too, the Proclamation of 1763, by drawing the boundaries of the province close in around the limits of the seigneuries,[6] created the impression that the province, if not already settled, was not so unsettled that the heirs of the present population would not fill it.[7]

...

... Immobility thus became not only a way of life for rural French Canadians, but also an ideal for the intellectuals, French Canada's educated leaders.[8]

In these circumstances colonization appeared not as a way of creating a new world but of preserving an old one. The church especially, concerned for the souls of its children, saw in colonization a way to maintain the old, parish-centred society of peasant farmers. This society seemed ideal not only because it promoted the Catholic virtues but because it conformed to the agricultural romanticism which Quebec's priests, like the lay intellectuals, had picked up in the classical colleges. Thus, colonization propaganda was largely priest-written, and church-sponsored societies raised money to help young farmers get started on new lands. An un-frontiersman-like attitude was natural here. Settlement was not a new start, but a way of preserving the old society of the St. Lawrence Valley. While the frontiersman went off to start a new, materially better life, French-Canadian colonizers saw in settlement very different goals: 'Prévenir l'émigration de nos compatriotes; ramener dans le sein de la patrie ceux dont la Foi est exposée à l'étranger; fixer notre peuple au sol; le détourner du luxe, de l'oisiveté, de l'ivrognerie, du blasphème; lui faire aimer la vie simple et paisible des champs ... .[9]

...

If colonization was to have as its aim the preservation of a certain type of society, a qualitative selection of settlers would be necessary. Families were preferred to single men, and the ratio of men to women, therefore, had to be kept even.[10] ...

Notes

1 The first statement of the idea is still the most dramatic. It's in Turner's essay, 'The Significance of the Frontier in American History,' in *The Frontier in American History* (New York, 1921), p. 4.
2 See, for example, C.T. Morgan, *Introduction to Psychology* (New York, 1956), p. 241. For the relevance of this to colonization, see the quotation from Gaston Bouthoul in O. Mannoni, *Prospero and Caliban: The Psychology of Colonisation* (London, 1956), p. 109.
3 J.B. Bury, *History of Greece* (London, 1959), p. 86.
4 Herbert Heaton, *Economic History of Europe* (New York, 1948), p. 72.
5 The mediaeval Russians, thrown out of their Kievan kingdom by the Tartar invasion, had not only to repel the Swedish and Teutonic Knights in the North, but also to learn to live in the Muscovite forests – a pair of accomplishments which eventually enabled them to regain and colonize an empire. In the West, the mobilization of peoples to escape and then repel the invasions of Magyars, Saracens, and Norsemen, prepared the colonizing activities of the twelfth and thirteenth centuries.
6 For example, in D.G.G. Kerr, *Historical Atlas of Canada* (Toronto, nd), compare plates 27 and 41.
7 See, for example, Carleton's report in P.B. Waite, ed., *Pre-Confederation* [(Scarborough, c. 1965)], pp. 52–3.
8 It is interesting that Pierre Chauveau, Quebec's first prime minister, was the author of the novel *Charles Guérin*, whose heroes, a group of city intellectuals and professionals, find peace and personal fulfilment only by abandoning the city for pioneer farming in the Eastern Townships.
9 C.A.M. Paradis, *Société des ... missionnaires colonisateurs ...* (Montréal, 1890), p. 13.
10 For example, [Public Archives of Canada], Cartier Papers, correspondence, MG 27, I, D4, vol. 5, Joseph Royal à George Cartier, St. Boniface, 1 juin 1872.

Some Quebec Attitudes in an Age of Imperialism and Ideological Conflict

A.I. SILVER

(December 1976)
CHR 57, no. 4: 440–60. Excerpt: 455–60.

...

Thus, if Quebeckers rejected the imperialism of the westward expansion of settlement, their newspapers did not reject the imperialism of the westward expansion of Catholicism. In fact, conscious of the religious-conservative imperial idea of the day, they saw the Northwest in its terms. When the Northwest Rebellion broke out, *Le Monde Illustré* associated it with imperial wars in Asia and Africa,[1] and *Le Nouveau Monde* compared Macdonald's position in Saskatchewan with that of Gladstone in the Sudan and Ferry in Tonking.[2] And, just as France, in Mexico, the Levant, or Indo-China, fought for justice, equity, and Christian principle, so Quebec, in defending the Métis, had on her side 'justice,'[3] 'droit,'[4] 'honneur,'[5] and 'l'union, la concorde et la paix' of Canada.[6]

Does it not seem, in fact, that the observation of French Canada's attitude toward the imperialism and ideological conflict of the age throws an interesting light upon Quebec's attitude toward the minority questions in Canada? Here was a province that considered itself to be the geographical and political expression of the French-Canadian nationality, the French-Canadian *patrie*,[7] that felt that Confederation, by establishing it as an autonomous province with its own parliament, was recognizing French Canada 'comme nationalité distincte et séparée,'[8] whose leaders refused to encourage settlement of their people in the Canadian West because it would mean an emigration of French Canadians away from their own country.[9] And yet, it was a province whose Parliament passed a formal resolution on behalf of the Manitoba Métis Ambroise Lépine; which, in the Métis affair, the New Brunswick and Manitoba school questions – indeed, whenever the French-Catholic minorities were embattled – intervened beyond its borders in their defence.

And it *was* Quebec that acted thusly – the autonomous province of Quebec – even when its attitudes were expressed by members of the federal Parliament. For federal MPs were not simply representatives of Canadian constituencies, of Canadians as *Canadians*; rather, in the autonomist view, they were representatives at Ottawa of the province of Quebec ...

While it was the prime minister of Quebec who was the 'représentant principal des catholiques dans la confédération,'[10] federal ministers had a duty to ensure that 'les justes reclamations de la Province de Québec seront entendues dans le Cabinet.'[11] Not least of these *réclamations* had to do with the defence of French Catholicism outside Quebec. It was that province, for example, 'un peuple tout entier,'[12] that demanded an amnesty for Riel and Lépine. The failure to obtain the amnesty was a defeat for Quebec: 'C'est bien cela. Québec veut l'amnistie, Ontario n'en veut pas. Québec cède et tout est dit.'[13]

Here was a view of Canada as world-in-miniature, divided between the two great hostile camps, each with its provincial champion: 'Ontario est le grand protecteur du fanatisme et des intérêts protestants,'[14] while, for the French and Catholics of Canada, Quebeckers were 'ceux qui, par la constitution et par les circonstances, doivent les protéger.'[15] Was it not that Quebec was a Christian nation, and that Christian nations had a duty to act as protectors of the weak and of the Truth, whether in Africa, in Asia, or in the other provinces of Canada? Catholic countries were bound to be imperial countries.

Quebec, then, in an age of imperialism, appeared to be an imperial country; her empire was in North America, though she might intervene elsewhere ...

Nor was it only the *language* of the military that was kept up in this connexion. The vigour of the Zouave tradition was shown in an 1874 proposal to create a Zouave militia regiment, complete with old Zouave uniforms and banners,[16] as well as in the warm reception given to the NWMP recruiting drive organized in 1873 by the ex-Zouave, E.A. Brisebois. Those who joined would, as in the Italian campaign, be 'les fidèles et loyaux soutiens de l'autorité.'[17] Such a rôle apparently attracted young French Canadians more than that of settler, for the proportion of French Canadians in the 1873 expedition of the Mounted Police was more than twice as great as the proportion of French Canadians among the Manitoba settlers in that decade.[18]

It was typical of the age that the great minority questions in Canada concerned the place of religion in schools and the impact of agricultural expansion on aboriginal hunting populations. The former was the chief ground on which the ideological conflict was being fought in Europe, and the latter was, as Professor Stanley has shown, a common problem of frontiers of imperial settlement.

When *La Revue Canadienne* compared the 1890 Manitoba school act with the 'néfaste' and revolutionary school law of France,[19] it was seeing the Canadian question in terms of the international ideological conflict. Both the Equal Rights Association and the Catholic school supporters discussed the question in these transcendant terms, confronting the Catholic conservative and the modern views of the purpose of education, the responsibilities and limits of the state's authority, and the rights of the family.[20]

...

What we have done here has been to try to look at French Canada as not just 'in' but 'of' the time and world community in which she acted. Viewed in this way, she does not seem to be at all the inward-looking and isolationist society she has often been thought to have been. Aware of world events, feeling involved in them, her politically-aware class, at least, judged Canadian issues as special cases of world-wide phenomena. At the base of their conception of their own society was Catholicism, and this not only dictated a particular involvement in ideological conflicts in Canada and abroad but also a positive response to the conservative and religious current in colonial imperialism, some of whose tendencies they manifested in their own social and political positions.

To stress this 'international' aspect of French-Canadian awareness is not only to challenge the view of French Canada as an isolated and isolationist society. It is also to raise questions about particular issues in Canadian history. Can the minority issues be explained more readily by this view of a highly autonomist Quebec acting beyond her borders as a special protector of Catholicism than by theories of a bicultural Canada, a transcontinental 'patrie' in which French Canadians would be at home from coast to coast? What does the noting of French-Canadian involvement in foreign adventures – particularly in something like the Sudan expedition – imply for traditional interpretations of the Boer War and World War I crises? Can one explain French-Canadian reactions in those cases by an assumption of *a priori* opposition to foreign adventures in general and British wars in particular? Is it right to contrast English-Canadian imperialism and desire for foreign involvement with French-Canadian isolationism, or should we rather suggest that English and French-Canadians tended to support different imperialisms, and often stood on opposing sides of the ideological conflict?

...

The influence of the international Catholic awareness in French Canada, then, was not limited to any one party or group. It touched, directly or indirectly, the generality of the political-professional-journalistic class which ran Quebec's affairs and directed its sympathies at home and abroad. It should not need to be said that questions discussed in this article were not the main preoccupations of that class. The fate of Catholic Poland, French Indo-China, or even the northwestern Métis could hardly occupy the main attention of men busy seeking power, distributing and receiving patronage, or trying to build railroads. But neither could it leave them unaffected. There were times when these questions would force themselves upon their attentions, and at such times their perception of the world and the main currents of its affairs inevitably affected their own sympathies and actions, both abroad and in Canada.

Notes

1 *Le Monde Illustré*, 4 avril 1885
2 *La Nouveau Monde*, 31 mars 1885
3 *L'Opinion Publique*, 9 oct. 1873
4 *Le Nouveau Monde*, 15 avril 1874
5 *La Presse* (Montréal), 17 nov. 1885
6 Ibid., 11 nov. 1885
7 Above, 449. [For elaboration, see p. 449 of the original article.] Also, e.g., *La Revue Canadienne*, xx, 1884, 249; xvii, 1881, 254; *La Vérité*, 15 jan. 1888; Oscar Dunn, *L'union des partis politiques dans la province de Québec* (Montréal, Desbarats, 1874), 14
8 *La Minerve*, 1 juil. 1867
9 For example, see the speeches of Ferdinand Gagnon and Oscar Dunn to the 1874 National Convention at Montreal, reported in *L'Opinion Publique*, 2 juil. 1874.
10 Above, 453. [For elaboration, see p. 453 of the original article.]
11 *Le Pionnier de Sherbrooke*, 19 juin 1874
12 Ibid., 29 jan. 1875
13 *Le Courrier du Canada*, 15 fév. 1875
14 *La Revue Canadienne*, viii, 1871, 319
15 Ibid., xxviii, 1892, 478
16 *Bulletin de l'Union-Allet*, déc. 1874, avril, mai 1875
17 Ibid., nov. 1873, 31. Also, *Le Franc-Parleur*, 7 oct. 1873
18 List of 'originals' made available by Mr S.W. Horrall, RCMP historian
19 *La Revue Canadienne*, xxvi, 1890, 281 *et seq.*

20 For example, D'Alton McCarthy, *Speech ... Delivered on Thursday, Dec. 12, 1889, at Ottawa, under the Auspices of the Ottawa Branch of the Equal Rights Association* (np, nd), especially 6, on the principles of liberty and equality; Equal Rights Association for the Province of Ontario, *Address by the Provincial Council to the People of Ontario, dealing Mainly with Separate Schools* (Toronto nd), 6–7; A.-A. Taché, *Denominational or Free Christian Schools in Manitoba* (Winnipeg, Standard Printing, 1877), 71; Taché, *Pastoral Letter by His Grace the Archbishop of St. Boniface, on the New School Laws of Manitoba* (St Boniface 1890), 3; *La Revue Canadienne*, XXVI, 1890, 386, 456; *La Vérité*, 28 juil. 1883; *Le journal des Trois-Rivières*, 27 mai 1872

Speaking Modern: Language, Culture, and Hegemony in Grocery Window Displays, 1887–1920

KEITH WALDEN

(September 1989)
CHR 70, no. 3: 285–310. Excerpt: 285–8.

Historians are beginning to acknowledge the crucial role of language in cementing social and political hegemony. An understanding that meaning emerges though language is hardly profound. What is new is a recognition of the complexity of meaning, and, by extension, of the agents which embody it. Part of this complexity stems from the fact that meaning is never self-evident. It is an ideological construct continually debated by different groups, each striving to impose a mental attitude towards the world by shaping and inventing appropriate texts. Language is a contested terrain. It is a ritual process which can be understood only in the context of specific frameworks of power relations. Dialogue exists, however, not simply among the parties in an ongoing discourse but within each utterance. Any communication contains traces left by previous speakers and any particular text, therefore, represents an accommodation between existing structures of meaning imposed on or accepted by the speaker and what it is that she or he ideally tries to say.[1]

As well, recognition of the complexity of meaning has grown with an understanding that texts encompass many things besides words. Language is only one kind of sign system and many different media can contribute to the same discourse. Even human behaviour, according to anthropologist Clifford Geertz, should be understood as symbolic action which attempts to communicate. The analysis of cultural forms, he has argued, should be thought of in terms of penetrating a literary text. Not what is being done but what is being said through it is the important thing to establish. As meaning – its creation, dissemination, and deciphering – has become the central preoccupation of many scholars, its intricacies have become boggling.[2] The text, as semioticians are wont to say, is infinite.

All this, at first glance, seems dense and remote, more appropriate to a few elite productions than the experience of ordinary people in the workaday world. Yet here, too, linguistic theory provides insight. Change occurs across the whole spectrum of human activity; people at every social level are faced with consequent adjustments of meaning. This kind of analysis is particularly useful because it demonstrates that response to change is not monolithic; that different groups generate different strategies to accommodate the same developments; and that the creation of meaning is rooted in concrete situations, not abstract possibilities. While it encourages historians to recognize that not everyone understands the world the same way, it can also help them glean new perspectives on their own discipline by knitting together a variety of approaches to the past that often remain quite separate.

An example of a struggle for meaning and hegemony which joins business and social history with intellectual and cultural history can be found in the grocery trade in Canada in the late nineteenth and early twentieth centuries. Though not as spectacular as the large urban department stores which have tended to preoccupy historians,[3] groceries too were culturally influential, not least because they were so numerous and close to home. At the end of the nineteenth century, Eaton's and Simpson's may have dominated their commercial horizon but Torontonians were far more likely to patronize on a day-to-day basis one or more of their city's 900 food stores. As with department stores, what people saw and did there established, defined, and conditioned an acceptance of modern life.[4]

Those sights and actions are extraordinary difficult to recapture. The existence of these marts – usually small, with few employees, often short-lived – was taken for granted. Customers did not confide to diaries or share with correspondents the pleasures of buying a pound of cheese or a jar of pickles. Surviving account ledgers reveal little about human activities in and perceptions of the stores. One source, however, does shed some light on food shops in Canada – the weekly trade paper, the *Canadian Grocer*. Founded in 1887 by John Maclean to keep merchants abreast of availabilities and prices of commodities, it also tried to foster all aspects of the business. To a large extent it was a repository of platitudes about successful merchandising but it frequently carried descriptions, photographs, and critiques of real establishments, especially those in Toronto where it was published. In the absence of other records, the *Grocer* is invaluable.

It indicates that from the 1880s to the First World War and well beyond, food-store window displays had considerable significance. Subscribers were continually admonished to mount well-thought-out trims, and many did. Since any form of human organization reflects an effort to impose meaning on existence, its study can suggest a lot about whoever spawns it. What this article tries to do, then, is explore why the grocery window was emphasized so much and what it communicated. Window displays constituted a series of texts in a discourse about the character of modern life. Like any sign system, they were shaped by previous constructions and were a ground of contention. The displays comprised, in effect, a language of modernity – a language promoted by merchandise producers, trade journalists, and some grocers, though not necessarily for entirely the same reasons. These groups used this language to mould an understanding of industrial society and, with different degrees of success, to buttress their authority within that system. Displays are worthy of consideration because they suggest not just what changed in the modern era but how particular versions of reality were made credible and how the contest for meaning was actually fought.

Notes

I would like to thank David Monod, George Rawlyk, and the two anonymous CHR assessors for their helpful comments, as well as Thelma Chuter for typing assistance.

1 T.J. Jackson Lears, 'The Concept of Cultural Hegemony: Problems and Possibilities, *American Historical Review* 90 (June 1985): 589–93; John E. Toews, 'Intellectual History after the Linguistic Turn: The Autonomy of Meaning and the Irreducibility of Experience,' *American Historical Review* 92 (Oct. 1987): 881–2, 885; Dominick La Capra, *Rethinking Intellectual History: Texts, Contexts, Language* (Ithaca and London 1983), 292–324

2 William J. Bowsma, 'Intellectual History in the 1980s: From History of Ideas to History of Meaning,' *Journal of Interdisciplinary History* 12 (autumn 1981): 279–91; Clifford Geertz, *The Interpretation of Cultures* (New York 1973), 10, 448; Bernice Martin, *A Sociology of Contemporary Cultural Change* (Oxford 1981), 27–52

3 See, for example, William R. Leach, 'Transformations in a Culture of Consumption: Women and Department Stores, 1890–1925,' *Journal of American History* 71 (Sept. 1984): 319–42; Susan Porter Benson, *Counter Cultures: Saleswomen, Managers and Customers in American Department Stores, 1890–1940* (Urbana and Chicago 1986); Michael B. Miller, *The Bon Marché Bourgeois Culture and the Department Store, 1869–1920* (Princeton 1981); Gunter Barth, *City People: The Rise of Modern City Culture in Nineteenth-Century America* (New York 1982), 110–47; Rachel Bowlby, *Just Looking: Consumer Culture in Dreiser, Gissing and Zola* (New York and London 1985); Rosalind H. Williams, *Dream Worlds: Mass Consumption in Late Nineteenth-Century France* (Berkeley, CA 1982); Elizabeth Ewen and Stuart Ewen, *Channels of Desire: Mass Images and the Shaping of American Consciousness* (New York 1982), 57–71.

4 The figure comes from the *Canadian Grocer* (CG), 22 Feb. 1895, 32. Very little has been written about the history of the grocery store, especially in the nineteenth century. See J.M. Blackman, 'The Corner Shop: The Development of the Grocery and General Provisions Trade,' in Derek Oddy and Derek Miller, eds., *The Making of the Modern British Diet* (London and Totowa 1976), 148–60; Michael J. Winstanley, *The Shopkeeper's World, 1830–1914* (Manchester 1983); Gerald Carson, *The Old Country Store* (New York 1954); Dorothy Davis, *Fairs, Shops and Supermarkets: A History of English Shopping* (Toronto 1966); Chester H. Liebs, *Main Street to Miracle Mile: American Roadside Architecture* (Boston 1985), 117–35; W.I. Walsh, *The Rise and Decline of the Great Atlantic & Pacific Tea Company* (Secaucus 1986); Michael Bliss, *A Canadian Millionnaire: The Life and Business Times of Sir Joseph Flavelle* (Toronto 1978). Literature on European stores is often concerned with defining the class status of the small grocer. See, for example, Alain Faure, 'The Grocery Trade in Nineteenth-Century Paris: A Fragmented Corporation,' in Geoffrey Crossick and Heintz-Gerhard Haupt, eds., *Shopkeepers and Master Artisans in Nineteenth-Century Europe* (London and New York 1984), 155–74.

PART FOUR

REFLECTIONS

COMMENTARY

The *CHR* periodically published retrospective articles, surveys, historiographical essays, and review forums that summarized the Canadian historical profession and its concerns. A number of these captured turning points in the discipline and opened up debate and discussion within the journal about directions for Canadian historical writing. Articles excerpted below provide windows on the state of the field at particular points.

Given recent denunciations of the historical profession for its lack of attention to political history, George Brown and D.G. Creighton's article (December 1944) on the *CHR*'s first twenty-five years is remarkable in its emphatic statement that history is more than just politics. Their case rested on the content of the journal's index for 1930–9. Such headings as 'Constitution, Law, Custom' had long lists of articles, but so did 'agriculture, fisheries, fur, transport, trade and commerce, and the Canadian north,' and there was evidence of rapidly growing interest in the history of education, churches, literature, and art. The *CHR*'s editors strove to promote a stronger understanding of Canada's past, and the journal encompassed broad-ranging fields.

As this volume has shown, however, the Second World War was followed by a decade and a half of widespread efforts to redefine and reshape the Canadian nation. In the wake of the Cold War, the desire to bolster the values of Western civilization contributed to an emphasis on political history and biography. By the mid-1960s, this project began to unravel, and the 1970s saw a more diverse historiography, like that of the interwar period. In 1974, *CHR* editors invited H.J. Hanham, a distinguished historian of nineteenth-century Britain, to discuss Canadian historical writing. In his article (March 1977), he explained that practitioners in young countries such as Canada tended to chronicle a national history – a task that included not just praising famous men, but exploring national character and the only half-conscious development of national myths. He observed that Canadian historians had been taking on that role since 1867, usually self-consciously. Whether English- or French-speaking, many of them wrote nationalist or interpretive studies, patriotic essays, or homilies designed to assist the work of royal commissions. As Canada was a multi-polar state, their task was difficult because there was no single national mould.

The result, Hanham concluded, was that Canadian historians' writing reflected the diversity of Canadian aspirations for the future, not just a single-minded quest for nationhood. Since the mid-1960s they had been enjoying a sense of liberation – preoccupation with the British heritage was only a sentimental tie, and the pioneering days were over. Nevertheless, English- and French-Canadian historians were still too disposed to think of history in narrow terms, exacerbated by divisions, and ought not to be constantly preoccupied with the mystery of what Canada is.

As their interest in political history waned, many historians also lost touch with the political economy tradition and, consequently, with economic history. In the meantime, a melding of Innisian and Marxist theories reinvigorated political science in Canada. Perhaps because Harold Innis had always stressed social scientists' disengagement from political programs, this new trend prompted concern – and even some hostility – within the Canadian historical profession. W.J. Eccles was concerned about the long-standing influence of Innis's interpretation of the fur trade, which he thought terribly flawed. His 'belated' review (December 1974) of Innis's *The Fur Trade in Canada* contended that the author had overemphasized the fur trade at the expense of political, military, religious, and missionary factors. Hugh Grant, then a doctoral student in economic history, countered (September 1981) that Eccles failed to understand that Innis was articulating a conceptual framework within which historical problems were to be perceived – the spatial extension of European empires in their search for staple products and the resulting discrepancies between the centre and the margin of Western civilization.

In a piece on political scientists writing history, John English (March 1986) sought to explain the decline of political history. The problem began in the 1960s when the traditional came to represent not only authority but also 'fustiness or even repression.' The counterculture, the New Left, and the war in Vietnam were also factors, according to English. Political historians' loss of esteem among fellow historians was soon reflected everywhere and reverberated even in the high schools. Moreover, the close ties once linking Canadian historians and political scientists withered as political scientists turned away from political theory and historical analyses to voting behaviour and other kinds of 'scientific' approaches.

Kenneth Dewar (December 1991) employed new trends in cultural history to examine narrative structures in historical writing – in particular, in the work of Donald Creighton. He endeavoured to dispel the notion that traditional narrative history had no intended political content or intent. His analysis showed that in Creighton's work narrative was only one of many ways of writing history, and its use also entailed conceptual choices.

Since the mid-1990s, more Canadian historians have been urging colleagues to build bridges between various specializations. Usually, they have discussed methodological approaches, but Allan Greer (March 1995) went a step further. He denounced the 'historiographical apartheid' between French- and English-Canadian historians, especially in regard to one of the most important political events in Canadian history – the Rebellion of 1837–8. Until the 1970s, the Rebellion had been a focal point of pre-Confederation history. But a teleological mode of explanation had depicted it as a necessary losing battle in Canada's evolution towards responsible government. In recent decades, empirical research on the Rebellion and a rich literature of social history had concentrated instead on down-to-earth particulars, although reflection on the conceptual level had not kept pace. Worse, non-specialist readers did not know even what the Rebellion was, or when and why it occurred. Accordingly, Greer called for a new synthesis to overcome two major obstacles – the isolation of Canadian historiography from larger international currents and the failure of studies of Lower Canada and of Upper Canada to recognize the links connecting the two provinces.

Significantly, Greer's plea echoed the concerns and hopes that had always infused and animated the *CHR* – to interpret and explain the Canadian past in all its dimensions while confronting divisions within Canadian society and the historical profession itself. And, like many Canadian historians, past and present, he emphasized the need to attune this project to global developments and international currents in scholarship.

ON CANADIAN HISTORY

Canadian History in Retrospect and Prospect:
An Article to Mark the Completion of the First Twenty-Five Years
of the *Canadian Historical Review*, 1920–1944

GEORGE BROWN and D.G. CREIGHTON

(December 1944)
CHR 25, no. 4: 357–75. Excerpt: 362, 364–6.

...

III

It is as well to begin with the proposals which have to do with the scope of the *Review* and of Canadian historical studies in general. There were a great many of these proposals. Those who answered the circular letter were generous in their praise of the achievements of Canadian history during the past quarter-century; but, on the other hand, they were also prolific in suggestions for the more intensive cultivation of the field and the progressive enlargement of the boundaries during the quarter-century to come. There was an insistent demand for new approaches, fresh interpretations, novel points of view. There was an emphatic assertion of the need of an active and independent spirit of historical enquiry. 'The *Canadian Historical Review*,' wrote a correspondent who perhaps summed up these general requests most completely, 'must somehow try to keep the philosophical interest alive ... It should systematically foster and cherish an interest in new points of view and interpretation ... New points of view are not welcomed in such a country as Canada, but without them the fields of history and of the social sciences are sterile except for a few highly trained cataloguers ... Somehow the *Canadian Historical Review* must detect the difference between a new point of view supported by a new vested interest and a new point of view representing the continued fevered search for truth.' Another writer, pursuing a similar theme, warned that an over-emphasis on modern trends is 'a special pitfall for historians,' and urged a greater concern with philosophy which, he declared, is 'the real storm centre of the social sciences.' ...

If, however, the value of local history had its champions, the importance of social history received even more vigorous support. 'You might do a lot worse,' wrote one correspondent, 'than crusade for meaningful social history during the next interlude between wars.' There was, on the whole, general agreement that Canadian historians had made at least a fair beginning in this field; but there was equally general agreement that a lot more could be done. In several letters the request for social history was put in very general terms; but in others, there were particular demands for religious history, literary, and scientific history, the history of ideas. 'It is true,' one writer admitted, 'that in this matter of ideas we are mainly in the condition in which the Director of the National Research Council says we are in the matter of technological research and invention; we exist on blood transfusions from the United States and Great Britain. But in the present age, when all our political, economic, and social ideas are going through a crisis, there should be some historical interest in investigating as to how we got these ideas in the past.'

...

While a good many writers insisted on the necessity of a wide programme of social historical studies, there were a few who emphasized the difficulties of its realization. It was pointed out that Canadian historians had been singularly late in attacking the field – that many of their efforts could scarcely be regarded as better than 'ghost-like antiquarianism.' In one letter it was argued that these weaknesses might have their origin in certain basic deficiencies of training and intellectual equipment on the part of historical students. 'Historians,' this writer observed, 'have probably done their most effective work in the field of political and constitutional development where they began with the advantage of a thorough familiarity with principles of political and constitutional organization. Impatience with a narrow political approach has led to an increasing interest in economic and cultural developments, but such a broadening of the field of history has not effectively met the competition of the social scientist as the historian too often has possessed an insufficient understanding of principles of economic or social organization. The *Canadian Historical Review* ought to advocate, as a basic training in history, a thorough disciplining in the social sciences. With such a disciplining, the historian would be more aware of the limitations of the social sciences as well as more familiar with social science methods.'

...

Along with this popular interest in social history there went an active, though less general, concern for military history. These two new preoccupations can probably be regarded as complementary rather than contradictory. They are both characteristic of modern historical studies, for they both represent a move away from history's original home base of politics. The variety and richness of military history and its intimate and vital relationships with other aspects of national development were particularly stressed by one correspondent ...

Most of the suggestions so far considered had to do with the more effective cultivation of the home field of Canadian history – the field which has admittedly been the chief concern of the *Review*. But there remained the question of expansion – of the expansion of Canadian historical studies in general and of the *Canadian Historical Review* in particular; and it was this topic which aroused most discussion and provoked the sharpest differences of opinion. Obviously a good many of those who answered the circular letter were deeply impressed with the conception of Canada as a not unimportant part of a closely interdependent world. Several of them were willing to agree that the *Review*'s concentration on Canadian history had probably been justified in the past. Others were quick to recognize that considerable expansion outward had already been achieved through articles, reviews, and review articles on fields related to Canadian history. But, even so, it was plain that some thought a more definite change of policy was now due. 'It may be trite,' one commentator observed, 'to say that the history of Canada cannot be divorced from world history, but I think that in the future more attention will be paid to the impact of American, European and Asiatic factors upon Canadian life and the influence of Canada across the Pacific, Arctic, and Atlantic oceans as well as in this hemisphere.'

Canadian History in the 1970s

H.J. HANHAM

(March 1977)
CHR 58, no. 1: 2–22. Excerpt: 2–3, 6.

Harold Innis was no doubt thinking of Canadian historians when he remarked in 1948 that Canadians were especially endowed by nature with long arms for patting themselves on the back.[1] For historians of new nations are expected to do just that: to peer into the past and to discern in the shadows the shape of great things to come, to weave scattered incidents into a tapestry revealing the more flattering characteristics of the national life. This is not just a matter of praising famous men and 'our fathers that begat us': it involves the simultaneous creation of a national chronicle and the exploration of national character and the only half-conscious development of national myths. The historians of the new nations of the eighteenth and nineteenth centuries – the United States, Germany, Italy – were, indeed, in terms of the mind as much nation builders as Washington, Bismarck, or Cavour. Canadian historians have been called upon to fulfil the same role since 1867 and have usually been quite self-conscious about it. Canada has been in the making, and Canadian historians, whether English-speaking or French-speaking, have wanted their share in the process, some by writing nationalist histories (*Colony to Nation*), others through intepetative studies (*Canada's First Century*), patriotic historical essays (*Notre Maître, le Passé*), or homilies and studies allegedly designed to assist the work of royal commissions.[2]

What gives the process a special interest for the non-Canadian is that Canada, like Switzerland, is a multi-polar nation. If there is a 'Canadian principle' it is that there shall be no single national mould: neither the long-expressed Toronto belief that Ontario is destined to set the pattern for the whole of Canadian life, nor the more recent Ottawa belief that the whole of Canada can be remade as a bilingual and bicultural replica of Ottawa and Hull, shall be allowed to achieve fulfilment. Canadian historians must, therefore, reflect the diversity of Canadian aspirations for the Canadian future, not just a single-minded quest for nationhood. And they have begun to do so with a new vigour.

During the last ten years Canadian historians seem to have enjoyed a new sense of liberation. The peoples of Canada, though still divided as they have been from the beginning, have achieved a new sense of self-confidence. The British connection, only a generation ago one of the basic preoccupations of both English- and French-speaking Canadians, is now little more than a sentimental tie. The pioneering days are over, the economy is prosperous and diversified. Historians need no longer complain, along with the farmers, that the country has been, or is being, destroyed by the politicians. Complaints about 'the fundamental corruption of Canadian public life'[3] and expressions of dislike and distaste for Mackenzie King, once endemic among Canadian academics, have largely given place to a growing awareness that corruption, like Mackenzie King, may have been part of the price to be paid for the emergence in Canada of a distinctively Canadian self-awareness – as Bismarck was part of the price to be paid for German unity. There is still too much name-calling in Canadian history, often based on a vulgar reworking of old campaign slogans, and an intolerance of human weakness. But the flogging of corpses is now mainly confined to non-academic historians.

Even imperial and diplomatic history, the longest-established branches of Canadian history, are in the process of transformation. The main theme is still the gradual emancipation of Canada from British and American dominance, but most of the best recent books have been as much concerned with the interconnection of domestic and international politics a with imperial and diplomatic negotiations *per se* ...

... Yet there has been little serious attention to the possibility that Canadians, though North Americans, have always been closer in many of their assumptions to Europe than to the United States. If, as has been alleged, Canadians have 'remained in cultural formation Europeans overseas,'[4] then one would expect Canadian–American relations to resemble European–American relations more than Canadian historians have hitherto conceded (interesting parallels might perhaps be drawn between Canada and Mexico). In any case, historians of French Canada in the late nineteenth century would gain a useful, new perspective if they were to pay more attention to parallels between French Canada and Ireland, Portugal, and Italy, rather than to the more obvious parallels with France. This would enable them, I suspect, to find for the first time an adequate means of exploring the psychological, social, and economic consequences of the fact that in 1900 just about as many French Canadians lived outside Quebec, chiefly in the United States, as within Quebec.[5]

I raise these issues because Canadian historians, though their interests have broadened in recent years, are still disposed to think of Canadian history in too narrow terms. The historical profession is divided on linguistic lines, which encourages English-speaking historians to concentrate their attention on English Canada and French-speaking historians to concentrate their attention on French Canada. The result is that Canada emerges from many recent books as if it consisted of two insular societies: even more insular in their attitudes than France and England. Nor has recent writing about Canadian history helped much. French-Canadian history is still coming to terms with the consequences for French Canada of the Abbé Groulx' use of history as the instrument of a francophone crusade and of the rivalry between the historians of Quebec and Montreal.[6] And English-Canadian historians emerge from Carl Berger's delightfully low-key account of them[7] as inhabitants of a world populated by politicians and academics whose primary interest was not in the forces that shape history but in the politics of English Canada. If Canada were to break up, Canadian historians would find it easy, too easy, to carry on business just as usual.

Notes

In 1974 the *Canadian Historical Review* invited the distinguished historian of nineteenth-century Great Britain, H.J. Hanham, to write an article on Canadian history viewed from the outside. We wish to thank the *Revue d'Histoire de l'Amérique Française*, *Acadiensis*, and Canadian publishers for their generous cooperation.

1 Harold A. Innis, *Essays in Canadian Economic History*, ed. Mary Q. Innis (Toronto 1956), 399
2 A.R.M. Lower, *Colony to Nation* ... (Toronto 1946, revised ed. 1964), Donald Creighton, *Canada's First Century, 1867–1967* (Toronto 1970), Lionel Adolphe Groulx, *Note Maître, le Passé* ... (3 vols., Montreal 1924–44)
3 Innis, *Essays*, 386
4 Maurice Cranston in *Times Literary Supplement*, 4 June 1976, p. 669
5 The Quebec French-Canadian population in 1901 was roughly 1,370,000; the number of ethnic French Canadians in the United States in 1900 was roughly 1,200,000.
6 For example, Marcel Trudel, 'Les Débuts de l'Institut d'Histoire à l'Université Laval,' *Revue d'Histoire de l'Amérique Française*, XXVII (1973–4), 397–402
7 Carl Berger, *The Writing of Canadian History: Aspects of English-Canadian Historical Writing, 1900 to 1970* (Toronto 1976)

A Belated Review of Harold Adams Innis, *The Fur Trade in Canada*

W.J. ECCLES

(December 1979)
CHR 60, no. 4: 419–41. Excerpt: 419–20, 440–1.

A reappraisal of the Canadian fur trade is long overdue. For this to be done adequately there are two prerequisites: first, past misconceptions have to be cleared away; then the trade has to be placed in its historic and not just its economic context. This communication addresses itself primarily to the first of these presumptions.

Harold Adams Innis's major work, *The Fur Trade in Canada*, has long been regarded as the definitive work on the subject, an impeccable piece of scholarship, and a landmark in Canadian historiography. Robin W. Winks stated in his foreword to the 1962 edition, 'The book is of the greatest significance because of Innis's fundamental reinterpretation of North American history and because of the effect of that reinterpretation on subsequent scholarship.'[1] The statement is certainly true, but Professor Winks then went on to state that Innis 'never wrote an inadequately researched or thoughtless book.' A little farther on, however, he qualified this encomium with the *caveat* 'his method of citation was somewhat quixotic,' as indeed it was.[2] The sweeping generalizations and conclusions of this work have been accepted uncritically by too many later historians. Unfortunately, neither his premises, both stated and unstated, his use of historical evidence, nor the conclusions drawn will stand up to close scrutiny and all too many erroneous interpretations of North American history have been made in consequence.

Innis saw clearly enough that in the early sixteenth century the trade in furs began as an adjunct of the cod fishery and that the coming into fashion of the beaver-felt hat had made the fur trade viable in its own right. His brief studies of the ecology of the beaver and of the manufacture and marketing of felt hats are certainly well done, albeit the latter study was derivative, being based on the work of French and British economic historians.[3] It was certainly the profits to be made in the garnering of furs from the Indians and their sale in France at a high profit that first enabled the French to establish permanent settlements in Acadia and the St Lawrence valley. Innis, however, took economic determinism to extremes and grossly exaggerated the role of the fur trade in the history of both North America and Europe. He stated, for example: 'The economic and institutional life of France undoubtedly suffered material disarrangement through the importation of furs on a large scale from New France.'[4] He produced no evidence in support of this claim and it is necessary only to examine the volume and value of the fur trade relative to the kingdom's total trade for it to be immediately apparent that the statement is, to say the least, a gross exaggeration.

Statistics are available for the years 1718–61 for furs imported at La Rochelle, the main port of entry for Canadian produce. These imports average out at roughly one million *livres* worth a year.[5] After 1739 some ...

... The conflict was not directly over furs but for control of the region where the fur brigades obtained the essential supplies of pemmican. Elsewhere he declares: 'To a very large extent the American Revolution and the fall of New France were phases of the struggle of settlement against furs.'[6] The causal connections of these great events to the fur trade he sees as the French occupation of the Ohio valley and the Proclamation of 1763. He failed to grasp the fact that the French did not occupy the Ohio valley for its furs. The Montreal traders had never shown any interest in the area. The French occupied the region, over the objections of the Canadians, for purely political and military reasons.[7] Similarly, the Proclamation of 1763 was a political document enunciating political decisions made to serve political ends. Any connection these decisions had with the fur trade was incidental.

The assertions that 'Canada emerged as a political entity with boundaries largely determined by the fur trade,'[8] that 'It is no mere accident that the present Dominion coincides roughly with the fur trading areas of Northern North America,[9] that the North West Company was the forerunner of the present confederation,[10] and that the present boundaries were a result of the dominance of furs,'[11] are all further examples of economic determinism carried to the extreme. Significantly, this assertion is the final conclusion of the book.

When the case is subjected to scrutiny it quickly collapses. The present border from the Atlantic to the western end of Lake Superior was in no way connected with the fur trade. In fact, if the fur trade were to have determined the border in the Great Lakes areas then it would presently run from the western end of Lake Erie south of Lake Michigan to the Mississippi. In 1783, despite the strong opposition of le comte de Vergennes, the French foreign minister, Britain ceded to the United States the territory south of the Great Lakes to the Mississippi for political reasons.[12] When, after the Louisiana Purchase, the border west of the Great Lakes had to be determined, it was only in the Columbia territory that the fur trade was a factor in the negotiations. Had the western boundary been determined by the fur trade it would today run along the Saskatchewan river to the Rocky Mountains, rather than the 49th parallel of latitude, for the fur trade country lay to the north of that river, and west of the Rockies it would follow the lower reaches of the Columbia River.

In a critique of a major work a detached, judicious balance has to be maintained in the rendering of judgment. It is, therefore, disturbing that virtually nothing can be found on the credit side of the ledger in this instance, except that Innis's *The Fur Trade in Canada* was a pioneering work which brought the Canadian fur trade to the attention of a wide audience. Unfortunately, it gave a distorted view of the trade and at the same time inhibited further investigation. The work contains a great mass of information, much of its presented in chapters that lack cohesion, and frequently the evidence presented contradicts the book's conclusions. The end result has been the establishment of myths as conventional wisdom.

The basic flaw in the work is that Innis manifestly approached the subject with certain *a priori* premises and conclusions already formed and he chose to disregard any evidence that pointed to different conclusions. Historians, if not economists, today begin – or at least they should – the study of any topic with a question, or series of questions, and study all the available evidence in search of answers. They may have some notion before they begin as to what the answers will be, but if the evidence subsequently indicates that they were wrong then they have to draw the conclusions that emerge from the evidence. Frequently it happens that the original questions are found to be of less significance than other questions that emerge from the evidence and have to be pursued. Innis, however, began with answers, not with questions, and thereby he went sadly astray. All too often his arguments defy both the evidence and logic, the latter sometimes being akin to asserting that wind is caused by the trees waving their branches.

For half a century this work has been regarded as definitive, and hence historians have, until very recently, shied away from a re-examination of the fur trade. This is most unfortunate since the trade played such and important role, not just in the economy of New France, but in the framing of its social structure, in military affairs, and in the execution of colonial policy that, in the final analysis, determined the fate of both the French and the British empires in North America. All of these aspects of the fur trade are long overdue for thorough investigation.

Notes

1 All references are to the 1962 reprint of the revised 1956 edition, it being the most readily available today. The book was first published in 1930.
2 Harold Adams Innis, *The Fur Trade in Canada* (Toronto 1962), 83. The operative word in this statement is 'inadequately.' Professor Winks later noted (xiv), 'His only serious lack was failure to obtain access to the closed archives of the Hudson's Bay Company ...' This implies that he attempted to gain access but was refused. It is difficult to see why this should have been since F. Merk was permitted to study documents in the archives of the company relevant to his work *Fur Trade and Empire*, published in 1931, and A.S. Morton made good use of those archives for his *History of the Canadian West to 1870–71*, published in 1939. Nor did Innis consult the great mass of fur-trade documents in the Archives judiciaries de Montréal. He did make use of some of the correspondence between the royal officials at Quebec and the Ministry of Marine, but only the transcripts of the documents at the Public Archives of Canada. Had he consulted the original documents in Paris he would have discovered that a considerable number of them were not transcribed for Ottawa. A list of those not to be transcribed, mostly dealing with economic affairs, was affixed to the inside of the cover of each volume. A considerable proportion of them dealt with the fur trade.
3 Innis, *Fur Trade*, 76, notes 132, 133
4 Ibid., 83
5 La rochelle, Archives de la Chambre de Commerce, Anciennes archives, carton 27, Récapitulation de ... marchandises entrées dans ... La rochelle, 1718–1761. Cited in A.J.E. Lunn, 'Economic Development in New France, 1713–1760' (unpublished PhD thesis, McGill University, 1942), 464–5. In 1715 Ruette d'Auteuil estimated the Canadian fur trade to be worth upwards of a million *livres* a year. See *Rapport de l'Archiviste de la Province de Québec, 1922–23*, 59–60. Fur and hide imports at La Rochelle, taken from the same source and for the same time span are cited in Emile Garnault, *Le Commerce rochelais! Le Rochelais et le Canada* (La Rochelle 1893), 15–16. Emile Salone, *La colonisation de la Nouvelle-France* (Paris 1905), 397–8, reproduces Garnault's figures with an amendment, the deduction of entry for hides since these, he states, most likely came from the Antilles, Moose hides, deer, and seal skins were, however, a not inconsiderable item in Canada's fur trade exports.

There is a fairly consistent but puzzling discrepancy between Garnault's figures and those cited by Dr Lunn.
6 Innis, *Fur Trade*, 178
7 See [W.J. Eccles, *Frontenac, the Courtier Governor* (Toronto 1959)], 334–6; *France in America* (New York 1972), 178–81; [Guy Frégault, *Le Grand Marquis: Pierre de Rigaud de Vaudreuil et la Louisiane* (Montreal 1952)], 329ff.
8 Innis, *Fur Trade*, 393
9 Ibid., 392
10 Ibid., 391
11 Ibid., 401–2
12 W.J. Eccles, 'The Role of the American Colonies in Eighteenth Century French Foreign Policy,' *Atti del I Congresso Internazionale di Storia Americana* (Genova 1976), 163–73

One Step Forward, Two Steps Back: Innis, Eccles, and the Canadian Fur Trade

HUGH M. GRANT

(September 1981)
CHR 62, no. 3: 304–22. Excerpt: 304, 308–9, 322

In a recent revisit to *The Fur Trade in Canada*, the work of Harold Innis has been subjected to intense examination by a meticulous and determined historian. The verdict has been something less than favourable. W.J. Eccles has concluded that the reverence bestowed upon this book is wholly unwarranted: 'Unfortunately, neither his premises, both stated and unstated, his use of historical evidence, nor the conclusions drawn will stand up to close scrutiny and all too many erroneous interpretations of North American history have been made in consequence.' Before the fur trade can be placed in the appropriate historical context, Innis's misconceptions must be 'cleared away.'[1]

...

Unquestionably we have reached the point at which some review of Innis's study is in order. Fifty years have passed since the publication of *The Fur Trade in Canada* and the field has seen no shortage of research during this time. This past decade has witnessed a renewed interest in

Innis within a variety of academic disciplines, such that many have been able to affirm the general premises of the ground-work which he developed. To one commentator, this re-examination has brought Canadian historiography, or more properly indigenous political economy, to the verge of a 'renaissance.' Perhaps we are now sufficiently secure on this original ground that we may proceed beyond Innis, a progression which no doubt includes a more critical evaluation of Innis's work itself.[2]

With all this said, however, the question still remains as to the basis for this next step forward. When we turn our attention to the detail of *The Fur Trade in Canada*, how are we to benefit from its analysis and what aspects should we reject? Our purpose here is to suggest how this rereading of Innis's writings on the Canadian fur trade should take place; and when this reflection is complete, we shall find that the thrust of Eccles's criticism constitutes a serious step backwards in our approach to both Innis and Canadian history.[3]

...

The Canadian fur trade then cannot be dealt with as an isolated economic event; instead, Innis analyzed its integration into the overall trade and industry of European empires. France sought to establish the St Lawrence as an agricultural base able to contribute foodstuffs to the sugar plantations of the West Indies, and to the fishing regions centred first at Placentia and later at Louisbourg. These efforts failed, however, largely due to the increasing demands of the St Lawrence region.[4] Innis emphasized that the rapid penetration of the fur trade into the interior accentuated the existing weaknesses in the agricultural development of New France. The fur trade not only inhibited further settlement but was also a drain on the labour and capital resources of the colony.[5] Despite efforts to diversify the economy, Canada continued to rely upon the production of furs as its primary commercial activity, to the detriment of the larger interests of the French régime. As Innis stated the matter: 'Fortunate was the nation without an extensive fur trade.'[6]

English colonialism, in contrast, experienced the balanced development of the fur trade, the fishing industry, shipping, agriculture, and commerce in New England, which in turn fostered intercolonial trade with the fisheries of Newfoundland, and the sugar, molasses, and rum producing areas of the West Indies. This even development aided the mother country in two ways: first, by encouraging settlement it provided England with a more substantial market for its manufactured goods; and second, it did not burden England with having to provide for the colonies' foodstuffs.[7]

It is within this broad context that one aspect of French–English competition in the fur trade is to be understood. Innis argued that the growing supremacy of English manufactures, of which woollen trade goods are an operative example, was a decided advantage in the competition for furs ... [T]he relative importance of price and non-price competition, the wage-labour relations – all are topics which would benefit from further study.

...

It is important to keep in mind the relationship between Innis and later historians. In Eccles's review Innis is by implication held responsible, first, for inhibiting further research and, second, for errors made by subsequent authors in the field.[8] Innis, however, was probably the first person to point out the need for more analysis and the tentativeness of his own conclusions ...

The Fur Trade in Canada is not, nor was it intended to be, the final word on the subject. What Innis did provide us with is a study which opened up a number of issues, solved some, and left others unresolved. Thus, we are certainly correct in challenging and rethinking several of Innis's specific propositions, but to do so we must first understand the broader subject of our critique. In the process, we may just find that the framework set out by Innis is the most useful avenue for future research on the Canadian fur trade.

Notes

The author wishes to thank Abraham Rotstein and Mel Watkins for reading an earlier draft of this paper, and especially Ian Parker for making numerous corrections. Tom Walkom's insights were invaluable.

1 W.J. Eccles, 'A Belated Review of Harold Adams Innis, *The Fur Trade in Canada*,' *Canadian Historical Review*, LX, 4, Dec. 1979, 419–41
2 Ian Parker, 'Harold Innis, Karl Marx, and Canadian Political Economy,' *Queen's Quarterly*, LXXXIV, 4, winter 1977, 545–63. Evidence of this renewed interest in Innis can be found in the *Journal of Canadian studies*, XII, 5, winter 1977, an issue devoted to a review of his work.
3 The main corpus of Innis's work on the fur trade can be found in *The Fur Trade in Canada: An Introduction to Canadian Economic History* (rev. ed., Toronto 1956); his so-called trilogy of essays composed of his 'Foreword' to Murray G. Lawson, *Fur: A Study in English Mercantilism, 1700–1775* (Toronto 1943), 'Imperfect Regional Competition and Political Institutions on the North

Atlantic Seaboard,' and 'Decentralization and Democracy,' the latter two reprinted in Mary Q. Innis, ed., *Essays in Canadian Economic History* (Toronto 1956), 321–36, 358–71; and finally, 'Interrelations between the Fur Trade of Canada and the United States,' reprinted in M.Q. Innis, ed., *Essays*, 97–108.

4 Innis, *Essays*, 360–3, 365. The drain on resources which the fur trade represented to the French empire is also discussed in Innis, *The Cod Fisheries* (rev. ed., Toronto 1954), 90–1, 136–7. The inability of Canada to supply enough foodstuffs to Cape Breton is noted by Christopher Moore, 'The Other Louisbourg: Trade and Merchant Enterprise in Ile Royale 1713–58,' *Histoire Sociale/Social History*, XII, May 1979, 90; and by J.S. McLennan, *Louisbourg from Its Foundation to Its Fall* (London 1918), 44.

5 Eccles's argument regarding the retardation of agriculture in New France rests upon demographic and climatic problems, factors which he implies Innis ignored ('A Belated Review,' 437). This certainly is not the case, however, for Innis was merely pointing out the economic events which deepened these existing weaknesses (*Essays*, 143–4). Among other things, the fur trade companies inhibited settlement before 1663 since immigrants represented potential competition in the fur trade (*Fur Trade*, 37). Second, the heavy imbalance in cargo resulting from bulky trade goods being shipped from France and light furs being sent in return also hindered immigration, in contrast to the timber staple, for instance, where unused capacity on the trip to North America encouraged European immigration (ibid., 58–9; *Essays*, 237; 'Foreword,' x). After all, the entire fur exports of New France for a single year could be shipped in one 'good-sized merchantman' (James Pritchard, 'The Pattern of French Colonial Shipping to Canada before 1760,' *Revue française d'histoire d'autre-Mer*, LXIII, 231, 1976, 192). Third, as Innis cited Du Chesneau: 'Two years absence of five hundred persons [coureurs de bois] (according to the lowest calculation), the best adapted to farm work, cannot increase agriculture...' (*Fur Trade*, 63).

6 'Foreword,' xix

7 Innis, *Essays*, 322–3

8 Eccles views in unfavourable light some of Ray and Freeman, *'Give Us Good Measure'* and attributes its shortcomings to an unquestioning acceptance of Innis's conclusions on the fur trade ('A Belated Review,' 428–9). Aside from the question of the merits of this study, it bears no marked resemblance to *The Fur Trade in Canada* either in terms of its initial premises or mode of analysis.

The Second Time Around:
Political Scientists Writing History

JOHN ENGLISH

(March 1986)
CHR 67, no. 1: 1–16. Excerpt: 1–2.

The troubles for political history began in the 1960s when the traditional came to represent not authority but fustiness or even repression. In Canada, political history was pre-eminently the tradition of Canadian historical writing. 'Nation-building' formed character, and politicians shaped circumstances. The historian, indeed, seemed to be the guardian of national tradition. William Kilbourn, for example, suggested in his article on historical writing in the 1965 edition of the *Literary History of Canada* that 'Such has been the preoccupation with the question of Canada itself and with a search for a national identity in a nation where it does not exist in as palpable and obvious a way as in Europe and the United States that one is sometimes left with the odd sensation that Canada is nothing but a figment of the historical imagination, a concept nurtured in the minds of a small minority of Canadian leaders in each generation, aided and abetted by a few historians.[1] The young historians had often shared classrooms with future prime ministers and statesmen, and if they did not always share later political affiliations, their style, their companions, and their ethos remained quite similar.

In the 1960s some historians did continue to aid and abet Canadian politicians and those politicians' attempts to define once again Canada's national identity. J.T. Saywell introduced *Federalism and the French Canadians* to English Canada, and Ramsay Cook was the book's leading interpreter.[2] Nevertheless, the setting was changing, as the university became swollen with undergraduates and new faculty. The faculty often came from the United States, either as native Americans or as graduate students returning home to their first job, and they brought with them the American intellectual's suspicion of politicians, an old wariness much enhanced by Lyndon Johnson, Richard Nixon, and Vietnam. For them, and for others whom they influenced, politics had lost their charm; they seemed too much the administration of things and too often sordid. A classical scholar has recently argued that this perception has prevented modern historians generally from understanding – or wanting to accept

– the 'primacy' of politics in earlier times, when the 'polis' was regarded as a memorial to those who had shaped it. In part this inability derives from the expansion of the economy and of the scope of a modern state, which has acted to make the private sphere 'the chief locus of human endeavour' for all but a few by limiting direct involvement in the affairs of the 'polis.' What Plato had deemed the noblest human activity and the ultimate expression of reason, the ordering of the state, became remote from daily experience. The result was resentment and alienation from politics.[3]

Whatever the cause, there can be no doubt that this mood affected younger scholars in their approach to political history. Moreover, there were new approaches to historical study which promised to open rich lodes which had been closed to earlier scholars. Sometimes these approaches involved technique, as in the case of computer analysis of census material, and sometimes they involved ideological innovation, as in the case of the studies of working-class culture which passed through Britain and the United States to Canada. Simultaneously, young francophone historians were reading from or even studying under French historians of the *Annales* school who had launched the most devastating of all attacks on narrative political histories, the type which Canadian historians had usually written. In Quebec and elsewhere, there was another political ingredient: the attack on Ottawa and 'centralization.' Among historians this attack fitted neatly into a new focus on 'limited identities.' In limiting identities, historians normally avoided the political and focused upon cultural, social, and economic concerns which seemed to offer definitions of these more limited identities more effectively.

...

Notes

1 William Kilbourn, 'The Writing of Canadian History,' in Carl Klinck, ed., *The Literary History of Canada* (Toronto 1965), 497
2 J.T. Saywell, Introduction, in Pierre Trudeau, *Federalism and the French Canadians* (Toronto 1968); and Ramsay Cook, *The Maple Leaf Forever* (Toronto 1971), especially 23–45. Saywell's contributions to the *Canadian Annual Review* in the 1960s are notable as skilled essays in contemporary history.
3 Paul Rahe, 'The Primary of Politics in Classical Greece,' *American Historical Review*, LXXXIX, 2, April 1984, 266 and passim

Where to Begin and How:
Narrative Openings in Donald Creighton's Historiography

KENNETH C. DEWAR

(September 1991)
CHR 72, no. 3: 348–69. Excerpt: 348–51, 368–9.

Was Donald Creighton a narrative historian? The question might be thought purely rhetorical, for surely it is a commonplace among historians not only that he was but that he was a master of narrative historiography. It is worth asking, nevertheless, in view of the renewed interest among philosophers and literary theorists in narrative as a form of prose discourse and of recent claims that contemporary historical writing is experiencing a 'revival of narrative.' In the former case, discussion has focused particularly on the epistemological import of narrative, in the latter on the practical implications of certain innovations observed in current historical study.[1] A reconsideration of Creighton's work in light of the new 'narratology' may help to illuminate his historiographical practice and enhance our appreciation of his mastery. It may also assist in clarifying some of the issues with which all historians must deal in choosing the way they write their histories.

Debate in recent times concerning the value of narrative history has been confused by uncertainty as to its nature. There are those, on the one hand, for whom all history is narrative history and historiographical narration is the representation in prose form of what one has discovered about the past through the study of its remains. In this view, the term narrative history is a redundancy. On the other hand, there are those for whom the term evokes a set of distinctive characteristics, including descriptiveness, chronological organization, attention to individual character, and a focus on particular actions and events. In this view, narrative history is considered, often critically, to be history of a specific kind. In everyday usage, moreover, the term is often simply associated with a colourful prose style.

Disputes over what history ought properly to be about have further clouded the issue by identifying narrative with 'political' or 'traditional' history. The conception of history as past politics has been the model against which newer conceptions – social history, for example, or total history – have staked their claims as alternative or superior approaches to the study of the past. Critics have wedded the particular form in which political history has commonly been written to its contents and methods, in the interests of affirming the value of a different content and method. Narrative has thus served polemically as a code-word for 'old-fashioned,' while defenders of the old-fashioned have been content to accept the usage of their critics.[2]

...

This confusion abut the nature of narrative history derives, I believe, from our conventional approach to historiography. Historiography is usually conceived not in its original meaning, as the writing of history, but as the study of the history of historical study, including the development of different 'schools' of interpretation and various conceptions of historical knowledge. As J.H. Hexter pointed out in an essay written some twenty years ago, historians have tended to be preoccupied by questions of content, method, procedure, and point of view when examining their discipline. Matters concerning the craft of writing have either been subsumed in debates over the scientific status of history or left to the creative intuitions of individual historians. For all the care that many exercise in writing their own histories, few have paid systematic attention to what Hexter called the 'rhetoric of history,' or historiography, properly speaking.[3]

In Creighton's case, for example, his writing, while much admired, is little studied. In what is now the standard history of English-Canadian historiography in the twentieth century, Carl Berger emphasizes Creighton's 'Artistry.' Indeed, he says, 'No other Canadian historian was so concerned with history as a literary art as Donald Crieghton.'[4] Yet Berger is more concerned with what Creighton wrote than the way he wrote it ...

One result of this approach to historiography is that we have only an impressionistic awareness of the variety of modes in which history may be written, their possibilities, and their implications for historical understanding and the communication of meaning ...

... I have found especially useful a distinction made by many narrative theorists between 'discourse' and 'story.' In fiction, that is between the 'order of telling' and a postulated 'order of the told': in history, between the historian's ordering of the past and the 'real' order of the past, as recorded in documents, artifacts, photography, and so on.[5] Narrative, in this view, is an order of telling that honours certain properties of temporal sequence, interconnectedness, and closure. It is neither assumed to be 'found' in the aspect of the past to be recounted, nor is it assumed to be necessary to the recounting. The mode of a historiographical discourse, therefore, is in some measure optional. In the words of the philosopher Nelson Goodman, 'although every narrative will survive some reordering, and some narratives will survive any reordering, not every narrative will survive any reordering. Some stories when reordered in certain ways are no longer stories but studies.'[8]

This definition of narrative is not confining but allows for a degree of flexibility that is missing from definitions that rely more narrowly on content and chronological order. When examined from this perspective, Creighton's histories exhibit a variety of rhetorical strategies. While their mode is predominantly narrative, it is not, contrary to common opinion, uniformly so, nor are his narratives always narrativistic in the same way. The range of his historiographic practice may be observed in the different ways in which he begins his histories ...

... In criticizing our conventional notions of narrativity, I have shown them to be at once indefinite and unnecessarily restrictive. Conditions and circumstances, setting and character, and human actions, intentions, and experiences may all be elements of a story rendered as narrative. Yet they are seen together in manifold relationships – spatial, temporal, explanatory, genetic, and so on – by means of a discursive form constructed by the teller. The chronology of the story elements is established by the telling but does not order it, while the recounting of particular doings and events need not be at the sacrifice of collectivities and general processes.

Seen as a way of ordering a discourse, narrative has no necessary 'political' content, nor does it require the use of particular kinds of evidence. Creighton's interests, the fullness of his sources, and his confidence in the pastness of the past allowed him to construct certain sorts of narratives, some of which were political in content. As Mark Phillips has argued, however, other sorts of narratives may well be constructed on more fragmentary sources and may give voice to more self-consciously subjective historical accounts of other matters.[7] ...

At the same time, narrative is only one among many ways of writing history. Character studies, interpretative essays, cross-sectional portraits, and so on offer alternative models of historiographical discourse. Adoption of the narrative mode is a matter of judgment. Such judgment, however, entails conceptual choices. When theorization or classification, for example, serves as the governing ideal of historical inquiry and understanding, some other kind of representation is called for, if only because the articulation of presuppositions required of these approaches cuts across the shared 'common sense' of writer and reader on which narrative is commonly grounded. Such approaches, in applying theories, or in posing and testing hypotheses, or in manipulating data and abstracting factors and characteristics, will find a narrative order of telling inappropriate to their needs and purposes.

These conclusions should encourage a fresh consideration of the relationship of form and content. Historiographical narrative, in its structuring of human agency in the context of time and space, would seem to presuppose a domain of human choice and purposive action that is often neglected, hidden, or denied in theoretical and typological approaches to the study of the past. This may help explain its pejorative association with traditional political history and its more positive association, in putative revival, with the new cultural history. In both cases the underlying issue, for many, has been the extent to which people's lives are shaped by natural, structural, and systemic forces beyond their control. Narrative, in short, is a way of ordering a discourse; it may also be a way of thinking, whose virtues historians will need to reconsider if narrative is truly to experience a revival.

Notes

I would like to thank Brian W. Dippie, William H. Dray, Pierre Payer, and Mark Phillips for their helpful comments on earlier drafts of this essay.

1 A useful guide to the narrative trend in the philosophy of history is Hayden V. White, 'The Question of Narrative in Contemporary Historical Theory' [1984], in *The Content of the Form: Narrative Discourse and Historical Representation* (Baltimore: Johns Hopkins University Press 1987), 26–57, while the narrativity of current historical writing is queried by Mark Phillips, 'The Revival of Narrative: Thoughts on Current Historiographical Debate,' *University of Toronto Quarterly* 53 (winter 1983/4): 149–65.
2 Hayden White makes this point with respect to *Annaliste* criticisms of narrative history ('Question,' 31–3); Gertrude Himmelfarb's liberal defence of political history is no more precise in its usage ('History with the Politics Left Out,' in *The New History and the Old* [Cambridge, Mass.: Harvard University Press 1987], 14, 25); while J.L. Granatstein simply claims narrative as the exclusive preserve of political history, 'broadly defined' (*Toronto Star Saturday Magazine*, 24 June 1989).
3 J.H. Hexter, 'Historiography: The Rhetoric of History,' *International Encyclopedia of the Social Sciences*, vol. 6 (New York: Macmillan and Free Press 1972 [1968]), 369–93

4 Carl Berger, *The Writing of Canadian History: Aspects of English-Canadian Historical Writing, 1900 to 1970* (Toronto: Oxford University Press 1976), 208
5 The theoretical literature pertaining to fictional narrative is usefully summarized in Seymour Chatman, *Story and Discourse: Narrative Structure in Fiction and Film* (Ithaca: Cornell University Press 1978), 15–42. For a humanist critique of the extremes to which recent theory has taken the 'textuality' of the text see M.H. Abrams, 'How To Do Things with Texts,' *Partisan Review* 46 (1979): 566–88.
6 Nelson Goodman, 'Twisted Tales; or Story, Study, and Symphony,' in W.J.T. Mitchell, ed., *On Narrative* (Chicago: University of Chicago Press 1981), 111
7 Phillips, 'Revival,' 153

1837–38: Rebellion Reconsidered

ALLAN GREER

(March 1995)
CHR 76, no. 1: 1–18. Excerpt: 1, 3–7.

There was a time when historians thought they understood the events of 1837–38. They did not much *like* the Rebellion, and their accounts of the event itself were often sketchy in the extreme, but they knew where it belonged in the broad sweep of Canadian history: they could explain why it happened and what it meant. For the generation of academic historians writing before the deluge of the 1960s, the less said about the illegal machinations of Louis-Joseph Papineau, William Lyon Mackenzie, and their followers the better.[1] And yet, curiously, the Rebellion formed a major – I think it would be fair to say *the* major – focal point in their writings about the pre-Confederation century. Like the ghost of Hamlet's father, it brooded over a stage that historians proceeded to furnish with political backgrounds, social and economic causes, and imperial results. Developments converged on 1837, and then moved off in novel directions after 1838, but the tumultuous turning-point itself did not seem a worthy object of research once its essential character had been identified.

...

All these interpretive schemes that dominated Canadian historical writing through the middle decades of the twentieth century were built on the assumption that history had a discernible direction and flow. Canada was moving towards a goal in the nineteenth century; whether this end point was the construction of a transcontinental, commercial, and political union, the development of parliamentary government, or the preservation and resurrection of French Canada, it was certainly a Good Thing. Thus the rebels of 1837 were quite literally on the wrong track. They lost because they *had* to lose; they were not simply overwhelmed by superior force, they were justly chastised by the god of History. (The narrative structure in these older accounts resembles the revolutionary triumphalism then prevalent in American, French, and Soviet historiography, though, in the Canadian case, the form is inverted.) The Rebellion was the necessary anomaly in this providential account of the past, the sorry fate of the insurgents serving to validate the larger pattern, as well as providing Canadians with powerful moral and political lessons.

These teleological modes of explanation continue to resound down to the present day, even though historians long ago abandoned the confident overview genre favoured by Creighton, Groulx, and the rest. Original scholarship in the last few decades has veered in the opposite direction, away from overarching themes and towards specialized research on down-to-earth particulars. Moreover, since conflict and violence have ceased to be taboo subjects, empirical research on the Rebellion itself has made great strides since the 1960s. Military specialists have told us about troop movements and casualties;[2] imperial historians have shown us how Whitehall viewed the affair.[3] Meanwhile, research on the economy has revealed the financial and agrarian distress that helped to poison the atmosphere of the times.[4] A rich social-history literature has concentrated attention, as never before, on the ordinary people who formed the great majority of those caught up in the Rebellion;[5] even the religious background to 1837 has been explored.[6] The result has been a great advance in empirical knowledge: myths have been punctured, generalizations have been qualified, and a wealth of factual data has been accumulated.

However, reflection at the conceptual level has not kept pace with the progress of empirical and microscopic research. One can only pity the poor student or non-specialist reader who wanders into this historiographical terrain in search of answers to fairly basic questions about the Rebellion: What exactly was it? Was this a single phenomenon with various aspects and phases – the Rebellion – or were there two or more distinct rebellions? Why did it (they) occur and why did it turn out as it did? Was it a minor disturbance or an important event with lasting consequences? The student or reader will encounter a literature that seems more concerned with interpretive fine points than fundamental issues.

...

The time has come, I believe, for some basic rethinking about the Rebellion of 1837–38, and I will suggest lines on which such a reconsideration might proceed. In my view, we should pause in the search for causes and effects and concentrate first on identifying more clearly the phenomenon that is to be explained. Surely the 'what' question is prior to the 'why' question. We can best approach this definitional problem, I would argue, by looking more closely at the crisis of 1837–38 as a complex series of events, one involving the actions and interactions of several parties, not just those identified as rebels. Rather than focusing on a one-dimensional act of revolt, we should recognize the contingency of events. Choices were made, actions taken, not as the inevitable result of metaphysical forces or of rigidly determining structures, but in response to rapidly changing circumstances. Placing the accent on complexity and contingency may seem a recipe for chaos rather than definitional clarity; nevertheless, as I hope to show, this is the only way to achieve an integrated view of the Rebellion and to grasp its essential nature.

Two major obstacles stand in the way of any synthetic initiatives of the sort outlined above: the comparative isolation of Canadian historiography from larger international currents, and the yawning chasm separating studies of Lower Canada and works on Upper Canada. The historiography of this country, strong in many other areas, lacks precisely the language and conceptual tools needed to make sense of revolutionary matters. Given Canada's history, as well as the historiographic traditions mentioned earlier, this is hardly a cause for wonder; what is surprising is the failure of Rebellion specialists to make fuller use of the enormous literature, empirical and theoretical, on revolutionary episodes in Europe and the Americas in the late eighteenth and early nineteenth centuries.[7] ... Indeed, we can hardly find the words to describe the events of 1837–38 without drawing on the histories of other revolutionary outbreaks.

While a broader international view might provide useful concepts and points of comparison, any attempt to construct an integrated account of the Canadian Rebellion is still bedevilled by a particularly advanced case of historiographical apartheid. Creighton was quite prepared to encompass Upper and Lower Canada in his classic work, but since his time, researchers on the two sides of the Ottawa River have been pursuing different issues using different methods and, on the whole, ignoring one another.[8] The Canadian Historical Association, following the prevailing trends but also awarding them a sort of official stamp of approval, commissioned two Historical Booklets on the Rebellion: one devoted to Upper Canada, the other to Lower Canada. This gap, mirroring the separation of French- and English-Canadian historiographies, greatly magnifies the effects of fragmented views and specialized research – a situation prevailing in almost all fields of history – and makes consideration of larger questions particularly difficult. Above all, it tends to obscure the links connecting developments in the two provinces.

Notes

1 For the sake of brevity, I am confining my attention here to influential works belonging to what might be called the academic mainstream. Dissenting interpretations that never received the attention they deserved include S.D. Clark, *Movements of Political Protest in Canada, 1640–1840* (Toronto: University of Toronto Press 1959), and Stanley B. Ryerson, *Unequal Union: Confederation and the Roots of Conflict in the Canadas, 1815–1873* (Toronto: Progress Books 1973). My own approach owes much to these writers, particularly Clark.

2 Elinor Kyte Senior, *Redcoats and Patriotes: The Rebellions in Lower Canada, 1837–38* (Ottawa: Canada's Wings 1985); Mary Beacock Fryer, *Volunteers and Redcoats, Rebels and Raiders* (Toronto: Dundurn 1987). Please note that, in this note, and in those which follow, only a few of the more significant recently published books are included. This is not a comprehensive bibliographic essay.

3 Peter Burroughs, *The Canadian Crisis and British Colonial Policy, 1828–1841* (Toronto: Macmillan 1972); Phillip A. Buckner, *The Transition to Responsible Government: British Policy in British North America, 1815–1850* (Westport, Conn.: Greenwood 1985), 205–49. Imperial history of a different sort can be found in George Rudé, *Protest and Punishment: The Story of the Social and Political Protesters Transported to Australia, 1788–1868* (Oxford: Clarendon Press 1978).

4 The relevant literature is vast, but the works of Fernand Ouellet are particularly noteworthy; *Economic and Social History of Quebec, 1760–1850: Structures and Conjunctures* (Toronto: Macmillan 1980) and *Lower Canada 1791–1840: Social Change and Nationalism*, translated by Patricia Claxton (Toronto: McClelland & Stewart 1980). See also the highly perceptive discussion by Douglas McCalla in *Planting the Province: The Economic History of Upper Canada, 1784–1870* (Toronto: University of Toronto Press 1993), 187–93.

5 In addition to the works by Ouellet cited above, see Leo A. Johnson, *History of the County of Ontario, 1615–1875* (Whitby: County of Ontario 1973), 95–127; Colin Read, *The Rising in Western Upper Canada, 1837–87: The Duncombe Revolt and After* (Toronto: University of Toronto Press 1982); Bryan Palmer, *Working-Class Experience: Rethinking the History of Canadian Labour, 1800–1991* (Toronto: McClelland & Stewart 1992), 69–75; Allan Greer, *The Patriots and the People: The Rebellion of 1837 in Rural Lower Canada* (Toronto: University of Toronto Press 1993).

6 Richard Chabot, *Le curé de campagne et la contestation locale au Québec de 1791 aux troubles de 1837–38* (Montreal: Hurtubise 1975); Gilles Chaussé, *Jean-Jacques Lartigue, premier évêque de Montréal* (Montreal: Fides 1980); Albert Schrauwers, *Awaiting the Millennium: The Children of Peace and the Village of Hope, 1812–1889* (Toronto: University of Toronto Press 1993)

7 A qualification is in order: on particular themes, Rebellion specialists have indeed drawn on a comparative literature covering such matters as riots in eighteenth-century Britain or the agrarian economy on the eve of the French Revolution, but they have shown hardly any interest in revolutionary episodes per se and in their integrity.

8 Mea culpa!

Index

Aberhart, William, 18
Abraham, Plains of, 9
Acadia, 115, 116, 318
Acton, Lord, 9, 11, 91
Adair, E.R., 9, 66, 82–3
Adams, Henry, 87–8
Adams, Herbert, 75
Aboriginal populations, 131. *See also* European–Amerindian relations; Natives
African Canadians, and segregration in schools, 25, 275
agrarian radicalism, 18
agricultural crisis (Lower Canada/Quebec), 27, 197, 233–4
agriculture, 119, 159–60, 220, 233–4, 264, 296, 323
agriculturisme, 238
Aird Commission, 165–6
Alberta, series on Social Credit movement, 18
Algonkians, 267–8. *See also* Natives
Allen, Hugh, 225–6
Allen, Richard, 200
American Civil War, 9, 87, 95, 106, 108

American Historical Association, 6, 24, 67, 75; annual meeting in 1932, 9–10
American Historical Review, 6, 10, 28, 75–6
American Revolution, 45, 90, 93–5, 101, 115, 117, 122, 206, 319
ancien régime, 112, 113. *See also* New France
Annales school, 24, 26, 39, 236, 260, 327
Annexation crisis (1848–50), 24, 123
anthropology, 13–14, 20, 32–4, 45, 51, 69, 129–30, 200–1, 268, 270, 273, 275
anticlericalism, 23
anti-étatisme, 238
antiquarianism, 313
antique industries, 3
archaeology, 13, 276
archives, use of, and preservation of material, 7, 20, 65–6, 74, 76–8, 84
Aristotle, 105
Arnold, Benedict, 90–1

Asquith, Herbert Henry, 98
assimilation, 174, 275
Atlantic provinces: and Confederation, 36; historians' neglect of, 14. See also regionalism
Atlantis, 35
Atwood, Margaret, 3
Australia, 42, 96, 101–2; historians and historical scholarship, 42
Axtell, James, 35
Aylen, Peter, 247–50

Bailey, Alfred G., 13, 14, 33, 69
Baldwin, Robert, 251
Banque du Peuple, 181
Barbeau, Marius, 13
Barraclough, Geoffrey, 31
Beard, Charles: purpose of history and role of historian, 9, 67
Beckwith, Walter, 249
behavioural science, 65
Bercuson, David, 28, 37–8
Berger, Carl, 199, 317, 329
Berlin (Kitchener, Ontario), 253
Bibaud, Maximilien, 270
biculturalism, 23, 300, 315
bilingualism, 21–2, 175
biography, 19–20, 25, 66, 136, 147–8, 153–5, 280, 309; historians' attitudes towards, 16, 18; and popular history, 8, 38–9
biological supremacy, 13–14, 20
Bitterman, Rusty, 33, 196
Black, J.B., 71–2
Bland, Salem, 293
Bleus, 224–5
Bliss, Michael, 200; review of *Radical Politics and Canadian Labour* (Martin Robin), 30–1
Bluenose, 217

Board of Railway Commissioners, 210
Boas, Franz, 13
Boer War, 96, 300
Bond Head, Sir Francis, 40–1, 198
'bonne entente,' 7, 68, 175
Borden, Sir Frederick, as minister of militia, 243
Bothwell, Robert, 28, 37
Bouchard, Gérard, 236
Bourget, Ignace, 226
Boyd, John, 226
Brandt, Gail Cuthbert, 36, 44
Brantford (Ontario), 253
Brebner, J.B., 41; on Harold Innis, 13
Brisebois, E.A., 299
Britain, 136, 181–2, 188; and colonies, 90, 93–7, 99, 108–10, 116, 128–9, 186, 207, 233, 263, 274; and constitution, 24; and First World War, 8, 97–8; historians and historical scholarship, 75, 149–50, 183–4, 198, 200–1, 260; immigration to Canada, 122; influence in Canada, 18, 30, 68, 75, 101–2, 108–11, 137, 142–3, 189, 250, 293, 313, 327; and Magna Carta, 141
British Broadcasting Corporation, 165
British Columbia, 196, 201, 212, 214, 216; and Confederation, 14, 108; and economic development, 32–3; fur trade in, 14; gold rush, 14; radio stations in, 164–5; and Spanish exploration, 14
British North America, 77, 101, 106–8, 112–15, 120–3, 154, 206–7, 233; colonial government in, 95–6; defence of borders, 95
British peace delegation, 99
Brock, Sir Isaac, 9

Brown, Craig, 26
Brown, George, 7, 108, 156, 309; as editor of *CHR*, 7, 10, 14, 17; on primary documents, 7
Brown, Jennifer, on *Company of Adventurers* (Peter Newman) and popular history, 39
Brunet, Michel, 22-3, 137, 177, 196-7, 226, 236-7
Brydges, C.J., 225
buffalo, 69, 147, 159-60. *See also* fur trade
Bulletin des recherches historiques, 6, 19, 73
Burpee, Lawrence J., 9, 217-18

Cadigan, Sean T., 40, 198
Cairns, John, review of *Main Trends in History* (Geoffrey Barraclough), 31
Canada: A People's History (CBC-TV series), 3
Canada First movement, 123, 162
Canada français, 6
Canada Land Company, 78
Canadian Broadcasting Corporation, 3, 137
Canadian Committee on Labour History, 31
Canadian Council, 28
Canadian Forum, 163
Canadian Historical Association, 26, 138, 335; founding, 7, 76; membership, 19; relationship with *CHR*, 7
Canadian Historical Review (*CHR*), 73, 184; and Cold War, 16; control of, 6-7; editorial policy, 5-7, 10-12, 14-15, 17, 20-2, 24-6, 28-9, 31, 35-7, 44, 46-7, 65, 135; founding of, 6; and French Canada, 7, 11, 19-20, 24, 39, 196-7; impact of First World War on, 6; and Native history, 13-14; and popular history, 10, 35-6; readers' surveys, 16, 28-9, 36-8; and regionalism, 14; relationship to anthropology, 12; relationship to ethnology, 12; and Second World War, 15-17; and University of Toronto Press, 28; University of Toronto history department, domination by, 28
Canadian Journal of Economic and Political Science, 184
Canadian Journal of History/Annales canadiennes d'histoire, 24
Canadian League, 163
Canadian National Railways (CNR), 164
Canadian Pacific Railway (CPR), 101, 164, 166
Canadian Radio Broadcasting Commission, 165-6
Canadian Shield, 12, 118, 128
canals, 186-8
Canniff, William, 99
Cape Breton, 101, 221-2; coal mines, 244
capitalism, and capital investment, 29-32, 141, 180-1, 187-8, 198, 214, 216, 219, 236-8, 253, 255, 259-61
Careless, J.M.S.: 'limited identities,' 25, 195; rejection of frontier thesis, 18, 136
Cartier, George-Etienne, 196, 244
Casson, Dollier de, 81
Cawthorn, William, 117
census, 203, 204
Chapleau, Adolphe, 21
charivari, 228, 231
Charter of Rights and Freedoms, legal cases involving, 38

Chateaubriand, vicomte de, 270
Chown, S.D., 290–1
church, 88, 138, 250, 264, 289–91, 292–4; in Quebec and French Canada, 26, 169, 173–4, 197, 224–5, 227–9, 236, 239, 296, 298. *See also* clericalism; Roman Catholic church
Cité libre, 23
citizenship, 4
civics, 4
Clark, S.D., 222
class. *See* social class
Claxton, Brooke, 163
clericalism, 169, 181, 182
Cleverdon, Catherine, *The Woman Suffrage Movement in Canada*, 35
Cobden, Richard, 109
Cold War, 16, 18, 30, 309
collective bargaining, evolution of, 30
colonialism, 68, 79, 173, 175, 323
colonization, 116, 295–7
Committee on Public Information (U.S.), 9
commodities, 13, 125, 127
communism, 148
computers (use of, in history), 27
Confederation, 68, 95–6, 100, 107, 109–11, 152, 157, 164, 184, 209, 319; anniversaries of, 8, 25, 195; Atlantic provinces' role in, 36; British Columbia's entry into, 14; and English Canada, 107–8; and French Canada, 11, 224–6, 296, 298; and influence of Native culture, 131; Montreal after Confederation, 225
Conference on Imperial Defence (1909), 97
Conquest, British, 77, 136, 138, 177, 179–80, 237–8, 319; impact on French Canada, 22–4; and popular myths, 9
conquest theory/hypothesis, 22, 24
conscription crisis. *See* First World War
consensus history, 4, 25, 26
conservatism, 113
Conservative Party (of Canada), 21, 137, 156
constitution (of the United States), 111
constitutional history, 10, 184, 275, 313–14; and British traditions, 110–11; of Canada, 112, 120–1, 184, 235, 244, 275, 313–14; historical scholarship on, 10–11; and influence of geography, 12, 69
continentalism, 18
Cook, Ramsay, 22, 24, 25, 195, 326
Corbett, Percy, 16
Cordillera, 212, 216
Corrigan, Philip, 40, 198
counterculture, 310
crafts, 255–6, 264
Craig, Sir James, 112
Creel, George, 8–9
Creighton, Donald, 17–19, 39, 41, 68, 136, 180, 221, 226, 309, 310, 333–4; as editor of *CHR*, 10, 14, 17–18; on Lower Canada, 11–12
Creighton, W.B., 289–90
critical theory, 201
Cross, Michael, 26, 31, 197
Crow's Nest Pass, 209
cultural hegemony, 41, 201
cultural history, 41, 46, 200–1, 275, 285, 311
cultural relativism. *See* relativism
cultural studies, 199
cultural theory, 44

Index

culture, 13–14, 130, 162, 215, 268, 269–71, 282–4, 303
Culture, 1941 survey, 16
culture, popular. *See* popular culture

Dafoe, J.W., 22
Dalhousie, Lord (George Ramsay), 112–13
democracy, 145, 175, 182
demography, 203, 279, 280; demographic history, 195
Denison, Lt-Col. Septimus, 246
Department of National Defence, 242
Dewar, Kenneth C., on Creighton, 41, 310
disciplines: disciplinary autonomy and boundaries, 12, 20
'distinct society' (Quebec as), 235
domestic servants, 280
Douglass, W.A., 293
Drawback Act (U.S., 1845), 157
Dubinsky, Karen, 199
Dubofsky, Melvin, 30
Duncan Commission, 209–10
Duplessis, Maurice, 235
Durham, Lord, 68, 251, 262
Durocher, René, 238

eastern Canada, 164, 196; 'golden era,' 217–20; relationship between Natives and Europeans, 14. *See also* regionalism
Eccles, W.J., 23, 26; on Innis, 32, 310; on New France, 27
Ecole pratique des Hautes Etudes, at Université de Paris, 23
economic determinism, 32
economic history, 20, 26, 32, 36, 74, 78, 196
economics, 16

electoral riots, 263
Elgin, Lord, 251
emigration, 101, 115, 282–4, 295, 297
d'Enghien, duc, 90
English Historical Review, 6, 10, 43, 75
English, John, 37–8, 310
Enlightenment, 71–2
environmental theories, 20, 78, 130, 136–7
Equal Rights Association, 300
equality (and inequality), 27, 219
ethnicity, 33, 45, 195–6, 215–16, 237–9, 250
ethnohistory, 34–5, 69, 270, 273, 275–6
ethnology, 13, 34–5; and uses of folklore, 7
Europe, 198, 200–1; capital in North America, 212–13; and colonization, 121; historians and historical scholarship, 78, 260; influence in Canada, 314; as market for colonial goods, 122–3; nationalism, 105; Upper Canadians' interest in, 108–9; and working-class history, 29
European–Amerindian relations, 270–1
Eurocentric (view of history), 271–2, 275
evangelicalism, 293–4
Expo 67, 5
exports, 214, 219, 233–4

family history, 195, 203, 280, 283
farming communities, 218–19, 220, 221
federal government, 38, 137, 146, 156, 162, 165–6, 209–10; and militia, 244

federalism, 111, 244
feminism, 199
feminist theory, 286. *See also* gender history; women's history
First World War, 21–2, 90, 94, 96–8, 100, 136, 141, 145, 148, 162; conscription crisis, 7, 21–2; impact on Canada's colonial status, 96–8; impact on society, 6, 8, 21, 65, 67, 145; and nationalism, 11, 30, 67, 104; outbreak of, 7–8; peace conference, 163; peace treaty, 98; and postwar reconstruction, 291; and working class, 30
Fisher, Robin, 37
fishing industry, 33, 159–60, 212–13, 216, 217, 218, 220
Flenley, R.O., 66
folklore, 7, 227
Forbes, Ernest, 196
Ford, Thomas, 248
Foucault, Michel, 45, 286
Foulché-Delbosc, Isabel, 14, 66
Fowke, Vernon, 18
'fragment cultures' (Louis Hartz's theory of), 25
fragmentation, 26, 43, 137
France, 256; and colonies, 274–5; and First World War, 97
freedom of information legislation, 38
free trade, 218
Frégault, Guy, 19, 22, 26, 177
French Canada, 11–12, 26–7, 77, 94, 112–14, 130–1, 196–7, 200, 300; and Conquest, 22, 24, 296; craftsmen's associations, 31; historians and historical scholarship, 11–12, 19–20, 29, 37, 39–40, 66–7, 73, 176–7, 200, 227; involvement in foreign adventures, 300; and nationalism, 11, 22, 26–7, 29, 107, 171, 226, 233–4, 274; reliance on Native knowledge, 130–1; society, 26–7, 29; and timber industry, 47, 249, 251; universities, 174; and western expansion, 29
French–English relations (in Canada), 11–12, 39–40, 68, 113, 138, 170–1, 178–9, 200, 224–6, 233, 237, 296, 311, 317; *CHR*'s attempts to ameliorate, 6–7, 39–40; in fur trade, 324; in historical profession, 19–22
French Revolution, 12, 90, 93, 174
frontier thesis, 13, 18, 121, 137, 159, 295
fur trade, 13–14, 27, 32–5, 66, 85, 123–6, 131, 159, 161, 188–9, 212–13, 233, 267–8, 279, 310

Gagan, David, 27
Galt, Alexander, 224
Garneau, François-Xavier, 237, 244
Geertz, Clifford, 200, 303
gender, 199, 282–4
gender history, 4, 199, 285–8
genealogy, family, 3
General Education in a Free Society, Harvard Committee ('The Harvard Report'), 17
geography, 12, 69, 121, 123, 171, 216
geography, historical, 12, 20, 32–3, 69, 196, 216, 273
George, Henry, and single tax, 293
German research tradition, 74–5
Germany, 105, 141; and First World War, 98, 100; historians and histori-

cal scholarship, 75, 260; influence in Canada, 74
Gibbon, Edward, 71-2
Glazebrook, G.P. de T., 135-6; on political history, 17; on role of historian, 15
globalization, and impact on history, 4
Globe (Toronto), 18, 68
gold rushes, 14, 33, 212
Goodman, Nelson, 330
Gordon, Col. W.D., 246
Gramsci, Antonio, 30, 260
Granatstein, J.L., 4, 36, 38
Grand Trunk Railway, 224
Grant, Hugh, on Harold Innis and W.J. Eccles, 32, 310
Grant, W.L., 78
Gras, N.S.B., 157-8
Great Depression, 30, 138, 189-90, 280
Great Lakes, 118, 233, 319-20
'great man' theory (of history), 16, 147, 148
Great War (The). *See* First World War
Greene, John Richard, 75
Greer, Allan, 40, 237, 311
Grey, Edward, 148
Groseilliers, Mme de, 85
Groulx, Abbé Lionel, 19-20, 22, 171, 177, 236, 317, 333
Group of Seven, 68, 162-3
Guelph (Ontario), 253
Gutman, Herbert, 30-1

habitants, 27
Halifax (Nova Scotia), 116-17; British garrison in, 243; merchants in, 195
Hamelin, Jean, 23, 26
Hamelin, Marcel, 238

Hamilton, George, 249
Hamilton (Ontario), 253-5; street railway strike, 246
Hanham, H.J., 309-10
Hardwood Hill (Nova Scotia), 219
Harris, Cole, 26, 32-3, 196
Hart, Albert Bushnell, 76
Hartz, Louis, 25
Harvey, D.C., 217-18
health care, 281
heroes (and heroines), 8-10, 14, 66, 84, 92, 274, 280; (as) saviours, 80-4
Heron, Craig, 31, 197-8
Hexter, J.H., 329
Hincks, Sir Francis, 224
Histoire sociale/Social History, 27
historians, popular, 3-4, 8, 19-20, 38-9, 66
historical criticism, 73
historical fiction, 3
historical geography. *See* geography, historical
historical institutes, 4
historical relativism, 7
Historical Studies: Australia and New Zealand, 42-3
Hitler, Adolf, 141, 148
Hobsbawm, E.J., 30, 260
Howay, F.W., 14
Howe, Joseph, 117
Howell, Colin, 36
Hudson Bay, 213
Hudson's Bay Company, 95, 119, 125, 126; archives, 66
Hume, David, 70
Hume, James Gibson, 65
Hurons, 80, 267-8, 271, 276. *See also* Natives

Iacovetta, Franca, 199

iconoclasm, 8–9
immigration, 264, 275
Imperial Defence Committee, 97
imperial federation, 123
Imperial Oil Company, 164
Imperial War Cabinet, 67, 98–9
Imperial War Conferences, 74, 97
imperialism, 29, 107, 110, 298–9
Incarnation, Marie De l', 81, 83–4
India, 96
individualism, 136, 140, 293
industrialization, 12, 22, 27, 30, 36, 40, 45, 65, 128, 172, 187, 190, 207, 212, 220, 225–7, 236–8, 254–5, 260–1, 279, 281, 292; in Quebec, 22–3, 227, 236
industrial relations, 30; and conflict, 198, 259
industrial revolution, 29, 36, 112–14, 160
Innis, Harold, 32, 213–14, 216, 276, 310, 315; influence of and reactions to, 18, 20, 32–3; and Native history, 13; review of *The Vertical Mosaic* (Porter), 25; on role of social scientist, 16
Innisian theory, 32–3, 127–9, 213, 216, 310, 322–4. *See also* staples, and theory of (Canadian) development
Institut Canadien, 226
Institut d'histoire de l'Amérique française, 19
intellectual history (history of ideas), 16, 25, 29, 41, 46, 196, 200, 279, 313
Intercolonial Railway, 209
International Labour Conference, 98
international relations, 15, 17, 100, 135

Ireland; historians and historical scholarship, 239–40
Irish Canadians, 186, 247–9
Iroquois, 85, 267–8, 274; Battle of Long Sault (1660), 9. *See also* Natives

Jackson Lears, T.J., 201
Jaenen, Cornelius, 34–5, 198; on Bruce Trigger and James Axtell, 35
Jameson, Franklin, 76
Jamieson, Stuart Marshall, 253
Jefferys, C.W, 66
Jesuits, 267
Joan of Arc, 83
Johnston, Wayne, 3
Jones, Gareth Stedman, 30, 260
Journal of American History, 43–4
journalism, 102. *See also* media, popular

Katz, Michael, 27, 195
Kealey, Gregory S., 38, 255
Kealey, Linda, 36
Keats, John, 287
Kennedy, W.P.M.: on nationalism, 11, 68
Kessler-Harris, Alice, 38
Keynes, John Maynard, 236
Kilbourn, William, 326
Kingsford, William, 78, 82
Kipling, Rudyard, 75
Kuhn, Thomas, 45

labour, 187–8, 212–13, 214, 219, 260–1, 282; labour and the left, 28
Labour/Le Travailleur, 31, 197
labour history, 28, 30, 138, 183, 197, 260–1. *See also* social class; working-class history

labour relations, 187
labour unrest (and strikes), 186, 197, 242, 244, 245, 247, 249, 253–7
Labrador, and Basque whaling stations, 213
LaCapra, Dominick, 200
Lachine Strike (1843), 30, 138
Lafontaine, Louis H., 224
laissez-faire (doctrine), 113, 141
Lambert, John, 228
Lanctôt, Gustave, 8–9, 11, 65–6
language, 105, 302
Lartigue, Mgr, 24, 181–2
Laurentian thesis (of Canadian development), 12, 118–19
Laurier, Sir Wilfrid, 22, 168–9
La Vérendrye, 9
League of Nations, 98, 100, 163
Legendre, Napoléon, 270
legends, 8
LeGoff, T.J.A., 27, 196
Lepine, Ambroise, 298–9
Le Travail. *See* Labour/*Le Travailleur*
liberalism, 136, 140–1, 182
Liberal Party (of Canada), 17–18, 21, 137, 156, 168
'limited identities,' 4–5, 25, 28–9, 38, 195, 260, 327
Linteau, Paul-André, 39, 237–8
literary theory, 44
Lloyd George, David, 98
local history, 15–16
Logan, H.A., 30, 197
London (Ontario), 253
longue durée. *See* Annales school
Loo, Tina, 200
Louisiana Purchase, 320
Lowell, A. Lawrence, 76
Lower, Arthur M., 19, 39, 69, 135–6, 138, 180, 183; on Laurentian thesis, 12; on Neatby and Royal Commission on National Development, 19; on role of historian, 15–16; on *The Commercial Empire of the St. Lawrence* (Donald Creighton), 15; on *The Vertical Mosaic* (John Porter), 25
Lower Canada, 11–12, 122, 156, 224, 249, 311; and struggle for financial control, 68; treatment by historians, 334–5
Lowie, Robert, 13
Loyalists, 94, 101, 110, 117, 122, 206–7, 263–4, 265
lumbering, 119

McArthur, D., 67
McCalla, Douglas, 36–7
Macaulay, Thomas B., 91
Macdonald, Charlotte, 282
Macdonald, Sir John A., 17–18, 136, 224–6, 298
MacDonald, L.R., 27
McGill poets, 68
McGill University, 13, 76
McIlwraith, T.F., 13, 34
McInnis, Edgar, 19
Mackenzie, William Lyon, 262–3, 332
Mackenzie King, William Lyon, 152, 165, 316
McKillop, A.B., 4, 200
MacKinnon, Robert, 33, 196
Mackintosh, W.A.; on Harold Innis's *Fur Trade of Canada*, 13; staples theory, 12, 46, 69
McLaughlin, Andrew, 76
McMartin, Daniel, 247–8
MacMechan, Archibald, 68
McMullen, John, 274
McNaught, Kenneth, 32, 197; biography of J.S. Woodsworth, 20–1

MacNutt, W.S., 14
Mance, Mlle Jean, 84
Mandrou, Robert, 26
Manitoba, 18–19, 21, 298; and First World War, 22; and Laurentian barrier, 119; and Militia Act, 246; schools question, 169, 298, 300
Mann, Susan (Trofimenkoff): review of *L'Histoire des femmes au Québec depuis quatre siècles*, 35–6
Maritime provinces: 'golden age' of, 33, 217–19; radio stations in, 164
Maritime Rights Movement, 209
marriage, 282
Martin, Chester, 39, 136, 159
Marxism and Marxist theory, 27, 29, 31–2, 40, 183, 198, 236, 260, 310
Massey Commission. *See* Royal Commission on National Development in the Arts, Letters and Sciences
Massicotte, E.Z., 82
Masters, D.C., 136
Mealing, S.R., 25
media, popular, 3, 29, 66, 91, 102, 136–7, 145, 164–5. *See also* journalism
Meech Lake Accord, 240
memory, 3, 65–6, 214
mentalité, 279
mercantilism, 13, 178, 207
messianisme, 238
methodology, 20, 79, 195, 200
Métis, 13, 35, 160, 198, 298, 301
metropolis and hinterland (theory), 18, 156–8
metropolitanism, 128, 207, 209–10, 213
Michaels, Anne, 3
Micmac, 271, 274. *See also* Natives

Middle River, 219
migration, 14, 25, 33, 68, 130, 183, 205, 212, 215, 217, 225
military history, 16, 31, 36, 75, 78, 136, 147–8, 183, 314; A.E. Prince on, 16–17
Militia Act, 243–5
Miller, Jim, 35
Minerve, La, 226
mining industry, 212, 214–15, 216; and strike in British Columbia, 245; and strike in Cape Breton, 244
minorities, 299
missionaries, 267–8
Mississippi Valley, 122
Mississippi Valley Historical Association, 10
Mississippi Valley Historical Review (Journal of American History), 10, 44
modern (ideas of), 16, 41, 44, 108, 187, 203, 302–4, 313, 327
modernism, 44–5
Molson, William, 225
monarchism, 179, 263
Monet, Jacques, 24; on *Histoire économique et sociale du Québec, 1760–1850* (Fernand Ouellet), 24
Montagnais, 271. *See also* Natives
Montgomery, David, 255
Montreal, 27, 233, 244, 246, 293; and battle with Iroquois, 80–4; historians and historical scholarship, 22–3, 317; merchants in, 188, 207; radio stations in, 164
monumental art, 3
Moogk, Peter N., 31
morality, 9, 15, 67, 87, 90–2, 264, 280
moral philosophy, 200
Morehouse, Frances, 14, 68

Morley, Lord, 7–8
Morton, A.S., 9, 39, 66, 136, 156
Morton, Desmond, 31, 197
Morton, W.L., 21, 39; analysis of Red River settlement, 18–19, 136; criticism of Fowke, 18
Motley, John L., 91
museums, 3

Napoleon III, 90–1, 109
narrative, 41; narrative history, 4, 71, 77, 311, 328–31
national consciousness, 22, 26, 67, 99–100, 137, 162–4, 171, 234, 326
national flag, 100
national history, 4–5, 16, 25, 29, 37, 41, 46–7, 315
nationalism, 68, 76, 104–7, 109, 115, 137, 145, 178–82, 195, 233–4, 291; in historical interpretations, 10–11, 14, 19, 22–4, 25, 27, 37–8, 42–3, 123, 143–4, 176–7, 180, 233–4, 239, 274, 310, 315, 326, 333
National Policy, 21, 30, 137–8, 162, 166, 189–90, 209
national unity, 25, 79, 104, 166, 175
nationhood; ideas of, 4, 206, 298, 310, 315
Native history, 33–4, 198, 267–76
Natives, 13–14, 33–5, 69, 77, 119, 124–6, 128, 159, 198–9; and European relations, 34, 77, 130–1, 198–9; after First World War, 20, 34; and fur trade, 13, 35, 279, 318
Neatby, H. Blair, 21, 137
Neatby, Hilda: and Royal Commission on National Development, 19
Neilson, John, 113
Nelles, H.V., 36
neo-nationalism, 26, 176

Nesbitt, William, 116–17
New Brunswick, 101; militia in, 242–3; schools question, 226, 298. *See also* regionalism
New Deal (United States), 142
New Denver (British Columbia), 214–15
New England, 116, 123, 206–7, 323
Newfoundland, 323
New France, 11, 66, 78, 177, 197; battle with Iroquois, 9; economic development, 23, 32, 121–3, 178–9; French policy towards, 27, 32; fur trade and settlement, 27, 32, 34–5, 318–21, 323; *habitants*, 27, 80; impact of Conquest, 22–4; mercantilism, 27; military in, 27; nationalism, 24; relations with Natives and Métis, 32, 34–5; women, 14, 66
'New History,' 31, 147
New Left, 29, 251, 310
Newman, Peter C., 39
New York, 157
New Zealand, 96; historical profession in, 42
Niagara Falls, 253
Nine Hour Movement, 187
'normal' society (Quebec as), 40, 236
North-West, 13, 157–8. *See also* regionalism
North West Company, 160, 161, 188–9, 319
North West Mounted Police, 126, 299
Northwest Rebellions, 13, 296. *See also* Métis; Riel, Louis
Nouveau Monde, Le, 226
Nova Scotia, 68, 101–2, 106, 244; colonial relations, 115–16; 'golden age' of, 33; provincial politics, 14;

segregation of African Canadians, 25; tourism, 221–2

objectivity, 15, 17, 25, 136
October crisis, 26
Ohio Valley: French occupation in, 319
Oman, Sir Charles, 148
Ommer, Rosemary, 38
Ondaatje, Michael, 3
Ontario, 101, 198, 315; bilingual schools issue, 21–2; Confederation, 209; economic development, 36; First World War, 21–2; historians and historical scholarship, 37; and Laurentian barrier, 119; migration to prairies, 295; Natives, 274; segregation of African Canadians, 25
Ontario Workman, 190
Orange Order, 198, 242, 250
Ormeaux, Dollard des, 9, 66
Oshawa (Ontario), 253, 255
Ostry, Bernard, 21
Ottawa, 209; and attacks on centralization, 38
Ouellet, Fernand, 23–4, 26–7, 54, 137, 233–4, 236; review of *Les Canadiens après le Conquête* (Michel Brunet), 196
Oxford Historical Society, 75

Pacquet, Gilles, 27, 233–4
Palmer, Bryan D., 4, 31, 197–8, 263; review of *Labour and Capital* (H.C. Pentland), 138
Papineau, Louis-Joseph, 27, 182, 332
Paris (Ontario), 283–4
Parizeau, Jacques, 40

Parkin, Sir George, 153
Parkman, Francis, 101, 175
Parr, Joy, 40, 199; and gender history, 40
Parti patriote, 181
Parti Québécois, 40
paternalism, 262–4
(la) patrie, 298
patriotism, 107, 274, 291
Peel County (Ontario), 27
Penman's Company, 283
Pentland, H.C., 30, 138, 264; on *Essays in Canadian Working Class History*, 31
peripheries, 68
Perth (Ontario), 247–9
Peterborough (Ontario), 253
Phillips, Mark, 330
Pierson, Ruth Roach, 198
Plato, 327
pluralism, 21, 40
political economy, 13, 32, 310, 323
political history, 17, 21, 25–6, 28–9, 36–8, 47, 68, 75, 78, 136–7, 149–51, 169, 184, 196, 200, 275, 279, 309–11, 313–14, 326, 328–9
political science, 20, 28, 310–11
political scientists, 12–13
Pope, Sir Joseph, 153
popular culture, 103, 228–9, 232; films, 102, 279; influence of American popular culture on Canada, 103, 136, 164–5
population growth, 225, 234, 264
Porter, John, *The Vertical Mosaic*, 25, 138
postmodernism, 36, 44–6
pragmatism, 7, 45
Prang, Margaret, 21, 137; on *The Vertical Mosaic* (John Porter), 25

Prairies, 101, 196; settlement of, 67. *See also* regionalism
primitivism (ideas of), 13, 18, 128, 137, 159, 274
Prince, A.E., 136; on military history, 16–17
professional historians, 39, 275
professionalization (of history), 6, 7, 74–5
professions (liberal), 180
Progressive Party, 209
proletarianism. *See* radicalism
propaganda, in United States, 9
Protestantism, 140. *See also* church
Protestants, in Lower Canada, 224, 228
providential (notions of), 174
provincial history, 21, 25, 78–9, 169
psychohistory, 280
psychology, 7, 16, 65, 295, 316
Public Archives of Canada, 38, 73, 78, 153
Puritan settlers, 130–1

quantitative history, 27, 31, 195, 236, 327
Quebec, 101, 116, 137–8, 224–6; economy, 27; and First World War, 21–2; government in 1657, 11; historians and historic writing, 19–20, 22–3, 26–7, 39–40, 137, 196–7, 327; impact of Conquest, 22–4; and imperialism, 29; industrialization and urbanization, 22–3, 40; influence of Annales school, 26; and Laurentian barrier, 119; nationalism, 22–4, 27, 30, 40, 137–8; and Natives in, 274; October crisis, 26, 196; political history of, 21–4, 137; politicians' use of past, 40; separatism, 23, 40; society, 26. *See also* French Canada; Lower Canada; New France
Quebec City: and battle with Iroquois, 80, 82–3; historians and historical scholarship, 317; merchants in, 207
Quebec Conference, 95
Queen's Quarterly, 218
Queenston Heights, 9
Queen's University (Kingston, Ontario), 76
Quiet Revolution (Quebec), 23, 39, 227, 238–40
Quincy, Thomas de, 8

race, 271, 275, 285
racial conflict, 113
radicalism, 18, 20–1, 30, 113, 189–90
radio broadcasting, 137. *See also* Canadian Broadcasting Corporation
Radio League, 165–6
Railway Act, 210
railways, 96, 124–5, 162, 186–7, 209–10, 212, 226, 301
Ranke, Leopold von, 6
Raynal, Abbé, 270
Rebellion Losses Act (1849), 251
Rebellions (1837–8), 27, 197, 233, 251, 311
reciprocity, 108, 157, 218
Redfield, Robert, 13–14
Red River, 18–19, 124, 137, 147, 157; and Confederation, 108. *See also* North-West; regionalism
Reformers (Upper Canada), 40–1, 108, 198, 262–4
Reformistes (Lower Canada), 181
regional history, 196
regionalism, 5, 14, 16, 25, 29, 37, 46–

7, 68, 143, 166, 195–6, 206–10, 213, 260–1, 327; eastern Canada, 14, 33, 36, 123; Quebec, 39; western Canada, 13–14, 18–19, 29, 33, 123
relativism, 7, 44, 45–6, 89
religious history, 25, 29, 75, 191, 200, 313
responsible government, 22, 311
retrofashion, 3
Review of Historical Publications Relating to Canada, 6, 73–6, 78
revisionist historians: Quebec, 40, 197, 236–40
Revue canadienne, 6, 300
Revue d'histoire de l'Amérique française, 19–20, 200
Rideau Canal, 249
Riel, Louis, 35, 168–9, 198, 226, 299
Riot Act, 246, 248
Robert, Jean-Claude, 40, 237, 238; review of *Canada since 1945* (Robert Bothwell, John English, and Ian Drummond), 39
Robertson, William, 71
Robin, Martin, 30–1
Roe, Frank G., 69
Roman Catholic church, 224–6, 227–9, 250, 296, 298–301; and Conservative Party, 169; as foundation of French-Canadian life, 26–7; and historical scholarship, 11, 22, 236–9; and Orange Order riots, 242
romanticism, 175
Root, Winfred Trexler, 45
Rosenberg, Rosalind, 38
Rouges, 226
Rouillard, Jacques, 237
Roy, Pierre-Georges, 73
Royal Commission on Dominion–Provincial Relations, 218

Royal Commission on National Development in the Arts, Letters and Sciences (Massey Commission), 19
Royal Proclamation (1763), 180, 296, 319
Royal Society of Canada, 19
royalism, 175
Rudin, Ronald, 40, 197
rule of law, 262
Russell Resolutions, 182
Russian Revolution, 30, 189

Sage, Walter, 14
St Catharines (Ontario), 253
St Laurent, Louis, 224
St Lawrence (River), 118–19, 121, 206–7, 213, 225, 233; canals, 157; and French settlements, 318, 323
Saskatchewan, 298, 320; and Laurentian barrier, 119
Sault Ste Marie (Ontario), Italian community in, 199
Saunders, Richard, 20, 26
Sayer, Derek, 40, 198
Saywell, John T., 21–2, 25, 137, 326
scientific history, 6–8, 17, 26, 66, 72, 78–9
scientific management, 256
Second World War, 15, 20–1, 39, 135, 137, 141–2, 145, 148, 236; and historians and historical scholarship, 15–17, 20–1, 135–6, 140; postwar period, 309; and postwar reconstruction, 135
Séguin, Maurice, 20, 22, 177
Seguin, Normand, 40, 237
seigneurialism, 26–7, 180, 296
self-government, 175
Selkirk Settlement (Red River), 159
semiotics, 201

separatism (Quebec), 23
settlement, 125, 295–6, 298
Seven Years' War, 122, 170. *See also* Conquest, British
Sherbrooke, Sir John, 112–13
Shiners' War, Ottawa Valley, 31, 197, 247–52
shipping industry, 217, 219, 220
Shorter, Edward, 256
Shortt, Adam, 76, 78
Shotwell, James T., 65
Silver, A.I., 29, 200
Silverman, Eliane Leslau, 36, 198
Slocan Valley, 212
Smith, Adam, 145
Smith, Goldwin, 76, 101, 103
social class, 184, 196, 216, 219, 245, 247, 250–1, 264, 282; class-based theory (of history), 25, 30, 183; class consciousness, 31, 138, 195, 261. *See also* labour history; working-class history
Social Credit movement, 18
social history, 14, 26–9, 31, 35, 37, 40, 42, 47, 84, 136, 149, 189–200, 260, 275, 311, 313, 328, 333; historians' attitudes towards, 4, 16–17
Social History, 35, 196
Social History Project in Hamilton, 27
social reform, 29
social regeneration, 293
social sciences, 16, 18, 20, 22, 28, 33–4, 45, 65, 135–6, 183, 239, 313–14
Social Sciences and Humanities Research Council of Canada, 38
social scientists, 140, 145, 171–2, 174–5, 183, 276, 310, 313; arguments on role of, 15–16, 135–6; and French Canada, 174–5

social welfare, 183–4
sociology, 13–14, 16, 51, 53, 78
Soffer, Benson, 255
Somme, Battle of the, 98
South Africa, 96
sovereignty (Quebec), 40
Spanish exploration, 14
specialization, 4, 28, 42–3, 311
Spicer, Edward, 276
Stacey, C.P., 19, 68
Stanley, G.F.G., 13–14, 136, 137, 159, 299; on *La Guerre de la Conquête* (Guy Frégault), 22
staples, and theory of (Canadian) development, 32, 46, 120–3, 129, 213–16, 310
staples trades, 212–16, 217
state (ideas of), 162, 166, 198, 260, 285, 327. *See also* National Policy
state intervention, 162
states' rights, 111
Stephens, Morse, 75–6
Stone, Lawrence, 27
Strachey, Lytton, 8, 155
Strong, Josiah, 294
Strong-Boag, Veronica, 199
student protest movement, 38, 260
suburbia, 199
'survival,' 296
Sutherland, David, 195
Sydenham, Lord, 251

Taché, Bishop Alexandre, 295
Taine, Hippolyte, 78
tariff, 102, 162, 209–10
temperance movement, 31
Thelen, David, 43–4
theme parks, historical, 3
theocracy, 182. *See also* anticlericalism; clericalism

Thirteen Colonies, 101, 106, 170. *See also* British North America
Thompson, E.P., 30–1, 138, 197, 260
Thompson, John: review of *Le Québec depuis 1930*, 39
Tilly, Charles, 256
timber industry, 33, 119–20, 212, 216, 233; and Irish Canadians, 197, 247–51
Tories (Upper Canada), 40–1, 109, 262–4
Toronto, 224–5, 253–5; and cavalrymen in Hamilton, 246; and consumerism, 303; radio stations in, 164
totalitarianism, 151
Toynbee, Arnold, 17
Trades and Labour Congress, 30
transportation, 212–13. *See also* railways
Treaty of Paris, 207
Trigger, Bruce, 20, 34–5, 198
Trotter, Reginald, 68, 135; on role of historian, 15
Trudeau, Pierre Elliott, 3
Trudel, Marcel, 26, 200
Turner, Frederick Jackson, 76, 124. *See also* frontier thesis

Underhill, Frank, 17, 20–1, 68, 138; review of *La présence anglaise et les Canadiens* (Michel Brunet), 23; review of *The Woman Suffrage Movement in Canada* (Catherine Cleverdon), 35
Union government, 21–2
Union Pacific Railway, 124
unions, 30, 187, 198, 214–15
United States, 69, 98, 105, 115, 125, 136, 157, 184, 196, 206–7; American exceptionalism, 43; Americans in Canadian universities, 38, 326; Canada's relationship with, 17, 95, 100–1, 162, 164–6, 184, 196, 206–7, 263; comparison to Nova Scotia, 14; *Equal Employment Opportunity Commission v. Sears, Roebuck*, 38; historians and historical scholarship, 8–9, 12, 26–7, 29–30, 42–4, 73, 75–6, 87, 183–4, 195, 198, 200–2, 260, 274–6; influence of Germany in, 75; influences on Canada, 11, 18, 30, 33–4, 68, 101–4, 110, 142–3, 189, 236, 313–14, 327; Native history in, 33; propaganda in, 9
Université de Montréal, and Montreal historians, 19–20, 22–3, 26, 196
universities, 102, 145; expansion of, 24, 78
University of Saskatchewan, 24
University of Toronto, 13, 21, 28, 65–7, 69, 163; Gray Lecture Series, 22; history department, 6–7, 21, 74, 76; and studies in political economy, 32
University of Toronto Press, 6–7, 21, 28
Upper Canada, 18, 40–1, 108–9, 156, 198, 311; and social attitudes, 108–10; treatment by historians, 334–5. *See also* Ontario
urbanization, 22, 27, 40, 172, 190, 220, 225, 260, 264; in Quebec, 22–3, 237–8

Vancouver Island and mining strike, 245
Van Kirk, Sylvia, 35, 279
Victoria, Queen, and diamond jubilee, 74

Victorianism, 172
Vietnam War, 29, 38, 42, 260, 310, 326
violence, 25, 197, 247–51, 261–2
Virginia, 93, 122–3

Walden, Keith, 41, 200, 260
Wallace, Stewart, 8, 10, 12
Wallace, W.S., 7, 65, 67, 153
Wallas, Graham, *The Art of Thought*, 71
Wallot, Jean-Pierre, 27, 196, 233–4
war, 148, 150
Warkentin, John, 33
War Measures Act, 26, 143, 196
War of 1812, 122, 264, 274; and popular myths, 9; and postwar period, 264, 274
Watt, Frank W., 21, 30, 138
welfare state, 150–1
Wells, H.G., 8, 66
western Canada, 69, 108, 122; and Hudson's Bay Company, 125. *See also* regionalism
western (Canadian) history, 14
'Western civilization,' 16, 145
western expansion, 29, 121, 298; and displacement of Native populations, 124–6
West Indies, 116, 207, 323
Whigs, 109
White, Hayden, 41
Williams, Raymond, 30, 260
Wilson, Daniel, 13, 69

Wilson, Woodrow, 11, 76
Winks, Robin, 25, 318
Winnipeg (Manitoba), 164
Wissler, Clark, 128
Wolfe, General James, 9
women's history, 28, 35–6, 40, 66, 199–200, 276, 278–81, 285; historians of, 35; Métis women, 35; and postmodernism, 36
Wood, Henry Wise, 18
Wood, William, 7
Woodsworth, J.S., 20–1
working-class culture, 30, 260–1, 327
working-class history, 4, 21, 25, 29–32, 35, 40, 138, 183–4, 197–200, 275, 327; debates surrounding, 4, 31–2; radicalism, 30. *See also* labour history; social class
Wrong, George, 6, 13, 65, 67, 74; and constitutional history, 10; and Laurentian thesis, 12; purpose of history and role of historian, 9–10, 67
Wynn, Graeme, 33, 196

Young, Brian, 40, 196–7, 237–8
Young, Walter, 30
Ypres, Battle of, 9, 83

Zeitgeist, 75, 90
Zollverein, 123
Zoltvany, Yves, 26
Zouaves (Canadian Pontifical Zouaves), 299